God's Purpose, the Cross, and Me

A True Story

Jane Carole Anderson

The Thread of Gold: God's Purpose, the Cross, and Me
by Jane Carole Anderson

Editing by John R.D. Anderson
Cover designed by Jane Carole Anderson with Stephen Sandlin

All Scripture quotations, unless otherwise indicated, are taken from the New King James Version®. Copyright © 1982 by Thomas Nelson, Inc. Used by permission. All rights reserved.

Bible abbreviations used:
ASV, American Standard Version
AV, Amplified Version
CLV, Concordant Literal Version
KJV, King James Version
NASV, New American Standard Version
NIV, New International Version
NTRV, New Testament: Recovery Version
RV, Recovery Version

Typographical changes have been made to some Bible verses to fit with the style of this publication.

All rights reserved. No portion of this book may be reproduced or transmitted in any form or by any means without the written permission of the publisher, except for the inclusion of brief quotations in a review.

ISBN 978-0-9769835-7-6

Copyright © 2005, 2020 by Jane Carole Anderson

Protus
Publications
TheThreadOfGold.com

DEDICATION

Jimmy Farest Allen, 1941–2005

This book is dedicated to Jim Allen who passed away unexpectedly one week before it went to press. As a result of a difficult church experience, Jim carried a great weight of sorrow in his heart for many years. He loved my husband and me and prayed for us faithfully during his final years. He was eagerly awaiting the publication of this book. I saw him the day before he went to be with the Lord. There were eleven of us who, without any plan on our part, all arrived to see Jim during the same ten minutes. We encircled his bed at the hospital and prayed for him, lifting him up to the throne of grace. When his sister, Lanell, began to pray for him, speaking the words of Psalm 133, it was as if Jim was being anointed with the oil that ran down from Aaron's head to the skirts of his garments. We sensed that we were on holy ground and felt that the Lord had done something wonderful in that room, something that we didn't fully understand.

I felt hopeful that the Lord would restore Jim's health so that he could remain with us, but the next day, I was stunned to learn that he had passed away. After a little time, I realized that during our time of prayer for him, God had been putting his finishing touches on the heart of this man, Jim Allen, whom He loved and for whom He died.

Throughout his life, Jim knew God and was known by Him. As those who knew him testified, He shared His Savior's love with all around him. On August 22, 2005, God took Jim, one of His precious, unique children, to be with Him. As my tears came, I understood that Jim was like a first fruit. His wounded heart was fully healed, cleansed, and set free by His heavenly Father before he passed from death to life to be with His Lord forever.

TABLE OF CONTENTS

My Heartfelt Thanks To v
Foreword vi
A Letter from the Author vii
Disclaimer ix
About the Author x
Writing Conventions xi
Part 1—God's Everlasting Love: A Sure Foundation 1
    Chapter 1 Into the Pit 3
    Chapter 2 Have No Fear 7
    Chapter 3 Much Sooner Than I Thought 22
Part 2 Satan's Subtle Deception Wood, Hay, Straw 39
    Chapter 4 The Church of No Name 41
    Chapter 5 Door Into Another World 49
    Chapter 6 Initiation Into "God's Best" 58
    Chapter 7 A Frog in the Pot 76
    Chapter 8 Don't Leave Me Out 98
    Chapter 9 Would We Submit? 115
    Chapter 10 A Campus Harvest 135
    Chapter 11 Everything Is His 152
Part 3 God's Wisdom Trial by Fire 167
    Chapter 12 Impending Trouble 168
    Chapter 13 The "Sisters' Rebellion" 189
    Chapter 14 Ongoing, Inward Torment 198
    Chapter 15 Bruised Reeds and Smoking Flax 206
    Chapter 16 Walking Out the Door 231
Part 4 God's Masterpiece His Purpose, the Cross, and Me 247
    Chapter 17 The Withdrawn Hand of Fellowship 248
    Chapter 18 The Master Weaver 274
    Chapter 19 The Cross 289
    Chapter 20 In God's Tapestry 296
    Chapter 21 You and Me 311
    Chapter 22 The Worthy Lamb 316
Part 5 God's Deliverance Freedom from Deception 321
    Chapter 23 About Deception 323
    Chapter 24 The Ax Laid to the Root 333
    Chapter 25 Faith Is the Victory 403
Index to Hymns, Psalms, and Poems 407
Bibliography 408
Glossary 411

My Heartfelt Thanks To ...

My dear husband, John, for his loving support, his invaluable help in authoring, his faithful editing and editing management, and for the many, many days of his life that he shared his wife with a computer.

My sons, Todd and Matt, for their invaluable feedback and encouragement; and my daughters-in-law, Janet and Danielle, for their love and support.

My mother, whose unexpected monetary gift was used to complete the publication of this book.

Lanell Allen for her undying friendship and for her many hours reviewing numerous book drafts, providing me inspiration and insight, and especially for her suggestion to use writer's comments.

Karen Robinson for asking to read about my experiences as a Christian, doing an unsolicited edit of my writing, and encouraging me to publish when I had no such intention; and Fritzeen Scott, Sally McPherson, and Janet Daniels for reviewing initial book drafts.

Marny Bishop, my dear friend and new sister in Christ, for her love and support and for insisting that I publish my writing.

Dave Edwards, whose timely re-appearance into our lives and encouragement to publish, helped us make the final go-ahead decision.

Karen Johnson, Rusty and Ann Powell, and Dave Edwards for their skillful, final editing; Dave Edwards, Oliver Peng, Fred Malir, Jodi Anderson, and Judy Albrecht for final book reviews; Barbara Rinkenberger, Cindy Pater, and Jonathan Smith for cover assistance; and John Wachs for printing consultation.

The Author and Finisher of our faith, who, by causing all things to work together for good, is the One who is ultimately responsible for this publication and the One I thank most of all.

Foreword

This story is for everyone. If you are not a Christian, in it you will see how God dearly loves people, including you, and how He wants to work in your ordinary life to make it an extraordinary one of eternal significance. If you are young in your life with God, you will learn how He wants to bring you into a mature relationship with Him over your lifetime. If you seek a deeper knowledge of God, not only will you find encouragement, but also in your pursuit, you will discover a wonderful secret as you learn about the deeper meaning and working of the cross as it applies to you in your Christian living. If you have been confronted, or know anyone involved, with the church in the author's story, or with a similar group, you can gain an invaluable insight into the nature and workings of such communities. And especially you who have "been there and done that," only to come out of the experience much older and brokenhearted, you will find among these pages much comfort in seeing how He is able, and indeed desires, to heal everything within you that has been broken or wounded. Whatever your case may be, God in His love and wisdom has placed this book into your hands.

May God bless you richly, dear reader, even as I was blessed with His speaking to my heart, in the reading of this book. While you commune with God and consider the wonder of His ways, you will find between these covers applications of divine truth to a life uniquely your own. My prayer is that as you turn these pages thoughtfully, He will engrave this infinitely wonderful and living truth on your heart. He did on mine.

— David Edwards

A Letter from the Author

Dear Reader,

I began writing in the early 1990's when I discovered that writing not only had great therapeutic value for me, but also helped me clarify and give voice to many matters in my heart and mind. Over a period of time, I came to believe that God had inspired me to write in order to leave a record of my spiritual history for my children and grandchildren. I believed He wanted me to tell them about His love and faithfulness to me during my lifetime, especially through times of suffering. I was hopeful that they would see the great and tender love God had shown to me and also be drawn to love Him. After about ten years, the Lord began to indicate to me that my story was not for my family alone. However, for a number of reasons, sharing it on a broader scale was not something I was ready or willing to do. But as God has done throughout my life, He once again brought me in His own way to the place where I was able to obey Him.

As much as I would like to tell my story in a form that would allow you to see just my God, my wonderful treasure, and not have to spend too much time looking at this earthen vessel, I have found that feat quite impossible. Be assured that on these pages the beautiful character is God. The other one, the one with all the needs, the flaws, and the hurts, is me. You will see how God makes Himself known to me and weaves a beautiful thread of gold into my little, common, unexceptional, often fearful, and seemingly purposeless life.

You may find that my life, at its core, is much like your own, in that whenever we are quiet and reflect a little, we know we live each day on shaky ground. Deep down, we know that we really have no guarantees about anything … unless there is God.

My story shows that God does indeed exist, and that He loves us with a love that far surpasses our ability to understand. It demonstrates that His love is readily offered and easily obtained. It doesn't have to be earned because it is already given. When we accept His love, it sets us on a rock from which we can never be dislodged. It gives us a deep, unshakable knowing that not only are we safe in this dark and distressing world, but also we each have been placed here with a special and wonderful purpose.

You will not find a textbook Christian life on these pages—one that moves along nicely from point A to point Z as if following a "how-to-be-a-Christian" manual. You will not find a neat, systematic, theologically-defined, orthodox experience. Instead, you will find a typical person who seeks God through the twists and turns of a messy human life and finds Him, or should I say, is found by Him. This book reveals the wonderful secret that every difficulty in life, every human suffering or tangled circumstance, is actually a gateway waiting to open and usher us into God's presence and His plan for our lives.

As you read, I hope that you will find Him, the One who not only brings us through every hardship to a place of triumph, but also makes us channels to others of His great love. Our faith in Him, which grows through all our experiences with Him on our journey through life, will remain for our eternal joy—the beautiful thread of gold which was woven through the dark-colored threads of our afflictions.

— Jane Carole Anderson

Disclaimer

This is a true story and is the author's personal testimony. Her experience in the Local Church and her insights from the Bible are part of her Christian experience. Any statements made by the author about the Local Church and its beliefs are based on her experience and reflect her own opinions and conclusions after having been a member for twenty years. Readers, of course, are free to research the Local Church and the Bible in order to form their own opinions. All matters related to the Local Church have been presented as accurately as possible. The author's intention in this book is to share her experiences and insights for the benefit of others.

The names of people in this book have been changed for their protection. The names of the author, members of the author's immediate family, and Lanell Allen, Joan Craig, and Dale and Helen King were not changed. The founder of the Local Church in the United States was Witness Lee, and his name is also used in this story. Witness Lee is now deceased, but the Local Church still exists.

Any spoken words or thoughts that are presented as quotations for literary effect are according to the author's recollection of the events. Such quotations may not be exact, but the meaning is as close as possible to what the author remembers. Also, some of the dates may not be exact but reflect the author's best recollection and research.

About the Author

    Jane and I met when we were both young coeds adjusting to university life. My first impression of her was of amazement—she was actually *reading* one of the course books she had just purchased from the bookstore, even though classes had not yet begun! In the two years following, I learned what a fun-loving, creative person Jane was. Whether she was writing entertaining skits for her pledge class of our women's service club or supervising the construction of a homecoming parade float, Jane was full of enthusiasm and total focus on the task at hand. She participated in such projects while maintaining grades to earn her a place on the Dean's List. In the years since then, I have grown to appreciate how God has blessed Jane with remarkable gifts of perception and application. In turn, her willingness to be transparent and share her experiences has been, and continues to be, a blessing to many people.

— Karen Johnson

Writing Conventions

Terminology: Terms that will be unfamiliar to most readers are explained by the author in the text, in a writer's comment, or in a footnote the first time they are mentioned. A glossary is available at the end of the book with the meanings of these terms.

Writer's Comments: Writer's comments, set in italic type, are interjected throughout the story from the author's current perspective to clarify, inform, and provide insight.

References: References to the "Bibliography" are like these examples: The reference (Kennedy, 182) refers to page 182 of the only book by Kennedy. The reference (Nee, Back, 11) refers to page 11 of one of the books by Nee, Back to the Cross.

Footnotes: Footnotes appear at the end of the subsections in which they occur.

The Lord will silently
plan for thee,
His purpose He'll
to thee unfold;
The tangled skein
shall shine at last,
A masterpiece
of skill untold.

— E. May Grimes

Part 1

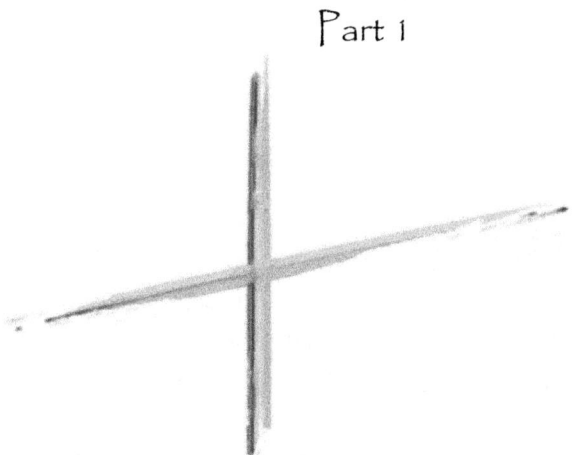

God's Everlasting Love

A Sure Foundation

Loved with everlasting love, led by grace that love to know;
Gracious Spirit from above, Thou hast taught me it is so!
O this full and perfect peace! O this transport all divine!
In a love which cannot cease, I am His, and He is mine.

Heav'n above is softer blue, Earth around is sweeter green!
Something lives in every hue Christless eyes have never seen;
Birds with gladder songs o'erflow, flowers with deeper beauties shine,
Since I know, as now I know, I am His, and He is mine.

Things that once were wild alarms cannot now disturb my rest;
Closed in everlasting arms, pillowed on the loving breast.
O to lie forever here, doubt and care and self resign,
While He whispers in my ear, I am His, and He is mine.

His forever, only His; Who the Lord and me shall part?
Ah, with what a rest of bliss Christ can fill the loving heart!
Heav'n and earth may fade and flee, firstborn light in gloom decline;
But while God and I shall be, I am His, and He is mine.

— W. Robinson

Chapter 1
Into the Pit

> The LORD has appeared of old to me, saying: "Yes, I have loved you with an everlasting love; therefore with lovingkindness I have drawn you." (Jer. 31:3)

IN THE SPRING OF 1977, MY HUSBAND AND I DRAGGED our bodies home after a church meeting in Houston, Texas. During that meeting, I was publicly humiliated; and after it, I was further shamed, censured, and ostracized. I had sensed God's nearness throughout everything that had transpired until that night, and then it seemed that He had abandoned me to this horrible experience. Those I loved had cast me into a pit of spiritual darkness and left me there to languish alone. I went to bed still sobbing as I continued to relive what had happened.

That Meeting

I was upset, nervous, and fearful as I sat there, waiting for Dan Williams to speak. I had been in this condition since the time I had been told, several days earlier, that my attendance in this meeting was mandatory. Dan was an elder and regional leader from a church in another city who had traveled to Houston with the purpose of holding this meeting. He was a tall, thin man who always wore a longsleeved white shirt, a thin tie, and dark pants. He was sitting forward in his chair on the front row jiggling one of his legs up and down periodically. Then he rose and began to speak. He asked that the tape recorder be turned off. This request was extremely unusual and, therefore, foreboding.

Because of events in the preceding weeks, I knew whatever was coming wasn't going to be good. When Dan began to speak, he announced that there was a "sisters' rebellion" in the Texas churches and that the sister leading this rebellion was in the Houston church. According to him, this sister had committed serious offenses against the church. She and others with her had encouraged people to open up and talk about their problems. According to Dan, this was the same as encouraging people to vomit. He disapprovingly said that when these sisters had told people to pray and wait for direction from the Lord, they were advocating "passivity."

As I had sat there listening to him, I had no doubt that I was the person about whom he was speaking. Though he didn't mention my name, many people in the church had already heard I was in trouble and had stopped speaking to me because of what was considered to be my "leprous condition."

Dan declared that these rebellious sisters had opposed the Lord's present move in the church and had caused a serious division. He proclaimed that they were seeking to be spiritual giants and that this was unacceptable in what he called the age of the body, the corporate expression of Christ. Because of their spiritual self-seeking, they had become deceived. Satan had used them to cause serious error and trouble and, hence, to damage the church. At one point, he stated his belief that sisters didn't have any spiritual discernment, and that they were, therefore, easy prey for Satan's deception. He also stated his belief that sisters could not receive revelation from the Bible. He continued speaking for a long period of time, informing church members about the evilness of the sisters' rebellion and stating that any evidence of such rebellion would not be tolerated.

A large knot of nausea and almost pain was throbbing in my stomach as I sat there listening, feeling like time had been cruelly suspended so that the wound I was receiving would be the deepest possible. When I ventured a glance around the room, hoping for anyone, anything that might be able to stop this nightmare, all I saw were faces glancing back at me with looks of pity. Dan finally concluded his message: "One of these sisters hasn't repented or talked to us. You know who you are. After this meeting, come to the fellowship room." My husband and I knew he meant me. It apparently hadn't been enough to put me in a public coffin; he needed to nail it shut.

The Inquisition

With many eyes on us, we crossed the meeting hall and entered the fellowship room. I felt like I was being summoned to the Inquisition. Dan was waiting there with a number of others who had been invited to attend as witnesses. Most of the local elders were present. One of their wives was present. An elder from a third locality was also there. A number of sisters were there, including some that had become members of the church through our efforts and had lived in our home for a long period of time. It appeared that the elders wanted them to be clear that I was not to be trusted. I was directed to sit down on the end of a couch. Most of the people present were sitting on folding chairs in a semicircle across the room from me. My husband was given a seat with them. Others were standing.

A folding chair was on my right side, about a foot away from the couch. Dan turned it to face me and then sat down. Looking at me, he began repeating in judgment of me his pronouncements from the public meeting. He offered no specific facts and no clear examples of my "rebellion." He asked me nothing. I did not understand his vague accusations. One of these was, "... and the shameful downfall that you caused to one of us." I had no idea what he was talking about, but thought that by "one of us" he might mean one of the elders. I wondered if his comment referred to a local elder named Steve Smith, who had broken down and wept in front of me and a few others several months before this. Steve was not present in the room that night.

Dan informed me that he knew all about the "secret meeting" we had planned for the spring. However, this was news to me because I didn't know anything about it. He said that all my rebellious, negative speaking had "come to their ears," revealing a conspiracy among the sisters that was undermining the elders and church oneness. Maybe he used the biblical phrase "come to our ears" to try and give scriptural support to what he was doing. He wasn't interested in learning whether I realized I was the leader of what he was calling a sisters' rebellion. He told me emphatically that I needed to repent for my offense to the church, and from that day forward, I was to "stop all my talk and be quiet."

I sobbed throughout his monologue. His non-specific accusations left me feeling that my person was being attacked. Near the end of the torment, I said, "The only solution I can see is just to dig a hole about six feet deep and put me in it. I think the problem is just who I am."

I also told him, "Whatever has happened, it isn't my husband's fault. It's mine." At this point, another of the elders present, who always seemed to be lurking in the background, Sam Jones, chuckled and said, "I always wondered why the Lord put you two together, and now I know." I had no idea what he meant by this strange statement. Why had he always wondered this? What did he now know? I certainly didn't understand his apparent amusement. How could anyone find anything funny in what was happening at that black moment in that room? I was weeping and in extreme distress, yet he found humor in the situation? Sam's comment, at best, was thoughtless and cruel.

Later that night at home in bed, I tried to pray, but I couldn't. I was experiencing an internal, spiritual, and emotional agony. How had such darkness swallowed us? I had belonged to Jesus since I was a child, and He had never failed me. Where was He now? I felt like I was suffocating in a deep, dark pit filled with blackness.

Chapter 2
Have No Fear

> When I was a child, I spoke as a child, I understood as a child, I thought as a child; but when I became a man, I put away childish things. (1 Cor. 13:11)

Born Afraid

I WAS BORN IN MEMPHIS, TENNESSEE, the oldest of three girls and named Jane Carole Hart. My earliest childhood memories were of fear. I had terrible nightmares in my room alone at night, so I would fight going to sleep. Whenever I closed my eyes, I would see slithering snakes like a border around the ceiling of my bedroom. I was awakened once to find what appeared to be some animal-like things sitting on my bed staring at me in silence. Every night I would cry and fight my parents to keep from being put to bed, from having to go alone into my little chamber of horrors. My parents, tiring of this ongoing problem, finally decided to leave me crying in the dark. They told me that no amount of my crying would bring them to my room. I survived, but the horror of it is still vivid to my mind's eye.

At about the age of five, I sat on the old quilt on my bed and asked my mother questions that were troubling me because I had been thinking about death: "Momma, what happens when you die? Is there nothing? How can there be nothing? Isn't *nothing* something?" She didn't have any answer for me.

When I was seven, my father, an airline mechanic for Delta Airlines, was transferred from Memphis to Atlanta, where we lived for about six months. He then requested a transfer to Dallas, where I spent my remaining childhood years. In Dallas, I switched schools once in the second grade and twice in the third grade before my parents finally bought a home. I was disturbed by all the changes. When my mother would leave me at school, I would put my head down on the desk and cry silently. After the last move, I began to settle in and make friends. Annie became my best friend.

Have No Fear

When I was about eleven, my friend Annie's big sister, Bonnie, who was twenty, asked me to go horseback riding with Annie and her. This was her gift to us for graduating from sixth grade. I loved horses and was excited about the invitation. When I asked my mother for permission to go, she said I could go only if I had enough money. I told her I did have enough but didn't volunteer the information that Bonnie was paying for us because I thought Mother wouldn't like it and might not let me go.

Later she asked me how I had been able to pay for the horseback riding. I told her that I didn't have quite enough money and that Bonnie had loaned the difference to me. For the next few weeks, when Mother reminded me to pay Bonnie back, I would tell her that I was going to, hoping she would soon forget about it. One day, she told me to ride my bike over to Bonnie's that very minute and pay my debt. I said, "Okay," and rode off, pretending to do what she said.

The lies had started out innocently, but they weren't innocent anymore. I began to feel extremely guilty. I was wrong to lie to my mother. The guilt wouldn't go away. It followed me everywhere. When I played with my friends, it was with me. I couldn't find anything that would drown it out. I couldn't face Mother. I felt like I had the weight of the whole world on my shoulders. I thought I now understood what adults meant about having to grow up and carry all of the burdens of life. Weeks later, one night while my mother was at work, I was feeling so guilty I couldn't go to sleep. I called my father into my bedroom and said, "Daddy, if I tell you something that's really bothering me, will you please not tell Mother?" When he asked me what, I said, "I lied to her about having money to pay for horseback riding. I really didn't have any money, and Bonnie paid for it!" He told me to go to sleep.

The next day, my mother called me into the kitchen to talk to me while she was peeling potatoes at the sink. Why had I done this? Why had I felt that I had to lie to her? Then she spoke words that burned deeply, "Jane Carole, I just don't understand why you thought you had to lie to me. Now I don't know if I will ever be able to trust you again." I had thought I had a problem before I confessed to my father—now I was really in deep waters. I was only eleven and needed the love and trust of my mother, which I had now lost. What if she found out about all the other things I had done wrong? I always swam in the forbidden deep end of the public pool. I accidentally came across a paperback romance novel on top of the refrigerator and had read some shocking parts of it! I couldn't be in the room with her without my face flushing. I couldn't let her look me in the face, or she would read my guilt!

One night, my guilt and I went to bed. The guilt was at its absolute worst at night. As I lay there, a thought came into my mind, "God forgives." I started to talk to God. I said, "Dear God, my momma won't forgive me for lying. Please, will You?" I fell asleep. The next morning when I woke up, I felt a wonderful peace. What was this? My constant companion, the black cloud of guilt, was nowhere to be found. A little voice echoed in my heart, "Have no fear, I am with you." I knew it was God. I was amazed. The next night I said, "Dear God, I know that You have forgiven me, but what about all the other bad things I have done. Do I need to confess those to my mother?" Instantly I heard a little inner voice, "No, I've taken care of it all." I was so happy. I was free.

It was many years before I comprehended what had happened to me that night. I had been born of God. He had come into my heart when I had confessed my sin to Him. He had given me His forgiveness and a new life. Years later when my mother heard my salvation story, she didn't remember her statement to me and felt badly about it. I told her she shouldn't feel badly at all. God had mightily used her to show me the consequences of sin! Some years later, I came across these words in the Bible, "Fear not, for I am with you" (Isa. 43:5) and recognized them to be the words God had spoken to my heart the night of my new birth.

An Answered Prayer

While growing up, I had a tremendous fear of not being normal. I always felt that there was something wrong with me, that I wasn't like other people. I would pray at night to "Dear God," as I affectionately called Him, that He would please let me be normal. When I was twelve, I begged my mother to let me shave my legs as other girls my age did. She adamantly said, "No. Forget about it. Your legs are fine." When I was thirteen, I still hadn't started my monthly cycle like most of my friends, and I was afraid I wouldn't. I began praying about this. One night, I believed that God had answered my prayer and had told me my cycle would start that week. I was happy and waited patiently the whole week, but nothing happened. However, four weeks from the day of His promise, the answer came. Then it dawned on me that He had actually answered my prayer as promised the week I prayed, because the twenty-eight-day cycle had begun then.

The way God answered this prayer characterized the way He would answer many others over the next forty-plus years. I would learn to count with certainty on promises He gave me in answer to prayer, even though the fulfillment was delayed. Years later, when one of my friends read this story, she asked about God teaching me to believe His promises, even when the answers were delayed. She wondered if He always did this. I really didn't know how to answer this except to tell her that there were a number of specific instances in my life when I simply knew He had answered my prayer. On the other hand, there were also times when I prayed and didn't get a clear answer. The important thing is that somehow, He did teach me to trust Him, even when answers were slow in coming.

A Face Like Alfred's

I was at a very difficult age and was struggling to grow up. Whenever I looked in the mirror, I saw a very ugly, big, round, freckled face surrounded by a thick, straw-like mess of hair looking back at me. If I had been under the "perming" hand of my mother, the straw was frizzed. I hated what I saw, especially when I went into the restroom at school and happened to look in the mirror and saw other faces looking back as well—those of the beautiful, blond-haired, blue-eyed, flawless-skinned creatures who walked the halls of my school.

One weekend, I rode the bus with my best friend, Annie, downtown to a movie. On the way there, two boys sitting in front of us on the bus began to talk to Annie. She was cute and they thought so too. One of them looked at me with my big round face and said, "You look like Alfred E. Neuman" (the face on the cover of *Mad Magazine*). They started laughing and Annie laughed as well. I laughed too. What else could I do? I knew what I looked like. The boys ended up sitting in front of us at the movie, where they laughed at the movie and also at my face a few more times. I guessed they got their money's worth. My face was laughing too, but inside I was in terrible torment, wishing I could run away and cry.

Annie decided to try out for the junior high school drill team, so I did too. My tryout number was 92. Annie's number was 90. I hoped that I would be far enough away from the judges so that they wouldn't see my big face well or my hairy legs, and I might somehow get picked. When I practiced in front of a mirror, I noticed that if I held my arms out straight, they curved downward from the elbow. I would consciously try to hold them slightly crooked, so they would appear straight. Maybe I could fool the judges about that too. Then the trials were over, and they began calling the numbers of those who had been selected, "... 85 ... 87 ... 90" (a scream of joy from Annie) "... 94" (a choking in the throat and a holding back of tears from me while giving congratulations to Annie).

When I consider now how much God has done in my life to let me know Him, I can laugh when I remember that time. He was keeping me for Himself. I was made happy so easily, and when I was happy, I forgot all about Him. When I had troubles or was unhappy, I always drew close to Him. He really was my very best friend. Because I didn't always get what I wanted, He helped me to learn what was important in life. Because I wasn't a beauty, as I grew older, He kept me from a lot of trouble that the "beautiful" girls went through. Because I thought I was abnormal, I needed Him to help me be normal.

I need to explain something about boys and me. In the first and second grades, they loved me. Up until about third grade, I actually was beautiful (and have the pictures to prove it!). They brought me presents and chased me at recess. When the boys chased me, I would come home every day and tell my mother about it, showing her all the little dime store necklaces and bracelets they had given me. One day, she looked at me and said, "You don't like those little boys." And from that day on, I didn't. Her comment made me feel strange and ashamed. I never again told my mother a word about boys.

Then the freckles came, and the long gawky body, and my days of popularity were over. As I got older, I wanted to be normal and have a boyfriend like other girls did! What would it be like to go steady? It appeared I would never know because I couldn't like anyone who showed any interest in me. I would get the same sick feeling I got the day my mother spoke those few words about boys to me. In the ninth grade, I had a crush on Mike until I found out he liked me too. Then I couldn't bear the sight of him. I denied that I had ever liked him.

Insomnia and God

At fourteen, I began having insomnia so badly that I would have to drag myself exhausted to school every day. I went to bed only to remain awake most of the night. Many times, I called to my mother in the middle of the night, crying because I couldn't sleep. One night she said to me, "You must have a guilty conscience. Don't ever wake me up again." I thought and thought but couldn't discover the guilt she suspected. Along with not being able to go to sleep, I started to recognize other things about my body that weren't fully automatic. As with sleep, I could interfere with their function. I even started having difficulty urinating. I became afraid I was either going to die from lack of sleep or lose my mind and end up wetting all over myself in a mental institution for the rest of my life. I said, "Oh God, if You will only help me, I will give myself to You to help mentally ill people."

I prayed every night for God to help me and took my Bible to bed with me, reasoning that somehow the Good

Book would help me. One night, as I was lying awake in my misery, dwelling upon the misfortune of dying at such a young age and asking God why this was happening, a little thought came to me, "You love yourself too much. So what if you die? What if I want to take you to be with Me? What if that is what I want for you?" I thought about that and then made a decision. If God wanted to take me, that was okay with me. I told Him so. I had decided I was willing to be sleepless unto death, if that was what He wanted. With this new attitude, I was able to quit trying to go to sleep, and I slept. From that time forward, as long as I kept the position that it was up to Him whether I slept or not, lived or died, I slept normally. But whenever I started wanting something too much, such as looking forward to an upcoming event, I would find myself thinking, "I've got to sleep, or I won't be able to enjoy this." I would be unable to go to sleep until I finally said, "It doesn't matter if I get to enjoy this or not. It's up to You, Lord."

I experienced this pattern for many more years. I later heard a Christian teacher say that the root of mental illness was self-love, and my experience confirmed that this was true.

I realize now that God was beginning to teach me something about the cross because it was when I decided to put what God might want above what I wanted that I experienced His peace. This was the first lesson of many to come in which He would teach me to love Him first and to put Him before myself.

End of an Affliction

The summer before I started high school marked the end of two years of suffering inflicted on me by my peers. During those two years, I had begged my mother to let me shave my legs, but she wouldn't allow it. I had obeyed her, but now I was rethinking my position. I was preparing to spend a few weeks with my cousin in Florida and then, in the fall, I would be going to high school. I made up my mind that no matter what penalty my mother would impose, the hair was coming off my legs. I wasn't going to Florida with furry legs to see my beautiful cousin, nor was I going to high school that way and endure the agony of sitting in my chair trying to hide my legs from the roaming eyes of my blond-haired, blue-eyed, smooth-legged inspectors. How many times during my junior high years had those eyes landed on my legs and then moved up to my face with a look of pity! I suffered every day with my hairy-leg affliction. Why didn't I just shave them anyway? Maybe the memory of my guilt after lying to my mother when I was eleven held me back. I think I was afraid of disobeying her and incurring more guilt. That summer, when I approached my mother and asked her one last time, she insisted again that I didn't need to shave my legs. I told her emphatically that if she didn't let me, I wouldn't go to high school! She marched up the hall to her room, went in for a few minutes, came out, and marched back down the hall to my room. She threw an old electric razor of my father's on my bed and said with disgust, "Shave them! You'll be sorry. Once this starts, it never stops!" I gladly committed the deed and delivered myself from the stares of my peers. Thank You, God!

I went to Florida and, miracle of miracles, I met a boy who liked me and one who I was actually able to like in return—maybe because my mother wasn't there to know. I purposely overlooked the fact that he was my cousin's ex-boyfriend who was trying to make her jealous. Anyway, I thought he liked me, and I had my first kiss or two. I was very naïve and only realized later that my cousin and her friends were into a lot more mischief than kissing. God went with me on that trip, protecting me through what could have been a very bad experience. From my view, I went home a real woman: I had been kissed!

Don wrote me a few letters, but I tried to hide the fact from my mother. If she knew about him, I wouldn't be able to like him anymore. Maybe I was subconsciously afraid my mother would make a poor comment about him. On top of this, I simply didn't know how to relate to anyone who openly expressed care for me in words. This was unfamiliar territory that made me feel uncomfortable and embarrassed.

Why was this unfamiliar territory? Possibly because I have no recollection of either of my parents ever saying that they loved me while I was growing up. I also have no memory of being hugged or cuddled. I have no doubt that they loved me, but my parents just didn't express care or love for me verbally or by physical touch. Instead, their care was expressed mainly by material provision. This was probably because of their own experiences as children.

Am I Jewish?

When I was fifteen, I realized that I was a Christian. At night, I prayed as my mother had taught me: "Now I lay me down to sleep. I pray the Lord my soul to keep. If I should die before I wake, I pray the Lord my soul to take. God bless Mother and Daddy, Dorothy and Julia, Grandmother and Granddaddy, and Aunt Emma. In the name of the Father, the Son, and the Holy Ghost, Amen." Then I would start talking to Dear God about my day and about whatever might be bothering me. I always prayed to Dear God. One night after starting to talk to Dear God, I had the thought that it would be much easier to be Jewish. Probably I was Jewish because I just believed in one God. After all, the "in the name of the Father, Son, and Holy Ghost" just didn't make any sense to me. So I asked Dear God, "Am I a Jew? I think I am because I just believe in You." Then I heard in my heart, "You believe in the God that Jesus brought." I thought about this and knew that it was true. Jesus had shown mankind the God of love. Since this was the God I believed in, I decided that this meant I was a Christian.

Not long after this, I read a book, *The Robe,* by Lloyd C. Douglas. While reading that book, I fell in love with Jesus. I thought if I could have lived when He was on the earth, being a Christian would have been really exciting. How wonderful it would have been to have lived with the early disciples and be excited about Jesus together. I had never met another person who claimed to be a Christian or who even talked about God on a personal level. My parents took us to a Disciples of Christ church, but I never heard the gospel preached there. I heard sermons with a lot of good stories and jokes that were about social issues of the day, but I didn't hear anything preached about Jesus. I never took a Bible to church until I decided to take a Bible credit course that the church offered which counted towards high school graduation. This was my first time to study the

Bible. Both in church and in the Bible class, I always was struck that no one seemed to be that interested in God or in what it really meant to be a Christian. It seemed to me that the greatest interest was in the donuts served between services. Going to church was just something you were supposed to do, like going to school or going to a dentist or going on family vacations. It was just a routine part of life.

A Window into My Little World

I believe that a glimpse into my experience as a child, especially with my father, is necessary to understand what happened to me later in life. Only in retrospect did I come to understand how much my childhood left me in need of love, acceptance, and appreciation.

No one in my family ever talked about God. Actually, my parents didn't talk much about anything with us children. We were to be seen and not heard. The most important thing in life to my father was money. It was at the root of many problems in our family and certainly made our life with him miserable.

If I left a light on in my room, I would get in trouble. If I turned the light off and then turned it back on too soon, I would get in trouble. This was because turning a light off and then turning it back on too soon cost more money than leaving it on. When my mother cooked dinner in the heat of Texas summers, he would shut the kitchen door so that the window air conditioners would not have to cool the kitchen. My mother would be sweating and overheating while cooking; but saving the money, not her, was more important to him. I thought this was terrible and sometimes begged him to think about her, but this resulted in him getting mad at me.

It was very important to my father that I made good grades. If I made straight A's, he gave me five dollars. If I made all A's and one B, he gave me nothing. I routinely made A's in my academic subjects, but periodically I made a B in Physical Education. That B would cost me my five dollars. One time, I made a C in English. Mrs. McCrane graded all our tests and papers, not with numbered grades as other teachers did, but with checks, check pluses, and

Chapter 2—Have No Fear

check minuses. You never were sure what your semester grade was until she verbally averaged it in front of the whole class one person at a time. During one such public grade-averaging session, she said, reading from her grade book, "Miss Hart. Let's see. Check. Check. Check minus. Check minus." When she completed her verbal tallying she said, "Let's see. That will be a C." When my father saw that C, he was furious and told me to go and talk to the teacher to find out what I needed to do to make an A. Her answer was, "Honey, if you are a C student, you are a C student." This made my Daddy livid. He marched up to the school and demanded a meeting with the principal and that blankety-blank excuse for a teacher. He told her in no uncertain terms that her job was to teach, not categorize her students. At her next public grade-averaging session, when she reached my name in her grade book, she paused, looked up at me, and said, "Miss Hart." She then proceeded, "Check. Check minus. Check. Check. Let's see. That will be (another long pause while looking up at me over her glasses) a B. I'm *sure* your father will be happy with that." "Yes," I thought, "but there goes my five dollars."

Because my father worked shifts for an airline company, every third shift he had to work nights and sleep in the daytime. If we made any sound in the house that woke him from his sleep, he would come out of the room like a raging bear and spank all of us. I wish I could say otherwise, but my childhood memories of my father are mainly of his anger. Mother told me she was thankful that we were all girls. She said that although he was very hard on us, if we had been boys, it would have been worse.

My father was very prejudiced against black people and frequently used a derogatory term to refer to them, usually mixed with curse words. When I was in high school, he made a lasting impression on me during dinner one night. After he had made an ugly racial comment to which I had responded, "Some *white* people are really bad, Daddy," he came out of his chair across the table at me and hit me, screaming at me, telling me I didn't know what I was talking about. I escaped to my room, where he followed me and hit me some more. I never said anything like that to him again, but he is responsible for my lifelong determination not to be prejudiced toward any race.

One sad memory has always stood out in my mind. I was dressed and ready to go somewhere with my high school girlfriend and her family. The event had been planned for some time. After I finished fixing my hair and getting dressed, I went out on the back porch to say goodbye to my father, who was watering plants with the garden hose. As we talked, I said something that he didn't like. With a sudden turn, he hosed me down from head to foot. I became hysterical because my hair was ruined and my clothes were all wet. He then grounded me. When they arrived a few minutes later to pick me up, I had to answer the door and tell my girlfriend that I couldn't go. This wasn't the first time I was grounded just prior to leaving the house to go somewhere with friends—it was a regular occurrence. This, however, was the only time I was hosed down.

Although I have other similar memories, there really is no point in sharing them. It is fair to say that I basically was afraid of my father because I never knew when he was going to get angry. I have tried to think of good or special memories with him when I was a child, but I can't remember any, other than that he enjoyed Christmas time.

His practice was never to say he was sorry for anything. The first time I ever heard him apologize was when he was seventy-three years old and I was forty-five. A short time before he died at the age of seventy-nine, he prayed the sinner's prayer and received Christ. He even asked the Lord to forgive him for his prejudices. His salvation truly was a miracle for which I am very thankful.

As I grew older, I learned more about my father's childhood and parents. He had begun working at age five to help buy his own clothes and had worked from that time forward. His father and older brother had been alcoholics. He didn't know how to make us feel loved or appreciated, but he worked hard and was faithful in meeting all of our material needs.

All things considered, my father had turned out remarkably well. After I was grown and married, he loaned us some money for the purchase of our first home. This was momentous for him. It was also the first time I remember him sitting and calmly talking to me, trying to explain something about himself. What he said helped me understand his high regard for money. He said, "Jane, I'm glad I have this money available for you. Do you know that in my whole life, not one person has ever given me anything, not even a nickel? I have worked for every penny I have." I felt very sad for him that day. I had not walked in his shoes, so I couldn't understand what his life had been like. Even though he did not give me the advantage in life of growing up in a close loving relationship with him, he did give us much better care than his own father had given him.

When I look back at some of the experiences I had with my father, I find it amazing that I didn't retain any bad feelings toward him. My father didn't know how to make me feel loved, but God did. The Bible says God is a father to the fatherless. Emotionally, I was like a fatherless child, but God faithfully stepped in to fill the gap. I think this may be why I never felt blame or anger towards my father. As a child, I always tried to please him; but if I ever succeeded, other than my five dollar reward for grades, he didn't let me know about it. He was just my daddy, and like any child, I loved him and wanted him to love me.

My best memory with him came not long before he died. I was visiting him in the hospital. As I returned to his room from a visit to the ladies' room, I met him on his required walk up and down the hallway. He stopped me and voluntarily gave me a big hug. He said in my ear, "You always were my smartest one." I said, "Thank you, Daddy." Thinking about that makes me cry.

When I think of my mother, I think of self-sacrifice. She worked hard for the family and tried her best to take care of us. Until I was around twelve years old, she would fight with my father to protect us from his upsets. Then one day, she decided not to do this anymore. In many ways, life was harder for us after that, but things were better between them.

Mother had a few nice dresses hanging in her closet. Other than those, she had her nurse uniforms. Whenever we asked her why she didn't get any new clothes, she insisted she didn't want any. The truth was that my father had her on a budget, and she chose to spend the money on our clothes instead.

She worked as a nurse from 2:00 p.m. to 11:00 p.m. a few days a week until I was in junior high, and then she started working five days a week. She got up in the morning, made breakfast, made our lunches, and sent us to school. She planned dinner before she left for work. When I came home from school, she would have detailed, written instructions that told me exactly what to do to prepare the evening meal. I followed the instructions and cleaned up the kitchen afterwards. Like my father, she was gone from home a lot because of work. I felt like a substitute mother for my two younger sisters.

My mother had a compassionate heart and was a very caring person. She wanted us all to be healthy and happy. Although my father often treated her very poorly, most of the time she accepted her lot in life. Occasionally, it would get too much for her; but because she didn't want us to know she was upset, she would just go into her room and shut the door. She had a Bible in her room that she read, but she never talked to us about the Bible. Mostly, she just did everything she could to keep my father happy.

It took me many, many years to realize that my family was extremely dysfunctional and that there was no proper discipline or emotional nurturing of the children. My sisters and I had abnormal relationships with one another and many resultant conflicts in our childhood. We carried the scars from our childhood into our adult lives. We became Christians and were helped by this to understand our parents and their backgrounds, to forgive them for their failures, and to love them. Becoming Christians, however, didn't automatically change the bad patterns of interaction we had developed as sisters.

Growing up, I wrongly learned that if your material and practical needs were met, then this meant you were loved, even if none of your emotional or psychological needs were met. My material needs were met, but in the emotional and psychological areas, I was on my own. Everything in our family was about work and survival. I didn't know this was abnormal, and I never had any complaint in my heart against my parents. I think my emotional and psychological neediness is what helped me find

Jesus at a young age. It is also probably the reason I was susceptible to serious spiritual deception as a young adult.

The best memories I have of growing up were about Christmas. This was the one time of the year that we children were made to feel special. Of course, the main attention we received at Christmas came from being given presents, but that was good enough for me. It made me happy, and receiving things made me feel loved. My mother did attend a few school events of mine, but my friend Annie's parents took me to everything else and even took me on a few of their family vacations.

Except for the constant conflicts I had with one of my sisters and the meanness I sometimes experienced from my father, I wasn't consciously unhappy. Like any other child, I had no other point of reference from which to evaluate my life. I just accepted my little world for what it was.

Chapter 3
Much Sooner Than I Thought

> But He gives more grace. Therefore He says: "God resists the proud, but gives grace to the humble." (Jas. 4:6)

Honking at Boys

IN HIGH SCHOOL, ALYSA BECAME MY BEST FRIEND. Her parents were fairly well off, and she had her own car. Her father drove a nice car, wore suits, and worked as a salesman in an office building. My father drove a ten-year-old, immaculately-kept car, wore khakis, and worked as an airplane mechanic in a hangar. I was embarrassed by this and always tried to hide it.

Years later, he would comment that I was always either the first one out the door or the last whenever he picked me up after school. He never figured out why. The truth was this: I would wait and come out last unless I could run fast enough to get out first and make a getaway before anyone saw my father wearing his khakis and driving his ten-year-old Chevy.

He wouldn't let me drive his car (not that I wanted to drive that old thing), but Alysa would let me drive hers. We cruised all over town just for fun. My parents, of course, were unaware of this.

Alysa and I loved to drive to Charco's (a hamburger drive-in), get a Coke, and wait around for some cute guys to show up. We'd strike up a conversation with them and usually manage to get them to follow us as we drove away. Alysa was the bait with her blond hair and drill team jacket. (I had decided not to try out for the high school drill team. I wanted to be on it, but I didn't want to run the risk of the big rejection, so I rejected it first. Alysa tried out and made it, so she had the all-important drill team jacket.) For fun, we would let the boys follow us awhile and then lose them and go home. One day, we were driving on a street in Dallas when a car with two boys passed us traveling the opposite direction. I leaned over and honked the horn because the boys' car had a decal from a prestigious local high school. We started laughing and went on to the ice cream parlor.

We parked, went in, and were buying our ice cream when suddenly Alysa said, "Jane, it's those guys. They turned around and came back." They entered the store and stood next to us to order some ice cream. I was thoroughly embarrassed. We lowered our heads and, as soon as we had our ice cream, ran out to our car where we began laughing hysterically. We left quickly, but they managed to follow us. As we neared our high school, against my objections, Alysa pulled over. Even though I was arguing with her that this wasn't smart, she was determined to meet them. After talking to them for awhile, Alysa gave them her phone number.

That night, Alysa called me saying, "Jane, the guys we met today called me tonight!" She was particularly interested in one of them. His name was Ricky, and he had asked her for a date. Alysa had responded that because she didn't know him, she could only go out with him if it was on a double date with me. The next day, Ricky came to her house with John to ask her out again, saying that they were going to my house next for John to ask me. I got a frantic phone call from Alysa saying they were on the way to my house and that I had absolutely no choice in the matter: I had to go out with John so she could go out with Ricky. Alysa was going to tell her parents that they were friends of mine, and I was supposed to tell my parents that they were friends of hers. It was evident to me that they both were interested in Alysa and that John was going with me just so Ricky could go with Alysa. They came to the door and asked me to go. I agreed. The end. How embarrassing that was!

They took us to their high school basketball game. That night was the first of many dates over the next few years for John and me. Ironically, it was one of only two dates Alysa ever had with Ricky. I don't know why I liked John. Maybe it was because he didn't seem to really like me. Yet, he did like to kiss me. That was what I liked too—none of this talking stuff. That made me too uncomfortable. John didn't say he liked me. He didn't even say my name. I was comfortable with that. My father never talked to me either, unless it was to discipline me.

Through the rest of my high school years, John and I dated. He usually called every other week. Sometimes there would be longer periods of time between calls. I knew that if he really acted like he cared about me, I would be true to my pattern and wouldn't be able to like him anymore. I had been able to get over what my mother thought, but I still had problems with what my peers thought, and with what I thought. John went to another high school, so I didn't have to deal with anyone knowing that I liked him. For me, it was the best of both worlds: I had someone who took me out, and I didn't have to face my problem of others thinking I liked him.

Not long after I began dating, I started to let my moral standards slip. There still was a line that I planned not to cross, but as long as I respected that line, I felt that it was okay. One night, after having been on a date where I behaved according to this belief, I went to bed and closed my eyes to go to sleep. Immediately, I envisioned a long, long slide stretching out before me going downward into a great blackness. I was at the top of the slide and was moving down it. I cried out to God to save me. I didn't want to go down that slide. I am absolutely certain now that in the following years, God intervened in my life to protect me. That memory always serves to remind me that God saved me. He warned me of the danger of my behavior and then answered my cry for rescue. If He hadn't rescued me, I am certain that I would have gone down that slide into the blackness of sexual sin.

Existentialism

When I wrote my term paper on existentialism during my senior year in high school, I had to read several books written by existentialists. One of them was *The Age of Reason,* by Jean Paul Sartre. By the time I finished reading these books and studying the beliefs of existentialists, I was unable to talk to God. I had talked to Him in bed at night for many years about whatever was going on in my life. He had been my best friend. Now, I began to find such conversation impossible. When I started to talk, thoughts flooded my mind about the childishness of even believing there was a God.

The existentialists said that God hadn't created man, but rather that man, sensing his own weakness and frailty, had created God. God was only something in his mind. Life was actually meaningless. There was no meaning to all of the random events that happened during a man's lifetime. Because man needed a crutch, something to lean on, something to explain all the occurrences in his life, he made up God—a being who was bigger than the weak little man was, who knew what all the things in the little man's life were about, who was in control of them, and who comforted the little man. Well, hadn't I believed in God as a child? Hadn't I started believing at a time when I was in great need? Maybe this God thing was just a childhood experience. It really wasn't logical. How could there be a God? If He existed, why wasn't He visible? Why didn't He do something to make His reality unquestionable? I couldn't escape the logic of the existentialists. To become an adult, I would need to lean on logic and not fairy tales. I decided it was time to grow up and face life as it really was without my imaginary friend. After reaching this conclusion, I discarded my childish, illogical belief in God. My frustration with not being able to talk to God ended because I quit trying.

For many months I was in this new frame of mind. I gradually became more and more unhappy and very moody. Alysa kept asking what was wrong. Where was the old Jane? Where was her friend? Eventually, she told me she didn't enjoy my company and, unless I could snap out of it, she couldn't take being around me. I wasn't happy, but I figured it was just par for the course of growing up. I had a lot to complain about, and if she wasn't friend enough to hear it, I wouldn't bother her.

My unhappiness was growing and even beginning to bother me. One night in bed, I found myself longing to talk to my old imaginary friend. A tremendous war waged in my mind. I would start to say something to Him, and then I would stop and say to myself, "You are so stupid. You are talking to the air. There is no God. You are so weak that you want to stay a child all your life." Then something else would be almost crying out saying, "Dear God, please be there! I want You to be there!" Then, "How can you beg something to be there that you made up? Stupid!" I don't know how long this war went on that night, but in those hours, the final war-ending battle occurred. As I lay there in my misery, all of a sudden, a thought came into my mind and caught my attention. The thought was, "You want to be logical; you want to be right; you want to be an adult; you want to believe what is really true; so you have chosen to believe the existentialist philosophy. Why don't you take note of the existentialist misery?" I began to think about this. All the existentialists I had read and written about in my term paper were a sorry lot of humanity. They were miserable and admitted it. All of a sudden, this seemed stupid. Then another thought came, "I wasn't miserable before I believed all the existentialists had to say. Now, I have become like them." Then I heard, "You were afraid of appearing to be a fool and believing in something that wasn't logical." All at once, I had a very clear thought and made a very big decision. "It's better to be a fool who believes in God and is happy than to be an existentialist, who is logical and seems to be right in his analysis of life, but is absolutely miserable." The war was over. I was going to live out my days on this earth as a believing, happy fool. I was filled with peace again, and existentialism went the way of all trash—into the garbage.

Once again, God was teaching me. He had shined His light on my desire to appear wise and my fear of being or looking foolish. When I gave up this desire and was willing to be a believing fool, I found Him again and His peace returned.

The summer before I went away to college, I met the boy who lived next door. He asked me out. I was crazy about him. He was a weight lifter, and I thought he was beautiful. I didn't care that he had a terrible reputation around high school. I would be different. I thought about no one but him for most of that year. I also didn't care who knew that I liked him. When we went to our separate colleges, we wrote; and I saw him some on weekends. I didn't care that he had a girlfriend at college. Gradually, however, I learned what he was interested in and realized the only reason he kept seeing me was that he hadn't yet conquered me. I talked and wrote to him about God. Then one night while talking to God about the boy next door, I knew I was not supposed to see him again. He had been showing his true colors and God simply told me, "No." I took that little word and never saw him again. Somehow God was more important, and I knew He had to have first place.

I was learning another lesson: putting Him first in something that was really important to me as a young girl—boys!

The Berlin Wall

My adult cousin, Louise, was married to an Air Force dentist. She and her five small children were stationed with him in Wiesbaden, Germany. For my high school graduation present, they invited me to spend the summer with them in Europe. My father, who could obtain a discounted airline ticket because of his job, said he would pay for the ticket if I would earn my spending money for the trip.

So during my senior year in high school, I began working after school at a five-and-dime store. The store manager, a middle-aged man named Mr. Hill, began to treat me poorly after a few days on the job. It was apparent that he expected the same level of performance from me that he got from another high school student who had been working for him for some time. He became easily exasperated with me from day one and would roll his eyes when I didn't immediately know something. This made me extremely nervous and prone to more errors. I had never been made to feel stupid before. I completely lost whatever self-confidence being a good student had given me. I usually cried on the way home each day for relief. If it hadn't been for the carrot of the trip to Europe, I would have quit in a heartbeat. The thought that in the not-so-distant future I would have to "work for a living" made me feel sick. I wasn't quite sure what that meant, but if it entailed facing more "Mr. Hills," I dreaded the prospect. At the end of the school year, I happily picked up my final paycheck, knowing that I never had to return, and packed my bags for overseas.

That summer in Europe as my relatives took me to various countries, my little world expanded into a great big world filled with unusual places and people. One week, Louise took me and another young girl to Berlin. There was a heavy feeling of fear and darkness that hung in the air in East Berlin when we toured behind the Berlin Wall. The silent, deserted streets were in stark contrast to the hustle and bustle of West Berlin. One night, Louise took us out on the town in West Berlin. After she had too much wine, she ended up taking us into a nightclub with an awful show. That was another eye-opening experience—one I wanted to forget! God went with me that night and helped me find a seat that enabled me to have my back toward the so-called entertainment.

The visit to Berlin left a lasting impression on me. I didn't have utterance to say this then, but that day I had observed two extreme results of the devil's hatred for mankind. On the eastern side of the wall, people had lost their freedom and were restrained to such an extent that the oppression in the city's air was palpable. On the other side, people still had their freedom, but they had thrown off all restraint and were involved in hideous expressions of that freedom.

When it came time for me to fly home at the end of the summer, there was an airline strike in progress. This was a potentially serious problem because it was just a little over a week before I was to start college. For the next week, as a standby passenger, I failed repeatedly in my attempts to catch a flight. When I finally was given a seat, I prayed every minute before the plane took off that they wouldn't remove me. When I finally felt the plane lift off, I breathed a long sigh of relief and began to pray that I wouldn't be "bumped" off the flight during its stops on the way home. At the last stop, when I realized I was not losing my seat, I said to the stewardess, "I am so glad you didn't take me off!" She responded, "I didn't know you were a stand-by passenger! We need your seat." She proceeded to de-board me. I sat crying in that little airport for many hours before they managed to get me on another flight.

And that wouldn't be the only time in my life that my big mouth got me in trouble!

I still have a picture in my mind of landing in Dallas and my parents and sisters standing at the airport terminal window. They were waving at my airplane as it stopped at the gate. I was an older, wiser world traveler who was glad to be home barely in time to make it to college.

Grace to the Humble

I had been determined to go to college. My father hadn't planned on his girls extending their education, but he decided to send me because I had persisted in begging him to do so. My desire was to major in art, but my father convinced me that art wasn't practical and that nursing was. I wanted to go to Baylor University, which was a very expensive school. Much to my surprise, my father agreed to send me. So in the fall of 1965, I headed for college in Waco, Texas.

My trip to Europe had been my first experience away from home, but at least I had been with relatives. Now I was petrified by the prospect of living in a new place completely surrounded by strangers. My roommate, whom I had never met until she appeared in our dorm room, had a perfect wardrobe. Every piece of clothing was in a plastic bag. Each outfit had matching shoes, slip, and underwear. I felt like one of the "Beverly Hillbillies" in comparison to her. As if the wardrobe wasn't intimidating enough, she decided to schedule our activities in our room. Did I want the mirror and sink from 7:00 a.m. to 7:15 a.m. or at another time? Please! I knew I couldn't take this. Mercifully, I soon ran into a girl I had known in high school and found out she wasn't happy with her roommate either. We managed to make a swap. Whew!

I walked across campus every day praying to Dear God, asking Him to take care of me and help me. I felt lost. The whole environment of college was different from anything I had ever known. My parents had dropped me off at Baylor on the first day of the term, and I didn't see or hear from them until Thanksgiving. I didn't call home because I didn't want them to think I couldn't handle being away at school. Everyone else seemed self-assured and confident.

I understand now that it was the Lord who always arranged things to let me know my need. This was His blessing to me because it caused me to pray and depend on Him. Frankly, I would have preferred to be strong in myself; but if I had been, I might have missed out on getting to know Jesus in small, daily situations.

John, the boy I had met with my friend Alysa during high school, was now away at another college. He wrote occasionally. Actually, he would write me a letter and say he wanted to see me when it was time to go home for a holiday. Before the Thanksgiving holiday during my second year at Baylor, I received a letter from him in which he asked if I wanted to do something with him over the holidays. I thought, "No, I don't. You take me for granted." I had been invited to go home over the holidays with a college friend, so I decided to accept her offer instead. I would show him. I sat down and began a letter telling him that I had other plans. That felt good. He needed that. My Bible was on my desk. For some reason, I picked it up and read, "God resisteth the proud, but giveth grace unto the humble" (Jas. 4:6, KJV). I sat there for a few minutes while that verse spoke to me. My decision to not go home and the letter to John had come from my pride. I tore it up and wrote another telling him I would be glad to see him. Our relationship had changed some. We had begun having long philosophical conversations. Actually, John talked and I listened and pretended to agree. I didn't have the guts to tell him I believed in God and that I even talked to Him. I knew John would laugh at me, and I didn't want that. I also was afraid he wouldn't be interested in me anymore if he knew I believed in God. He was very cynical about God and faith. He had told me that he didn't care at all about what happened to a person after death, but he was concerned about truth in this life.

Struggling with God

As my second year at Baylor continued, I became unhappy. I went to bed each night thinking about my life. I really cared about John, but I was sure the feeling wasn't mutual. I was just someone for him to date. Did it matter that John didn't believe in God? Deep down in my heart, I knew it did. A Christian should marry another Christian. Because the people you date are the people you marry, I had begun having the thought that God wanted me to stop seeing John. I argued, "But I really care for him, and it is

Chapter 3—Much Sooner Than I Thought

so hard for me to like anyone." I decided to make a deal with the Lord, one that was all in my favor. I would stop seeing John if God would do these things: (1) take away my feelings for John so it wouldn't hurt, (2) let me meet someone else whom I really liked and who liked me, and (3) let this person be someone at my own college. If God would do these things, then I would stop seeing John (quite a one-sided deal!).

The next day, while I was in the campus bookstore, I stopped to look at some acrylic paints. I was planning to start painting, so I picked out some colors, brushes, and a canvas. Someone started talking to me, asking me if I painted. I told him I was learning. He struck up a friendly conversation and asked me my name. The next day, he called and asked me to go to a play on campus. Later, I found out that he was a "somebody" on campus. On the first date, I also discovered that he was a Christian. We had a great time. After the play, we had a long walk and a long talk. We ended our date by spending several hours in a late night coffee shop laughing and talking. He asked me out again. I liked him, and the feeling seemed to be mutual. We dated the rest of the school year. He was going to a ranch for a summer job in Wyoming and made plans to come through Dallas for a visit on the way home to Louisiana at the end of the summer.

Of course, I was very aware that this was the answer to my prayer about John. The school semester ended, and my mother came to take me home for the summer. On the drive home, I thought about what the summer would hold without John to date. I knew I needed to keep my end of the deal, but I didn't want to. John called and asked me to go out, and I accepted. By the time he came to get me, I was feeling terribly conflicted. I stood in my room before leaving and told God I was sorry I couldn't keep my end of the deal. As I went down the hall to the living room where John was waiting, I said in my heart, "Dear God, if You want me to end my relationship with John, You will have to do it for me. I can't."

That night was strange. I couldn't talk at all. I had absolutely nothing to say. I was so quiet that it was even bothering me. John kept asking if something was the matter, telling me I was acting strangely. All of a sudden and to my surprise as well as his, I blurted out, "I don't think I can see you anymore. We are too different. This year I dated someone who believes like I do about God. I didn't know that this was possible before now. Now I know I can never be happy hiding what I believe. I haven't been honest with you when we talk. I do believe in God. I know you think that is a crutch, and maybe it is; but I need one." We talked a little more. Finally, he sat there looking at me and said, "Well, I don't want to continue seeing you if you believe like that." When he walked me to the door that night, He didn't say, "Goodnight," but instead he said, "Goodbye."

I went into the house, closed the door, and leaned against it, ready to cry. Instead of crying, I realized that I had an incredible feeling of peace. Not one tear came. In fact, I felt wonderful. What was this? I knew it was God. He had done what I couldn't do. He had kept my end of the deal for me! I went to bed and woke up the next morning with the same peace. I had an amazing sense of expectancy. Something wonderful was going to happen to me. I didn't know what or when; but I knew it was going to happen, and I knew it would be something from God.

That summer, having completed the two-year academic portion of my nurse's training at Baylor University in Waco, I began the two years of practical training at Baylor Hospital in Dallas. I moved into the nursing students' dormitory beside the hospital. After I had been at school for several weeks, I received a phone call from John, who asked me if I would go to lunch with him to talk. He told me this wouldn't be a date. I felt like I should go, so I did. He had some questions about what I believed, but I wasn't able to explain very much because I didn't know the Bible that well. He asked, "What do you have to do to be a Christian?" I said, "You have to believe in Jesus." He asked, "Believe that He lived two thousand years ago?" I said, "Well, yes, but you also have to believe that He lives now." John said that believing in the historical Jesus was one thing but the alive now part was ridiculous.

John began calling again after that day, and we started going out to eat and talk. After a little while, we were back in the same old dating rut. I had hoped he was going to change and start believing. Not so. One night, we were sitting in the dorm lobby. He looked depressed. I asked him what was wrong. I tried to comfort him by saying that I loved him. I asked, "Do you love me?" (He had said he did one time before, and I just wanted to hear it again.) He looked at me and said, "I don't know." I said, "What? How can you not know?" He said, "It depends on how I feel." I said, "On how you feel?" I was horrified. I said goodnight and went to my room. I lay in the bed crying and praying. "Dear God, why am I here again? What kind of person loves when they feel like it? Please help this poor person. Can't You do something to help him? And please help me! I'm back where I was before You helped me to stop seeing him!"

A Notch on My Belt

Several days later, I ran into an old friend from high school who was very happy and excited about life. She had recently heard the gospel through Campus Crusade for Christ and had become a Christian. Even though I had attended a Baptist university, I had never before heard of anyone *becoming* a Christian. Actually, she was the first person I had ever met who talked openly about the subject. I told her I was a Christian and shared with her my "John story." She encouraged me to stop dating him. It was easy for her to say, but I knew it wasn't easy to do. I told her, "I've already done that once. It's not that easy to give up someone you really care about." She proceeded to tell me how she had accepted Christ a week before her wedding date. When her fiancé, who wasn't a Christian, rejected the gospel, she had broken off the engagement. She shut my mouth with that story. Then she asked me to go with her to a Campus Crusade for Christ Leadership Training Institute, a week-long program in California at the end of the summer. She told me it would be good for me to be around other Christians and see how many young people there were who were serious about God. I decided to go.

I prayed that, if possible, God would work it out for John to go, but decided I wasn't going to ask him. Several days later, John noticed some of my literature about the California trip and began asking me questions. He decided he also wanted to go, telling me the trip was a great deal ($50 for one week's room, board, and transportation).

Later, my new Christian boyfriend from Baylor, Andy, came to see me on his way back from Wyoming as planned. His visit happened about a week before I was to leave for the Campus Crusade for Christ event in California. John was out of town at the time, and when he got back, he found out I had gone to an amusement park, Six Flags Over Texas, with Andy. John called repeatedly until I got home that night and then had a lot of questions about who my friend was. I think he was actually jealous.

John and I left the next day on our group bus trip to Arrowhead Springs, California, where Campus Crusade held these events at a mountain resort. The first night, we all met together in a large outdoor amphitheater to hear several people speak about Christ. After a few training meetings, we were all supposed to board buses and go to the California beach to preach the gospel. I thought, "If I am a Christian and am scared to do such a thing, what will John feel?" At the end of that meeting, everyone stood together and prayed the prayer in a little booklet by Bill Bright called, "Have You Heard of the Four Spiritual Laws?" This was done so that anyone who wasn't yet a Christian could have an opportunity to become one. I stood when everyone else stood. Out of the corner of my eye, I could see John, still sitting. That made me mad. Why couldn't he just try! When the prayer was over, I turned and ran out, making a beeline back to the girls' dormitory.

I went to my room and, in the dark, got down on the floor between the bed and the wall and started crying. What was I going to do? Obviously, John wasn't going to change. I couldn't resolve my conflict with God as long as John, the non-Christian boyfriend, was in the picture. In a flash, I knew what I was going to do. I made up my mind. I started to pray, "Dear God, I'm going to choose John over You. I can't do this anymore. I know that I will come back to You one day, but for now, this is just how it has to be. I can't do this try-to-give-him-up thing anymore."

But then, suddenly, I cannot explain how, I knew that John was going to become a Christian. It was a certain fact to me. I didn't know when, maybe it would be ten years in the future, but it was going to happen. I might not even be around to see it, but that was okay. In my heart and mind, I had a complete turnaround. I was going to stop seeing

John and follow Jesus. He would take care of everything. The incredible peace from the beginning of the summer returned. I got up from the floor a different person. The thought came into my mind, "This is God's grace."

And it was His grace. This experience was the beginning of my learning that whenever I was struggling with God, there was a secret help available. I learned I could talk openly and thoroughly to Him about my struggle. I learned that it was all right with Him for me to say things that were blunt, even things I thought He might prefer I didn't say. The secret was not to hide my struggle or try to suppress it, but to go to Him and lay it out in front of Him as honestly as I knew how.

The next day, when I met John before the first meeting, I found him the skeptic as usual. He said that it was no wonder everyone there believed. In a place like that, everyone psyched each other up and only talked about God. To my surprise, and his, I didn't say anything. He wanted a response. I shrugged and smiled. John wasn't in my hands anymore. We went to a couple of meetings during the day and back to the amphitheater that night. On Sunday afternoon, John approached me and said, "Well, you can put another notch on your belt." When I asked him what he meant, he said, "I did the 'pray to God' thing. If this is being a Christian, it feels like hell." My first thought was, "Oh no, he prayed, and it didn't work." But instantly a voice in my heart said, "Don't worry, I am in him now."

Are We Communicating?

The next morning, we boarded the buses and headed for the beach. John had started reading the Bible the night before and had actually enjoyed it. On the bus, everyone started singing, and John joined in. I noticed a difference in his countenance. He looked happy. As the day went on, he started getting happier and happier. It was amazing. The rest of the week was wonderful. About midway through the week, we sat down together one afternoon on a bench and began to talk. In the past, I would always tell him, after we had been talking philosophically, that we just didn't communicate. He would say that was stupid. How could I say we weren't communicating when we had just been talking for two hours? On this day, after a few minutes, John looked at me and said, "Are we communicating?" I started laughing. "Yes!" John was a new man in Christ:

> Therefore, if anyone is in Christ, he is a new creation; old things have passed away; behold, all things have become new. (2 Cor. 5:17)

This memory always helps me understand what it means to be born again. Before John was born again, his spirit was deadened. When we talked, there was no communication on a deeper level. When he received Christ, his spirit was made alive, and he was brought into the fellowship of the Son. Because of this, we could communicate on a level not possible before. What a wonder! I was also amazed by the fact that to become a Christian was an actual experience of new birth. I had previously thought that becoming a Christian was simply a matter of deciding to believe differently. I had no idea that Christ Himself would come into a person's heart when invited! What I saw happen to John totally changed my understanding.

I marvel now at how God worked in all those circumstances to prepare John for his salvation, even to the extent of bringing another boy on the scene with whom John was in competition, one who was a Christian.

Riding back to Texas on the bus, I was happy. As I was looking out of the window, talking to the Lord and wondering what lay ahead, I heard in my heart the Lord telling me that John and I were going to be married. The phrase I heard Him saying was, "Soon, very soon, much sooner than you think." I believed it.

Much Sooner Than I Thought

Two days after we got home, John asked me to marry him. He believed this was what God wanted. I did also. I accepted. We decided I would change schools and go to North Texas State University where he was. We would get married in a year, after he graduated. When I told my parents that John and I were planning to marry and that I wanted to change schools, they exploded. When I told my mother that John had become a Christian, she was

Chapter 3—Much Sooner Than I Thought

mortified. She was standing at the kitchen sink peeling potatoes. She turned and waved her hand at me saying, "John has always been a Christian, so he can't become one!" I tried to tell her what had happened, but she became more upset and started crying. My father put his foot down and said he wouldn't pay for my education if I changed schools.

John and I decided that I would change schools anyway. When I inquired about housing, I found out that all the dormitories were full. However, they would try to find approved off-campus housing. While I was waiting to hear the result of their efforts, I began feeling uneasy about what we were doing. I kept pushing the uneasy feeling down because I wanted things to work out. I prayed, "God, I am not sure we are doing the right thing. If You want me to stay at Baylor and wait for things to work out with my parents, please let there be no off-site housing here for me." If there were no approved housing available, then I would take this to mean I was to go back to Baylor and wait. When they did locate off-campus housing for me, I was as surprised as they were to hear my response, "Thank you, but I won't need it." I left the campus housing office surprised by how I had responded but with a tremendous sense of relief.

I told John, "They had a room for me, but I didn't take it. I am going back to Baylor and wait." I explained my prayer and my surprise at what I had done. John said, "Before you went into the office, I also prayed. I told God that if you didn't get housing, I would take it to mean that we were supposed to get married now." John took what had occurred to mean we should not wait to marry. I happily agreed. In this unusual way, God had let us know what we were to do.

Before John went to ask my father for permission to marry me, we sat in the car outside and asked God to help us. We were both afraid of how my father would react because he had already told me I couldn't marry until I finished school. To our great surprise, my father calmly said, "Yes, when?" John told him we were going to get married that week. We were in favor of a small ceremony and were willing for them to do whatever they wanted within that time frame. My mother started crying and asked, "What are you going to wear?" We were married the next Sunday, much sooner than I had thought, just as the Lord had told me on the bus coming back from California.

During the week before our wedding, John and I prayed about each thing we had to do. When we had a need, we didn't pray out loud but sat together and prayed silently. We hadn't been able to find an apartment in the crowded college town, but after we prayed, one opened because of a last-minute cancellation. We hadn't been able to agree on wedding rings, but after we prayed, we were able to agree on simple wedding bands. When we selected the rings we wanted, the jeweler told us how long it would take for them to be ready. We said, "But we need them by Sunday!" He raised his eyebrows and said, "I see." He pulled open a drawer full of loose wedding bands of all shapes and sizes. We selected two of them that fit and bought them! My mother put together a small wedding, dressed me in white, and managed to have all my college friends present. The ceremony was on September 17, 1967, in the "Little Chapel" at my family's church, and the reception afterwards was in my family's home. Considering the time constraint, my mother did an amazing job.

During the first week of our marriage I received a forwarded letter from Andy, the boy I had been dating at Baylor. I realized it was going to be a big shock to him to receive a letter back from me, only a few weeks after I had last seen him, telling him I was married, but there was no other option!

Part 2

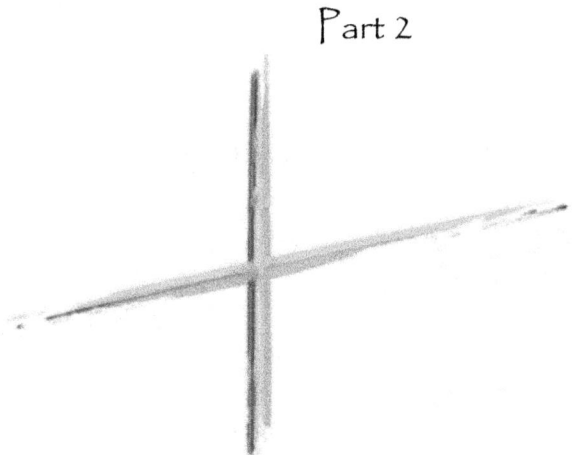

Satan's Subtle Deception
Wood, Hay, Straw

The Lord will silently plan for thee,
   Thou object of omniscient care;
   God undertakes Himself to be
Thy Pilot through each subtle snare.

The Lord will silently plan for thee,
   So certainly, He cannot fail!
   Rest on the faithfulness of God,
In Him thou surely shalt prevail.

The Lord will silently plan for thee
   Some wonderful surprise of love,
Eye hath not seen, nor ear hath heard,
   But it is kept for thee to prove.

The Lord will silently plan for thee,
   His purpose He'll to thee unfold;
The tangled skein shall shine at last,
   A masterpiece of skill untold.

The Lord will silently plan for thee,
   A happy child kept in His care
As though no other claimed His love,
But thou alone to Him wert dear.

            — E. May Grimes

Chapter 4
The Church of No Name

> Now if anyone builds on this foundation with gold, silver, precious stones, wood, hay, straw, each one's work will become clear; for the Day will declare it, because it will be revealed by fire; and the fire will test each one's work, of what sort it is. (1 Cor. 3:12-13)

Looking for Fellowship, Finding Ballet

SO MUCH HAPPENED IN THAT SHORT SUMMER that I felt like I was in a whirlwind. When it stopped, John was a Christian; we were married and living in Denton, Texas; and we were enrolled in North Texas State University. God had become very real to us. We were both anticipating an exciting life with Him. We wanted to become involved with Campus Crusade for Christ, but because no Campus Crusade organization had been established there, we started looking elsewhere for Christian fellowship.

We visited several churches in Denton, but nobody was particularly interested in us or in John's salvation. Jesus didn't seem to play much of a part in the Sunday morning ritual. One church we visited, after we inquired, invited us back to a Wednesday night supper where we saw an amateur ballet that thoroughly bored John. He asked if this was what church was supposed to be. He said, "If I wanted to see ballet, I would go to a real ballet. Why don't they talk about Jesus or the Bible?"

We soon gave up on traditional churches and decided to visit a Christian coffeehouse on campus. After eating there one night, we stayed for an event in which they showed two movies back to back: "Death of a Salesman" and "The Grapes of Wrath." We could hardly believe that afterwards they simply dismissed everyone for the evening. The extremely depressing movies had set the stage for presenting the gospel, but the evening had ended without anyone even mentioning Jesus or God's wonderful salvation. We were both puzzled. Where was Jesus?

After we had been living in Denton a few weeks, a girlfriend from Baylor named Katy, who had just transferred from Baylor to Texas Woman's University in Denton, called me. She was very interested in hearing about John's salvation. When she heard we were looking for a church, she invited us to go with her to a Christian meeting in a home, one she had discovered in her own quest for Christian fellowship.

Fellowship in a Hundred-Year-Old House

Thus we went to our first meeting at David Washington's house on Carroll Street, just north of West Oak. David and Alice had three little girls and one little boy. David, an ex-military officer and an ex-pastor, was in graduate school at North Texas and hosted a small group of Christians that met regularly in his home. By this time, John and I had become very discouraged about finding Christian fellowship. When we went to the Washingtons' meeting, we entered through the back door of a hundred-year-old white frame house with a large porch surrounding it. We passed under several lines of wet clothes, through Alice's kitchen, into a big hallway, and then into a room with no furniture except for about fifteen metal folding chairs in a circle on a hardwood floor. A few women with big scarves on their heads were sitting in the chairs and praying out loud. They seemed to be moaning, saying, "O, Lord" at the beginning of each sentence, with emphasis on the *O*. I was uncomfortable. I hoped they weren't expecting us to pray out loud. I had never heard of such a thing and had no intention of participating. I didn't. Neither did John. Sometimes, their manner of praying seemed funny, but they were sincere, and I was too uncomfortable to laugh. I just sat there quietly, occasionally looking at the old wallpaper on the walls that was curling up and peeling off in places.

After about fifteen minutes, the door opened and in walked several men. John was so glad to be saved from spending the morning in a room with these moaning women that he relaxed after they appeared. We sang some

Chapter 4—The Church of No Name

songs, and then they each started to share personal testimonies. David Washington, a fatherly, mild-mannered man, talked about some Bible verses. It was very interesting, and I had to admit afterwards that I had enjoyed the Bible teaching, the personal experiences they shared, and especially the singing.

They all were very friendly and eager to hear why we had come there and rejoiced with us about John's salvation. That was a first. We both enjoyed this taste of real fellowship, which stood in contrast to what we had experienced watching ballet and movies. I told one of the ladies that I liked the meeting but that I was too shy to ever participate and didn't want to do so. She laughed and said that didn't matter. No one had to participate. I felt relieved and thought that I might want to come again. John also enjoyed it and inquired about other meeting times. I had never experienced fellowship like this. I was reminded of how I had felt when I read *The Robe* many years before. It was exciting to me that these people seemed to be like those in the early days of Christianity.

One of the things which attracted us to the group and kept us coming back was their meetings. They taught and tried to practice what the apostle Paul talked about in the Bible in 1 Corinthians 14. There, Paul says that every member of the body can prophesy (speak about Christ).

> For you can all prophesy one by one, that all may learn and all may be encouraged. (1 Cor. 14:31)

To this day, I still believe that, as Paul said, every believer can speak something about Christ in Christian gatherings.

I had grown up in a typical church in which we sat in pews and listened for an hour and tried to stay awake. In that church, at best we only remembered the anecdotes and jokes the preacher shared. In contrast, these meetings were full of biblical truth and personal experiences coming from almost everyone present. In the second meeting we attended, to my surprise and that of every one else, I said something! Because the meetings were so small and informal, I was surprised by how easy it was to speak when God gave me something to say. There was no program or set agenda to follow, so the Lord was free to lead the meeting by inspiring each of us to share our experiences or tell about what we had been reading in the Bible. Each one was free to ask for a song to be sung, offer a prayer, give a teaching, or share a testimony. There was, however, one long-winded brother; but since he wasn't the only one who spoke, the experience overall was enjoyable and fulfilling.

Not long after we began attending these meetings, I started to realize that God was speaking to me during the day through what I was hearing in those meetings. He also was speaking to me through the words of the songs we sang. In my traditional church background, I had been accustomed to just singing the first and last verses of songs. The songs there had been mainly just music and rhymes to me. Now we sang every word of every verse. I never had noticed before this time that the words to Christian songs had so much meaning.

Our New, Unique Church

After our first few meetings, John told me he wanted to begin attending all their meetings each week. I think there were four—two on Sunday, one on Wednesday, and one on Friday. I said I would go on Sunday but not on the other days. That was too much for me. I wanted to have a marriage full of time with John alone.

One night while John studied at the kitchen table and I was putting curlers in my hair in the bedroom after showering, I heard a noise. As I turned to see what it was, I saw a hand coming through the bathroom window curtains. My own sudden scream scared me even more! I met John at the door to the bedroom saying over and over, "A hand, a hand!" We called the police, who surmised that a regular peeping Tom had been frustrated because I had put a clothespin on the bathroom window curtain to shut it completely. Apparently, he had visited before and, when he found the curtain pinned shut on this night, he tried to remove the clothespin. My scream sent him running, knocking over a garbage can and leaving the telltale clothespin behind.

After this, I was too afraid to stay in the apartment alone. Now, I had no choice but to go with John to all those weekly meetings. I began to enjoy attending them as the Lord continued to use Scriptures and songs to help me. We began spending more and more time with our new Christian friends. Whenever John was at his part-time job at a soda pop canning factory, because of my fear of being home alone, I would spend time at the sisters' house. (They called the women "sisters" and the men "brothers" because we were all brothers and sisters in God's family.)

A Freezing Baptism

Not long after we began to regularly attend our new church, the brothers decided to have a baptism meeting at Lake Dallas. John needed to be baptized, and there were others as well who wanted to be baptized. They decided to go ahead and have the baptism in February because it was too long to wait until the water became warm. My high school friend, Alysa, happened to come to this baptism meeting, the second meeting she had attended. Upon arriving at the lake, we left our car engines running with their heaters turned on, so we could quickly warm ourselves after coming out of the freezing water! I was one of those who decided to be baptized a second time. I did this because I wanted to make a public declaration of my faith and because my first baptism had merely been a required church ritual. Alysa sat quietly and watched with wide eyes. After witnessing this unusual event, she stopped calling me. Apparently, I had become just too strange for her. I didn't pursue her either.

The Church of No Name

The church had a bookroom that sold books mostly by Watchman Nee and Witness Lee.[1] It escaped my notice that there were very few books by other authors. The church group had been using the name, "The Church of the Resurrection," but they told us that the Lord had recently led them to stop using any name at all. They also told us about Watchman Nee's revelation concerning the scriptural "ground of the church" or "ground of locality." This revelation was based on how Paul addressed his letters to the churches in the Bible. When he wrote a letter to a church, he addressed it to a city (or locality), for example, "Unto the church of God which is at Corinth...." When he wrote to more than one church, he addressed his letter to a province or region, for example, "... unto the churches in Galatia." Because of this, Watchman Nee believed that there should only be one church in each city. This belief was supported by the fact that the book of Revelation was written to seven churches which were referred to by their city names (Rev. 1:11). Watchman Nee believed that God viewed all Christians in a city as part of the one church in that city. There should, therefore, be no other basis or ground for meeting as a church, other than the fact that believers lived in the same city.

---

[1] Watchman Nee (1903–1972) is best known in the United States for his writings on the Christian life. He was responsible for a Christian movement in China referred to as the "Little Flock." In 1952, he was put in prison by the Communists because of his Christian faith. He died in 1972. (See "One Under the Umbrella" in chapter 8 for more about Watchman Nee.) Witness Lee (1905–1997) was a coworker with Watchman Nee in China. He continued Watchman Nee's movement, referred to as the Local Church, on the island of Taiwan and later in the United States and elsewhere. His writings, mostly transcribed from spoken messages, are published by Living Stream Ministry. (Information compiled from various Internet sites.)

We were taught later that additional support for the one-church-per-city belief was found by putting two verses together: Titus 1:5, where elders were appointed in every city, and Acts 14:23, where elders were appointed in every church. We were told that together these verses indicated that there should only be one set of elders per church and per city.

Watchman Nee also believed that there should be only one name associated with the church—the name of Jesus. This meant that denominations were wrong because they denominated themselves with other names and were thus dividing the body of Christ. In the same way that Mrs. Smith wouldn't take another name and call herself Mrs. Duncan, Christians should simply be Christians and not refer to themselves by other names such as Baptists, Methodists, and so forth. He taught that God wanted all believers to receive one another in the name of Jesus alone and meet with Christians according to the city where they lived.

Chapter 4—The Church of No Name

We thought all of this sounded very interesting. Because we were beginning to believe that there was something wrong with most churches, especially those we had grown up in and the ones we had recently visited, we began to wonder if the Lord had not led us to His real church.

A California Connection

We soon learned from the Denton church that there were two other churches in Texas that believed the same about the ground of locality as the people in Denton. One church was in Lubbock, and the other was in Waco. These three groups all believed what Watchman Nee taught about the local ground of the church. They kept their meetings open to every believer in the city where they lived because they believed that everyone who was born of God was automatically a member of His church. They said that God had set up the church in this way so that Christians could have a genuine, practical oneness. By "practical oneness," they meant oneness that could be seen by people in the world, one that was not just an invisible spiritual oneness. They said that Jesus had prayed for this kind of oneness because unbelievers needed to be able to *see* Christian brotherhood.

These three small churches occasionally traveled to one another's cities to have meetings together, especially on weekends. They were also in touch with a similar church, located in Los Angeles, California, where Witness Lee was now living and ministering. This church was much larger than all the Texas churches combined. We also learned that many people had moved to Los Angeles from all over the country to become a part of the Church in Los Angeles. John and I were favorably impressed by all of these things.

Local Administration Only

Not long after we began regularly attending their meetings, we learned another interesting thing about the Texas churches. Before John and I had come in contact with the Denton church, a middle-aged brother named Leon had gradually maneuvered himself into a position to exercise his influence over all three small Texas churches with their youthful membership. Because Watchman Nee and Witness Lee taught that there should be a completely separate administration or eldership in each city, with no extra-local influence or control, the California church's leaders soon helped the Texas brothers understand that Leon was violating this principle. When the Texas brothers tried to correct Leon, he wouldn't listen to them and ultimately left. After this, the churches in Texas decided to stop visiting one another for a period of time in order to establish themselves more clearly as locally independent entities.

Leon's influence in the Texas churches foreshadowed a similar situation that would happen in coming years, only it would be on a much larger scale. There was a lesson here, but we didn't learn it. At that time in Denton, John and I were very new to the group and as yet had no thought that any of the brothers were considered to be elders.

My friend from Baylor decided to travel with John and me to Waco for the Baylor homecoming weekend. The Denton brothers and sisters took our trip as a sign from the Lord that it was time to re-establish fellowship with the Waco church. They made arrangements for us to stay in the home of Stephen and Trudy Thompson, one of the couples in the Waco church. We met all the people in the church there and attended their meetings that weekend. John enjoyed talking to the men in the church, but I was a little intimidated by the women. They seemed so spiritual. Several of them had children or were pregnant, and they were all several years older than I. I was uncomfortable around them; but because I was usually shy when I first met people, I expected to get over this discomfort in time. All in all, we were happy because we had found real Christians whose primary focus in life was Jesus.

Chapter 5
Door Into Another World

> Be sober, be vigilant; because your adversary the devil walks about like a roaring lion, seeking whom he may devour. (1 Pet. 5:8)

The Revenge of the Flying Kitten

AFTER SEVERAL MONTHS OF MARRIAGE and life in our new church, I began to face the fact that our marriage relationship wasn't doing well. I wanted John to tell me he loved me and treat me like Prince Charming was supposed to treat his new princess. It just wasn't happening. One day, I asked him if he loved me, and he told me he didn't know if he did or not. What? Hadn't we solved that? Didn't he become a Christian? Wasn't this the answer to every problem? Weren't we supposed to live happily ever after together in our castle? I soon found out the simple, resounding answer to these questions was "No."

All I wanted was to be happy. That would about sum up my goal in life. It didn't take much to make me happy. I just needed a little love, kindness, and thoughtfulness from my new husband. All I wanted was for us to get to know each other better and find things to do together that were fun. I had no idea how much pain had been in John's life before this, nor did I realize that he possessed finely developed coping mechanisms to handle this pain.

In brief, John's father wasn't home much when John was a young child. When John was about eleven years old, his father completely deserted the family. John had been deeply hurt by this abandonment and had learned from an early age to shut down his real feelings.

He could tune me out and go to sleep in the middle of an argument. Afterwards, he would act like nothing, absolutely nothing, had happened. That was beyond me! How could he sleep when we were at odds? That was impossible for me. One evening after an unresolved argument, John lay sleeping and I sat in a chair by the bed staring at him and stewing. The little white kitten he had given me was playing at my feet. I reached down, picked it up, and started petting it. How could John sleep? How could he be so cruel and thoughtless? I pretended to be an innocent observer as the little kitten flew through the air and landed on John's sleeping face with a big meow and its claws out! John came out of his sleep like a roaring tiger. I said, "How can you sleep when we have a problem?" He dismissed my question, turned over, and went back to sleep.

Later as I lay awake, I prayed for God to wake him up and make him face the issues. Then I heard the familiar voice in my heart, "I will not cater to your self." Self? Did He say self? Was He talking to me? I remembered a hymn we had sung about the cross at a meeting. It talked about the "self" being something that hinders us from knowing God. I began to think about what this might mean. I had grown up believing it was right to put my self first. I was taught from kindergarten upwards that my self was something wonderful: I needed to educate it, improve it, appreciate it, defend it, love it, and work to give it all it wanted in life. Wasn't life's purpose to pursue individual happiness? But now a new thought was present in my mind: "There is something about 'self' that is a problem to God." Gradually, light began to dawn: God wanted me to understand something about my self-centeredness. I wanted John to love me because *I* loved me. I was unhappy because I wanted John's love, needed his love, no doubt had a right to his love, but I wasn't getting it. John didn't seem to have much to give.

One night, the Lord said to me, "If you will let Me, I will give you the love you are seeking from John. I will meet your needs for a loving husband." I knew He was telling me to stop making an issue with John about whether or not he loved me. I couldn't lose by taking God up on His offer to meet my needs for love, so I said, "Okay, Lord." The issue with God was settled, but many times, even though I tried to stop focusing on myself and my needs, I just couldn't help getting on John's case.

God also sent a word to help me through David Washington. He was very kind to us and treated us in a fatherly, caring manner. One night after giving us a ride home from a church meeting, he talked to us about marriage. He told us that, as human beings, we were made up of three parts, and that marriage was related to oneness in all three parts. He said that together as a married couple, God would make us one in spirit and soul and body. By marriage, we had become one flesh or one in body. Because we were Christians, he said that we were already one in spirit. He then explained to us that becoming one in soul was something that would take a lifetime of God's work in our lives. He also cautioned us not to have children too soon. His words about marriage encouraged me and gave me hope that, even though we were having some problems now, in the long run, everything was going to turn out okay.

My Education Is His

I had enrolled in school at North Texas, changing my major from nursing to sociology. I hated it. I didn't like any of my classes and didn't want to be in school. I kept thinking the Lord wanted me to quit. However, I was afraid. If something happened to John and I needed to support myself, I wouldn't have any way to do so without a college degree.

The girl in the apartment next door had a sweet little baby. They looked so wonderful together. I entertained a small thought that if I had a baby and John realized it loved me, he might become jealous and also start to love me. When the doctor switched me to a stronger birth control pill, it made me violently ill. John told me to stop taking it, so I did. Bingo, baby number one was on the way. I was secretly thrilled. So not long after our conversation with David Washington, I gleefully announced after a meeting that we were going to have a baby!

Although I had been helped by David Washington's wise words about marriage oneness, I'm sure that my announcement made him think that we had not paid the least bit of attention to him. I look back now in horror at how selfish, immature, and out of touch with reality I was at that time. We were basically oblivious to the realities of economic survival and parenthood.

John's mother was supporting us so that John could finish school and graduate that year. John had a part-time job for some extra money. My parents had refused to pay for the rest of my education, but because they had given me the remainder of the money in my educational savings account, I had been able to enroll in school that semester. We were in serious need of a reality check, but we probably wouldn't have recognized one if it had come. When I found out I was pregnant, John and I decided I should quit school so we could use the remainder of my school money to pay for the baby's birth. I was really afraid about not finishing school, but as I prayed about it, the Lord gave me a promise: If I ever needed to work, He would provide a job. I took His promise by faith, surrendered my education, and headed down the road of being a full-time mother.

I spent a lot of time thinking about the little baby in my womb. Was I going to be a good mother? I took a pen and paper and sat down at the table and wrote a letter to my baby.

Dear baby,

You don't know me yet, but one day soon you will. I love you and Jesus loves you. I want you to know that I have given you to Him. One day you will love Jesus, too.

Love,

Your mother

A Dead Pizza

When I was about four months pregnant, I cooked a pizza for dinner and set it on the corner of the little kitchen stove in our apartment. When it fell off and landed upside down on the floor, John made some ugly comment that infuriated me. I looked at the back side of the pizza for a minute and then raised my foot and stomped it to death. Crying, I ran out the door into the field next to the apartment and sat down under a big tree. Because I was wearing a thin little housedress and it was very cold outside, I started shivering. What a pathetic sight! I waited for John to come after me. He didn't. Well, I would just sit there and freeze to death. That would teach him. I could see the headlines, "Pregnant wife found frozen in field while husband sleeps in his bed with a dead pizza on the kitchen floor." After about thirty minutes, I decided I wasn't cut out for martyrdom. I went back into the house where I found John in bed asleep. I buried the dead pizza.

I hated John for his ability to totally tune me out. Eventually, I began to realize the Lord was using experiences like these to break me of my temper tantrums. My fits weren't getting the desired result. I got nothing back for all that expenditure of emotional energy. I knew John had problems, but it seemed like God wasn't listening to my complaints about John. Instead, He was working on me.

I am thankful for this now. If my tantrums had worked, I would have mastered the art and become a real pro, able to apply my skill to anyone whom I thought needed it.

No More Movies

One day, John and I walked by the Washington's house on our way to go to a movie in downtown Denton. Their home was just a block or so away from downtown. We were talking about our new church and how happy we were in it. As we approached the downtown square, we both began to feel uncomfortable about going to the movie that night and decided instead to stop by to see David and Alice. We liked being around them and their big family. We took a turn to the left, walked to their door, and knocked. They were thrilled to see us, and we spent the evening with them. What seemed to be just a simple turn off our pathway that night was actually a first big step toward exiting from the world we had grown up knowing. It would be almost twenty years before we went to another movie!

If that statement is surprising to you, no doubt much of what happens to us during the coming years will be also.

A Life Out of Almost Death: Todd

In August of 1968, John graduated from North Texas State University with a Bachelor of Arts in English. He had prayed and decided to teach, but he couldn't find a teaching job because he didn't have his teaching certificate. Finally, he was offered a job at a private, correctional-type boarding school in Desoto, Texas, south of Dallas. Included in his salary would be a house to live in near the school. One or two emotionally maladjusted boys would live with us in the small two-bedroom house as a part of the package. I told John I wouldn't do this under any circumstances. I was about to have our baby. John was desperate for work, so he took the low-paying job, without the housing, and we moved in with his mother in Dallas.

How little I appreciated his mother's sacrifice for us! She was a very good woman who did everything she could to take care of John and me. She told me how glad she was that John had married me. She revealed that John had never had a real family when he was growing up and told me more about his father abandoning them. She had worried about John and his future, so she was thankful for our marriage and believed my family would be good for him. While we lived with Nana for about four months, she gave us her bedroom and let me redecorate.

My obstetrician was in Denton, so when I went into labor while John was at work, my mother drove me to the hospital. John made it to the waiting room before our beautiful 8 lb., 9 oz. baby boy, John Todd, was delivered on September 11, 1968.

After returning to John's mother's house, I wasn't recovering well. My mother told me I was acting like a baby, but I couldn't help it. I had no energy, and if I stood very long, I felt dizzy. One day, I became frightened when I had a large amount of fresh blood pass from my bowels. I called my mother, who hurriedly drove me to my doctor in Denton. When he recommended putting me in the hospital to run a test on me, my mother, who was a nurse, grabbed my hand and said to him, "You will do nothing of the kind." She knew that this particular procedure could be fatal if there was fresh internal bleeding in progress. Because I had not seen further rectal bleeding since I called my mother, I think the doctor may have doubted my story.

My mother called a rectal specialist with whom she had worked. Because I was no longer bleeding and because I was nursing my baby, he instructed us to see my pediatrician to get the baby on formula. After this, I was supposed to make an appointment to see him. If, however, I saw any more fresh bleeding before then, I was to come to his office immediately. The next morning while at the pediatrician's office, I began to hemorrhage. Mother immediately called the rectal surgeon's office. He had just happened to stop in his office on his way out of town for the day. He had found a patient there who was waiting to see him who had come on the wrong day for his appointment. The doctor went ahead with the appointment, and just as he was about to leave the office, he received my mother's call.

Mother immediately got me into her car and headed for the hospital. Somehow, she managed to hold Todd and drive down Central Expressway while slapping me on the back of the head, trying to keep my head down because I was blacking out whenever I sat up. She dragged me through the doctor's office lobby and onto an elevator, carrying baby Todd all the way. When we reached his office floor, his staff met us at the elevator. About fifteen minutes later, he located the tear in my rectum and rushed me across the street to Baylor hospital for emergency surgery. Mother informed me later that the doctor said that if he hadn't been unexpectedly detained at his office that morning and prevented from leaving on his trip, I most likely would have bled to death. I was thankful that God wasn't ready to take me yet and that He let me go home to my one-week-old baby boy, Todd.

As a light aside, my mother used to scold me as a child for wearing shorty-pajama bottoms as underwear. She used to say, "Take off your pajama bottoms in the morning and put on real underwear! One of these days, you are going to find yourself in an emergency situation and you're going to be embarrassed to have on those shorty-pajama bottoms instead of underwear!" Mother was present that day to see my yellow pajama bottoms and her prophecy fulfilled!

The Denton obstetrician had unwittingly sewn one of the episiotomy stitches through my rectal wall. It had ripped through, tearing the rectum severely. After surgery, the surgeon told my mother and John that in about eighty percent of these kinds of cases, they had to do the surgery again and give the patient a colostomy so the rectum could heal in the absence of infection. They didn't tell me this. I was in the hospital for another week and spent three to four more weeks healing. Thank the Lord: I was in the twenty percent.

My parents encouraged us to sue the Denton doctor, but John and I didn't think that would be the Christian thing to do. Interestingly, for the whole hospital stay and surgery, we received only one bill for $220. Our insurance wouldn't pay anything because of a technicality in the fine print. John and I went to a credit union in Denton and got a loan for the $220, which we paid off at $15 a month.

While writing this story, I began thinking about that bill. Surely that wasn't enough to cover the cost, even in 1968. So twenty years later, I asked, "Mother, did you and Daddy pay for that hospital bill without our knowing it?" When I told her how much we had been charged, she couldn't believe it. She said they hadn't paid anything and always wondered how we had managed to pay those bills. She asked me who had sent us the bill for $220. I had no idea but thought it was the hospital. Someone had obviously done us a tremendous kindness. I'm sorry that I didn't realize this then and that I never thanked anyone. Maybe our small bill had to do with the hospital's and doctor's kindness to my mother who worked at that hospital, and to me for having been a nursing student there.

That Boy Doesn't Love You

During the week I spent in the hospital, my mother had a little talk with me. She said, "Jane, do you know what John said when I called him and told him you were going into emergency surgery and were hemorrhaging?" I said, "No." She said, "He asked if he should come! Jane, that boy doesn't love you." I told her she just didn't understand John and not to ever talk to me like that again. I didn't let her know how much her comment hurt me.

I was becoming aware that there was more going on inside John than he talked about and that I really didn't know him very well. He was having a hard time with his teaching job. One morning, when I gave him orange juice for breakfast, he said, "Don't ever give me orange juice again. My stomach is upset enough going to work without drinking that." Whenever we were having a communication problem and I pressed him for a response, he would either become silent or escape to slumber-land. One night, I was supposed to be packing for us to go to a California church conference to which the Denton group had invited us. It was being held in Los Angeles over the Christmas holidays. I wasn't feeling well and wasn't sure I wanted to go. I hadn't started packing yet, and it was really late. We were supposed to leave early the next morning. I was whining, complaining, and stalling. Out of the blue, John blew up. He shouted that we would just stay home, and then kicked the wall, accidentally making a hole in it. I had never seen him like this before. I got up and started packing. In some ways, as my mother had said, it did seem to be true that John didn't love me; but deep down, I knew it wasn't that simple.

Chapter 6
Initiation Into "God's Best"

And let us consider one another in order to stir up love and good works, not forsaking the assembling of ourselves together, as is the manner of some, but exhorting one another, and so much the more as you see the Day approaching. (Heb. 10:24-25)

No More Christmas

MY PARENTS WERE UPSET BECAUSE we weren't spending Christmas with them. Christmas had always been my favorite time of the year, and I really wanted to go home. Instead, we did what we believed the Lord was asking of us. We traveled to Los Angeles for a winter conference being held by Witness Lee.

Little did we know at that time that we would go home for Christmas only one time in the next twenty years. Why? During those twenty years, there would always be a long church conference over the Christmas holidays, and we would be expected to attend. We would learn that Christmas and Easter originated from pagan holidays which were introduced into Christianity at the time of Constantine. Since these holidays came from a pagan source and had many pagan practices, we would come to believe that it was wrong to celebrate them. Actually, no one would ever tell us we couldn't celebrate; however, these teachings would be frequently repeated and supported by testimonies. This belief provided us another reason to justify our going to conferences rather than going home to see our families. In retrospect, I realize our decision to stop celebrating these holidays wasn't a result of personal conviction or of the Lord's personal speaking to us. Rather, it was a result of the group dynamic.

The number of people attending the conference overwhelmed me—probably six to seven hundred. The place in which we met was a very large room filled with

Chapter 6—Initiation Into "God's Best"

folding chairs set up in concentric circles. In other words, everyone was facing the center and one another. They all were shouting, praising the Lord, and standing to give testimonies. We were caught up in it all.

Unlike in our little church, the Los Angeles meetings included a lot of bona fide hippies. They had just become Christians and were fired up for Jesus. They had long hair and some were barefoot.

Over the next few years, they cut their hair, put on regular clothes, got jobs, and got married. It was evident to anyone who watched this transformation happen that Jesus was responsible for bringing them out of a degenerate and dangerous lifestyle into more healthy human living. This was also evidence to us that God was blessing the Local Church.[2] Such indications of God's blessing in our early years were common.

---

[2] Although Local Church was not used as a name by its members, I refer to it as the Local Church. I also refer to it as the church, which was the common usage among members. I use the term Local Church to refer not only to a single Local Church, but also to all the Local Churches collectively.

The speaker at the conference was the older Christian teacher to whom I referred earlier, a Chinese brother named Witness Lee. His knowledge of the Bible was remarkable to us, especially considering that we had difficulty understanding his broken English. People in the church referred to him as "Brother Lee." We soon began to do the same thing.

This conference, as I recall, was about Christ and the church in the Psalms. Brother Lee showed us that there was a progression in the book of Psalms, beginning with psalms about Christ, continuing with those about God's house and the city of Jerusalem, and finally ending with psalms about God's praise filling the whole earth. We spent a lot of time in the meetings shouting, "Christ, House, City, Earth!" and "O Lord, Amen, Hallelujah!"

During our time there, I heard someone talk about an older Chinese brother in the Church in Los Angeles who was a very close coworker with Brother Lee. Someone told me that he, like Brother Lee, was so full of the Lord and was so transformed that, if you were in a room with him, he could see right through you and know what you were thinking. I believed this and decided that this old Chinese brother was someone I didn't want to meet!

The Big Circle and the Little Circles

The first time I heard formal teaching about the ground of the church was at a conference meeting in Dallas held in a community building in a park. At that time, Brother Lee was in his early sixties. He told us about an experience that Watchman Nee had with some pastors in the city where he lived in China. These pastors had become concerned with what they termed the "Little Flock" led by Watchman Nee. Many believers had left their traditional churches and were meeting with the Little Flock. In an attempt to remedy the situation of losing people from their congregations, the pastors met with Watchman Nee and asked him about what they considered to be his proselytizing. They told him that rather than promoting unity, he was causing further division.

Brother Lee told us how Watchman Nee answered them: Watchman Nee told all of these pastors that he was so desirous that there be a real, visible testimony of oneness in Christ's body that he was willing to go back to the place where the Little Flock was meeting and lock the door, never to meet there again. He asked all the pastors to do the same. He told them that he and all those with him would then come together and meet with all of them and their congregations in a new place as one church. In addition, Watchman Nee said that he would take no leadership position among them. They were all shocked by this. Ultimately, they were unwilling to do it. This change would no doubt have been too costly for them. Watchman Nee then asked them who it was that was causing the division.

I was very impressed by this story. Also, Brother Lee drew a big circle on the blackboard, representing a city. He then drew several smaller circles inside it, representing churches. He put little dots in the circles, representing believers. He told us that each little circle represented the ground upon which each group of Christians met. They all had the same foundation, Christ, but the ground on which they put their foundation was different. The ground of the Baptists was baptism by immersion. The ground of the Methodists was the teachings of John Wesley, and so forth. The problem was that these groups of believers were building the church on the foundation of Christ plus something else. Brother Lee told us that if all the little dots would leave all the little circles and meet together, they would be meeting on the ground of locality—the city. He said that everyone needed to keep Christ, drop their "plus" items, and simply meet together as Christians within the big circle of the city. This message was very enlightening to me and very persuasive.

At the same conference, for the first time I heard Brother Lee speak about Christianity in a derogatory manner, referring to it as "poor, degraded Christianity." By Christianity, he meant all churches other than the Local Church. I also heard him refer to what he called "sugary Christianity" for the first time. He explained that the goodness in Christianity was like sugar; it was natural, not spiritual. As Christians, we needed spiritual goodness. He told us that God was always good, but not all good was God. He also said disparagingly that those in Christianity had stopped at the cross and just remained there instead of going on to see the glorified Christ of Revelation who was walking among the churches with burning eyes, judging them. While listening to him speak, I sometimes felt that he was boasting and was somewhat prideful. However, I quickly dismissed this as my own judgmental thought. When I compared my youth and inexperience to his age, experience, and impressive Bible knowledge, what did I know?

A Runaway

While living in Dallas with John's mother, we met in the home of some Christians to whom David Washington had introduced us. One of the leaders in the Dallas meeting was overbearing and difficult to be around, so after about three months, John and I decided we wanted to go back to Denton and meet at the Washington's house again.

John also decided to go back to North Texas and get his teaching certificate, so he could get a real teaching job. He got a part-time job at Denton State School making $8 an hour, a small fortune to us, and re-enrolled in North Texas. In January of 1969, we rented an apartment near the campus and began spending most of our free time with the Denton church.

Shortly after this, I told my sister, Dorothy, about the group of Christians we had found. When I was about fourteen years old and Dorothy was about nine, I had tried to answer some questions she had asked me about God. From what she told me later, I believe that she probably was born again during that time. Our interest in God was the one thing we had in common. We fought about most other things. At my suggestion, she had read the book, *The Robe*, and was as affected as I had been by the story. When we started meeting with the church group in Denton, I told Dorothy that I was having an exciting experience like that of the early disciples about whom we had read in *The Robe*, and I invited her to come and see. After one visit, she also was very attracted to the group, but she was reluctant to come again because she had a boyfriend who wasn't a Christian.

Dorothy's story is a long one, but I will sum it up by saying that after she graduated from high school, she ran away from home, came to live with us, and became part of our new church. She abruptly ended her relationship with her boyfriend. We had nothing to do with her decision to run away. We had never even thought of such a thing. She did it on her own, after a big fight with our father. The first I knew about her departure from home was when she called to say she was on her way to our house with all her belongings. This deeply hurt my parents, and it took many years for those wounds to heal. They felt that I was responsible for what Dorothy had done. Because I believed that the Lord wanted her to be a part of the church and had allowed this to happen so she could be in it, we didn't send her home. About a year later, she married someone from the Church in Los Angeles.

A Three-Week-Long Conference

During the summer of 1969, we went for about three weeks to a summer conference hosted by the Church in Los Angeles.

It took all the extra money we had to travel to the conferences and to contribute to our hosts' expenses. We stayed in the homes of members of the Los Angeles church, not in hotels. We called this practice "taking hospitality." Many of the people in the three churches in Texas were school teachers who had the summer off from work and were free to use their time this way.

We took Todd with us, who was then nine months old, so I had to take turns babysitting with two other sisters during the meetings. At this conference, several hundred chairs were set up on three sides facing one side of the room where a podium and blackboard for the speaker stood. Brother Lee would give a message in one meeting, and then in the next meeting, he would call on people to come to the front of the room and repeat portions of it. John and I were assigned seats that were on the third row, directly in front of the podium. I was terrified by the thought of being called on to repeat something. I had trouble understanding all of what Brother Lee was saying and knew I could never repeat it. One of the elders in the Los Angeles church sat beside Brother Lee and helped him select people to be tested in this way. I thought we were safe because he didn't know our names; however, when we were leaving a meeting one day, this elder greeted us by name. I almost fainted, but God was merciful to me, and I wasn't called on that summer.

At one such conference, Brother Lee called a sister from Texas named Dana to the front and asked her to give a short message on a point he had covered. He sat down and waited. She stood at the front with a blank look on her face as time passed. Repeatedly, he told her to go ahead and speak. I don't know how long this went on, but it seemed like forever. I felt like throwing up. I prayed that he would let her sit down. It was humiliating. She stood there speechless for a long while, appearing to be frozen with fear. Finally, he told her to sit down and called someone else. As far as I could tell, Dana was never the same after that day. I thought this was terrible, but reasoned that Brother Lee knew the Lord and also knew what he was doing. Surely he was trying to help us learn and mature as believers.

We Move for the Church

During the conference that summer, the brothers from the three churches in Texas decided that, for the sake of having a larger church with more impact, all of the churches in Texas should move together to one city in Texas. Apparently, some of the brothers had talked with Brother Lee about doing this, and he had agreed. Afterwards John was invited to attend a meeting with the other brothers from Texas and heard that the Lord was "moving us to Houston." So in August of 1969, we moved. Most of us were young people and found it fairly easy to pack up and head for Houston. Some were older and found the move harder, but they still did it.

To my recollection, John and I didn't personally pray about moving but just did what the rest of the church was doing. I understand now that many times as Christians we should follow others, but we should never do this without praying and asking for our own personal conviction about what the Lord is asking of us. We were beginning to practice blindly following others.

John and I loaded up our things and headed south with everyone else. There were a lot of amazing stories during the move about how people found jobs and places to live, so it seemed the Lord was really directing this move. We all settled into three places: two apartment complexes (one in northwest Houston on a street named T. C. Jester and one in the southeast) and an older residential area in the central part of the city west of downtown. John and I lived in the north complex along with about ten other families. Many of the brothers were schoolteachers, and they all got teaching jobs immediately—except for John. He was eligible to be drafted and sent to Vietnam if he didn't find teaching employment. It was nearly three weeks into the school year, and he still didn't have a job. I was very upset that the Lord would give teaching jobs to some who didn't need deferments from military service and wouldn't give one to John who did. Every night in bed, I cried and prayed. I begged the Lord to give him a job. Deep down, I was afraid that God had in mind for me to lose my husband in a war and be left to take care of my baby all alone so that I would have to learn to depend on Him more. With John unemployed, it wasn't long before we ran out of money. The very next day, a brother showed up at our door and handed us a few hundred dollars that someone had asked him to give us.

About three weeks into the school year, a job became available teaching remedial reading at a middle school in northeast Houston. This school called early one morning and said they wanted to talk to John. He already had left for the day, having decided the day before to start looking for some other kind of employment. The school wanted John to call back immediately. Frantically, I tried to figure out how to find him. I had no idea where he was going, nor did I have a car to drive and look for him. Finally, I was reduced to sitting down and praying that the Lord would bring him home. A very short time later, John showed up, having forgotten something. He phoned the school, interviewed, and was hired.

This experience shows I was still praying and talking to the Lord about what was happening in my life. However, by this time, because of what I was learning in the church meetings, I was beginning to believe that this way of praying wasn't what the Lord really wanted from believers. Instead, I thought what He really wanted was for us to "eat Jesus."

Eating Jesus

While still living in Denton, we heard for the first time a teaching about Christ being our life. I really appreciated this teaching because it placed emphasis on having a relationship with Jesus, which matched what we were seeking. I believed in my heart that God wanted us to have a close relationship with Him. We heard more about Christ being our life during our first few years after moving to Houston. In line with this teaching, we learned that there were three different Greek words used in the Bible that were translated into the English word *life:* These are *psuche, bios,* and *zoe.* We were told that *psuche* was our soul or psychological life, *bios* was our physical life, and *zoe* was God's eternal life. We focused on the many Bible verses that contained the word *zoe*. God wanted us to experience Christ as our life and not just follow dead doctrines.

How could we do this? By "eating Jesus." We were taught that the Bible refers to Jesus as the "living bread" for us to eat (John 6:51). Jesus said, "...he that eateth Me, even he shall live by Me." (John 6:57, KJV). Jesus didn't say. "Study me"; He said, "Eat me." Brother Lee taught us that those in Christianity were busy studying and learning about Jesus, but they weren't eating or enjoying Him. This was illustrated in an allegorical fable that I think someone in the Local Church wrote. It was called "Hunky and Dory in the Kingdom of Food." The story line went something like this:

> Two fellows named Hunky and Dory lived in a kingdom that was filled with every imaginable kind of wonderful food. This excellent food had been placed everywhere throughout the kingdom by its wealthy king who loved His subjects and wanted them to have the very best food. But amazingly, in the Kingdom of Food, no one ate the food! Most people stood about and discussed it. Some were more diligent and spent their time studying it to find out all about it. They got their information from the king's recipes. They proclaimed their knowledge about the food. However, surrounded by a wonderful feast filled with nourishing food, they were blind to its real purpose.
>
> But then one day, Hunky did the unthinkable. He picked up a spoon and ate a bite of casserole. Wow! What a taste! It was great! So this was food! Hunky instantly understood. Food was to be eaten and enjoyed! He ate more of the casserole and then, full of energy, ran to find Dory. He convinced Dory to take a taste. Dory also instantly understood. He then realized that all the subjects of the king were in darkness regarding why their king had gone to so much trouble to supply them with so much excellent food! He meant for them to eat it, not study it.

We likened ourselves to Hunky and Dory who were eating and enjoying Jesus. The Kingdom of Food was poor Christianity which was filled with hungry subjects. John and I had found this to be the case both in the churches in which we had grown up and in those we had visited just prior to the Local Church. These churches certainly seemed to be filled with subjects who weren't enjoying the King's food.

We Find the Switch

Brother Lee also gave messages about *how* to eat Jesus every day. He said that all of the practices we learned in Christianity were "old and religious," not something new and fresh in the Spirit. God might answer old, religious ways of praying, but there was a better way. God had made man with three parts: a spirit, a soul, and a body (1 Thess. 5:23). The human spirit was the key to eating Jesus and experiencing Christ as our life. We heard many messages about this and about the importance of learning to, as Brother Lee phrased it, "exercise our spirit," our human spirit, to contact Christ.

How did we exercise our spirit to contact Him? By "calling on the name of the Lord," as mentioned in the verse, "For 'whoever calls on the name of the Lord shall be saved'" (Rom. 10:13). Brother Lee told us that the root of the Greek word for *call* in this verse was *kaleo* (Strong, G2564), which meant to "call aloud" or "call out." For example, he used Acts 9:14 to show that Saul (later Paul) was able to find Christians to arrest because they were calling on the Lord's name out loud. He also showed us other verses in which early Christians were calling aloud (Acts 22:16, Rom.10:12–14, 1 Cor. 1:2, 2 Tim. 2:22). In our meetings, we began to practice calling on the name of the Lord. We would loudly call out in unison, "O Lord Jesus! O Lord Jesus! O Lord Jesus!..."

Brother Lee compared calling on the Lord to flipping on a light switch. He said that we received initial salvation when we turned on the switch for the first time (Rom. 10:13). Now we should continue by using the switch and being saved daily. He told us that when we called "O Lord Jesus," we contacted Christ in our spirit where we were "saved by His life" (Rom. 5:10). We were supposed to do this every day, throughout the day. I practiced this and tried not to do my old kind of praying; but inevitably, when I was in need, I would break down and revert to talking to

God, telling Him how I really felt and asking Him for what I needed.

This always worked for me, but because of the teaching I was now hearing, I began to believe it was wrong!

We Find the Best Way to Eat

In addition to learning about calling on the Lord, we also were learning about the best way to really eat Jesus—"pray-reading." Pray-reading meant to pray using the actual words of the Bible (Eph. 6:17–18), rather than to compose a prayer with our own words. We were told to intersperse the words in a verse with these other biblical words: "O Lord," "Amen," and "Hallelujah." We began to practice pray-reading the Bible in all our church meetings. One person would pray, "O Lord, we have this treasure ..." Another would pray "Amen, we have this treasure ..." Another would pray, "In earthen vessels, O Lord, earthen ..." Another would pray, "Hallelujah, Lord! We have this treasure in earthen vessels." In between these prayers, everyone would loudly say together, "Amen." After awhile, we would move on to the next part of the verse, "That the excellency of the power ..." and so forth.

Pray-reading did help us focus on a Bible verse and not rush over its words too quickly. However, under constant teaching about pray-reading being something new to save us from the old ways of doing things, we began to believe that this practice was the only way to be involved with the Bible.

We were taught that we were not supposed to use our mind to understand the Bible because that was not what God intended. The words of the Bible were "spirit" and "life" (John 6:63), so we had to contact the Word with our spirit by praying rather than with our mind by thinking. We were told, "Get out of your mind and into your spirit," so that we could enjoy the Lord and experience His life. By "enjoy the Lord," we meant being joyful or excited about Him as opposed to studying or learning about Him. We frequently said something like, "We just need to enjoy the Lord!"

Before this, I had enjoyed simply reading the Bible by myself. Now, whenever I started to read it, I felt guilty that I was practicing something old or that I was using my mind instead of my spirit. If I just *read* the Bible, I felt like I wasn't really eating or receiving life from the Word or enjoying the Lord. So I would try to pray-read instead. Because I felt silly doing this alone, I usually ended up doing neither. The only time I really tried to pray-read the Bible was when I was in a group setting with others who were pray-reading.

Babysitting—A Torture

We began having our church meetings in a room at the YMCA in downtown Houston. The sisters, most of whom had small children, formed babysitting groups in our apartment complex. My group had eight children in it with most of them four years old or under. I passionately hated babysitting. It was like being tortured for three hours until you could get all of the children to go to sleep on pallets. Babysitting usually lasted from 6:30 to 10:30 or 11:00 p.m.

I look back on those days with tremendous regret. I hate writing about this because it makes me ashamed and sorrowful. I don't ever remember sitting with Todd at night, cuddling him and reading to him. I was too busy struggling with a small army of children. He experienced the same thing night after night. Many nights, I wasn't with him because another baby sitter was. We were meeting at least four nights a week and on Sunday mornings during the time we lived at T. C. Jester. My children suffered in the long term because of this kind of neglect.

John and I were having problems getting along, but our arguing was kept at bay by staying busy with church events. When we did find time to talk, matters that needed attention surfaced, and we usually fought. John had become more verbal since the foot-in-the-wall incident back in Dallas. One day, when I made John angry again as I had in Dallas, he reached over, picked up my treasured clock radio, and crashed it to the floor, breaking it into several pieces. I was furious and hurt. I couldn't believe he had done that. I picked up the radio pieces and ran out of the apartment crying to my Christian sister and neighbor, Diane. I cried and cried. She comforted me and told me to go home.

I asked the Lord to please fix whatever was wrong with our marriage. I was clueless. I knew I nagged, but I also knew he needed it because he didn't take much interest in carrying responsibility for home and family matters. He went to work every day and brought a paycheck home, but that was about it. It seemed I had to worry about everything else while he worried about nothing. His not worrying meant I had to worry more. He hated making any kind of decision and went to great lengths to avoid doing so. More and more, I took charge of things. I knew this wasn't good, but someone had to do it. He didn't smoke or drink or carouse. He went to church—all the time. I had a lot to be thankful for, but deep down, I knew our relationship wasn't what it should be. Unfortunately, without free time together, it was impossible to work on improving it.

Building a Meeting Hall

In addition to spending time in meetings, we began to spend time planning and building our own meeting hall. (We didn't refer to the physical building as "the church," but as "the meeting hall," because, according to the Bible, the church is the believers, not a physical building.) All the brothers and sisters pitched in and came up with enough money to secure a loan and buy property in southwest Houston on Windswept Drive. We didn't hire anyone to build the meeting hall, but built it with our own donated labor. While holding down jobs during the day, the brothers worked late hours on the meeting hall night after night until it was completed. Most of us moved from the three areas of the city in which we had initially settled to an apartment complex called Fountainview Trace, which was near the new property.

After the meeting hall was built, we were meeting five or six nights a week plus Saturday and Sunday mornings. The ones responsible for this busy schedule were the "leading brothers."

Our original thought, to my understanding, was that all of the brothers in the church were considered to be on an equal status and that no one was a designated leader. However, by this time in Houston, we had begun the practice of recognizing a few of the brothers among us as our leaders. We referred to them as "the elders," "the leading brothers," or "the leading ones." We believed that a plurality of elders would prevent the possibility of being led astray that existed when following only one person. Over time, we began to acknowledge one of these leading brothers as the main leading brother who was looked to by all as the local leader with the final say.

The elders were the main decision-makers among us and were responsible for the administration of the church. Most often, we just referred to them as "the brothers." For instance, if someone asked, "Did you fellowship with the brothers about that?" it was apparent that the person was questioning whether or not you had talked to the elders about what to do.

On Sunday morning, we had a meeting for the children while the adults met for two sessions. (Everyone always attended both sessions.) On Sunday evening, we met at 6:00 p.m. for the Lord's Table, during which we took bread and wine to remember the Lord's death. On Tuesday evening, we met for Bible teaching. On Wednesday evening, we met for prayer. On Friday evening, we met for more teaching. From early Saturday morning until afternoon, we met for "service group"[3] functions. On Saturday evening, we held what we called a "love feast" because everyone brought food and ate together (Jude 1:12). The purpose of this gathering was to bring non-Christians, feed them, and then present them with a gospel message. Monday or Thursday evenings were left for service group meetings and service group leader coordination meetings. There was no time set aside for family bonding or for resting.

---

[3] A service group was, in essence, a committee of selected church members that was given responsibility to complete a special kind of church-related work such as gardening, cleaning, typing, book sales, and children's work. We did not hire people to do such things, but did them ourselves on a voluntary basis.

Most of the leading brothers in Houston had their own businesses. In Houston, the main leading brother was Dan Williams. He opened a day-care center for children so that he could spend his time working on church matters. A sister in the church operated this business for him.

Because of this business arrangement, he could have time during the day to see his family if he wanted to do so. The majority of brothers in the church, however, worked all day and then attended church meetings and performed service functions the rest of the time. This meant that for most of us, there was no time left for our families.

I know now that Satan was definitely behind the packed schedules. Because we were too busy to have time to rest and reflect, it was easy for him to lead us astray. This is a recognized mind-control technique. Another technique is constant repetition. We were bombarded with variations of the same teachings day after day, and week after week. Satan, who often appears as an angel of light and who is a master at misusing God's Word, was able to slip in more and more things that sounded scriptural but contained error. For example, over time we came to believe this: "If you take care of the Lord and the church, He will take care of your marriage and children." We obeyed this as if it was actually a verse in the Bible. Because we had come to believe that the church was the foremost thing in God's mind, it was easy to accept this as truth. We did not notice the entrance of this kind of unscriptural belief. Over time, this particular belief served to justify the neglect of our family relationships and to override the cry of our consciences against this bad behavior.

Dan Williams and his wife, Clara, also lived at Fountainview Trace. Clara and I had frequent contact because we lived in close proximity and were involved together in church-related matters. When Dan and Clara opened their day-care center in an old house, I volunteered to help Clara make large wooden cartoon characters to decorate the outside of the day-care center. We spent several days working together on the project. One day, to my surprise, Clara bluntly let me know that she disapproved of the babysitting arrangement that I had made for Todd during the Saturday night young people's meeting. I didn't think this was any of her business, and we had a little intense discussion about it, which she later reported to her husband. Dan made her apologize to me. I really appreciated his action. Because of this and several other experiences, I had a particular respect and appreciation for Dan.

Chapter 6—Initiation Into "God's Best"

Our First Burning

While living at Fountainview Trace, we participated in our first "burning." A burning was a big bonfire into which we threw material possessions that we loved more than the Lord. We also burned religious items that we had come to believe were idolatrous—such as pictures of Jesus or crosses. Burning them testified that we didn't love the world or idols but sought, rather, a heavenly city.

Although there is an account of book burning in the Bible by those in Ephesus who practiced magic, what we did wasn't the same. The Ephesians only burned occult materials (Acts 19:19).

We threw all kinds of things into the fire: stereos, televisions (after breaking the tubes), sports equipment, jewelry, record and book collections, and so forth. Once, my mother bought me three beautiful new pantsuits, the latest fashion rage, and I loved them. The next week, a burning was announced, and the beautiful polyester suits melted on the fire!

During a meeting, while I was home babysitting, Dan Williams spoke well of my pantsuit sacrifice in the message he gave. I liked the praise but lived in fear for the next few years that my mother would ask why she never saw those new clothes again. I was thankful that she never did. Another time, I ventured to decoupage a map of the world on a big piece of stained plywood and put a verse under it that read, "The earth is the Lord's, and the fullness thereof; the world, and they that dwell therein" (Psa. 24:1, KJV). I loved it and was hoping a spiritual decoration might be acceptable. I hung it on my bare dining room wall. I also ventured to buy a few colorful pillows to throw on my old couch. A few days later, another burning was announced. I went through my house to find things that the Lord didn't want me to keep, leaving the living and dining rooms until last. I stood there looking at my new decorations and finally decided they had to go. Why? Because I loved them. For the same reason, I also burned my wedding pictures and Todd's baby pictures. I even tossed in an expensive gold charm bracelet filled with gold charms from my school days and an expensive ring that John had given me for my birthday when we were dating.

I believed that material possessions, unless they were absolute necessities, were "worldly" items that were part of Satan's world system. As such, they were unacceptable for followers of Jesus. When I combined what I read in a book entitled *Love Not the World,* by Watchman Nee, with what I observed in the lifestyles around me in the Local Church, I came to the conclusion that anything beautiful or pleasant to look at, such as decorations, jewelry, and pictures, were worldly; they were vanities, not necessities.

It is interesting that I didn't pray about this or ask the Lord if I needed to burn something. I had already formed my own guidelines for these things, so I just followed them. Also, the fact that God in His creation gave us beautiful things to enjoy never occurred to me. I was practicing a form of asceticism, trying to please God and others. I did not want to appear to be worldly, so I tried to avoid enjoying physical or material things.

At one of the burnings, Todd was clinging to my leg as he watched me throw into the fire a big stuffed animal that John had given me when we were dating. Todd loved to play with it. He looked up at me and asked tearfully, "Mommy, why are we burning Tiger?"

I am ashamed now that we took children to these burnings. I am also sorry that this is one of Todd's childhood experiences. I now recall something else that went into one of those fires: the letter I wrote to Todd during my pregnancy. That letter was burned up, so I was never able to give it to him. However, I never forgot its contents, nor did God. I had consecrated Todd to Him, and He took me up on the offer. Today because of God's love and faithfulness, Todd also loves Jesus.

I felt badly standing there with him watching his little friend burn in the fire. I wished I had not brought Todd with us. I didn't know how to answer him so I said something like, "We'll get you another big stuffed animal, Todd. There is a reason we're burning this one, but I don't know how to explain it to you."

The truth was that in our lives we had already traveled some distance down a pathway that was heading into very serious spiritual deception. Jesus told the disciples, "Take heed that no one deceives you" (Matt. 24:4). This is a serious warning and has great meaning to me today. In Greek, the word heed means "to look, see, usually implying more especially an intent, earnest contemplation" (Vine, 540). We didn't do this. Being seeking, well-meaning Christians did not guarantee that we would be free from deception. If it weren't possible for a Christian to be deceived, Jesus wouldn't have warned us to watch out for deception.

At the beginning of this downward road, John and I had been young, trusting, idealistic Christians, loving our Shepherd and following His voice with no idea of the spiritual dangers that lay ahead of us. We didn't know that there would be other voices beckoning us to follow them and seeking to distract us from taking time with Jesus so we would come to know His voice clearly. While believing with all our heart that we were following the Lord, we would become more and more deceived by the great deceiver, the devil. As Jessie Penn-Lewis wrote:

> The knowledge that it is possible to be deceived, keeps the mind open to truth, and light from God; and is one of the primary conditions for the keeping power of God; whereas a closed mind to light and truth, is a certain guarantee of deception by Satan at his earliest opportunity. (Penn-Lewis 50; in abridged, 58)

Jesus never left us. He was there to deliver us, but it wasn't an easy deliverance. He would eventually have to present us with hard lessons in order to open our eyes so we could make choices that would bring us out of darkness.

Chapter 7
A Frog in the Pot

> I beseech you therefore, brethren, by the mercies of God, that you present your bodies a living sacrifice, holy, acceptable to God, which is your reasonable service. (Rom. 12:1)

John Loves Me

IN 1972, MANY COUPLES BEGAN MOVING into a neighborhood filled with rental homes in southwest Houston, primarily so that their children could have backyards in which to play. John and I started looking for a house in that neighborhood but soon realized we couldn't afford to move there. We were paying around $135 a month for our apartment with all the utility bills paid. The houses were $175 to $200 a month with no utilities included. We lived from paycheck to paycheck and couldn't afford such an increase in housing expense. Although as a teacher John brought home only around $225 semi-monthly, we continued to drive through the neighborhood looking for an affordable house and asking the Lord to please let us find one. We figured the maximum we could manage was $150.

One day, we saw a really nice house that looked empty. After walking around it and looking in the windows, we went next door to ask the neighbors about it and found out that they were the owners. Because they were particular about who lived in the house, they had not put up a sign in the yard. They decided that they liked us and offered to rent it to us for $150 a month. We were thrilled and made the big leap. I loved our new house on Navarro with its trees and grassy backyard. We had three bedrooms instead of two, so we could have both a guest room and a room for Todd. This was the eighth time we had moved in the four-and-a-half years we had been married, and I was ready to stay put for awhile.

After we moved in, I took an afternoon nap one Sunday. When I woke up, John was there looking at me. He said, "Jane, I want to tell you something. Remember how you always used to ask me if I loved you when we first got married? Well, I want you to know something now. I do love you." With that he left. I closed my eyes and cried silently, "Thank You, Lord." I had given up expecting John to say he loved me, but God hadn't. After almost five years of marriage, John was volunteering that he loved me. Some couples start out saying they love each other and, after several years, don't say it anymore. This was better.

The Day I Gave Up Saturday

Every weekend, I would hope that I could carve out some time for the family on Saturday; but due to our service group responsibilities, this never happened. I would set my sights on a few of John's hours in the afternoon, only to have those taken by some pressing church need. John believed that brothers should give their time to the church and not be hindered from their church duties by their wives' demands. If he ever did anything contrary to the Local Church norm in order to take care of me and my wishes, he always worried that he wasn't doing what was expected of a brother in the church. When he didn't have time for our family, I would end up angry with him. One day, I made a decision to give up Saturday, and I did. From that day, I never again asked for Saturday time for the family. After that, our Saturday arguments stopped.

We had begun committing everything in our lives to the Local Church—what we often labeled as God's best—because we had started to feel sure that we had found His true church and His purpose for our lives. As you read, if you haven't already, you will probably ask at some point, "Why? How could you stay in a church like this?" Although we weren't stupid people, it may appear otherwise. I ask you to keep in mind that the development of all our beliefs and practices, and the resultant changes in our lives, took place very gradually over a very long period of time. This is not easily conveyed in a story! Our first years were really wonderful. God's presence was very real, the Bible teaching was exceptional, and our experience of brotherly love in God's family was without parallel.

Contact with Our Parents

We usually visited my parents and John's mother in Dallas several weekends a year. I wanted to go more often, so they could see Todd, but it was difficult to get away from the church schedule. We were not encouraged to make such visits but were pressured to be faithful to attend all the meetings and to fulfill our assigned responsibilities in the church. There was always a good reason not to go. My parents rarely visited us in Houston. They did not like our church and refused to come to even one meeting. I faithfully wrote my mother letters after I was married until, after several years, she asked me to stop doing so because it was too difficult for her to keep up with responses. After that, my contact with my parents was mainly through long distance phone calls; however, that was infrequent because of our budget. John's mother came to see us more frequently and would attend meetings with us. I could tell she was puzzled by some of the things she observed, but she was very nonjudgmental and accepting of our unusual church.

As I mentioned earlier, we did go home to my parents' house one year for Christmas. That year, the annual winter conference in California was cancelled because of Brother Lee's health. As I prepared for that visit home, because of our belief that Christmas was a pagan holiday, I had two big worries: I was afraid I would offend the Lord if I gave my parents a Christmas gift, and I knew for certain I would offend my parents if I didn't. So finally, I violated my anti-Christmas belief and bought a small household gift for them. I couldn't, however, bring myself to offend the Lord further by wrapping the gift. So I left it in a paper bag. The night before Christmas, I agonized over whether to give or not to give and whether to wrap or not to wrap. Ultimately, I said to the Lord, "I cannot give my parents a present in a paper bag! Please forgive me if this offends You, but I'm wrapping it!" As I wrapped the gift, I sensed the Lord's presence and heard His voice in my heart, "I am with You." He and I wrapped my parents' gift and put it under their tree. Of course, I would never let anyone in the Local

Church know that the Lord had helped me wrap a Christmas present!

A Day in the Life of a Sister

In those days, I was one busy sister. During the day on Tuesday and Thursday, the sisters, ninety-eight percent of whom didn't work outside of the home, would meet in groups to pray for the church. We didn't share about our own practical needs or personal difficulties; rather, we just pray-read verses without any discussion beforehand. Our prayers were mainly for the Lord to bless His work in the church. The rest of the time, we were involved in various church projects, in taking care of needy "saints," or in babysitting each others' children so we could perform our various church services.

At some point, we began calling each other saints because Witness Lee emphasized the use of this Bible term. He explained that the term saint was wrongly used in Christianity to recognize exceptional believers and should rather be used as the Bible used it, to refer to every believer.

We were often asked to provide hospitality. This involved providing food and lodging in our homes for people who were visiting or newly saved, usually over a weekend. Sometimes we were asked to actually let someone move in with us. One time, the leading brothers asked us to allow a young single brother to live with us for an indefinite period of time in order to help "capture" him for the church. Interestingly enough, this young person was our own age.

We actually used the word capture *to describe helping people "see the church" and give themselves to it as we had done. John and I, a young married couple with enough troubles learning to live with each other and to care for a toddler, certainly didn't need the added complication of a male stranger living with us. We should not have allowed this young man to live in our home. But to the church leaders, this was one way to increase the number of people who were sold out for the church. Whenever the elders realized that an unmarried newcomer or a weak church member needed a living situation, he or she was placed into the home of a church family. There was little consideration for the needs of the families. That we would say yes to this proposition shows three things: (1) our belief that God expected this of us, (2) our desire to please the elders, and (3) our concern that if we refused, the elders and anyone else who knew about it would question our absoluteness for the church.*

The word absolute *is a term that we used to measure the loyalty of a member. You were either absolute or not absolute, meaning you were either completely, absolutely loyal or you were not. The status of our loyalty was always being monitored by the leaders. As members, we also monitored each other, believing it was our duty to report signs of non-absoluteness to the brothers.*

John told our live-in brother that he couldn't be at our home during the day while John was away at work. This brother had a job trimming trees for the city. One day he got off early, came home, and knocked on the door, expecting me to let him in. I don't think he was intentionally being obnoxious or going against the rules; rather, he just didn't realize the awkwardness of the situation. I let him in, but that evening, I got really mad at John for putting me in this uncomfortable position. I resented the brother's presence in our home. When I was cooking in the kitchen, he would come and stand by me at the stove and talk. He stood too close for my comfort, and I wanted to hit him with the spoon I was holding. John told him again that he absolutely wasn't to come home during the day. Shortly afterwards, he was there again at the door, knocking early in the afternoon. I opened it and he said, "I don't want to come in, I just need some soap so I can clean up." So, instead of having a man in my house, I had a man in my backyard, washing up with soap and water from the hose and then laying down in the grass and sleeping for all the neighbors to see through our chain link fence! I decided during those three or four weeks that I would never again let a brother live with us. If we had to have anyone, it would be sisters.

By this time, I had reached the point that I was beyond considering the option of not allowing anyone to live with us. I had given up my freedom to refuse this, but I didn't even think about it that way. Rather, I thought if we said, "No," we actually would be saying we loved ourselves more than we loved the Lord. To remain in the approval of the leading brothers and to serve the

Lord faithfully, we would have to be willing to open our home to let other people live with us. By deciding to allow only sisters to live with us, I was actually trying to manage the situation by choosing the lesser of two evils. It didn't occur to me that the problem I was having could become John's, as he would be sharing his small home with other women. My thinking had already so conformed to the Local Church mind-set that I had no such consideration.

Recently, when I asked John if he had wanted to have people living with us, he answered, "Yes." For him, it wasn't too much of an issue to have someone else living in our home because he wasn't home very much. He went to work and came home briefly before going to a meeting every evening. The real impact was on the wives, who had to cook, clean, and share their home with the live-ins.

A Gospel March

When Todd was about three-and-a-half years old, John and I considered having another baby. Todd needed a brother or sister, and we wanted another child. However, the bad experience after Todd's birth filled me with trepidation. Whenever I was with Sandra Brown, a sister whom I thought of like a spiritual mother, I would end up talking about whether or not to have another baby, and if so, when. She would answer me in her characteristic manner with a big smile filling her whole face, and say some variation of, "Jane, you already know the answer to what you are asking me." One night, I started praying about my anxiety. Bowing down on the bathroom rug, I sobbed, "Lord, I know you want me to have another baby, but I am so afraid. I can't!" As I prayed, suddenly I knew I could. I stopped crying and got up, knowing the Lord's grace had come, and that He would do for me what I couldn't do. I became pregnant again in May 1972.

Soon thereafter, the church organized a "gospel march" in downtown Houston. We wore white smocks with red-lettered slogans like these: "You Need Jesus," "Christ is Life," "O Lord Jesus," and "Jesus is Lord." Some brothers led the march playing snare drums and a bass drum and trumpets. Many other brothers and sisters followed the drummers and shouted slogans together, like cheers shouted at a football game.

Gospel marches like these occurred in the Local Churches in Taiwan. Years later, we found out that it was common in the Chinese culture to march on behalf of various causes wearing robes with slogans. This was not the Far East, however, and we were extremely unusual!

I was one of the few selected to be a runner. So I ran alongside the marchers and passed out gospel tracts. When I got home that day, I felt sick and was so tired I could hardly move. I fell into bed and went into a long, deep sleep. During the night, I woke up with cramps, nausea, and heavy bleeding. I was about two-and-a-half months pregnant and was having a miscarriage. I was very upset by this and believed that my running in the gospel march had caused the miscarriage. I eventually accepted that God had allowed this to happen for some reason. I comforted myself by thinking that maybe there was something wrong with the pregnancy, and the miscarriage would have happened anyway.

Service Groups

The leading brothers assigned us to work on the various church service groups so that we could be practically "built together."[4] I was assigned to the clerical service group, even though I didn't want to be on it. I felt that I lacked the ability to do the job well, but it really didn't matter whether we had any capability in any given area of service. In fact, the leading brothers preferred that we didn't have any capability. The premise was that if we had some ability in an area, we might do the job in our "self," in our own strength, and become "puffed up" (1 Cor. 13:4). Without natural capability, we would have to depend on the Lord to get the job done, and He would get the glory rather than us getting it. According to our belief, if it was "natural," it was bad.

---

[4] We were taught that God wanted to build us together, just like He had built the tabernacle in the Old Testament. The tabernacle was built with boards paired and standing together in silver sockets. A single board was not complete unless it was paired with another board. We were not complete as an individual but

needed to be paired with at least one other to make a useful unit. We were taught about the concept of building in the New Testament (Eph. 2:21; 4:11–16, 29; 1 Cor. 3:9, 14:26) and believed that God was building us together into His church.

There was one notable exception to this practice—the music service group. I don't suppose it would have been good to have the piano played by someone who didn't know how and had to depend on the Lord to help him or her pick up the skill while playing. I guess that was one area where it was worth risking that the person might be serving in the self. To us, the term self referred to whatever we could do in our own strength. If we said something was "natural," we meant that it was not spiritual but something from our human nature and, therefore, not something of God.

Although the main purpose of service groups was supposedly for us to be built together, we were certainly expected to accomplish work. We were allowed to express our preferences when we signed up to serve, but we understood that we would serve wherever we were placed. I hated typing because my typing skills were poor, and I always made errors. I got very nervous when I tried to type something important and made even more errors. Most of the time, we typed message outlines or songs onto stencils for the mimeograph machine. These had to be perfect, and it was very difficult to correct mistakes on the original stencil. I started over many times, using a new stencil each time.

The clerical service group was also responsible for the mimeograph machine. We normally typed during the week and mimeographed on Saturday mornings. Two people could easily operate the mimeograph machine, but we were supposed to find ways for more people to participate and work together. Many times, we would have six people around the machine. Each one was responsible to do some little thing, like press the ink, turn the crank, scan the copy, undo a paper jam, or load paper.

I can still picture four to six women standing around that mechanical nightmare with ink on our hands, pray-reading and calling on the Lord while we cranked away and inked the roller. When I remember this scene now, I laugh, realizing that we must have looked a little like a female version of the "The Three Stooges" trying to accomplish one of their jobs.

The machine was old and constantly jammed. I dreaded facing it. Sometimes, I was there late into the afternoon trying to finish the work. Some people loved working in service groups. I personally disliked it immensely, but felt I had no choice in the matter.

Sometimes I was called an hour before an evening meeting to mimeograph copies of a new song. Because we were not supposed to serve alone, I would call someone to go with me, leave dinner and the family, go to the meeting hall, run off the song, hurry back home, get the children ready for babysitting, and make it back to the hall in time for the meeting.

Hymns and Songs

I loved the hymns and songs that we sang in our meetings. We used a hymnal which some members in the Church in Los Angeles had compiled. It was simply called *Hymns* and contained mostly Christian hymns that had been written over the centuries by the Lord's people. It also included a number of hymns from Watchman Nee and Witness Lee. The hymnal had over a thousand songs in it, and we sang from it in almost every meeting.

I still have that hymnal and count it one of my greatest treasures. It is organized in such a way that I can easily find a hymn in its indexes if I know the first line of either the first verse or the chorus.

We also used what we called a "supplement," which was a loose-leaf notebook to which we could easily add new songs. We each had our own hymnal and supplement and carried them to every meeting with our Bible in various kinds of large briefcases, purses, or other types of bags. We called these our "book bags."

Anyone among us might write a song at any time, as we were encouraged to do by the leading brothers. Usually, someone would simply write new lyrics to an existing tune, oftentimes from a popular song of the day. Many times, these new songs were dropped off anonymously at the meeting hall. The lyrics were often inspired by the message that had just been shared in the previous meeting, so the leading brothers usually wanted to introduce the song in the next meeting. The clerical service group, then, would prepare copies of the new song to distribute in the upcoming meeting. This is why I sometimes would get called an hour before a meeting to type a song and crank up the mimeograph machine.

Some of the songs were wonderful. The singing was very enjoyable, and all joined in heartily. Here are a couple of example verses from supplement songs that I loved:

> From my heart comes a melody
> Of the One who gave His life to me.
> How can I turn away from Thee;
> Lord, I have seen Thy changeless love for me.
>
> — Author unknown

> Turn, turn my heart to you;
> Lord, I confess my heart is untrue,
> Turn, turn my wandering heart;
> Lord, unto me Thy love impart.
>
> — Author unknown

As time passed, the use of love songs to Jesus such as these began to diminish until, in our later years, they were rarely used. It was many years later, while writing this book, that the Lord brought songs like these back to my memory. I also realized that, as time went on, we used the classic Christian hymns in our hymn book less and less frequently. We gravitated towards those whose words had been written by Watchman Nee or Witness Lee.

Oneness

In the meetings, we read verses from Ephesians about oneness and building so many times that those pages in my Bible were loose and falling out. Brother Lee believed that through us God would bring about a truly biblical church experience. He told us that God was not interested in a group of individual Christians but wanted a "corporate expression" of Himself. We were saved to be part of His body, so we needed to give ourselves for this. In order for Him to express Himself, we needed to learn to deny ourselves and "take up the cross" (Matt. 16:24). There was no place in the body for anything of the self, so it had to go. Oneness was what Jesus prayed for—not just invisible spiritual oneness but externally visible oneness—a testimony that the world could see.

When I was first introduced to this concept of oneness, I understood that we were supposed to have unity without conformity or unity with variety. Rarely, if at all, did I hear such statements anymore. I was aware that there was a great deal of conformity among us, but then I wasn't sure what "unity without conformity" meant anyway. There was certainly no variety in our appearance. Everyone dressed alike. The sisters wore very, very plain clothing. Most wore blue jean skirts and plain blouses. Our shoes were usually black or brown flats or loafers. With the exception of watches and wedding rings, we didn't wear jewelry. Most of the sisters wore head-coverings. This practice came from the New Testament teaching about a woman having her head covered when she prayed to God (1 Cor. 11:5). This wasn't a requirement, but none of the sisters who were considered to be spiritual went to meetings bareheaded. There were two styles of head-coverings in use. One type of head-covering was a colored cotton bandana (usually blue, brown or black). It was folded into a triangle, placed over the hair, and tied at the nape of the neck. The other style was a crocheted, circular doily that was about five inches in diameter, usually white, tan, or black. The sisters from the Far East typically wore these, or some of the more "spiritual" Caucasian sisters among us. The brothers wore what I called "brothers' clothing"—a plain white shirt; a plain, thin, dark-colored tie (never wide, which was in style then); and a pair of dark-colored slacks. There were exceptions to this type of attire, but none of them erred on the side of being stylish. Many times, I found myself determining what kind of clothing was acceptable to wear by looking at the elders' wives. Whatever they wore, I could safely wear also.

We were taught that the visible practical expression of our spiritual oneness occurred primarily in the meetings. Because we were expected to attend every meeting, if someone missed a meeting, they would hear from one who attended, "Brother (or sister), where were you last night? You should have been there. I can't repeat for you what you missed!" Serious illness was just about the only acceptable excuse for absence. I was afraid to miss a meeting because a new "flow" in church teaching or practice might come. If I missed its introduction and supporting motivational rhetoric, I might not be able to "make the turn" and would be left behind. I actually worried about this when I had to babysit.

One way we used the word flow *was to refer to the direction that the leading brothers believed the church as a whole should be going. This flow was whatever they believed was the current move of the Spirit among us. A flow was typically the result of a teaching from, or fellowship with, Witness Lee. The flow changed directions when some new teaching or major practice was introduced. It was often called a "turn" and sometimes a "new move."*

Especially in our earlier Local Church days, the flow referred to the moving of the Holy Spirit in a meeting. We believed that the Lord had a purpose for each church meeting, and that we should be sensitive to Him to determine what that purpose was and participate accordingly. Since, in our meetings, any member could choose a song, pray out loud, or share a testimony, we thought it was necessary for everyone to be in the same flow.

Our Vision: The Lord's Recovery

Brother Lee was teaching us about God's recovery being our governing vision. We began to refer to ourselves as the "Lord's Recovery" or just "the Recovery." According to what we were taught, the church of the first century had been lost, degraded to the point that by the fifteenth century, the Bible was locked away in Latin and wasn't available for the common person. People were left with abundant superstition and no gospel or Bible truth until Martin Luther discovered and recovered the truth of justification by faith. Brother Lee said that this was the beginning of God's recovery. With the invention of the Gutenberg press and the publishing of the Bible in common languages, the Word of God was made available so that more previously lost Biblical truths could be recovered.

According to Brother Lee, we were in the final stage of God's recovery, and through us, God was recovering the last item, the church. He explained to us how Satan feared believers being one, so throughout history, he always sought to prevent real church oneness. He told us that Satan was responsible for combining the early churches, each of which had begun as a locally governed entity, into one world church with one leader, the Pope. From the time of the Reformation forward, Satan was also responsible for taking believers to the opposite extreme and dividing them into many, many churches based on different doctrines and experiences. Both of these were not according to the Bible.

Now the Lord was using us to recover the lost biblical practice of one church in a city. This would open the way for there to be true oneness and brotherly love as a visible testimony—one that would testify to non-Christians about Christ's reality and defeat God's enemy. We were called to stand on the ground of oneness and represent all believers. We in the Lord's Recovery were like the small number of those who rebuilt the temple in the Old Testament; we were the twentieth-century "remnant" (Ezra 9:8–9). The Lord was waiting for this oneness to be expressed on the earth before He could return.

From the time I saw the vision of the Lord's Recovery, I preached the gospel with a new focus. I was motivated to bring people into the Recovery. I believed that when people became Christians, they needed to become part of the Local Church or else they would miss God's "up-to-date move." Christianity only preached the gospel of being saved from hell, termed by Brother Lee as the low gospel, not the gospel of being "saved by His life" that we preached, which Brother Lee said was the high gospel.

We spent time with people on the outside as long as we felt they were good prospects, or what we called "good material," for the church. When it became clear they were not, we stopped spending time with them. We believed the

Lord still cared about other Christians but that they were not in His heart's desire. Those who came in contact with the church and decided not to take the way of the Lord's Recovery were not our concern. On several occasions, I was told by a leading brother not to waste my time on certain persons because not everyone would "take this way."

Deeds of the Nicolaitans

Brother Lee also taught us that the clergy-laity system was not pleasing to God because He intended that all believers be priests, serving Him directly without an intermediary class. We learned from chapter two of Revelation that the word *Nicolaitans* meant "to conquer the people" and that God hated the deeds of the Nicolaitans (Rev. 2:6). They were the beginning of the modern day clergy-laity system in which a few serve God and others watch passively. Instead, we were all supposed to be priests to God.

I still believe that God doesn't have so-called lay people! Every believer should be a living, functioning member in His body.

In addition, we were taught that the practice of having salaried ministers was unscriptural. Those who taught the Bible in our meetings were not hired. We were encouraged to give money to them individually as the Bible instructed.

Even though we did not believe in salaried ministers, I believe that eventually there were some of the leading brothers among us who routinely received regular amounts of money from the church in addition to designated gifts from individuals. We, however, would not refer to this practice as giving them a salary.

We were a church family with a common bond, belief, scriptural evidence, and purpose. God's purpose was first, above everything else in our lives. We wanted to please the leading brothers because we looked to them as God's "representatives or deputy authorities."[5] These things motivated us to keep up our brutal pace and unusual lifestyle. We heard the leading brothers comment that so-and-so is a "really good brother" (or sister) whenever they saw behavior that indicated absoluteness. Everyone wanted to be considered a *really good* brother or sister.

---

[5] Most of the beliefs we held about representative or deputy authority can be found in Watchman Nee's book, *Spiritual Authority*. (Witness Lee mentioned to us a few times that Watchman Nee had not wanted his teachings on spiritual authority to be published; however, others had done so.) The book contains statements like these: "Now since all governing authorities are instituted by Him, then all authorities are delegated by Him and represent His authority" (Nee, *Spiritual*, 61). "God sets in the church authorities such as 'the elders who rule well' and 'those who labor in preaching and teaching.' They are the ones whom everyone should obey" (Nee, *Spiritual*, 67).

No Questions or Negative Speaking

The leading brothers emphasized the importance of oneness, absoluteness, and our submission to God's authority. Anyone who really loved the Lord would be one, absolute, and submissive. Anyone who questioned Brother Lee's teaching or a church practice would soon be found to be "negative," "divisive," "spreading poison," or even "leprous." We were taught to be like a Nazarite in the Old Testament, who took a vow to God that he would keep himself pure. If someone, even a close relative, dropped dead beside the Nazarite and he touched the body, he would become contaminated, thus breaking his vow. We considered anyone who became negative as a spiritually dead person. We also read in the Old Testament about Miriam, who became leprous when she and her brother, Aaron, questioned Moses. Similarly, anyone in the church who asked questions about the leading brothers could easily become a "leper." It was necessary to stay away from such persons in order to protect the church. If anyone disassociated themselves from the church and had critical things to say, they were considered negative and were to be avoided. We were also taught not to read any material critical of the Local Church.

We were especially discouraged from asking questions. We were just supposed to say "Amen" to everything we heard or observed in the teachings and meetings of the church. We were told that Satan asked Eve the first question in the Bible; hence, questions were evil. The serpent, representing Satan, was even shaped like a question mark. It was even intimated that if we asked questions, we were "one with the serpent." Questions came from our fallen mind, so we needed to turn from our troublesome mind to our spirit where Jesus was. Questions were from the "tree of the knowledge of good and evil" and needed to be rejected. We were not supposed to consider either right or wrong, but rather, we were supposed to live by another tree that was in the Garden of Eden, the "tree of life" (Gen. 2:9). We were taught that this tree of life was food for our spirit. We were supposed to learn to live in our spirit, not in our mind. Comments like, "Brother, get out of your mind," or "Sister, you need to turn to your spirit," were commonly heard among us.

A Frog in the Pot

Someone reading this might be asking, "Hey, wait a minute. Why did you submit to all of this? Wasn't it your choice to attend all these meetings? Wasn't it your choice to let these people live in your house with you? Wasn't it your choice to work like a slave? Wasn't it your choice to submit to these leaders?" The answer is yes. Our participation was entirely voluntary. I don't think there is a way to explain this satisfactorily to anyone who wasn't a part of the Local Church, unless they have experienced another similar group dynamic. The bottom line was that we had become totally convinced that this was what God wanted from us. We believed that He had provided both this environment and any resultant hardships for our highest good.

On one hand, our daily life was difficult, but on the other hand, we were participating in very enjoyable meetings. Sometimes we would even describe them as being "in the heavenlies." It was worth the price we had to pay to get to a meeting. We had an enlarged family in which we knew everyone. We were involved with one another in our daily lives. We weren't just "going to church" anymore; we *were* the church—and not for just one day a week. We were experiencing brotherly love like the "church in Philadelphia," a church mentioned in Revelation of which the Lord spoke well (Rev. 3:7). The church was the most important thing in our lives. It was our purpose. It was God's "high calling" for us. We were willing to give up everything and to pay any price to give the Lord the church that He wanted. Our reward for any resultant suffering would come in eternity. We would rest then.

In many ways, we were like the proverbial frog in a pot of warm water that did not jump out when the heat was gradually turned up. The frog sat still as it was cooked to its death. The cooking time for us was many, many years.

"Christ as Life" Versus Religion

We were learning more about Christ being our life (Col. 3:4). We were supposed to let Him live in us rather than live by our own natural life. Our natural life was what we had by our physical birth. Christ's life was the life we had by our new spiritual birth. Brother Lee said that whatever we could do for God without experiencing Christ as our life was just "religion."

For example, Brother Lee said that God wanted us to love with His love, love that came as a result of experiencing the life of God, not with our own natural love. He reminded us that the kind of love found in degraded Christianity was not a product of true spirituality, but rather was a product of the natural, human life. God had no use for such love. How could we express God's love instead of our own? It was easy. All we had to do was to forget about trying to love and just focus on receiving God's life and being "mingled" with Him.

How could we be mingled with the Lord Jesus? By pray-reading and calling on the name of the Lord. Brother Lee said:

> The more we pray-read, the more something of the Lord Jesus comes out from Him and into us. It is thus that something of the Lord is mingled with us, and we not only have life, but have it abundantly. (Lee, *Christ*, 118)

As we received the Lord and were mingled with Him, God's love, as well as all of His other attributes, would spontaneously be expressed through us. Brother Lee told us that before expressing love in a situation, we should ask ourselves whether or not this was God expressing His love or us expressing our own love.

He repeatedly stressed that we should continually receive the life of Christ in order to be mingled with Him, and prescribed the only way for us to practice this:

> Now, if we would contact this Christ, we need to exercise our spirit to pray-read the Word or simply to call on His name. If we would do this, we would continually contact Christ and enjoy Him. There is no other way. (Lee, *Christ*, 105)

> You may say that whenever I speak I always return eventually to the matter of calling on the name of the Lord and pray-reading. It is really so. I have not found a third way. In all my years of experience with the Lord, I have only found these two ways: calling on the name of the Lord and pray-reading the Word. I do know of a certainty that this is the best way for the Lord to mingle something of Himself with us. (Lee, *Christ*, 118)

> There is no other way but by calling on His name and pray-reading. All the day we need to say, "O Lord, Amen! O Lord, Amen!" All the day we also need to pray-read the Word. (Lee, *Christ*, 119)

Calling on the Lord and pray-reading were given as the only way to produce a genuine expression of Christ's life in us. We didn't have to worry about trying to love or produce some other godly attribute. Christ's love would spontaneously be expressed as a result of these two exercises. What if we had trouble with our spouse? Brother Lee's answer was simple:

> Every day, every minute, open up yourselves to the Lord who is the Spirit within you. Always say, 'Praise the Lord! Amen! O Lord Jesus! I love You, Lord Jesus.' Open up yourselves to the all-inclusive Spirit in such a way. Behold Him. If you do this, life will be supplied into your being. Life will be given to your spirit, to your soul, and even to your mortal body to make you persons of life. If you as a husband practice this, spontaneously in every instance you will love your wife. That will not be your love but the Lord Jesus within you. The Lord loves your wife, so you will love her too because you are one with the Lord. As a wife, if you practice this, spontaneously you will submit yourself to your husband. Whatever your husband says would not bother you because you are filled with the Lord Jesus within you. Then you will have a happy marriage life. (Lee, *Divine*, 85)

> When I call, "Lord Jesus," the Spirit comes. If your wife bothers you, religion would teach you to be patient. But to keep this religious teaching does not work. What does work is to call upon the name of the Lord—"O Lord Jesus!"... To call upon the name of the Lord is to forget about the ethical teachings, to forget about our mind, emotion, and will, and to turn to the spirit. (Lee, *Divine*, 92-93)

It was of utmost importance that every day we were experiencing Christ being our life. He told us that when getting dressed, rather than choosing what *we* wanted to wear, we should ask the Lord what *He* wanted to wear. The example was given of a brother choosing a tie in the morning. He should pray, "Lord, which tie are You wearing?" I tried this kind of prayer a few times and then said to myself, "If I start doing this, I am going to end up in a loony bin."

... or end up wearing my husband's tie! It never occurred to me that such teachings, like asking the Lord what He was wearing, conflicted with the teaching about Christ being our life. If eating and drinking Jesus was supposed to result in God mingling Himself with us and spontaneously being our life, then wouldn't we be able to spontaneously choose the correct tie? Why did we need to ask? Things like this left people with a confused message: Pray about what tie to wear; don't pray about a marriage problem. Although I didn't practice praying like this about my clothing, I failed to notice this contradiction.

Pan-Banging

Brother Lee taught, when he gave messages on Christ versus religion, that Christianity as a whole was an old, dead religion. We needed to "get out of religion" and "get into the Spirit." Some of the songs that were written during this get-out-of-religion flow had lines like these:

> We are freed from the system, Praise the Lord!
>
> * * *
>
> He's offending all religious men
>
> * * *
>
> We're through with dead religious games
>
> * * *

Chapter 7—A Frog in the Pot

We are slaying the ord'nances, religion too

* * *

Bury that old dead religion

* * *

Overcome degraded Christianity!

Ultimately, what began to happen in our meetings showed that we understood getting out of religion to mean changing external things more than becoming inwardly, spiritually living. The way we conducted our church meetings was offensive to the average Christian in the early 1970's. Many times, everyone in the meeting would stand up and chant loudly "O Lord Jesus" together for a period of time. It was common for people to spontaneously stand up and shout, "Praise the Lord," or give a testimony.

The singing had always been loud and boisterous, but what was beginning to take place in our meetings went far beyond this. The messages about getting out of religion fueled a kind of frenzy as we sought to break through the deadness we had inherited from degraded Christianity. At one meeting, someone stood in his chair and shouted something like, "We are free from religion!" Many others followed suit. This began to be a regular occurrence in the meetings. At another meeting, someone brought a kitchen pan and banged on it with a spoon, shouting similar out-of-dead-religion slogans. More people brought implements, such as various kinds of pots and pans, kitchen utensils, or tools, with which they could make noise. Some of the young people used brooms and rubber strands to make instruments that made strange boinging sounds. Jug bands were formed. Strangely, we believed this bedlam was helping us get out of religion. We had a few meetings outside in parks where people would gather and watch these peculiar events. Some of the young people even took their jug band on the bed of a truck and performed their out-of-religion noises. I participated in some of these practices but felt very uncomfortable and often silly.

Once a group of ten or so sisters, myself included, asked a brother who owned an open flatbed truck to load up our sisters' prayer meeting and drive around the Montrose area in Houston. We were going to pray for that particular area of town! After our prayer-drive around the area, we stopped, got out on the sidewalk and shouted for the walls, spiritual walls, to fall down like Jericho's!

When I think about that whole scene now, I have to laugh. Ten very conservatively dressed women with bandanas on their heads were sitting on folding metal chairs in a circle on the bed of a large truck with wooden slat sides. We were being driven through a large metropolitan city, shouting and praying with our eyes closed! The shouting must have helped us shut out the reality of what we were doing. Closed eyes probably helped too. This is funny because of its ridiculousness and sad, too, because it shows we were being ushered by God's enemy into strange and peculiar behaviors that certainly wouldn't help us find favor with man!

In our church meetings, we usually sat on folding chairs placed in a semicircle or in a full circle. On one particular occasion, when many were jumping up and down, several people on the front row picked up a brother and threw him up in the air, catching him as he came down, and then pitching him up again. His glasses flew off onto the floor, and one of the jumpers accidentally broke them. At one meeting, some chairs were thrown around, and a chair was actually thrown out of the door of the meeting hall! I had hoped this strange stage the church was going through would come to an end, but instead, it was snowballing. All of this was happening about a year after my miscarriage, when I was about seven months along in another pregnancy. One night, I was in a meeting where people were jumping up and down and marching around. Chairs were being moved away so that people couldn't sit back down. I wasn't budging from mine, protecting the baby in my belly. Unexpectedly, a brother from behind me whacked me on the back and said, "Jump, sister!" I whirled around with a look that would kill, and he backed up looking like I had actually hit him. When I saw the opportunity, I made my way into hiding behind the piano until things settled down. I began to dread going to these meetings.

I actually hated what was happening, yet I still participated to a degree. This shows the conflict going on inside me. I was a double-minded woman, definitely unstable (Jas. 1:8), and certainly confused. No answers came to me from the Bible because I had come to doubt my own independent interpretation of it. I didn't feel good about what was happening, but I was afraid to question it. Why? Because oneness was so important to us. The church leaders were supporting and participating in this. If I questioned it, I wouldn't be "one" with everyone else. This was a most serious sin, and I didn't want to hurt the oneness. It was better to be unhappy and uncomfortable than to damage the oneness.

It had become very important to me to be considered as absolute for God and one with His church. Outsiders saw our behavior as blind following. If anyone accused us of this, we would deny it, insisting that no one told us what to do. This answer wouldn't be intentionally dishonest; we just didn't believe they could understand, as we did, what it meant to be absolute. The case of our pan-banging oneness is an example of how Satan used our belief to produce a twisted application of oneness.

About a month later, two leading brothers from Los Angeles spoke at a conference held in Dallas. I couldn't go because I was too far along in my pregnancy, so John went without me. Midway through the weekend, he called and said, "It's over." Apparently, when people showed up at these meetings with their pom-poms and noisemakers, the speakers concluded that things had gone over the edge in Texas. They spoke about Christ as life, what it was and what it wasn't. Pom-poms and pan-banging fell into the second category. We were delivered. Both speakers were Brother Lee's valued co-workers, so their assessment of the situation was accepted.

Chapter 8
Don't Leave Me Out

> That we should no longer be children, tossed to and fro and carried about with every wind of doctrine. (Eph. 4:14)

"God's Man on the Earth"

WE WERE BECOMING CONVINCED that Brother Lee was the one and only man God was using to lead His present-day recovery so that Christ could come back. Brother Lee told us that Paul was God's main leader in New Testament times, and from this, led us to the conclusion that God's way was to have one man in each time period to lead His up-to-date move. Our church leaders strongly believed this and insisted it was our responsibility to support Brother Lee one hundred percent.

During our first five to seven years in the Local Church, we had occasionally heard Witness Lee make reference to selected teachings of others such as Andrew Murray, W. H. Griffith Thomas, and John Nelson Darby. During those years, he frequently mentioned Watchman Nee. He also mentioned having some association with T. Austin Sparks; but he told us that when Sparks would not take the way of the Local Church, the effectiveness of his ministry stopped. As time passed, Witness Lee basically stopped referring to the teachings of others except, occasionally, for Watchman Nee. The leading brothers eventually told us that it was a waste of our time to read other authors' books or materials.

Because of our belief about who Brother Lee was, many of us began to accept his teaching without question and without checking it carefully against the Bible, believing he couldn't be in error.

One Under the Umbrella

Brother Lee had been a coworker serving under Watchman Nee in China for many years. He told us that Watchman Nee had a strong desire to see the church recovered to a proper scriptural state. Before they met, Brother Lee had received years of Christian training in China from a Christian group known as the Brethren.[6] As a result, his Bible knowledge was extensive and very impressive. When the Communists took over China and imprisoned Watchman Nee, Brother Lee fled to Taiwan. He told us that Watchman Nee had commissioned him to go to Taiwan to carry on the work of recovering the Local Church.

---

[6] The Brethren movement began in the early nineteenth century when small groups of Christians met in an attempt to return to New Testament simplicity. They took the Bible as their authoritative guide instead of the creeds and religious traditions of the denominations of their day. "They believed that the pristine purity of the early church must be restored by a return to the New Testament pattern, and that by their departure from this pattern the churches of Christendom had largely become apostate." (Miller, 1054).

When Brother Lee came to the United States and began starting Local Churches, he was in his early sixties. Periodically, he would tell us stories about the closeness of his relationship with Watchman Nee and how he followed him without question. Here is one of these accounts:

> In the eighteen years that I was involved in the work on mainland China, I did a lot but no one ever heard any opinion from me. They only heard my voice in giving messages all according to Brother Nee. Some brothers can testify that among all the co-workers with Brother Nee in those eighteen years I did the most. But I labored without voicing any opinion. In the co-workers' conferences sometimes Brother Nee would ask, "Witness, what would you say?" I had nothing to say. My attitude was that whatever Brother Nee told me to do, I would do it. It was that simple. From 1932 to 1950 no one ever heard me expressing any opinion regarding the work in mainland China.
>
> Actually, there is nearly nothing different between my understanding and Brother Nee's except for one thing. I never told anyone what this was, not even my wife or family, until I came to

this country and Brother Nee went to be with the Lord. The doctrinal item which I felt different from Brother Nee was regarding the two witnesses in the book of Revelation (11:3-12). This was the only difference between my understanding and Brother Nee's. My intention is to show you that I was not altogether the same in everything with Brother Nee. In this one thing I was not the same and I am still not the same. My point is this—in spite of this difference, I never uttered anything in my ministry that Brother Nee did not preach, and I did not teach anything that he had not touched.

One Flow

The Lord has opened my eyes to realize as I have told you in the past, that in the Bible, especially in the New Testament, there is only one current flowing from the throne (Rev. 22:1).... If North China were to be taken by the Lord, He would surely do it through the same flow. I had to jump into this current, to be one with this current to let the Lord flow. (Lee, *Book 7*, 83-85)

Whether intentional or not, by speaking in this way, he indirectly communicated to the leaders what he expected. They needed to aspire to follow him as he had followed Watchman Nee, absolutely and without question. Eventually, this "oneness" seed that he planted grew to be a great tree of unquestioning loyalty and submission to him.

Along this same line, he told us that Watchman Nee had received much persecution and criticism from the Christian community, but that Brother Lee and some of the other coworkers were sheltered from the criticism by being under Watchman Nee's umbrella. He told the leading ones in the United States that he was now the one receiving the criticism, and that all of them were sheltered under his umbrella.

Watchman Nee has been well-respected in the United States, and his books are available in many bookstores. Witness Lee claimed he was the number one co-worker of Watchman Nee in China and used this association to try to gain acceptability with American Christians. In 2013, however, the English version of a book was published entitled, My Unforgettable Memories: Watchman Nee and the Shanghai Local Church, *by Lily M. Hsu. As a young woman, Hsu was an insider in the Shanghai Local*

Church and also an eye-witness of Nee's trial by the Communists in 1956. Rev. Tsu-Kung Chuang of T.K. & True Light Ministry, Massachusetts, wrote concerning the book, "Just like the weakness and sinful actions of King David has [sic] been candidly recorded in I Samuel, this book might be viewed as Watchman Nee's 'prophetic biography.' If anyone wishes to know who Nee is and to evaluate his writing fairly, this is a must-read book." This book presents evidence that Nee had a hidden life of sexual immorality, that he plagiarized material from Jesse Penn-Lewis, and that he negotiated with the Communists in a way that violated the trust of fellow Christians and made them vulnerable to persecution, as well as evidence that he did not die a martyr's death, as was recounted more than once by Witness Lee (Hsu).

Spreading by Migration

In the early 1970's, my youngest sister, Julia, was in high school in Dallas. She had some friends that had recently received Jesus and were excited about Him. One of them, Linda, was the younger sister of Jackie, a friend of mine who was now a member of the Church in Houston. Linda and Julia started calling Jackie and me for fellowship. We talked with the leading brothers in Houston, and they decided that a group of us would travel to Dallas and meet with these young believers. One of Linda's friends offered to let us use her home for the weekend. Her parents, who were interior decorators, were going to be out of town on a business trip. Unbelievably, the parents consented to let a large group of us stay in their beautiful, spacious home that was filled with expensive furnishings, some with price tags on them awaiting sale. I still marvel that this family let a group of total strangers sleep, eat, and hold meetings in their home. We had some gospel meetings, and a number of high school students received the Lord and were subsequently baptized in the swimming pool of another participant's home.

My sister, Julia, didn't come to any of these meetings because my parents forbade her after they learned from my sister Dorothy's ex-boyfriend that Julia was planning to attend. My parents sent her to their pastor for counseling. After leaving the session with him, she was very upset and stopped at a phone booth to call and ask if some of us could meet her somewhere because she had been forbidden to come to see us. A handful of brothers and sisters met her, talked with her, and prayed for her. I did not go. The next time I talked to Julia, she was very distant and said she didn't want to ever talk about the church again. Struggling with what to do, she finally decided she couldn't hurt my parents as Dorothy and I had done.

After this, it would be about fifteen years before Julia and I would begin to have fellowship again.

We returned to Houston with a glowing report: A number of young people had received the Lord. They wanted to be in the "church-life," but there wasn't a Local Church in Dallas. The church-life was a term we used to indicate that church was more to us than just going to a meeting as a duty once a week. The church was a way of life, every day of the week. The church was Jesus living His life in us together with other Christians. We referred to our church experience as the "body-life" because we were living members of the Lord's living body on this earth. We were not an organization, but an organism. Christ was our life, and we were His way to express or show Himself on the earth today. Growing up in Christianity, I had never heard about or experienced anything like this.

Considering the condition of many churches with which we were familiar at that time, the Local Church was very attractive to people who were searching for God.

To our way of thinking, we were the only church that really knew what "church" was. Christianity couldn't really help anyone, and we believed it was a shame to Christ. The fact that we sang songs with phrases like "overcome degraded Christianity" shows we had adopted Brother Lee's belief about Christianity. He often said, "I am forced to tell the truth about the real situation in Christianity." He continued to refer to it as "poor degraded Christianity" and sometimes as "poor, poor Christianity."

After we reported all that the Lord had done in Dallas, the leading brothers decided it was time for some of the brothers and sisters to move there to take care of these new Christians. So shortly after this, in 1971, a group moved from Houston to Dallas. This was the first "migration," as we termed the move, out of Houston to another city.

Over the coming years, many brothers and sisters moved from Local Churches all over the United States to other cities to start new Local Churches. Usually, one particular church would be responsible for each migration and would send the largest group of people. Other churches might send a few more to join them.

John and I wanted to move to Dallas, but we knew if we did, he would lose his draft deferment. The leading elder recognized this as a serious problem and recommended that we not go, saying that it was better to be in the Church in Houston than in the military in a place where there was no Local Church at all.

Thus, there came to be a Local Church in Dallas. There was an official "taking-the-ground" meeting attended by both those who were moving there to start the church and those who traveled from Houston to support the occasion. In that meeting, we prayed, praised, and "claimed the ground." By this, we declared to the principalities and powers that there was now a Church in Dallas standing on the ground of genuine oneness and open to all genuine believers. The Recovery had spread to Dallas.

The Cross Removing Me

We were also hearing a lot of teaching about not loving the "soul-life." According to this teaching, a person's soul consisted of the mind, emotion, and will—in other words, the self or personality. We needed to lose the soul-life, so the Lord could build His church. This translated into not loving anything at all related to our selves, but loving only what He loved, which was the church. We were being taught to function in the church by applying the cross to the self-life. This was necessary because God's building must be built with the proper materials. He would ultimately judge with fire whatever we built that was from the self (1 Cor. 3:12–15).

> Thus we must function only by the cross and through the cross. Wood represents the human nature, and hay and stubble represent the things of this earth. We must learn to reject and deny all the human elements, all the things of this earth, by the cross....

If, however, we bring in wood, hay, and stubble, we will greatly damage the church life. We must learn to check ourselves by the cross in the way we function. In the church we must always act by the way of the cross. (Lee, *Vision*, 178)

My understanding of this and similar teachings was that God was using the Local Church environment like heat and pressure on a piece of coal to produce a diamond. He was doing away with my own individuality. We sang a song with these words: "We're locked up in this prison, no key to this here lock. They feed us bread and water, we're chained here to the Rock.... You'll never see us break out. We'll stay here to the end."

The words to this song are humorous to me now, but they do capture what I then believed. I felt that I had no choice but to submit to the hard things in the church and do as was expected of me. If I didn't, I was hindering the building of the church. I looked at myself through the eyes of church leaders and members to assess my situation before God, instead of asking Him myself.

I was learning that everything about me was unacceptable, and God did not want it. I had no rights, and it was wrong for me to express my opinions, thoughts, or feelings. I was supposed to accept everything that happened to me in the church and suffer any consequences without ever speaking a word.

I believed that anything I liked or enjoyed doing was inherently evil because it was of "the flesh," a biblical term for sinful, fallen human nature. If I ever had a really good laugh about something, I felt I had sinned. I denied my self as much as possible. I tried not to let down my guard for fear that I would be living and walking in the flesh. The personal experience of the cross, as taught in the Local Church, was a hard and joyless necessity.

The term cross *as used in the Bible is not easily understood. It does not refer only to the wooden cross upon which Christ died, but also to a spiritual truth, one that can be personally or subjectively experienced. I realize now that the Local Church teaching about the cross was actually causing me to practice asceticism ("austerity and self-denial, especially as a principled way of life" [Encarta]) and to confuse this with spiritual truth (Col. 2:20–23). It was actually causing me to practice something very close to self rejection. Because of my misunderstanding about the subjective experience of the cross, I constantly measured myself by degrees of abstinence and continually monitored my behavior for any form of self-expression. I always felt that others were measuring and monitoring me in the same way. I would learn in years to come that the subjective experience of the cross has nothing to do with practicing asceticism or self rejection, and that it is not a joyless necessity but is, instead, a joy producer.*

Don't Leave Me Out

In the fall of 1972, several months after my gospel-march miscarriage, I had conceived again. (I was in the final trimester of this pregnancy during the pan-banging days.) During this pregnancy, I had an amazing experience with the Lord.

The doctor who had repaired the rectal tear after Todd's birth had told me I should never again have a normal episiotomy (an incision to aid in childbirth). If the rectal wall were to tear again, it could be very serious. He had instructed me to tell any new doctor about this during any future pregnancies. Then, the new doctor could prevent a tear by giving me a *lateral* episiotomy. I felt it was important to be fully awake in the delivery room to remind my new doctor of this, so I decided to go to natural childbirth classes. An added benefit was that John, if he went to the classes, could go with me into the delivery room. Acknowledging my fear, John agreed to attend the classes, albeit reluctantly.

Spiritually, I was seeking to be obedient to the vision of the building of the church and the cross, but I was having an ongoing struggle because I believed that I was wrong to be enjoying my pregnancy and looking forward to having my second child. Surely this human matter was competing with what the Lord wanted. I was several months pregnant when I read one day in my Bible:

> A woman when she is in travail hath sorrow, because her hour is come: but as soon as she is delivered of the child, she remembereth no more the anguish, for joy that a man is born into the world. (John 16:21, KJV)

When I came to this verse, I became upset. I shoved my Bible across the table and said, "I know I'm not supposed to, but I want to enjoy having this baby!" The verse had made me think about the fact that I was secretly enjoying being pregnant. As soon as I said this, God calmed my heart saying, "There is nothing wrong with you enjoying having your baby—just don't leave Me out." I sank in relief, thanking Him, and telling Him that I would include Him.

This is an example of how much I was being affected by the teaching I was continually receiving. It is true that Christ told us to deny ourselves and take up our cross to follow Him, but this truth isn't learned by man teaching us. It is learned by God teaching us as He reveals Himself to us. Part of the problem I was having was related to how I understood this teaching; the other part was related to how it was being presented to us. I can say this because of the fruit in my life: I had come to consider God, the One who gave His own life for me, as a demanding taskmaster, not wanting me to enjoy anything. But in this situation, my genuine feelings surfaced and I let Jesus know how I really felt. When I did, He immediately answered my declaration with the truth: He wanted me to enjoy having my baby and getting to know Him more in the process. As a result, I didn't leave Him out. When time came to deliver my baby, I had an amazing experience with Jesus. However, I never told anyone in the church about this experience because it just didn't fit. But I didn't forget it. From that time, I started turning back to my original practice of going to Jesus and telling Him everything.

Shortly after I agreed not to leave Jesus out of my pregnancy, He showed me that I had been wrong in my approach to John about the natural childbirth classes. Deep down, I knew that if I asked him for his real feeling, he would have told me he really didn't want to go to those classes. When the Lord showed me that I hadn't given John a choice about this, He asked me if I would rather have my way or have His blessing on the birth of this child. When I chose to have His blessing, the Lord told me to go to John and ask him what he really wanted to do. John made it clear to me that he did not want to be in the delivery room, and he wasn't interested in the classes. So I released him.

A few days later, Sandra Brown, a sister who was a natural childbirth expert, offered to help me prepare. She would also go to the hospital with me to assist me while I was in labor. My doctor didn't want me to have the baby naturally and told me it was better to use a painkiller. Actually, a painkiller was better for him, not me. I was determined to deliver without painkillers, even if he didn't want to help. I began happily preparing for the coming birth, knowing it was going to be a blessed event!

In Need of a Better Word than Wonderful

A few days before my due date, it occurred to me that if labor started during the middle of the night, Sandra would have difficulty making it to the hospital because she and her husband had moved about forty minutes across town to Hall Two.

By this time, we had started meeting in a second location in the city in order to facilitate the spread of the church-life. We called our second meeting place "Hall Two."

I called and asked her what to do if I went into labor at 2:00 a.m. She assured me she would be there. She then made arrangements for another sister to drive with her, even in the middle of the night. At about 6:00 p.m. that same evening, a sister called me to ask if Todd could spend the night with her child. This was a first. Todd had never before been invited to spend the night with a friend. I let him go.

During the night, I awoke with sharp labor pains. John called Sandra, and we were all on our way at 2:00 a.m.! At the hospital, I was surprised to find out that my doctor wasn't going to take care of the delivery because he had been called out of town unexpectedly. The doctor who had taken his place was very much in favor of natural childbirth and made sure I had a nurse who was trained in the method and would help me. Sandra and John took turns coming in and out of the labor room helping me with my natural childbirth breathing patterns. John located a place on my back where he could press and relieve some of my pain. He marked the area with a pen and wrote in it "O Lord Jesus." The nurse and Sandra also took turns pressing the "O Lord Jesus" spot. Several hours later, after a doctor's check, he asked me where my husband was and then left. They took me to the delivery room.

Once I was on the delivery table, I looked down at the end of the table to see John standing there with the doctor! Later, John told me that the doctor had asked him, "Would you like to see the birth?" Of course, this was entirely against the hospital rules, and the doctor knew it. John told me that to his own amazement, at that moment, he realized how much he wanted to be there and see our baby born. He said, "Yes." The doctor got him gowned, scrubbed, and into the delivery room. I was overjoyed! For John, it turned out to be what he considers the most amazing experience of his life. Minutes later, Matt was born and they let me touch him. They asked me what the big (9 lbs. 6 oz.) boy's name was. They all laughed as I said, "Amy." (I had planned on having a girl.)

In the recovery room, tears kept filling my eyes as I replayed the events of the prior evening in my mind. The Lord had taken care of every detail of this birth. What kind of a God was this? Who was I that He would do this for me? I was just a little nobody, a woman having a baby like thousands of other women every day. How could the God of the whole universe have time to be so involved in such little things? He had prepared Sandra for the 2:00 a.m. call. He provided a place for Todd. He arranged for a different doctor to take care of the delivery and thus take care of my desire to have the baby by natural childbirth. In spite of the hospital rules, He had brought John into the delivery room with a changed heart, one that wanted to be there!

Lying there on the bed in the recovery room, I recalled my conversation with the Lord many months before when I had made the choice to have His blessing rather than my way. So this is what it meant to have His blessing! Why, it included everything, even having it my way but without any effort on my part to get it! I kept saying, "Lord, You are so wonderful." Then I thought of a song we sang in our church meetings and began singing it in my heart to Him, "Wonderful, wonderful, wonderful, wonderful, isn't Jesus our Lord wonderful?" Somehow that word wasn't adequate to describe what I was experiencing. I tried to find another one, but couldn't, so I just told Him, "Lord, I need a new word; *wonderful* is too common for You!"

Children Who Are Not Breathing Well

Once in my hospital room, I fell asleep. The doctor awakened me with a very grave look on his face. Our baby was having difficulty breathing and had been put into a special incubator to supply him with extra oxygen. I froze. The first possible explanation was a birth trauma that would go away in a short amount of time. Unfortunately, I already knew the next possibility: underdeveloped lungs. A sister I knew had lost two babies as a result of this irreversible problem. The doctor left, and I started crying and praying, "Dear Lord, please don't take my baby from me. Please. I don't trust any of these doctors here. They'll do their best, but his life is not in their hands. It is in Yours. You are the only One who can help my baby. Please let him live!" As I prayed, the Lord spoke gently to my heart, "I have children who aren't breathing well, and I need you to help them." "I will, Lord, I will." Day one passed. No change.

Day two came. When the new mother in the bed next to me received her baby for feedings, I turned over and looked the other way, crying silently. I kept praying that my baby would be okay. They put me in a wheelchair and rolled me down to see him in his incubator. Through the incubator's thick glass, his chest appeared very large and deformed. I ached for him, and I felt like my heart was breaking. They took me back to my room to wait. Day two ended. Again, there was no change. I cried myself to sleep. In the middle of the night, however, I was suddenly wide awake. I heard a verse plainly spoken in my heart, "weeping may endure for a night, but joy cometh in the morning" (Psa. 30:5, KJV). I slipped into a quiet sleep.

The doctor awakened me several hours later. Matt's breathing had normalized. As the Lord had promised, weeping endured for a night, but joy came in the morning. This was the morning of the third day, and these words came to mind, "After two days will He revive us; in the third day He will raise us up" (Hos. 6:2, KJV). Symbolically, my son had been given back to me in resurrection after two dark nights.

This experience with God was wonderful. Somehow, I knew it was in stark contrast to what I was learning in the Local Church. I knew how real God had made Himself to me in a seemingly unspiritual, common human event related to my own little family. I also knew deep down that this experience with God was something outside the scope of the Local Church teachings and practices. It wasn't something I could share in a meeting or talk about with others in the church. It was an individual, personal experience. Why had God done this in my life? It was wonderful, but it was also confusing because I was in the Local Church and was supposed to care only about things that were directly related to building up the church, not about things related to my individual, personal life.

Matthew Guy Anderson was born on June 20, 1973. Little did I know at that time that the blessing God promised when I gave up my way would apply not only to Matt's birth but also, in an amazing way, to Matt's whole life. From that experience, I learned that to choose God's way, not ours, is not a small thing but a big thing.

It is interesting that this experience with the Lord had begun with Him asking me to give up something of myself that I wanted very much—John's presence in the delivery room. I had been struggling with the teaching about losing my self-life for the church. God, however, didn't tell me to give up everything for the church, but rather to give up a specific thing that was in the way at that time, something that was preventing Him from showing me something about Himself. I was striving to get what I wanted by my own self effort. I realize now that God's request offered me the opportunity for a little experience of the cross in my life. When He asked me to give up my way and drop my attempt to get what I wanted in exchange for His blessing, He was actually asking me to take up my cross and follow Him. When I did, I lost something, but I ultimately gained so much more! I saw God at work in my life, and He was wonderful.

Afraid of a Friend from My Past

Something happened just before Matt was born that is in stark contrast to what I had just experienced with God and my baby's birth. My old high school best friend, Alysa, called me and arranged to come for a visit. I had not seen her since the freezing baptism five years before, and I felt wary of spending much time with her alone. What would I say? What would she think of my life? What would she think of my plain clothing and my undecorated home? What would she think of my having another child? Our lifestyle would make it plain that we could barely afford to take care of the child we already had!

I felt compelled to invite Sandra Brown to come over during Alysa's visit. I'm not exactly sure why I did this. Maybe it had to do with the fact that we were always encouraged to do things together so we wouldn't act in ourselves or fall prey to the devil and be trapped by something in the world. Maybe I thought having a sister with me would keep me in my spirit so I wouldn't be dragged back to my past life. I'm pretty sure that I wanted to avoid any probing questions. It proved to be a very awkward visit. Sandra's presence did keep Alysa from asking me any such questions. Alysa soon resigned herself to the situation and sat quietly and politely throughout her visit while Sandra, my shield, sat with us like some kind of a chaperone. Alysa and I never had any meaningful conversation. I flitted about like a scared, little bird, making small talk, mostly with Sandra.

I never heard from Alysa again. How shamefully I behaved. My behavior was not like Jesus. He loves. I didn't. I just wanted to protect myself. This certainly was not the Jesus who took care of me throughout Matt's birth. I hate now remembering how I treated her and pray that someday God will help me find her, apologize, and reconnect with her.

Inward Confusion from Church Experiences

It isn't easy to explain the Local Church. On one hand, the church was wonderful; on the other hand, it wasn't. These opposites existed simultaneously.

The church was wonderful to me because much of the Bible teaching we were receiving was amazing. I had never realized before how profound and complex the Bible was. Brother Lee knew it backward and forward and was adept at tracing a line of teaching through the whole Bible for several hours without any notes. We were shown things such as a garden, a river, gold, and precious stones in the beginning of the Bible as raw materials, and again at the end of the Bible, these very same items built up into a city, the New Jerusalem. We were told that this was what God was after: His habitation with man for eternity.

We learned about Adam and Eve being a picture of Christ and the church, and how Eve was made from a rib taken out of Adam when he was in a deep sleep, a symbol of death. We were taught that Eve's creation was symbolic of how the church was created by the life of Christ that was released for us when He died on the cross. This picture was also used to teach us that only God's life could produce God's building, the church.

We also learned that the good land that God gave to the children of Israel in the time of the Old Testament was a picture of the unsearchable riches of Christ that God gave to us in the time of the New Testament. The children of Israel had to labor on the land during the year and then, at the appointed time, bring the best of their produce to the one place that God had chosen to put his name, Jerusalem, and worship Him there by offering up their produce. This was also a picture of the Christian life—of laboring on Jesus and bringing the produce of our experiences with Him to the meetings to offer up our testimonies as worship to the Lord.

Most of us had never heard teachings like these before, and they were wonderful to us. We began to greatly appreciate Brother Lee. Most of the leaders in Texas began to openly praise him and his ministry.

Witness Lee was a very gifted Bible teacher. His love for God's Word was evident, as was his commitment to serve the Lord. I credit my familiarity with the books and verses of the Bible to the many years I spent hearing his ministry. By his example, I was encouraged to love the Word as well. In our first years under his ministry, his teaching was more Christ-centered. According to him, much of what he taught us then he learned from the Brethren. In those years, he always gave them credit; but in the latter days of his ministry, he ceased doing this as he began teaching from what he called his own "new light," or realizations from the Bible.

So on one hand, the Local Church was wonderful to me. On the other hand, it wasn't. Some of its practices and the application of certain teachings we constantly heard bothered me. But I dared not allow myself to admit I didn't like something, and I felt badly if I ever allowed myself to question something. To do so would be, no doubt, my self. It would mean that I wasn't staying in my spirit and that I was living in my flesh. If I wanted more time with my family, this meant I wrongly loved them more than the Lord and wasn't willing to pay the price for Him to have His church. I needed to give my all. I needed to learn to be in submission to God's deputy authorities, meaning the church leaders, so that the church could be built and the Lord could return. We were at the close of the age. Probably our children would never even grow up because the Lord's return to the earth was imminent.

This errant thought was an evil one that helped me feel justified in not investing that much of my time in nurturing and developing them. Todd and Matt were two precious and unique little people that God had committed to my care, and I was found sadly wanting! My parental failure had inevitable long-term consequences in their lives, and in mine and John's, and it is, to this day, one of my deepest regrets.

Brother Lee sometimes offered us illustrations of his teachings that would confuse or bother me. In one message, I heard him say that if you were really spiritual, you would not drive a new car. Driving a new car was an indication of your spiritual condition. After hearing this, a brother might sell his new car and buy an old car. Then a short time later, I would hear Brother Lee say that if you drove an old car, this didn't glorify the Lord. We should be driving new cars as a testimony of the Lord's love for His children! Brothers and sisters would then feel all right to buy new cars.

One illustration that still occasionally haunts me was about a piece of paper. Witness Lee said something to this effect, "If you can walk past a piece of paper lying on the floor and not pick it up, you are not spiritual." Only God knows how many times I have thought of that statement when I pass (or don't pass) a piece of paper on the floor.

Even though these things troubled me, I just couldn't bring myself to say, or let myself honestly think, that I didn't like something that was happening in the church. To do this would be the same as rejecting what God Himself had arranged to help transform me and grow me up into Christ and into oneness with all the brothers and sisters. I just had to bury any such thought and press ahead.

At one point, in the midst of these kinds of confusing experiences, Brother Lee gave us a serious warning. He said that we should be careful never to leave the way of life, referring to all the teaching we had heard about Christ being our life. In his warning, he repeated this phrase a number of times: "Treasure life." He told us that God had given him this word to share with us while he was convalescing from eye surgery.

Years later, someone told me that he believed God was speaking this to Witness Lee about his own condition at that time, and that maybe he was the one who was starting to veer off from the way of life. He felt that maybe Witness Lee's eye problem was God's way of warning him that he was losing vision with his spiritual eyes.

Chapter 9
Would We Submit?

> Stand fast therefore in the liberty by which Christ has made us free, and do not be entangled again with a yoke of bondage. (Gal. 5:1)

Embarrassed at Breakfast

I WAS EMBARRASSED ONE SATURDAY MORNING AT BREAKFAST with a number of other service group leaders and the four Houston elders. At one point, one of the elders introduced a topic that the four of them had been discussing in private—some of us needed to move to another city to start another Local Church.

In the years following the initial move to Houston, there had been more migrations throughout the United States. In Texas, the first migration out of Houston was to Dallas. Another was to New Orleans. I don't remember which move was being discussed that morning, but the topic was who would go.

One of the four elders looked at me and said, "How about you and John?" Knowing that I wasn't considering such a move for even a minute, I responded, "You'll have to ask John about that." He retorted, "Oh really? I thought you ran things at your house." Everyone laughed. I was humiliated and furious with him. How cruel and how unnecessary his comment was! He didn't live in my shoes. Who did he think he was? Granted, I wasn't a naturally submissive or quiet or meek sister, but I was trying to be. The rest of the day, I considered various things I could do or say to show him he was wrong. Then the Lord spoke, "Would you rather show him your self-made submission now or let him see Me living in you when I have finished My work in you?" After pondering that awhile, I decided to give up the self-improving, self-justifying route and hand myself over to the Lord to let Him do His work in me, in His time.

The House Swap

In August of 1973, after living in our wonderful little rental house for about a year and a half and attending meetings in Hall One, John told me that the leading brothers wanted us to move to Hall Two. They had decided that Stephen Thompson, one of the elders who was then living at Hall Two, needed to move back to be an elder at Hall One. They wanted us to swap rental houses with the Thompsons. How easy it was for them to take my house, my nest, where I was taking care of our six-week-old baby! I was being asked to go through a nightmarish move with a nursing baby! This would be our ninth move. I went to see the swap house and became even more upset with the request. Not only was the house ugly, it was on Howard Drive, a busy street which was dangerous for my four year old. It had two bedrooms and an enclosed back porch. I didn't want to move, but knew it was inevitable.

It never occurred to me to ask the Lord if that was what He wanted, or to ask John to pray about this. You simply didn't tell the elders that you had a different leading from the Lord. If you did, it would be obvious to them, and you would know also, that your leading wasn't from the Lord, but from your own self. That was just the way it was. If the brothers were asking us to move for the sake of the church, we felt that this was the same thing as God asking us to move.

Adding to my horror on the day we moved in, we inherited a young, carrot-juice-drinking brother who had already been living with the Thompson family. His room had boxes of carrot juice stacked on the floor. They had told him that he could stay on—easy for them to offer! Rather than move him out of his room, we made the enclosed porch into our bedroom. The house had only one bathroom, and we had to share it with this young man. I had no privacy and had to stay hidden in my bedroom until I was dressed for the day. This included going to the bathroom or kitchen—not exactly a convenient situation for a nursing mother.

Stressed Out by People Pleasing

In the Local Church, new babies were just a part of life, and mothers did not receive any special consideration after giving birth. I was expected to carry on as before, so a typical week with a young child and a nursing infant wasn't something to be desired. During the weekdays, I attended two prayer meetings where no children were allowed and for which I had to make babysitting arrangements. I was frequently called on to help with various needs among the brothers and sisters and was expected to do so. On Monday evenings, I attended a service group meeting; on Tuesday evenings, a teaching meeting; on Wednesday evenings, the church prayer meeting. On Thursday evenings, if I didn't have an additional service group meeting to attend, we were supposed to invite a church member or possible recruit over for dinner at our home.

Weekends were the absolute worst time for me and, no doubt, many other wives. Typically, I cooked, served, and cleaned up Friday's dinner, bathed the children and packed them for babysitting, nursed the baby, and went out the door by 7:00 p.m. When the church meeting and fellowship time that followed it were over, usually around 10:00 or 10:30 p.m., I picked up the children, rushed home, nursed the baby, and got everyone settled for the night. Then at 7:00 a.m. on Saturday morning, three service group coordinators knocked on my door to do the planning for the cleaning and arranging service group to which I had been assigned as a service group leader. (By now, I was no longer on the clerical service group.) They would leave my house just in time for me to finish getting the children ready to go with me to the meeting hall for the actual cleaning activities, which usually lasted until noon. We didn't believe in hiring any outsiders to do anything regarding the church property or affairs, so we didn't unless we had no way to do the work ourselves.

After helping to clean the meeting place, I rushed home and took care of Todd and Matt, who were screaming and crying by this time, ready for lunch and a nap. While they slept, I prepared a meal to be taken to the gospel dinner that night. When I finished, the boys were awake and needed further attention. I bathed them, fed them, and got them ready for the evening babysitting group by 5:30 p. m. The gospel dinner started at 6:00 p.m. and was followed by a meeting that usually lasted until 10:30 or 11:00 p.m. I repeated the get-home-and-get-them-to-bed routine and crashed on my bed. And, don't forget, I was nursing a baby and dodging the young man in our home throughout this process. What about John? John who? There was nothing left of me for him.

On Sunday morning, I was up repeating the feeding and dressing routine with one hand and preparing lunch with the other before we left for the meeting which began at 9:00 a.m. Oh yes, someone would be coming over for lunch after the morning meeting, which usually lasted until 12:30 or 1:00 p.m., because the speaker talked way past ending time, and then testimonies followed. Many times, we didn't leave the meeting hall until well after 1:00 p.m., at which time I gathered up my stuff, grabbed the boys, and rushed home to serve lunch.

After lunch and cleanup, I put the children down for their late naps; they were usually completely out of control by this time. At 3:00 p.m., I went to a one-hour singing practice with a group of brothers and sisters who sang gospel songs in malls. We didn't have any designated singers or choir in the meetings because that was considered to be a worldly method that Christianity used. I usually made it home just in time to get the kids ready for babysitting once more (unless, of course, it was my turn to babysit) and head out for the Lord's Table meeting, which began at 6:00 p.m.

One such weekend, after Sunday afternoon singing practice, I fell on the bed sobbing that I couldn't do one more thing that day. I told John emphatically that I wasn't going to the meeting that night. The pressure to attend every meeting was tremendous. John said, "You'll be there," and left to go to some pre-meeting meeting. I was furious and exhausted and hysterical. I lay on the bed and cried. Much to John's surprise, I didn't go to the meeting. I couldn't enjoy staying at home because of guilt, but at least I attempted to rest. Partway through the evening, after the boys had gone to sleep, I called a sister, one who didn't keep all the rules and wasn't considered by the leading brothers to be absolute. Her failure to conform was tolerated because she was unhealthy and had frequent physical difficulties. Through stifled sobs, I explained my schedule, my exhaustion, and my frustration with everything. She had one profound thing to say to me. "Jane, your problem is that you are a men-pleaser."

The Harvest House with Sisters

After about a month of living in the Howard Drive house, I finally turned the whole situation over to the Lord and asked Him to take away my resentment towards the brother who was living with us and to change how I felt about being there. He did both. Not long after this, the brother packed up his things and moved out. Things were looking up!

Then in December of 1973, the leading brothers approached John and asked us to move into a "single-brothers' house" with Local Church brothers who were students at the University of Houston. (Unmarried brothers sometimes lived together in "single-brothers' houses" and unmarried sisters in "single-sisters' houses.") The leading brothers thought it would be good to turn this single-brothers' house by the campus into a "corporate-living" situation so that there would be a married couple responsible for the household.

By this time, there were several married couples that had single brothers or single sisters living with them in their homes. We called these arrangements "corporate living." Sometimes, these living situations included only one unmarried person; oftentimes, three or four; and sometimes, nine or ten, but always of the same sex.

Because John was interested in being more involved with the brothers who were college students, he liked the idea. When he broached the subject with me, I said to myself, "I am drawing the line here." We had been living in the swapped rental house for about three months. I was still nursing the baby. I wasn't ready to move again, and I wasn't going to live in a house full of males and become their maid. I didn't respond to John's question, but started some serious thinking about a way out of this dreadful proposal.

I had been spending time with several sisters who were also students at the University of Houston, and I knew they needed a place to live closer to campus. So I said to John, "If you want to be near those brothers and near the campus, I am willing to move—but only to a sisters' house!" He understood my not wanting to live in the brothers' house and agreed to this as a workable compromise. The leading brothers were not excited about this idea and suggested to him that it was much better to move into the brothers' house. After all, it was available. They said that it was very difficult to find rental homes in that neighborhood, and that we probably wouldn't be able to find anything. Any house that became available was instantly rented because of its proximity to the campus.

John started driving through the neighborhood every day after work in hopes of grabbing up a new rental offering. I was hopeful he would fail in the endeavor and we would stay put. One evening, after driving through the campus neighborhood praying, he came home with the news that he had rented a house. After stopping to talk to someone, he had been directed to a house that was going to be leased while the owner went out of the country for a year or so. John was the first one to inquire about the house, so he got it.

This was the tenth move in our six-year-old marriage. Our new home was a two-story, yellow frame house with a screened-in back porch, by far the nicest house we had ever lived in. Because it was on Harvest Lane, we called it the "Harvest House." Two single sisters moved in with us. There were three bedrooms upstairs and a full bathroom. We gave the large master bedroom to the sisters and our family took the other two bedrooms. We all had to share the upstairs bathroom, which had a door into the hallway and another door into the sisters' master bedroom.

Although the living arrangements in the house were difficult, I soon recognized some benefits of moving there. The campus was far away from both meeting places and from where most of the people in the church lived. I didn't have a car. That meant my phone didn't ring during the day for church needs or sisters' prayer meetings. I was stuck at home with the children. I could learn to like this! Another couple moved into the brothers' house where we had been originally asked to live. The wife of that couple and I took turns babysitting our combined three children. I went to only every other meeting and had only one more child when it was my turn to babysit. What a treat!

A Brush with the Supernatural

Even though I was having problems with some of the things that were practiced in the church, I dearly loved the people, my brothers and sisters in Christ. Together we had a number of exciting experiences with the Lord. One such experience happened with a young couple named Ted and Beth Jefferson, who decided they also wanted to move into our neighborhood near the University of Houston and be involved in the campus ministry. Beth became discouraged when they couldn't find a home to rent in the neighborhood, so she asked me to drive through the neighborhood with her and pray for the Lord to give them a house.

She was a real live wire and always made me laugh. As we were driving, she suddenly ordered, "Stop, let me get out!" She jumped from the car and approached an elderly lady who was watering plants in her front yard. The lady's house looked like something from a horror movie. Huge cacti and century plants were growing everywhere, and vines covered most of the two-story brick house. After several minutes, Beth jumped back in the car and said, "That's it! This is my house!" When she had asked the lady if she knew of a house for rent, the lady had said, "Yes, this one is. My husband is very ill, and we need to move." Within the month, Ted and Beth were our nearby neighbors.

Shortly after they moved in, Beth became very frightened of living in the house. She said she was hearing strange sounds all the time and didn't like being there alone. Ted told her she was imagining things and needed to calm down. It was a big, spooky house, so I understood how she could feel afraid. Soon, she found out the real reason why the landlord was sick—he had been severely beaten by burglars during a house break-in a few months before!

One day, I received a call from a frantic, whispering Beth, "Jane, get down here immediately! Come now! Help me! There is someone downstairs. Just come beat on the front door and scare them away!" With my hair in rollers, I grabbed up Matt and put him in his stroller. I told Todd to get on his bike and follow me. I ran the two blocks to Beth's house, wondering all the way what I was going to do when I got there. I didn't think anyone was in the house, but what if someone was? I left the children in her front yard and ran to the front door calling, "Beth! I'm here." She came running down the stairs and said, "Come with me to the kitchen. They were in there!" When we got to the kitchen, the cabinet doors over the oven were standing wide open. There was a rolling pin on the floor across the room. Beth looked at it and said, "Jane, that was in the back of that cabinet," pointing at the open doors. "There is no way those opened by themselves and that rolled out!" No one was in the house, and the kitchen back door was locked. Beth said, "Jane, this house is haunted!" I tried to laugh it off, but thought to myself how glad I was that we didn't live there. When Beth told Ted, he was incredulous and began to make fun of her.

At midnight several days later, John answered the phone to hear Ted say, "John, can you and Jane come over right now? Something really strange is going on over here!" John said, "Ted sounds terrified. Let's go." When we got there, a white-faced Ted began to explain that he had been in the living room when he heard a strange noise coming from their enclosed back porch. When he walked into the porch room, he froze with fear as he saw the Venetian blinds moving from bottom to top, as if someone was holding them at the bottom, and shaking them up and down. All the windows and doors were shut. There was no wind. He had called for Beth and then immediately called us.

We had heard about things like this before but never had experienced them. We decided to walk through every room of the house, praying, in order to have a spiritual cleansing of the whole place. Room by room, we proclaimed the victory of Christ on the cross and bound the powers of darkness, commanding any demons present to leave that home.

We came to a small crawl door in the upstairs hallway that Beth had never opened. She said it was a storage room where the owners had left some things. When we looked inside, we found an assortment of occult artifacts. We picked them all up and moved them to the garage. The landlord agreed to take the items away.

This wasn't a typical Local Church experience. We had learned to do this kind of spiritual "house cleaning" in our earlier years in the church.

From that day, there were no more incidents, and Beth had no further episodes of fear.

Trained and Tested

In the mid 1970's, the Living Stream Ministry began having ten-day, semiannual trainings (instead of conferences), in which Brother Lee began to cover in detail each of the books of the Bible in a systematic way. These trainings provided him with a strictly managed environment in which he could teach us and test our retention of his messages. When we registered for a training, we were agreeing to submit to such discipline. He was the trainer; we were the trainees. He could do whatever he felt was necessary to train us.

The ministry's headquarters was moved from Los Angeles to Anaheim, and construction on a ministry center that seated several thousand people was started. Brothers from all over the country were asked to temporarily move there to help build the new facility. When the ministry center was finished, they also built a home as a gift for Brother Lee. The Church in Anaheim met in the new building except when Brother Lee used it to hold his semiannual training meetings. People traveled from all over the world to attend these sessions.

We hung onto every word Brother Lee spoke, believing that what we were hearing was God's present speaking to us. We were admonished and expected to attend these two trainings each year. Each training cost $50 per person for registration. We paid our own travel costs and also gave money to the families who provided us with hospitality.

There were several thousand people who attended and took hospitality in homes. Children were not allowed to attend. Some people left their children with relatives. Some sisters would take turns staying home to babysit. I made arrangements with a sister who could never go to the trainings because she was the caregiver for her infirm father, and paid her $50 to keep my children. I was, therefore, able to attend most trainings. (I never volunteered to baby- sit!) Typically, the trainees attended two meetings in the morning and one in the evening. In the afternoon, we studied the previous session's teachings and also did chores in the home where we were staying. We sat in assigned seats for the training sessions and wore name badges. If we were late, we were locked out of that session. If we missed three training sessions, we were dismissed from the training. I never heard of anyone missing three meetings!

We were called randomly, sometimes by seat number, to stand before the thousands of trainees and be tested on our retention of the previous session's teaching. This might mean repeating portions of Brother Lee's teaching or answering questions. He wasn't happy if we didn't use some of his exact phraseology and terminology. I disliked immensely this part of the training and lived in fear of it. I don't think I was alone in this feeling. I never forgot the time I had seen him humiliate the sister who stood frozen at the podium.

And to think, we were giving him our permission to do this and were even paying for the experience!

My fear of being tested drove me to buy a small flashlight so that I could study after bedtime under my bed covers.

An atmosphere of competition among the various churches and church regions began developing at the trainings because the leaders from each region wanted their churches to be recognized as churches that were following Brother Lee's ministry in the most absolute way. This recognition seemed to be especially important to the Texas elders, who heard Brother Lee declare publicly at his trainings how much he appreciated the Texas brothers' absoluteness.

The training itself was difficult enough, but the living arrangements sometimes added another dimension of discomfort. One such hospitality situation stands out in my memory: John and I were one of six couples staying in a young couple's small wood frame home that had only two bedrooms and one bath! One of the six couples was newly wed and had come to the training straight from their camping honeymoon! Because they had a tent with them, they set it up in the backyard and slept in it.

The logistics of this hospitality arrangement were unbelievable. All the sisters slept in one of the bedrooms and the living room. All the brothers slept in the other bedroom. Our beds were foam mats or mattresses laid on the floor. The bathroom was located between the two bedrooms, and each couple was scheduled for fifteen minutes together in the small bathroom, in either the morning or evening. The fifteen minute blocks were sufficient (barely) because sisters wore no make-up and most had no need of much more than a brush and a rubber band to fix their hair. The dining room table was turned up against the wall at night to make room for the sleeping mats and set up again in the morning for meals. Cooking, serving, and cleaning duties were assigned and posted for each meal. We were given a short time for afternoon rest or study. Everyone had to adhere strictly to the schedule to make this arrangement work.

Don't forget. On top of all of this, there was the pressure to be ready to be summoned by name or seat number to stand up, walk to the front of the room, and be tested—and possibly humiliated—in front of several thousand people!

The Heavenly Hebrews Training

As difficult as it was submitting to the training experience, there was a positive side. We were spending a great deal of time studying the Bible and were learning a lot about it. The training on the book of Hebrews was a particular time of blessing and insight for me. The heavens were truly opened for me during that time. It seemed that there was nothing between God and me. I learned that I could come "forward with boldness to the throne of grace" to find mercy and "grace for timely help" (Heb. 4:16, NTRV). I saw Jesus "made a little inferior to the angels because of the suffering of death" (Heb. 2:9, NTRV). In my mind's eye, I saw the long train of testimonies of the faithful in Hebrews 11. In Hebrews 12, I saw the great "cloud of witnesses" cheering us onward (Heb. 12:1, NTRV). I saw Jesus enduring the cross "for the joy set before Him" (Heb. 12:2, NTRV). I learned that the meaning of the word *Hebrew* was "river-crosser." Abraham, by faith, crossed a river to another place to which God had called him.

I and many others no doubt can testify that God certainly blessed what Witness Lee taught us during the Hebrews training. The things I learned from God's Word during the Hebrews training still speak to me today. The Bible says,

> So shall My word be that goes forth from My mouth; it shall not return to Me void, but it shall accomplish what I please, and it shall prosper in the thing for which I sent it. (Isa. 55:11)

It seemed, however, that every time we had a fresh visitation by the Holy Spirit in the meetings, some unusual practice would follow. The teaching about us being today's river-crossers triggered hundreds of baptisms which were intended to show that we were answering the call to come forward to God out of all deadness. Many were being baptized for the second or third time. From that time, to be baptized became something we could do whenever we felt the need to testify that we were passing out of a deadened state. It became an accepted practice to be baptized more than once. If someone felt their relationship with the Lord had become stagnant, the person might jump up in a meeting, repent, and request to be baptized again.

All the person probably needed to do was just repent of sin.

Accepting Local Training Meetings

Not long after Brother Lee began his trainings, we began holding weekly training meetings in the Church in Houston (as did other churches) in which the contents of his training messages were taught. Up until this time, we had tried to keep Brother Lee's ministry separate from the church. We had been taught that the church itself was to be primary and that any ministry was to be secondary. Ministry should be for and support the church, not vice versa. When we first began having these "ministry meetings," the leading brothers emphasized the importance of maintaining a clear separation between the church meetings and the local training meetings. At the first local training meeting, the leading brothers announced that this was not a meeting of the church, but a meeting for training us in Brother Lee's teachings. After a period of time, however, this distinction was lost, and no differentiation was made between the two types of gatherings.

When we began placing such a great importance on Witness Lee's ministry, the church members and church meetings were destined to become secondary in importance. We were still like the frog in the pot, and the water was so warm by this time that it made us feel very relaxed and drowsy. No need to think about what was happening. After all, could God's man on the earth today lead us astray? Even if we had wondered about this, we wouldn't have asked any questions—they might put us out of the pot!

After each training, Brother Lee's training messages were printed into small booklets which were called "Life-Studies." These were sold only among the Local Churches, not to the general public. There were approximately thirty messages per training, with each Life-Study publication containing one message. Those who could restate and repeat the training messages were highly regarded and praised. Personal testimonies that confirmed Brother Lee's teachings were well received. We were all encouraged to spend time in the Life-Studies and to get the full benefit of the trainings so we could be useful to the Lord. We had the unparalleled opportunity of being trained by Brother Lee, the modern-day Paul.

At the beginning of the trainings in Houston, all seemed to be going very well. We were heading into a new era that would hasten the building up of Christ's testimony on the earth and bring Him back sooner.

If we could have seen where we were headed, we might not have turned our focus to Witness Lee's ministry and disregarded our belief that the church and the work (the sphere of ministry outside the church, like the Living Stream Ministry) should be kept separate. Throughout the 1970's, Witness Lee's ministry grew in the United States and abroad. Many nationalities were represented at the trainings because Local Churches had now been started in many places. Then, Witness Lee agreed to move one of his semiannual trainings from California to Texas, so brothers from the churches built a Living Stream Ministry center in Irving for him, using the volunteer labor of church brothers. Members of various Local Churches in the area also began to help produce Living Stream Ministry publications out of the new facility.

Would We Submit?

Our regard for church leadership was increasing in tandem with the growing appreciation for Brother Lee's Ministry. We were placing more importance on the authority of the elders and were feeling ever-increasing pressure to submit to them. The roles of the leaders and the members with regard to authority were becoming more defined as patterns of behavior were repeated among us.

One evidence of this change was in our meetings. Unlike our earliest years in the church, the leading brothers began exercising much more control over the church meetings, to the extent that they corrected and adjusted us if, in their opinion, we were getting off the track of Brother Lee's ministry. For example, if someone chose a hymn that didn't seem to support the topic being covered that day, a leading brother would say something like, "Let's change that to hymn number 444," which he obviously thought fit better. If someone was saying something that seemed to be not quite on target or was too lengthy, one of the leading brothers might interrupt and admonish, "Make it quick, brother." Whatever anyone said in a church meeting was under their scrutiny.

Deputy authority was practiced not only in the conduct of the church meetings but in everything else. Three sets of verses were used to impress us about the seriousness of properly relating to God's deputy authorities: First, Genesis 9:22–25 showed that after one of Noah's sons,

Ham, discovered him drunk and naked in his tent, the other two of Noah's sons walked backwards to cover him with a garment and didn't look on his nakedness. The son who looked at and published Noah's sin was cursed. Second, 1 Samuel 26:5–11 showed that David wouldn't smite the "Lord's anointed," Saul, even when Saul was wrong. David left that to God. Third, in Numbers 12:1–10, when Miriam, the sister of Moses, spoke against him and questioned his authority, God smote her with leprosy. We were told that these verses showed how serious it was to deal wrongly with someone to whom God had given deputy authority.

Ultimately, this meant that if an elder was overtaken in a sin, it was best just to look away like Noah's sons did or leave it to God like David did. Once, Witness Lee said that if anyone had a complaint against an elder, it should be submitted to the elders in writing by two or more parties, but I never heard of this ever being done.

I now believe that the examples of Noah, David, and Miriam were misused. It is easy to see what an avenue this teaching opened for the devil's activities among us. Because of this teaching, church members could simply look away from serious sin in someone in authority over them, as if it didn't even exist. As a result of this belief, in the long run, there was no one to check and balance Witness Lee, who ended up at the top of the chain of authority, that is, except God Himself directly from heaven. In other words, there was nothing in place among us to help Witness Lee if he fell into error.

God's Economy

The teaching that seemed to be rising to the top in importance was something Brother Lee called "God's economy."

The teaching about God's economy rests at the heart of Witness Lee's ministry. It was, and still is, the primary teaching and main emphasis in the Local Church. His use of the term economy *is different from the common meaning and use of the word. To most people, the word* economy *immediately brings to mind the thought of finance and economics. This is not, however, his meaning.*

Brother Lee said that God's economy (Eph. 3:9, RV) was God's eternal purpose (Eph. 3:11). When I first heard his teaching on this subject, I found it very difficult to understand. In brief, God's economy was His purpose that "the processed Triune God dispense Himself into man" in order to produce His habitation. The term, "processed Triune God," indicated that God had gone through a process consisting of incarnation, human living, crucifixion, death, burial, resurrection, ascension, and outpouring as the life-giving Spirit in order to make Himself available to be dispensed into us as our life when we called on His name or pray-read His Word. This teaching was a further development of Brother Lee's teaching about eating Jesus so that He could be mingled with us.

The Kingdom, Overcomers, and Outer Darkness

Brother Lee would periodically mention that someday he would share with us what he had learned from Watchman Nee about the coming kingdom. However, he would always say that it wasn't time yet. Then unexpectedly, one day in a meeting, he told us that it was now time for this line of teaching. From that time, he began to give many messages on the kingdom.

The complex teaching about the kingdom contained numerous terms and concepts. In summary, Brother Lee taught us that this kingdom was a thousand-year period after Christ's second coming in which Christ would reign on the earth with His "overcomers." Only the believers who overcame in this life would reign with Christ in the coming millennial kingdom.

According to the letters to the churches in the book of Revelation (Rev. 2 and 3), an overcomer was one who overcame the fallen situations of the churches that were described in those letters. If we did not overcome, we would have to spend a period of time in "outer darkness," weeping and gnashing our teeth (Matt. 25:30) and being "beaten with many stripes" (Luke 12:47). Thus, this would be a thousand-year period of discipline for those who were not overcomers. Such persons would not perish eternally, but would "be saved, yet so as through fire" (1 Cor. 3:15). This meant that for a thousand years in outer darkness, they would be disciplined until they learned the lessons they should have learned during their comparably short lifetime on earth. They would, therefore, miss the thousand-year wedding feast of the Lamb (the millennial kingdom era). After the millennial kingdom was over, the non-overcomers, having been matured by their discipline, would then be included in the New Jerusalem with God for eternity.

We believed this teaching because it came from Brother Lee and because it offered an answer to some of the much-debated and seemingly irreconcilable verses in the New Testament about whether or not a believer could lose his or her salvation (a topic debated by Calvinists and Arminians). This teaching offered an explanation for the existence of verses in the Bible that sounded like Christians *could* lose their salvation. These verses were not referring to loss of salvation, but to loss of the reward of becoming an overcomer. In other words, God's children were like students who, if they were unwilling to study and learn their lessons, would be punished. God would not reject them permanently but rather would discipline them until they finally graduated. Such believers were still His children and would not lose their eternal salvation.

There were several Bible passages that supported his reward and punishment teaching. Matthew 25 was the one most often referenced. There, Jesus presented a parable about ten virgins—five who were wise and five who were foolish. All ten were believers because they all "trimmed their lamps" and went out to meet their Lord in response to the midnight cry, "Behold, the bridegroom is coming." But only five of them had enough oil in their lamps. The foolish five ran out of oil and begged the wise five to share. The wise ones, however, told them they had to go and buy for themselves. While they went to buy, the bridegroom came, took the wise five into the wedding feast, and shut the door. He would not open it to the foolish five when they returned, but left them in outer darkness. In other words, five were rewarded and five were punished.

Another parable supporting this teaching is also in Matthew 25. A lord gave money to three of his servants and went on a trip. Again, all three were believers because they were all servants. While the lord was gone, two of the servants wisely used their lord's money, but one of them buried his lord's money. When the lord returned, he rewarded the good and faithful servants, making them rulers over many things and letting them enter into his joy. However, he took his money away from the wicked and lazy servant and gave it to the one who had the most. To this, Jesus added:

> "For to everyone who has, more will be given, and he will have abundance; but from him who does not have, even what he has will be taken away. And cast the unprofitable servant into the outer darkness. There will be weeping and gnashing of teeth." (Matt. 25:29-30)

Brother Lee told us that Paul was an overcomer. He had "fought the good fight" and there was laid up for him a "crown of righteousness" (2 Tim. 4:7–8). He pointed out that Paul's crown was a crown of *righteousness,* not of grace. We were initially saved by grace, but the life of the kingdom was a life of righteousness. We had to be wise virgins who bought oil (the Spirit) now and were ready for Christ's second coming. We had to be good and faithful servants who were making profit for the Lord in His absence, as those had done in the parable.

Ultimately, these teachings left many among us fearful of being left in outer darkness. We understood that the kingdom life was different from the gospel of grace, but most of us didn't understand how to apply what we were hearing to our own lives, except to be in total submission to the church and the elders.

We would have fared much better without these teachings because they became very dominant and strengthened our submission to deputy authority. They turned our focus to becoming overcomers and caused many to despair of making the grade.

Males and Females

Most of the brothers with whom I was associated in the church considered women to be creatures who could easily be deceived and used to hurt others. Therefore, women needed to be carefully managed and held under authority.

Sisters who were intelligent or more vocal than others were handled cautiously and might receive looks or comments from brothers about any perceived forwardness. Brother Lee frequently talked about sisters and their out-of-control emotions. He also said that sisters with smart, quick minds were a source of trouble. He told us that the major heresies in church history had been introduced by women. Of course, Eve was at the top of the list for introducing trouble way back in the Garden of Eden. I was usually cautious and guarded around brothers, not wanting to say or do something that would be offensive or appear to be not submissive.

The Local Church environment was very hard on women. This was a spillover result of our beliefs about authority and submission. While there, I never forgot for a moment that woman was deceived first (1 Tim. 2:14).

Also, male and female relationships were carefully monitored. We were told that, as Christians, it was not proper to touch each other or display emotion by physical touch, even to those of the same sex. Of course, we could touch our own spouses and children, but we never dared to hug one another as brothers and sisters in Christ. A few times, I accidentally touched a brother or sister and had to immediately recoil with embarrassment and apologize. I felt there was something wrong with this practice even though it sounded spiritual.

I didn't think to look at what the Bible said about this. It is interesting to note that, in contrast to our practice, several times Paul told the brethren to greet one another with a holy kiss.

We were also strongly admonished never to be alone with a member of the opposite sex in order to avoid the "appearance of evil" (1 Thess. 5:22, KJV). Even visitors to our meetings were managed when it came to being with someone of the opposite sex. For example, if an unmarried visiting young man came to a meeting holding the hand of a young woman, in a short time, if possible, they were separated and seated in different places. This mainly occurred at gospel dinners.

One time, a young woman who had been to three or four of our meetings, was taken aside by Sam Jones, one of the Houston elders, into one of the church offices for a talk or "fellowship." He stopped me as I was passing by and asked me to sit in on the talk. Sam asked her if she was dating someone. She said, "Yes." He started talking about the importance of purity in following the Lord. She was looking at him somewhat blankly. This wasn't the response he wanted. Suddenly, he picked up a book and slammed it loudly on the desk. I was so startled that I literally jumped in my seat and had to regain my composure. He raised his voice and began ranting at her about the sin of fornication and its danger to her Christian walk. I was appalled. The young woman never returned to another one of our meetings. Sam's behavior made me feel sick inside; I knew there was something very wrong with it.

I guess, in a strange way, Sam's treatment was a blessing to this young woman. This was not the first time that I had been bothered by Sam's behavior. Many years later, after we were no longer connected to the Local Church, a brother told me how he also had an experience with Sam Jones similar to the one I just described. Sam had invited him into a private room at the meeting hall along with a young brother. He had proceeded to correct and rebuke this young brother about something. When Sam had become frustrated with the young brother's failure to respond as expected, he had picked up his book bag and thrown it, hitting the young brother with it! Also, after we were no longer in the Local Church, I heard a significant number of stories from other people whose exit from the Local Church was directly tied to bad experiences with Sam Jones. He certainly played a key role in what lay ahead for me.

Chapter 10
A Campus Harvest

Most assuredly, I say to you, unless a grain of wheat falls into the ground and dies, it remains alone; but if it dies, it produces much grain. (John 12:24)

Morning by Morning

WE WERE ADMONISHED YEAR-ROUND TO RISE EARLY and meet with a few others for "corporate morning watch" in order to pray-read the Word together. For two reasons, I never practiced this kind of morning watch. One, I simply didn't want to go! Two, my sleep difficulties that began in high school had resurfaced with a vengeance after Matt's birth. I had been helped to sleep in high school by being willing to die from lack of sleep if that was what God wanted. I couldn't say this anymore. It wasn't okay to die because I had two small children to take care of! Sleep had become a treasured commodity in my busy schedule. When I couldn't fall asleep, I would panic at the thought of having to face the next day with all of its demands without having had any rest. This, of course, made my insomnia worse. Many nights, I only slept a few hours.

One year while attending one of the trainings in California, after falling asleep late, I woke up at 4:55 a.m. I was wide-awake and felt drawn to read the Bible. Nothing like this had ever happened to me before. I had a wonderful time that left me feeling like the Holy Spirit had filled me to the brim. The next morning, I woke up again, wide-eyed at 5:05 a.m., and I had a repeat experience with the Lord and the Bible! This went on day after day with each morning's wake-up time being ten minutes later than the day before, until it reached 5:55 a.m. During the rest of the training, my eyes opened at 5:55 a.m. This experience continued after I returned home to Houston. Many times, I awakened to a few words of a song. When I got up and looked up the song in my hymnal, I found that the rest of the words were full of meaning and applied specifically to my current situation.

Mornings became my secret time with Jesus. I had no doubt it was Him who was waking me. This was happening not by my effort but by His grace. Living in the Harvest House with young sisters made keeping my secret time a special challenge. I had to be very careful not to wake them when I got up, or they would insist on joining me for a corporate morning watch. So I would quietly roll out of bed, step slowly across the creaking hardwood hall floor to the stairs, and then take one creaking wooden stair at a time, pausing for a few seconds on each step to recapture the silence. I usually successfully made it to the downstairs bathroom or living room where I hid for my private time with Jesus! One of those mornings, after fourteen years of battling insomnia, the Lord told me that the trial of my sleep difficulty was over.

Again, I can't explain how I knew He was saying this; I just did. The passing of time proved that what I had heard from Him was true.

One morning, I was having difficulty staying focused during my time with the Lord. I was telling the Lord I loved Him and trying to read the Bible, but He seemed to be elsewhere. Actually, my thoughts kept drifting across the room to a chair stripped of its old, worn-out fabric, which was waiting for me to finish a re-upholstering project that I had planned for that day. I had been given the old chair and was hoping to improve its appearance. I finally stopped praying and looked across the room at the chair and said aloud, "No, Lord, I don't love You. I love that chair! That's all I can think about, and that's all I really want to think about today!" The minute I finished my truthful statement, Jesus was there. He taught me something wonderful that morning: I shouldn't ever try to hide what is really in my heart from Him. My honesty was what mattered to Him, not some kind of religious verbiage.

I was also having some secret battles with a lurking feeling of spiritual pride. After all, God was visiting me in the mornings. I felt blessed on one hand, but I also had a feeling of pride that would creep up on me. I would confess this whenever I felt it, but it still kept sneaking back. I especially had these pride flare-ups around one of the sisters who lived with us who had begun to seriously get on my nerves. She came across as quite pleased with her own spirituality. She wanted me to call on the Lord and pray-read with her whenever we were together in the house. It seemed she was always in my space. I often felt that she was competing with me. I wanted to tell her to go away and leave me alone, but I knew that was out of the question. I began thinking about how much she was serving the Lord in her own strength and had no idea about grace. She needed a visitation of grace like I was having!

Thankfully, the little evil voice didn't find a place to settle down in me. It was just a little nagging, gnawing pest that kept me coming to Jesus. It kept me very aware of what a sick, deceitful, arrogant little heart I have without Him. Grace means just that—grace. Grace was not something I had somehow earned or deserved. How could I be proud of something I had nothing to do with!

A Fresh Consecration

As a result of my mornings with Jesus, I consecrated myself to the Lord in a very specific way. I wrote my consecration in the back of my Bible:

April 30, 1975

Lord Jesus, I offer myself to You without reserve to be trained by You in every aspect of my living: husband, children, money, sisters, service, meetings, and whatever else You know, to be trained in life and to be fully delivered from the tree of the knowledge of good and evil. Save me into Yourself.

Signed: Jane Anderson

I had begun to want above all else to know Him. Soon, I began to realize that He was taking me up on my offer. He was teaching me through experiences that I was His and needed Him for everything. I told the Lord that I wanted to see Him as Paul had. I, too, wanted to be captivated by His beauty as Paul had been. I loved these verses in Philippians and prayed that I could experience them:

But what things were gain to me, these I have counted loss for Christ. Yet indeed I also count all things loss for the excellence of the knowledge of Christ Jesus my Lord, for whom I have suffered the loss of all things, and count them as rubbish, that I may gain Christ and be found in Him, not having my own righteousness, which is from the law, but that which is through faith in Christ, the righteousness which is from God by faith; that I may know Him and the power of His resurrection, and the fellowship of His sufferings, being conformed to His death, if, by any means, I may attain to the resurrection from the dead. Not that I have already attained, or am already perfected; but I press on, that I may lay hold of that for which Christ Jesus has also laid hold of me. Brethren, I do not count myself to have apprehended; but one thing I do, forgetting those things which are behind and reaching forward to those things which are ahead, I press toward the goal for the prize of the upward call of God in Christ Jesus. (Phil. 3:7–14)

Through the Cross

Sandra Brown and a few other sisters, including me, loved to read Christian biographies and autobiographies. They found some that they had not read at libraries and bookstores, acquired them, and began passing them around. With more time on my hands while in the Harvest House, I started reading such books. I loved them. I read about Hudson Taylor, George Mueller, John and Charles Wesley, David Brainerd, George Whitefield, John Bunyan, John Newton, Charles Spurgeon, Amy Carmichael, Mimosa, and others. In all of these books, I saw people of faith in love with Jesus. The One I knew and loved, my dear Jesus, was on display in their life stories.

Biography reading was not a practice sanctioned by the church. The church bookroom sold only books by Watchman Nee and Witness Lee. In earlier years, the bookroom carried a few other books, mainly on "deeper life" teachings, but this stopped not long after we moved to Houston.

After we started reading biographies, the leading brothers began to mention things in church meetings to discourage us from reading such books. Why? We were told that they were too old and too religious, and hindered us from staying in Brother Lee's present-day light. I kept reading them anyway in my Harvest House hideaway.

I thoroughly loved living in the Harvest House because I was getting to know Jesus, and He was becoming my even better best friend. It was wonderful to have free time to relax and spend with Him. When I read the autobiography of Madame Guyon[7], I was amazed at how much she loved the Lord and how much she suffered in her walk with Him. She wrote about how the joy of knowing Him far surpassed any affliction she endured. She even welcomed experiences of suffering. She wrote about embracing and loving the "crosses" she was given to bear. I wasn't sure I could ever do that, but I did find myself drawn to want to know the Lord in a deeper way as she had. When I talked to Sandra Brown about Madame Guyon, I found that she was affected the same way. The following song, written by Madame Guyon when she was imprisoned for her faith, speaks volumes about her experience with the Lord:

> A little bird I am,
> Shut from the fields of air,
> And in my cage I sit and sing
> To Him who placed me there;
> Well pleased a prisoner to be,
> Because, my God, it pleaseth Thee
>
> Nought have I else to do,
> I sing the whole day long;
> And He whom most I love to please
> Doth listen to my song;
> He caught and bound my wandering wing;
> But still He bends to hear me sing.
>
> Thou hast an ear to hear,
> A heart to love and bless;
> And though my notes were e'er so rude,
> Thou wouldst not hear the less;
> Because Thou knowest as they fall,
> That love, sweet love, inspires them all.

> My cage confines me round;
> Abroad I cannot fly;
> But though my wing is closely bound,
> My heart's at liberty;
> For prison walls cannot control
> The flight, the freedom of the soul.
>
> O it is good to soar
> These bolts and bars above!
> To Him whose purpose I adore,
> Whose providence I love;
> And in Thy mighty will to find
> The joy, the freedom of the mind
>
> — Madame Guyon

---

[7] Madame Guyon (1648-1717) was known for her subjective experiences of the cross. It was written of her in the introduction to her autobiography, "Her sole crime was that of loving God" (Guyon, 5).

I also pondered over things I learned about a lady missionary to China named M. E. Barber, who helped Watchman Nee when he was a young believer. I decided I wanted to learn the same lesson she had learned in her walk with the Lord: obeying Him and waiting before the Lord for Him to work. She believed it was much more important to know Him and be known by Him than to work for Him.

I decided that the Lord wanted me just to live there in my house by the campus and focus on *Him,* not on *working* for Him. Yes, we were there to minister to the students on campus, but the Lord showed me I should do nothing except learn to obey Him in daily things and let Him reveal Himself to me. I was beginning to understand that if I really cared about others and wanted to help them know Christ, I needed to learn in my own experience what it meant to know Him and to know Him crucified.

Most assuredly, I say to you, unless a grain of wheat falls into the ground and dies, it remains alone; but if it dies, it produces much grain. (John 12:24)

So then death is working in us, but life in you. (2 Cor. 4:12)

God used three things to show me that He wanted me, as a member of His body on this earth, to learn what it meant to "supply life" to His believers: (1) parts of the book, *Spiritual Reality or Obsession,* by Watchman Nee, (2) parts of the book, *The Priesthood,* by Witness Lee, and (3) the story of M. E. Barber. Through these, I learned that any work that originated from Him would always be in the principle of a grain of wheat falling into the ground and dying, as Jesus illustrated in John 12:24. I learned that God's work was always the result of a believer subjectively experiencing the cross and functioning as a priest, one who brings others to God in prayer. I realized that much of my Christian experience was directly related to the experiences of many other Christians who had been like grains of wheat falling into the ground and dying, those who had been such priests to God. I understood that God wasn't as interested in my *doing* as He was in my *being,* and in my oneness with Him. I asked Him to work in my heart to conform me to His image as Paul wrote in Romans 8:29. I wanted to be a vessel fit for his use. I prayed, "Lord, make me a vessel you can pray through."

What God began teaching me during this time started to change my understanding about the cross. He began showing me how much He loved me as a person and how much He cared about my personal needs, while at the same time He began calling me to follow Him. Whenever He let me know He wanted me to lay down my way or what I wanted in a situation, I could do so, knowing that He would empower me to obey once I agreed. I began to wonder if this was what it meant to fall into the ground and die like a grain of wheat. Even though I was learning something new from God about the cross, my Local Church understanding of the cross, something that came close to total self-rejection, still managed to coexist with my new understanding for a number of years.

Our Money Is His

The Lord was definitely shining His light into my heart and teaching me in very specific ways to depend on Him. Just before we moved to the Harvest House, John quit his junior high teaching job because he wanted to work with brothers during the day and labor with his hands. He went to work for Sam Jones, who had a business installing floor coverings. John made a little more money than he had done as a teacher, but we were still barely able to make ends meet. Something I read in a Watchman Nee book about money struck a chord. He said that if you were having financial difficulties, the first thing you should check is your giving. We had been giving ten percent of our income to the church, but that was all. I never considered giving beyond that. I stretched every penny.

Imagine my surprise the day I kept coming up with $120 more than should have been in our bank account. That amount was a small fortune to us. Being a die-hard who would never give up until the checkbook balanced, I pressed on trying to find the $120 difference. Finally I prayed, "Lord, help me! Where is this money coming from?" Then I discovered $40 that I had subtracted from my checkbook two months before. As I scanned backwards through the check register, I spotted three of these amounts which totaled $120. Then I understood. Each $40 was supposed to have been withdrawn directly from our bank account to pay for the continuation of our health insurance after John quit his teaching job. Upon investigation, I learned the insurance company had denied our request. I was happy to solve my checkbook problem, but upset that we didn't have health insurance, considering the fact that we had two small children.

As I sat there, I heard the Lord asking that we give that monthly payment for insurance to Him. He would be our insurance. This was a scary proposition to me. I knew the Lord was speaking to us about giving, but this was an unexplored territory, so I asked the Lord to give me a trusting heart. I discussed this with John. We agreed to buy the heavenly insurance, so to speak.

A few weeks after this, John decided he wanted to start giving his mother an amount of money each month because of all the money she had given us over the years. That was fine, but we had no money to give her. She wasn't in need of it, so I suggested we do it later. He responded, "What about the money that was for health insurance?" Stunned, I said, "It is still going for health insurance! We're giving that to the Lord (that is to say, the church), and He is providing our insurance (by faith). That's not our money to give somewhere else!" So, like the defiant wife I was capable of being I said, "Did you pray about this or just think it up?" He answered, "No, I didn't pray. I just think we should do this."

Later, I went to my upstairs overstuffed armchair to have a talk with Jesus about this development. I asked, "Lord, what do I do? You told me one thing, and John is telling me another, contradicting You—and he didn't even pray about it!" The answer I got to that prayer has served me well for many years. The Lord brought the verses to mind which say that "Sarah obeyed Abraham, calling him lord," and was "not afraid with any amazement" (1 Pet. 3:6, KJV). I then read the related story in Genesis about Abraham letting another man have his wife, Sarah, in order to save his own skin. Sarah went along with what Abraham did, and God Himself intervened to protect her (Gen. 20). Immediately after this in the book of Genesis, the promised blessing of a son, Isaac, came. The Lord used those verses to make it plain to me that I should not ever let what He told me directly supersede what John told me. The way of blessing in our marriage was for me to go along with John and put my trust in God. I was free to communicate with John honestly about how I felt, which John always let me do, but whenever he made a decision, I had to go along with him and put my trust in God.

So we began sending John's mother $50 a month. About three months had passed when we received a call from his mother, Nana. As she spoke, she began to weep. She said, "I have three sons—two are successful and well-off, and one of them is poor as a church mouse. My two well-off sons have never given or offered to repay me anything, but you, my poor son, have given me this money, money that you don't have to give." She told us she didn't need the money and wouldn't keep it, but it had meant more to her than we could ever know because it showed her something about the God in whom John now believed. She sent the money back to us. John and I both felt that something very significant had happened to her. Sadly, Nana died suddenly two years later. John had certainly followed the Lord's will in clearing up our debt to her, and she had been blessed by seeing God in the situation.

About fifteen years later, Harriet Mays, a sister who lived in Dallas where Nana lived, told us that years before while she was cleaning at the Dallas meeting hall one day, she was surprised to look up and see Nana standing there. Nana had come to the meeting hall in a taxi. Having met our friend Harriet previously, Nana said to her, "I just wanted to come and see the place again where John goes to church." This happened in 1977, about a month before she died, when her health was failing after a surgery.

In Need? Ask Him

We had two cars. One was a little stripped-down Datsun that we had purchased new. We couldn't even afford air conditioning for it—a seeming necessity in hot and humid Houston! The other car was a used Ford station wagon that we had purchased with the school retirement money John had withdrawn when he quit teaching. He needed the Ford to carry his flooring equipment. One day, John called me to tell me it was not running and was sitting in the meeting hall parking lot. He had been given an estimate of $200 to repair it. We had no money. After I got off the phone, I started internally grumbling about how things weren't getting better financially, but were getting worse. Then I had the thought, "You have not because you ask not" (Jas. 4:2). So, I stopped and said in a kind of prayer-complaint, "Lord, we are giving to You and looking to You to meet our needs. John's car is broken, and he needs it to work. We don't have $200. So where is Your provision?" A short time later, John called again and said, "Jane, the car is fixed!" I said incredulously, "How?" He said, "Well, a brother came by and saw our car in the parking lot. He stopped and asked me to let him look at it. He bought a $14 part and replaced it. That fixed it!" As he related this, I was remembering my prayer-complaint, repenting for the complaint part, and thanking Him for the answer.

Another experience of God's provision soon followed. With $16 left after balancing the checkbook one month, I was eager to buy a new pair of shoes to replace my worn-out pair. As I arranged my day to get to the store, I began to feel uncomfortable about my decision. I felt like the Lord was telling me, "No." I said, "Lord, I need a pair of shoes, and I have some money, so what is the problem?" A mental picture of a pair of shoes boxed away in the upstairs closet came to mind—shoes John's mother had given me that I didn't like but had worn until they looked old. I retrieved them and realized that with a good polishing, they could be a replacement pair for my spent shoes.

Several months later, sitting in a meeting and looking down at these same shoes, I saw a hole in the sole of one. Later I complained, "Well now what, Lord? You didn't let me buy new shoes when I had the money, and now I really need a pair and have no money." The next morning, one of the sisters who lived with us appeared at the door of my room and said, "Jane, I was cleaning out some things, and I found these shoes my mother gave me that I have never liked. They've never been worn. If you like them, you can have them." I hadn't said a word to anyone about my need. I tried them on. They were a perfect fit and exactly the style I wanted. I thanked her. After she left, I cried and asked the Lord to forgive me for my bad attitude.

About two days later, another sister came to me with a box in hand and said, "Jane, I have a pair of shoes my mother gave me that I don't like and have never worn. Do you want them?" I found out later that she knew nothing about the prior pair of shoes I had been given. Inside the box, I found an expensive pair of brand name leather shoes, the kind I had always wanted, but never could afford. Another perfect fit! After she left, I really cried. "Lord, I don't understand. Another pair?" Then light dawned. My heavenly Father loved me and was giving me not only what I needed but more than what I needed. Because of the strict church and economical environment we lived in, I had begun subconsciously to think of Him as hard, demanding, and tight. By giving me a double portion of shoes, He made a major adjustment that day in my perception of Him. I am the child of a very rich and generous Father who is very aware of me, my needs, my wants, and even my preferences!

What Was the Affliction of Joseph?

I had other similar experiences during the time we lived in the Harvest House, as He was teaching me how real and near He was. What I didn't know, however, was that God was in the process of preparing me for some hard years that were just ahead. While reading in the Old Testament one day, I came across this verse:

> Woe to them.... that drink wine in bowls, and anoint themselves with the chief ointments: but they are not grieved for the affliction of Joseph. (Amos 6:1, 6, KJV)

The last words stood out. I kept thinking about them, so I wrote in the margin of my Bible, "Lord, what was the affliction of Joseph?"

God didn't answer me that day. He chose, rather, to answer my question in a unique way several years later.

A Campus Harvest

A young sister named Lana, from the nearby college campus, would visit our church meetings occasionally. I grew to love her and was praying for her. One morning, she came to see me, and we visited awhile. I was about to ask her to stay for lunch when I heard in my heart, "With such a one no not to eat" (1 Cor. 5:11, KJV). Whoa! Was the Lord telling me not to ask her to lunch? I didn't invite her. After she left, I realized what this verse coming to mind might mean. In these verses, "such a one" refers to someone practicing extra-marital sex. Was the Lord telling me that she was involved in fornication? I prayed about this and felt that the Lord wanted me to ask her if this was so. I considered how uncomfortable that would be. Yet the next time she came to see me, I just simply asked her. She looked embarrassed, hung her head, and said, "Yes." I talked to her about how serious this was and her need to repent. Several talks later, she told me she was in love with her boyfriend and couldn't stop her sin. I told her about

Scripture that strongly admonished believers not to associate with other believers for whom fornication was a way of life, and that I wouldn't be able to continue fellowshipping with her or even spend time with her until she stopped this sin. She made her decision in favor of her boyfriend and stopped visiting me.

About four months later, she called me and wanted to come over. During her summer vacation, she had done a lot of thinking and praying. She had finally repented and ended her relationship with her boyfriend. The Lord had responded to her and blessed her as a result. Excited about her new walk with the Lord, she had decided to give herself fully to Him. She was baptized shortly after this and began to attend all of our meetings. She moved in with us and started praying for her friends on campus. We now had three sisters living with us.

So after about a year of our living in the Harvest House, Lana was the only person from the campus who had come into the church (our way of saying that she had become a member). Because the leading brothers didn't consider this to be a very significant increase, they wanted us to move back to the Hall One area. John decided he would ask if we could stay a little while longer, so I prayed desperately that we would be allowed to do so. I was thankful when the leading brothers said we could have three more months. Just before those three months ended, a glorious harvest began. Wondrously, the Lord began to work on the campus. Day after day, the sisters returned home telling amazing stories about the gospel and the "seekers" (people who were seeking truth) that they were meeting. A number of students came into the church in a very short period of time. I secretly wondered if this little harvest was related to falling into the ground and dying with Jesus.

When one of my friends was reading a draft of this book, she asked me to explain what I meant by "dying with Jesus." I don't know how to explain this. I just know that He was shining His light on my self-centeredness and on my motives. In His light, I was beginning to learn to stop, repent, and turn my wants and actions over to Him. When I did this, He would come and give me a wonderful sense of peace and the joy of His presence.

What an exciting time this was! I was really happy while living in the Harvest House.

The Wheeler House with Seven Sisters

Impressed with the events happening on campus, the leading brothers assigned Stephen Thompson, the elder with whom we had swapped houses earlier, to take responsibility for what they were now calling a "campus work." In 1975, the leading brothers arranged for John and me to move to a different home by the campus, one that would accommodate more people living with us. They encouraged a brother who had the financial means to buy a duplex across the street from the campus and then rent it to us. John, our boys, and I would have two bedrooms and a bath upstairs on one side of the duplex, while the sisters would share the three bedrooms and two baths on the other side. This house was unattractive, and its location wasn't as good or safe as the Harvest House's location. I was hesitant about the move. It concerned me greatly that the back door had three or four locks on it, installed there by prior occupants. John was ready to go, but I was holding back. Finally, I decided to trust the Lord, and we took the plunge. We had been married for eight years now and were moving for the eleventh time!

We moved from the Harvest House to the "Wheeler House" (on Wheeler Street) along with seven sisters. The maintenance service group cut a door through the downstairs middle wall and joined the two living rooms of the duplex. Our living room served as the main living area, while the sisters' living room became the dining room. We built a huge oval dining table, which would seat approximately sixteen people, with a big lazy Susan in the middle for easily serving food.

It took military-like precision to accomplish all the household duties. Each sister had pre-assigned tasks to perform. One sister helped me cook every day, usually for twelve or more people. Another sister did the job of grocery shopping with me. I prepared five or six weeks of meal plans with matching grocery lists for each. The grocery items were listed according to the store's aisle arrangement. We would split the list, make a run through the aisles, and meet at the checkout lane with up to ten grocery carts. Because we had two kitchens, we sorted the groceries by kitchen location as they were bagged. We organized them in the same way when we put them in the car and then unloaded them through our two back doors into the proper kitchen when we got home. Managing food for the house was a colossal task.

Just writing about it makes me tired!

While living in the Wheeler House, several more sisters moved in with us. Under Stephen's leadership, we started holding young people's meetings and organizing visits to the campus. John and I participated mainly by providing a home for the sisters, a place for them to bring people for meals and conversation, and a place to have meetings.

A Visit From the Police

Three young women, who had just come into the church-life from the campus and were now living with us in the Wheeler House, had been dating young men who had also been brought into the church. They all stopped dating. (All of them ultimately married each other.) One of these, a sister named Louise, was newly saved and seeking to follow the Lord. She was from a Catholic family that was opposing her new Christian walk. They also did not like her boyfriend and did not want her to see him. They were very upset about her involvement with the Local Church and wanted to rescue her. They refused to hand over Louise's tax refund check when it was mailed to their house. Louise asked me to go with her to her home while her parents were out and help her search for the check. John went with us, and we found it hidden under her mother's mattress. I felt very frightened during the whole time we were in the house that they would come home and discover us.

I still cannot believe I did this! All that I can say is that we were young and totally committed to helping people get into the Local Church and stay in it.

Shortly after this, her mother brought the police to our door to try and take Louise away. She had apparently told the police that Louise was being held against her will.

Louise had to come to the door and convince the police that she was living with us of her own free will.

Greater than John the Baptist

A wonderful thing happened while we lived in the Wheeler House. Most of the time, when we attended the semiannual trainings in California for ten days, we left the children with a sister in Houston who remained behind to take care of her elderly father. One day, after John and I had returned from the training on the Gospel of Matthew, I was driving somewhere with Todd, who was now seven years old. He asked me, "What did you do at the training?" I told him that we studied a book of the Bible. After a few minutes he wanted to know, "Is that all you did? When other people ask you about it, you spend a lot of time telling them; but when I ask, you just say one thing." He was right. I prayed, "Lord, what can I tell him that he will understand?" One of the verses from the training came to mind, so I started to tell him what I remembered about it. I said, "Matthew 11:11 says that among those born of women, none is greater than John the Baptist, but he that is least in the kingdom of the heavens is greater than he. John the Baptist was a great person who lived at the very end of Old Testament times. He saw the beginning of New Testament times when Christ came. We are in New Testament times now when everyone who is saved is greater than John the Baptist." I elaborated a bit more about what I had heard. After a few minutes, Todd looked at me and said, "What does it mean to be least in the kingdom of the heavens?" I had no idea, so I told him I didn't know.

Several times that week, Todd asked me if he could go to the meeting on Saturday night. As a rule, we didn't take children to the meetings. Because this was a love feast, I thought Todd's interest might have been centered on the dessert table! He insisted that he wanted to go. Soon I began to think that maybe the Lord was stirring behind all Todd's persistence. Unlike a number of other parents, we had never pushed him to believe or pray or call on the Lord. Instead, I prayed for him to have a genuine, personal experience with God. I believed God would call him in His own time. So Todd went with us to the meeting that Saturday night.

After the meal, Steve Smith presented a gospel message. Amazingly, his message was about Matthew 11:11, the same verse I had told Todd about earlier in the week. At the end of his message, Steve asked anyone who wanted to receive the Lord to stand and pray with him. A number of people responded by standing up one by one to pray with Steve and accept the Lord. Todd had taken a seat on the front row of the large circle. I was sitting several rows behind him. I could see him shifting as though he was trying to stand up when he suddenly shot up out of his chair. He prayed with Steve and accepted Christ. He was the last one to receive the Lord that night. Steve sat down, but a few minutes later, he stood up again and said, "Something has just occurred to me. I just realized what the phrase, 'the least in the kingdom of the heavens' means." Amazingly, this was the question Todd had asked me earlier in the week that I had been unable to answer. Steve continued, "I believe that the *least* is the newest-born one."

So Todd, the last and newest-born child of God there that night, was the *least* in the kingdom of the heavens! God hadn't only answered his question, He also had arranged that Todd actually *be* the answer, at least for a few moments in that meeting. As such, he was also greater than John the Baptist. I cried. God's ways were truly amazing.

Chapter 11
Everything Is His

> But seek first the kingdom of God, and His righteousness, and all these things shall be added to you. (Matt. 6:33)

My Material Possessions Are His

HAVING PEOPLE LIVING IN OUR HOME WAS DIFFICULT, but the Lord made good use of it to teach me about who He is. I was very happy when we managed to save enough money to buy a brand new washer and dryer, until the multitude of sisters living with us began asking to use them for their wash, rather than go to a self-service laundry. I resented this and badly wanted to say, "No." But I knew I couldn't do that without appearing un-Christian-like. So my little cleaning machines began carrying a major load. I was filled with resentment every time I saw a sister carry a load of wash through my side of the house to my new washing machine! I finally had to pray about how much this was distressing me. The Lord reminded me of my consecration—my possessions weren't mine, but His. "But, Lord, they won't last very long; and we, not the sisters, will have to buy new ones!" "Jane, that is My problem. I will take care of it." Finally I was able to say, "Okay, Lord. They belong to You." Peace came.

Ultimately, those machines lasted so many years that I wanted them to break down so I could get new ones. They didn't break down, so I painted them to improve their appearance. Finally, I gave them to Todd when he got married. At last, I got new ones! Todd told me in 1999, some twenty-five years after our Wheeler House washing machine purchase, that he had just replaced the old washing machine with a new one! A few years before, he had sold and replaced the still functional gas dryer because their new home required an electric dryer!

Chapter 11—Everything Is His

My Marriage and Family Are His

After almost three years of living by the campus, with about a year of that time on Wheeler Street, I was tired. My quiet mornings with the Lord had suffered because of the busy schedule required to maintain the Wheeler House. Everyone involved was working hard to produce a successful campus work; however, it seemed to me there wasn't the same kind of blessing we had experienced the prior year. One night in the spring of 1976, John confessed to me that he was jealous of the time I spent coordinating activities with Stephen Thompson.

The Lord had put John and me near the campus as a couple; yet when the campus harvest began, the leading brothers back-shelved John and put Stephen Thompson, an elder whom they considered to be more capable, in charge of the campus work. The Lord had used John to lead us to the campus and, indirectly, through John's care for me, the Lord had brought about our living in a sisters' house. The elders had discouraged John from doing this and, at one point, had even tried to make us move away. In spite of this, God had worked and blessed us in that house. Yet as soon as they saw a harvest beginning, they called it a "campus work" and came and took over its management. No one asked what we thought. It seemed they didn't think God could follow through with what He had begun. I watched the campus situation change in the months after Stephen Thompson's assignment from one of amazing blessing to one of planning, organizing, and eventually overworking.

John proceeded to tell me that he was upset by my neglect of him. He couldn't take it anymore. All of my waking moments were spent taking care of campus things, church duties, the sisters, and the children. He got nothing. I knew this was true.

I had been practicing, as taught, "Just take care of the Lord and the church, and the Lord will take care of your marriage." I had come to believe that one of the reasons God needed marriages was so that we could better serve the church. Another reason was so that He could transform us by suffering. This thought came from the many derogatory things I heard whenever marriage illustrations were used in messages to clarify a point.

Everyone would laugh at the examples given. Marriage was referred to metaphorically as an oven, a frying pan, and a place of death. I had become convinced that it was wrong to desire or to try to have a happy marriage. I actually believed that a happy marriage was impossible because we were fallen human beings. I also had long ago given up my attempt to spend quality time with my husband or to focus on him and his needs. I had settled this matter when I gave up Saturdays.

I had believed God would take care of my marriage if I put the church first, but here I sat, looking at my very distraught husband. Hadn't I only been serving the Lord and doing what I had been taught? It occurred to me that there could be more to this. Perhaps I had been trying to fill a void in my marriage by spending a lot of time with the sisters who were living with us. I began to cry. I reached over and picked up my Bible and asked him, "Do you see this?" Pages were loose and the cover was cracking and breaking off in pieces. "This could fall into a bunch of little pieces and you would never even notice. You would never get me another one!" I was as surprised by my statement as he was. Where had that come from? As we talked, God began to open our eyes. Yes, I in fact I had neglected John. Yes, he in fact had neglected me. I didn't feel love for him. He didn't feel love for me. After that night, John began a campaign to win my love again. The next day, he brought me flowers for the first time in our nine years of marriage. Next, he bought me a brand new Bible. He was actually courting me, and his loving treatment brought about a matching change in my heart. Thus began a turnaround in our marriage.

Risking Having A Friend

I was spending a lot more time with a sister named Anne Andrews because of our church related duties. Anne had a vivacious personality and giggled when she talked. We enjoyed each other's company and were becoming friends. Because we were not supposed to have friendships, I knew this was somewhat risky territory. Friendships were considered to be something natural, soulish, and fleshly. As brothers and sisters in Christ, we were supposed to cultivate only spiritual relationships with one another. In spite of this prohibition, I was happy about my developing friendship with Anne. Several times, we jokingly told each other that we were probably going to get in trouble for our wrongdoing. I noticed in the Bible that Jesus was the friend of sinners and even called His disciples "friends" (John 15:15). Maybe it was all right to have a friend?

It was apparent to everyone that knew them that Anne and her husband had a very good marriage relationship. I began to confide in her about my marriage issues and about some of the problems that John and I experienced as husband and wife. I told her that we were both seeking to improve our relationship. She was very understanding and began giving me very helpful marriage advice. She told me that I just needed to love John and proceeded to give me a lot of practical help as to what that meant. Most of all, she helped me by example in the way that she related to her own husband. They had been married a number of years but were still very much in love. (They had been married before they became members of the Local Church.) They were delightful to be around. Anne would giggle when she talked about Guy and get a sparkle in her eye. John began to notice a difference in the way I was treating him and commented on it. I told him Anne was helping me understand more about what being a wife meant. He also was glad we were friends! Although I was truly afraid that we might get in trouble for being friends, I decided that the benefit I received from her friendship was worth the risk.

I really cared about her and knew she also cared about me. I felt safe with her and could open my heart to her without fear. I was glad that I could tell her about a problem and ask for help without being told I just needed to call on the Lord or pray-read. Of course, I knew Jesus was the only one who could actually help me with my problems, but it was a source of comfort to know someone else cared and was helping bear my burdens. The Bible said to bear one another's burdens, so even though friendships were not sanctioned in the Local Church, I felt it was all right with God.

One day, another sister talked to me about her marriage, and I ventured to share with her some of the help

Anne had given me. She was very interested and wanted to talk again. She was surprised and a little shocked with one piece of advice I had received from Anne. I suggested she go to the store and buy a new nightgown! As I thought about so many of the marriages in the church, I began to realize how much we all needed some practical help. I talked about this with John and also with Anne.

The Church in Baton Rouge?

Brother Lee had been teaching us from the book of Ephesians about the Lord slaying all the ordinances on the cross (Eph. 2:15–16). As a practical application of this truth, he told us that we should never insist on any specific practice in church meetings. (He was likening our treasured practices to the ordinances that were slain on the cross.) For example, if we moved to another city and found Christians whose meetings were open to all believers in their city, we should just join in with them and drop all of our own particular meeting practices.

Our understanding of this teaching and willingness to practice it were put to the test shortly after this when we came in contact with a group of Christians meeting in Baton Rouge, Louisiana. Members of this group had left various denominations and begun meeting together. They purposely had not adopted a name for their group, and their church meetings were open to all believers. John and I visited them several times with some other brothers and sisters from Houston. On one of these visits, Anne and her husband, Guy, traveled with us, and we stayed in the homes of the Baton Rouge group. We were blessed by their gracious hospitality and warm brotherly love. The time with them reminded me very much of our experience in Denton long ago. Their meeting practices were different than ours, but they definitely were open to all Christians.

Sometime later, one of the couples from Baton Rouge came to Houston to visit the Local Church and stayed with our main leading brother, Dan Williams. Those of us who had been to Baton Rouge were excited about their visit. After the weekend was over, however, Dan was unimpressed. He had talked at length with the couple and determined that they weren't clear about the ground of locality. His receiving of them was tied to their embracing our Local Church vision. This bothered me. Because they didn't see the importance of the ground of locality, Dan didn't recognize their validity as a church. I knew in my heart that they were truly practicing Christian oneness, regardless of their terminology.

Not Just a House but a Home

Things were changing for us. As John and I were trying to take care of our marriage more, we began to feel that the Lord wanted us to relinquish the big and abnormal corporate living situation by the campus for a normal family living situation that would be conducive to taking better care of our marriage and children. We decided that we wanted to buy a home of our own, but we had no savings. The money that the sisters paid us for food and lodging made it only barely possible for us to afford our rent. The amount we charged was as close as we could get to the actual cost of having them live with us. It mainly covered their food, but it also was used to help with the rent.

Although we were concerned that we couldn't move and live on our income, we decided that we should try anyway. We were surprised and thankful when my father loaned us some money for a down payment on a house. We looked unsuccessfully for an affordable house for a period of time. Then one night, a brother and his wife told us that they wanted to move near the campus and host a sisters' house. We four worked it out so that they sold their house near Hall One to us and then took our place in the Wheeler House.

It is interesting that we took this step without consulting or "fellowshipping" with the elders. Because of this, we would soon realize that our move didn't have their approval or blessing. We weren't supposed to do anything independently or act in any way that wasn't in full harmony with the church. We were expected to consult with the leading brothers about all important decisions in life—jobs, marriage, moving, and so forth. Their directives were always prefaced with something like, "Brother, we're not telling you what to do, but our feeling is ...." The elders would say that they didn't tell us what to do, but we knew that if we didn't act according to their "feeling," our state of absoluteness would be suspect. Wanting to please the Lord, we had consecrated our lives to Christ and *the church. Sadly, this had become a basis for more and more obedience to the leading brothers' requests, demands, or suggestions. It also became the basis for correction when they felt we were stepping out of line.*

Our new house was on Mobud Drive in a suburban neighborhood where a number of other Local Church members lived. Three of the Wheeler sisters wanted to move with us and did. So much for our family living alone, but at least the workload was greatly diminished. We now simply had a home on Mobud Drive, not the "Mobud House."

The Light Is On Me

I began once more to have time to spend alone with the Lord. My Bible reading times were wonderful. I started discovering more things about Jesus, His relationship with us, and our relationship with each other. I shared these things with John and Anne.

One morning, the Lord brought to my memory an old problem with a sister named Lynn Turner. He showed me that to keep the Lord's commanded blessing according to Psalm 133, I needed to go and talk to her and clear up the problem:

> Behold, how good and how pleasant it is for brethren to dwell together in unity! ... for there the Lord commanded the blessing—life for evermore. (Psa. 133)

The problem was this: When I was in the hospital following the miscarriage of my second child, Lynn had deeply offended me when she called and announced that she was pregnant. She had rejoiced about her good news and continued to talk about it, totally oblivious to my loss and pain. I didn't want to see or be around her after that. Afterwards, she asked me if anything was wrong because she had sensed my coolness toward her. I told her there was no problem. Now, several years later, the Lord was showing me that I had lied to her, so it was now my responsibility to go to her. Finally, I obeyed. As I talked with Lynn while her husband listened, I felt a great sense of relief. They forgave me and then, to my surprise, told me of another problem—one they had with me. One time when the leading brothers talked to me about Lynn, I had told them that she was a hypochondriac who used sickness to get attention. They had treated her accordingly, when she was actually quite ill, and had deeply hurt both of them. As I listened to them, I felt extremely embarrassed and ashamed. I repented to Lynn and her husband. We all wept and were reconciled. What a cleansing that was for all of us!

Through this, the Lord also exposed my ugly motivation for reporting to the leading brothers, a motive that wasn't at all pleasing to Him and one for which I also had to repent. I had not been concerned at all for Lynn when I had told the brothers she was a hypochondriac, but rather for myself. I had killed two birds with that evil stone—I had slandered Lynn, and I had made myself look like a good and useful sister to the leading brothers.

From that experience, I also realized how important it was that we obey the commands that tell us to go to one another to clear up offenses (Matt. 5:23-24, 18:15-17). While I had remained in a state of being offended by Lynn and unwilling to admit the truth to her, God's enemy had used me to wound both of them without my even realizing it. When I obeyed the Lord regarding them, the enemy's device was uncovered, and our fellowship was restored. Not long after this, I discovered the following hymn which described my experience with Lynn and her husband:

> How sweet, how heavenly is the sight,
> When those who love the Lord
> In one another's peace delight,
> And so fulfill His Word;
>
> When each can feel His brother's sigh
> And with him bear a part;
> When sorrow flows from eye to eye
> And joy from heart to heart;

> When, free from envy, scorn and pride,
> Our wishes all above,
> Each can a brothers' failings hide,
> And show a brother's love;
>
> When love, in one delightful stream,
> Through every bosom flows;
> When union sweet, and dear esteem,
> In every action glows.
>
> Love is the golden chain that binds,
> The saints Thy grace thus prove.
> And he is glory's heir that finds
> His bosom glow with love.
>
> — Joseph Swain

I told Anne and John about my experience with Lynn. In light of that experience, I started to think more about the things we had heard about the Lord's blessing. Brother Lee had told us that God's commanded blessing was on oneness. If we lost oneness, we would also lose the Lord's blessing. I told Anne that I was aware of other unresolved problems among some of the sisters and suggested this could be a hindrance to the Lord's blessing on the church. I suggested that we pray about this. I had read in a missionary's biography about a Christian meeting in which the participants realized that the Lord was not present. They had stopped the meeting and gone outside for a short period of time. Little groups of people had talked to each other under the trees. When they reassembled, immediately the Lord's presence flooded their meeting. Afterwards, they all marveled at what had been accomplished by confession and forgiveness under those trees. In light of what had happened with Lynn and me, I thought that there were probably a lot of us in the church that needed some time together under the trees!

Young Galileans

Another new flow began and the young people in the churches became very excited when Brother Lee started talking about the young age of the twelve disciples who followed Jesus. He said that because of their youth, they were crazy and bold enough to give up everything and follow Him. Brother Lee called these twelve disciples "young Galileans." He told us how the Lord always called young people because they were not set in their ways. Some of the disciples He chose were young fisherman who easily dropped their jobs and followed Him to become fishers of men. Brother Lee said that college campuses were like a sea full of fish. Jesus was calling the young people among us to become fishers of men. The young people began to refer to themselves as the "young Galileans" and, thus, a new flow was underway.

My friend Anne and I were both involved with the young people. One night after a young people's meeting, we talked about something we had both noticed—a hint of the unsavory flavor of the former pan-banging days. The young people had marched around the room shouting slogans and cheering forward the latest new move. Anne and I determined we wouldn't be naïve about this but rather learn from our past and not repeat it. We kept our observations to ourselves, deciding just to watch and pray.

As a result of the new flow, Bible studies were started on college campuses in order to have a way to connect with students and get to know them. In this way, the young Galileans could hook them, reel them in out of the campus sea, and gradually introduce them to the Local Church meetings. Because we had begun to encounter more opposition from other Christian groups who didn't like what they were seeing in the Local Church, the decision was made to keep secret the fact that the campus Bible studies were sponsored by the Local Church. We believed that the opposition had been instigated by Satan to frustrate God's move. Therefore, we had to be "wise as serpents and harmless as doves" (Matt. 10:16) in order to manage the opposition and successfully reach more young people.

The new flow also resulted in something the brothers called "outposts." Outposts were little groups of brothers and sisters who were sent to live in another city, usually near a campus, not necessarily to start a new church, but to catch people who would then move to the city of the sending church and join the Local Church there.

Daring To Ask Questions

One night, as John and I had dinner with Guy and Anne at their apartment, we began talking about current events in the church and ended up having a very long discussion. Concerning the latest flow, we wondered if all the young people's exuberance was really coming from the Lord or was just natural enthusiasm.

We reminisced about our visit to the group of believers in Baton Rouge and wondered if we were accepting and receiving them as we should. Dan Williams had dismissed them as a "free group"—meaning they were a loose affiliation of Christians who were not on firm scriptural footing regarding the Lord's purpose, the church. We questioned Dan's posture toward them, knowing it didn't match up at all with Brother Lee's recent teaching from the book of Ephesians about how we should receive other Christians.

We spent some time discussing my experience of repenting to Lynn Turner and her husband and the sweet experience of brotherly love that resulted. We also talked about how serious it was for us to have problems with one another. I questioned whether or not some long-standing problems that I was aware of between some of the sisters could be affecting the Lord's blessing on the Church in Houston. We four agreed that, according to the Bible, Christians should practice clearing up problems quickly.

We also discussed the need to give each other the freedom to follow the Lord and receive individual direction from Him, as John and I had done regarding living by the campus, rather than trying to conform to the latest church flow. We also acknowledged that we needed to be free to open up to one another honestly about our problems and personal situations, such as husband-wife relationships. After this meeting, Guy, who was an elder in the Church in Houston, said that he felt we should all get together with the other elders and discuss our concerns about these things.

A Weeping Brother

Guy arranged a meeting in his home with us and his fellow elders, Steve Smith and Sam Jones, and we repeated our concerns. (Prior to this event, our main leading brother, Dan Williams, had moved to help with the Local Church in another city, so Steve Smith was now the main elder in the Church in Houston.) As we were discussing our issues of concern, unexpectedly, Steve leaned forward, put his head in his hands, and began to weep. He didn't shed just a few tears—he sobbed. We all became very quiet and waited, not knowing what to think. Steve eventually said something to the effect that he felt responsible for the troubling conditions we had described. Most of us felt bonded together by that experience. Our hearts went out to Steve, realizing he had been very deeply affected by our open fellowship with him and each other. We didn't understand why Steve had been so strongly affected, but we were deeply moved by his reaction. Steve said that he and the other elders would get back with us at a later date regarding the things we had talked about, but they never did.

Years later, we learned from Steve that after our discussion at Guy's house, Sam Jones, the other elder in attendance, wasn't at all happy with what had happened in that meeting together. Sam had been primarily an observer throughout the session, not a participant. Immediately afterwards, he had called and given some kind of report about the evening to Dan Williams. I believe that whatever he told Dan played a key role in the actions that Dan shortly began to take towards John and me.

My Reputation Is His

I was reading a book by Watchman Nee entitled *Practical Issues of This Life*. The Lord drew my attention to two chapters from this book: chapter six, "The Lord is Never Discouraged," and chapter seven, "A Deeper Joy." The Lord wrote on my heart several truths from these chapters. The following passages made a strong impression on me:

> While the Lord was on the cross He was rejected by men and even forsaken by God.
>
> Were we ever put into such a situation, we doubtless would be disappointed, discouraged, and extremely hurt. Yet on the cross the Lord cried aloud: "It is finished"! (John 19.30).... All through His life our Lord took the Father's will as His satisfaction.... Hence for this reason, no matter how changeable were the people and things and events of the world about Him, nothing could discourage Him. Whoever therefore makes God his satisfaction shall never be disappointed. (Nee, *Practical*, 96-97)
>
> Now what would you do if, in your life and work, you too met with such an unfortunate chain of events perpetrated by the very people with whom you are associated? How could you help but be heartbroken and discouraged, judging that all is lost. Yet not so with our Lord.... There is no bitterness nor sorrow in His heart. He neither frets nor becomes angered. How about you and me, though? Could you and I still thank God even though we are being doubted, slandered, and rejected without cause?... Can you and I thank Him under such an adverse situation? (Nee, *Practical*, 113-114)
>
> Are you satisfied if God knows you?... If *God* only knows you, is that really enough for you? It is quite true that we need our brothers and our sisters; yet at the time when people do not know us, we will still be satisfied with only the Father's knowledge of us if we are truly those who live before Him....
>
> ... Only the one who is willing to be known by God alone will truly know God; and the one who truly knows God is able to lead other people to know God too. (Nee, *Practical*, 116-117)

I was sobered when I read this. These questions stood out to me: (1) What would you do if, in your life and work, you too met with such an unfortunate chain of events perpetrated by the very people with whom you are associated? (2) Could you still thank God even though you are being doubted, slandered, and rejected without cause? (3) If God only knows you, is that really enough for you?

My environment was soon to change in a way that would require me to answer each one of these questions.

Part 3

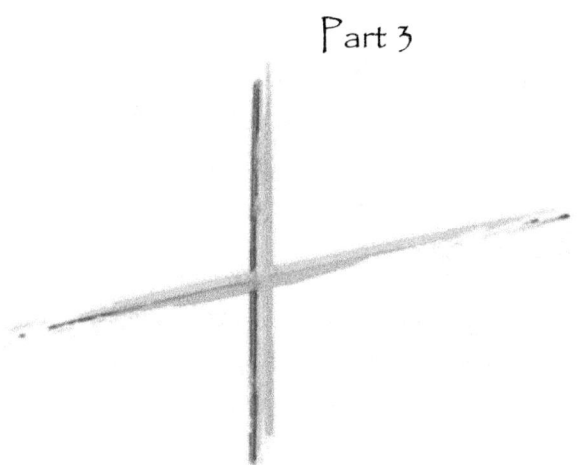

God's Wisdom

Trial by Fire

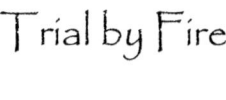

How firm a foundation, ye saints of the Lord,
Is laid for your faith in His excellent word!
What more can he say, than to you He has said,
To you who for refuge to Jesus have fled?

Fear not, I am with thee, O be not dismayed,
For I am Thy God, and will still give thee aid;
I'll strengthen thee, help thee, and cause thee to stand,
Upheld by My righteous, omnipotent hand.

When through the deep waters, I call thee to go,
The rivers of sorrows shall not overflow,
For I will be with thee thy troubles to bless,
And sanctify to thee they deepest distress.

When through fiery trials, thy pathway shall lie,
My grace, all sufficient, shall be thy supply;
The flame shall not hurt thee; I only design
Thy dross to consume and thy gold to refine.

E'en down to old age all My people shall prove
My sovereign, eternal, unchangeable love;
And then, when grey hairs shall their temples adorn,
Like lambs they shall still in My bosom be borne.

The soul that on Jesus hath leaned for repose,
I will not, I will not desert to his foes;
That soul, though all hell should endeavor to shake,
I'll never, no never, no never forsake!

— Author unknown

Chapter 12
Impending Trouble

> Beloved, do not think it strange concerning the fiery trial which is to try you, as though some strange thing happened to you. (1 Pet. 4:12)

Give Us Liberty

A BROTHER NAMED ED BLACK, who was relatively new to the Local Church scene and was in the Church in Anaheim, was steadily becoming more recognized by all the Local Churches and was beginning to be considered as Brother Lee's new right-hand man. The other elders in Anaheim, who had been with Brother Lee from the first days in California, appeared to be taking a back seat to him. Ed was a very charismatic, exciting, and entertaining speaker who was shaking things up with his earnest way of speaking and his bold teachings (they were progressive, almost a little too "real" for us). Many times, it seemed that part of his purpose was to help liberate Local Church members from their legalistic approach to the Christian life. It seemed that, because of his teaching and example, some brothers and sisters were venturing to do some "worldly" things from which they had been abstaining. The young people really appreciated Ed Black's inspiring speaking, and so did I.

One day, much to my surprise, I heard that some of the young people had played basketball together. I had no problem with this personally, but I wondered if it would actually be allowed to continue.

Prior to this period of time, to my knowledge, no one ever played sports or had much physical recreation of any kind while in the Local Church because we believed it was wrong.

I was surprised when I came across a whole chapter that was devoted to the subject of recreation in Watchman Nee's book, *Do All to the Glory of God*. He stated that recreation was good for families and for us as Christians, primarily for the purpose of physical and mental renewal. Because Watchman Nee's writings were sanctioned, I told others about this chapter, including some of the young people. I even ventured to talk to some of the young sisters about our tendency to be too legalistic.

A Baton Rouge Outpost

John and I were looking somewhat longingly at Baton Rouge. We couldn't forget what we had experienced on our previous visits there. The freedom and love we had seen in those Christian meetings and in their relationships with one another were very attractive. The leading brothers in Houston had been discussing the possibility of some going there to live. We had been in our newly purchased home for only a short time, but we were making plans to move to Baton Rouge. Two young couples, one of whom had come into the church through the Harvest House, were also ready to move with us. They were interested in a campus work. John and I saw the prospect of experiences like those we had while living by the University of Houston as well as those we had while in Denton years before.

While we were considering moving to Baton Rouge, Steve Smith called one night and invited John and me to come to his home to talk with him. He told us that he had been thinking about our talk at Guy's apartment and had realized there was a definite lack of helpful openness with one another in the church, and that this was greatly needed. When we met with him, I wondered about the fact that he did not invite the other elders. He talked to us more regarding openness, honesty, clearing up problems between members, and helping one another with personal matters such as our marriages. He said that he felt these things were important and wanted to give the Lord a way to address them among us. He admitted that there was a real lack in these areas.

In light of our conversation with him, we asked what he thought about our moving to Baton Rouge. He encouraged us to stay in Houston to help with whatever the Lord might want to do with regard to the things we had discussed. After hearing this, we decided to stay in Houston. The other couples who did move to Baton Rouge were ultimately considered by the church to be an outpost whose main purpose was to gain students from the campus. They associated some with the group of believers who were already meeting there, but treated them as a free group, not the church.

It is interesting that Steve's desire to provide practical help for brothers and sisters in the Church in Houston with their marriages and personal problems was never realized. Because Sam Jones did not like the discussion at Guy and Anne's, as a fellow elder, I believe that he did not support Steve's burden.

A number of years later, while he was still an elder in the Local Church, Steve Smith was discovered in sexual sin. I don't know what his moral situation was at the time of our discussion with him and the other elders, but his distraught weeping, which didn't appear to be directly related to the content of our conversation, and his admission to John and me that there was a need in the church for marriage help, may have indicated he was having some serious issues related to his own life at the time of our conversation with the elders at Guy and Anne's apartment. Considering what happened, it is a shame that Steve was never able to follow through in the church with what he had talked to us about that night.

An Embarrassing Confrontation

With the decision to stay in Houston made, I settled in to living in our new home. I began to use some of my time to start reading again. I read the biography, *Rees Howells, Intercessor*, by Norman Grubb. I was very moved by Rees Howells' love for people and his willingness to help them at great cost to himself. God taught him through the Bible and his experiences that intercessory prayer was different from asking God intensely for something. He learned that only a person who had become an intercessor could pray intercessory prayers. Jesus is an intercessor because of what he suffered on the cross on our behalf:

> Because He poured out His soul unto death, and He was numbered with the transgressors, and He bore the sin of many, and made intercession for the transgressors. (Isa. 53:12)

Rees Howells learned that an intercessor was someone who was willingly identified with a suffering one, even to the point of suffering the same thing, in order to gain a "position of intercession" for that one. For example, in order to become an intercessor on behalf of someone who was sick, Rees Howells became willing to, and did, experience the same illness in his own body. After a long process, which also involved failure and humiliation, he gained a "position of intercession" (Howells, 86–91). After this, all other sick ones for whom God burdened him to pray were healed as a result of his prayer. He learned by such experiences that intercessory prayer was always answered. He had many experiences of this kind of prayer throughout his life.

I told Anne about how much this book had spoken to my heart. We soon learned that some sisters in the Church in Anaheim had also recently read the book about Rees Howells. We heard that the Lord was working among them to heal offenses and restore their oneness. We both thought that perhaps the Lord might be starting to heal problems among sisters in all the Local Churches and restore our oneness, as we had recently discussed. Brother Lee had once told us that sisters were the "life-blood of the church." In one of our occasional church meetings that were for sisters only, Anne and I testified about the Rees Howells book. We shared that we had heard recently that the Lord was doing some exciting things among the sisters in the Church in Anaheim.

The next morning, we were in our regular sisters' daytime prayer meeting at Anne's house when, much to our surprise, the door opened and Dan Williams, our former elder, walked in with the Houston elders, Sam Jones, Steve Smith, and Guy Andrews. Dan stopped our prayer meeting and began to talk to us. Steve, the leading elder in Houston, looked down most of the time, never making eye contact with us. My blood ran cold as I realized Dan was speaking directly to Anne and me, correcting, adjusting, and chastising us regarding something he thought we were doing. He said, "We heard about the sisters' meeting last night. We know what you two sisters are doing. If the Lord is doing something with the sisters in Anaheim, it will come here through the proper channels—not through you two." Not only was I unsure what he was talking about, I was embarrassed, shamed, and horrified by the experience because there were ten or so other sisters present as witnesses. I was also bothered about why these elders had done this in front of others instead of talking to us in private.

"Well, I guess that is that," I declared to Anne after we left the meeting. She asked me what I meant. I asked her, "Weren't you in the same meeting I was in, and didn't you hear the same thing I heard?" She answered, "Yes." I said "Well?" She said "Well what?" I said, "Well, that's enough for me! I'm going to be really careful about what I say. What are you going to do?" She said, "Nothing any different than what I have been doing. We aren't doing anything wrong." I realized that in my conscience, before the Lord, I believed the same thing, so I decided not to change my behavior either. Anne and I then compared this situation to what we had heard Brother Lee teach about Joseph and Mary in the book of Matthew. He told us that after Mary conceived Jesus by the Holy Spirit, it took God time to bring Joseph to accept her condition and recognize that God was responsible for her pregnancy. Until He did this, Mary had to suffer Joseph's misunderstanding. Maybe in a similar way, we had to be willing to experience the misunderstanding of the leading brothers. Just as God eventually gave Joseph a different perspective on Mary's situation, He could also clear up our situation with the leading brothers.

I had another very strange experience that day, one I never told anyone about until thirteen years later. When the leading brothers were sitting across the room from us on the fireplace hearth in Anne's house, and as I sat there listening to Dan's admonishment, I had a strong sense of something black rising up behind him and the other elders with him. It is hard to explain this; but intuitively, I knew that there was a dark spiritual presence there. Afterwards, I didn't let myself think about this because it was frightening, and it made me think I was nuts. The reason I divulged it many years later was that I heard a story from a brother who had been in a different Local Church about how he had been treated in similar fashion by the leaders. At the end of his story, he described a strange thing he had experienced while they had been speaking. *As they were admonishing him, he had seen with spiritual eyes what he described as a black snake rising up in their midst.* He said that he knew that sounded strange, but it was the only way he knew how to verbalize what he had experienced.

But Have Not Love

I began working on a service group with a single sister named Judy. The brothers did not consider her to be a good sister because she was not submissive and had occasional emotional outbursts. They had corrected her verbally several times for not controlling her emotions. One time, one of the brothers had said something to her that greatly upset her, so she had knocked over a folding chair and had yelled at him. This was a terrible thing to do and one that wouldn't soon be forgotten by the elders.

I had been influenced by their thought about her; but as I got to know her better, I began to see her with new eyes. She really loved the Lord and had a sweet relationship with Him. I grew to love her and enjoyed her company. I knew that the elders had labeled her as a troublemaker, and I also realized that they seemed to be locked into their thought about her. My eyes told me she was an "uncomely" or unlovely member of the body of Christ, but my heart told me she was very necessary and was loved by God. Weren't we supposed to love her the same as any other member? (1 Cor. 12:22–25). In my own heart and mind, I became something of an advocate for her by speaking well of her whenever I had the opportunity. She was a weak and hurting member. I felt that the Lord was asking me to love and help her. He asked me if I was willing to be identified with Judy as Rees Howells had done for others. I told the Lord I was willing.

Not long after that, while reading the verses in the gospel of John about Mary wiping the feet of Jesus with her tears and anointing them with precious ointment, I realized that like Mary, we should love and highly value believers like Judy, those who seemed to be "feet" in the church. I wrote the following words to an existing tune. I sang this song many times to myself, but never shared it with anyone else; it just did not fit into the flow that was going on then:

> She kissed His feet, with tears she washed them.
> Her love for Him the deepest was.
> Thy feet, O Lord, there is the blessing
> To pour out love abundantly,
>
> To pour the ointment on the brethren
> Embracing them, we're loving Thee.
> Thy feet, O Lord, there is the blessing
> To pour out love abundantly.
>
> — Jane Carole Anderson

Risking Being a Mom

I had been taught and believed that God would take care of my children if I took care of the church. I also believed it was wrong for me to enjoy them or do fun things with them. As parents, we were supposed to meet their needs for food, clothing, shelter, and get them to school for their education. We were supposed to shape their characters by teaching and disciplining them so that they would grow up as people of good character that God could use one day. I believed that I wasn't supposed to do anything that would build up their self-images or encourage them to be worldly.

While living in the Wheeler House, my children mainly had known their mother as the captain of a tight ship. Every day was governed by lists and schedules. In our new home on Mobud, the daily demands on my time were less, and I began to spend more time with them. It seemed to me that things were changing for the better.

Things were definitely changing. We had moved without consulting with the elders. We had talked to the elders and dared to ask questions. We had talked to a few others about marriage and family issues, and I was actually focusing on my children to some degree. All these things show that, in spite of the strong, controlling atmosphere surrounding us in the Local Church, we were starting to think some on our own, to make some independent choices, and to risk the consequences.

We took a huge step and got a dog for the children, becoming one of the very few families in the Church in Houston who had a dog. I taught my youngest son, Matt, who was not in school yet, how to play chess! Once, when I realized that he had not yet learned to swim, I took a big risk for him. After trying unsuccessfully to find a place to get free lessons for him, as I had done for Todd, I decided that I should teach him myself. The problem was that I believed wearing a bathing suit in public was wrong. We had never been told that we couldn't go swimming or wear a bathing suit in public, but no one I knew did. Brother Lee had talked about how he always wore long-sleeved shirts to cover his flesh as much as possible. After hearing this, it wasn't hard to see the impropriety of wearing a bathing suit!

I discovered one day that I could have access to a swimming pool at the apartment of an older sister who was a new member of the church and didn't yet understand or fully follow all the church's practices. When I inquired about the availability of her pool to visitors, she insisted that I use her pool to teach Matt to swim. With the first hurdle cleared, I began to wonder what I would wear in the pool. With great trepidation, I went to Target and purchased a very modest maternity bathing suit. I wasn't pregnant, but I just needed to be covered in a major way. I felt that I was committing a sin, but I did it anyway because I felt it was important for Matt's sake. Matt stood on the side of that pool, refusing to jump to me because he was afraid I wouldn't catch him before his head went under. I did everything I could to convince him to jump. Just before giving up, I made one last plea, "Matt, if you jump now, I will buy you a big Hershey candy bar on the way home." Much to my surprise, he almost knocked me over in the water as he flew off the deck and leaped into my arms. That was my Matt, and that was one of the few special experiences we had together. I accomplished my mission, and Matt learned to swim without anyone finding out about my wearing a bathing suit in public!

One day, Todd's second grade teacher called me to talk about him. She told me what a sweet little boy he was and how he loved to talk to her. She said that every day he consistently sought her out for conversation. Then, she kindly asked me, "Mrs. Anderson, do you ever spend time listening to Todd?" I was embarrassed by her call and rightly so. I tried to make light of her question, but it wasn't a light question. It was a very revealing one.

I am very sad when I remember this. My dawning awareness of my children coupled with our move away from the campus show that the Lord was working in our hearts to bring us into obedience to Him and His Word regarding our family relationships. He had brought us to the place that, in order to do things that were important for our marriage and our children, we had begun to violate some of our deeply-ingrained Local Church beliefs.

Everything Has Come to Our Ears

Before the embarrassing confrontation by the leading brothers during the prayer meeting at Anne's house, I had earned a measure of appreciation and respect from them because of the campus work. Now, I was discovering that they weren't happy with me at all. Over a period of time, I was called by the elders into their "fellowship" room at the meeting hall several times so they could talk to me. Dan Williams was there each time. It was plain to me that they were watching me and felt I was off track in some way. These times were very upsetting and intimidating, but I always knew the Lord was with me.

On one of these occasions, John also attended at their request. After listening to them state that they were concerned about some things we were saying and that they were hearing (through the grapevine), John attempted to say there had been some kind of misunderstanding. Dan cut him off sharply saying, "There has been no misunderstanding! We know everything! Everything has come to our ears!" John and I were both amazed that Dan said, "Everything has come to our ears," as if they had discovered something we were trying to hide. The truth was that at the meeting Guy had arranged with the Houston elders, we had told them directly about our concerns.

During one of these sessions in the brothers' room, the Lord spoke a part of a verse in my heart, "as a sheep before her shearers is dumb, so He openeth not his mouth" (Isa. 53:7, KJV), instructing me not to try to vindicate myself. Another time, the Lord brought to my mind the phrase in a hymn, "hidden dangers near." This phrase prepared me for a call I received later the same day requesting my presence in yet another short session with the elders.

In all of these times, they talked to me in an accusing, warning way without giving any specifics. I usually said very little and just listened. They seemed to be trying to assess my condition. I think they may have been concerned that if I were not a hundred percent in agreement with everything Brother Lee taught, and was speaking differently than him, I might undermine the absolute loyalty of the many young people with whom I was very involved.

The truth is that during that period of time, I was absolutely loyal to Witness Lee's teaching. I never said one word against Witness Lee during all the years I was in the Local Church. Whatever I said or did that bothered the leading brothers during that time was simply my attempt to be faithful to what I understood from the Bible, Witness Lee's teaching, and Watchman Nee's books. I did not question Witness Lee; rather, I was concerned about some of the church's practices which did not seem to match, not only the teachings of Watchman Nee and Witness Lee, but also the Bible.

During this difficult period, the Lord continued His gracious visits in the mornings, giving me promises, encouraging me to trust Him, and comforting me through Bible verses and through the words of hymns. I found Him to be the God who "gives songs in the night" (Job 35:10), as many times He woke me during the night and spoke to my heart through the words of a hymn. When I later looked up all the words of the song, I would get a special measure of encouragement through them. I was also entering a period of "night" in my life and circumstances, during which all the hymns in the "Comfort In Trials" section of the hymnal were becoming my spiritual food. One day, Jesus spoke a promise to me through the following verse of a hymn, and I believed it:

Chapter 12—Impending Trouble

> The Lord will silently plan for thee,
> His purpose He'll to thee unfold;
> The tangled skein shall shine at last,
> A masterpiece of skill untold.
>
> — E. May Grimes

My situation with the leading brothers was very confusing and becoming more complicated. It was indeed like a tangled mess of yarn. I couldn't understand it or see a way out of it, but according to this hymn, God was in control. He would make sense out of everything in his own way and in His own time.

I wrongly assumed that the fulfillment of this promise was just around the corner. Not quite. It would not come until many, many years later.

In the following song, the line about the day being half done gave me a clue that the situation I was in was not going to be a short-term one:

> He giveth more grace when the burdens grow greater,
> He sendeth more strength when the trials increase,
> To added affliction, He addeth His mercy,
> To multiplied trials, His multiplied peace.
>
> When we have exhausted our store of endurance,
> When our strength has failed 'ere the day is half done,
> When we reach the end of our hoarded resources,
> Our Father's full giving is only begun.
> His love has no limit, His grace has no measure,
> His power no boundary known unto men,
> For out of His infinite riches in Jesus,
> He giveth and giveth and giveth again.
>
> — Annie Johnson Flint

In the following hymn, the final sentence assured me that the pathway I was on was one He had planned for me. There would be an "after" to all that was happening.

> Near after distant,
> Gleam after gloom,
> Love after loneliness,
> Life after tomb;
> After long agony,
> Rapture of bliss.
> Right was the pathway
> Leading to this.
>
> — Frances R. Havergal

Set, Settled, and Occupied

One of the three sisters who lived with us was abducted off the campus by a cult deprogrammer that her family had hired. We never saw her again. We received a note from her in the mail written on toilet paper that said, "Please don't try to contact me." We didn't. After a little more time, the other two sisters moved out. At last, we were alone and living a normal family life for the first time since Matt was born. He was four years old now.

In the meetings, we began to hear about a "wall" that brothers and sisters hit when they reached age thirty which made them "set, settled, and occupied" in suburbia—a category, no doubt, that John and I now fit into perfectly. The young people gave testimonies about never wanting such a thing to happen to them. Paralleling this, there seemed to be a move afoot to replace older elders with new, younger elders in Local Churches throughout the country. I believe Brother Lee actually called for this, encouraging the older elders to step down and let younger brothers replace them. Brothers and sisters, including elders, began moving all over the place as these changes occurred.

When I could forget about the pressure in the meetings to conform to the latest flow and the brothers' obvious unhappiness with me, I realized that I was glad to be living in a suburban neighborhood with other families and their children. Our children were also happy. Actually, I was secretly enjoying becoming more "set, settled, and occupied."

When Anne and Guy started a mom and pop typesetting business out of their home, they asked me to work for them part time. They bought a photo-typesetting machine and used their converted garage as their business office. This was extremely convenient for me because they just lived a few blocks away. I was able to take Matt to work with me, and Todd could easily walk there after school. I loved the job. It was fun to type on the amazing machine and then see the various typestyles as they printed out on photo paper. I learned how to do some layout paste-up for ads they sold. What fun! Not only that, I was working with my dear friend Anne. We joked and laughed about things. I knew deep down that Jesus wasn't at all bothered about any of this. He was walking with me. I was a little concerned, however, that the old, carefree, fun-loving person I had been during my college days might "over-emerge"!

Anne and the Red Car

I had told Anne about the times the brothers had called me in to talk to me, but she felt as I did: We weren't doing anything wrong, so we just needed to forget about it. We continued our friendship and fellowship. Once when we were talking about the legalism in the church, we discussed how we all conformed to each other in our dress and lifestyles. I told her that I had read in Watchman Nee's book, *Love Not the World,* that what is worldly to one Christian is not necessarily worldly to another. Worldliness was something in our lives that we each should allow Jesus to identify. We both agreed that we wanted to be afforded more freedom to follow the Lord individually. John was party to our conversations and had matching feelings.

One morning, I was shocked when Anne appeared for work in a brightly-colored, stylish pantsuit! I felt a little scared when I saw her, thinking I might somehow be responsible for this sudden change. She giggled and said,

"What? I love this outfit!" I didn't say more, but knew I certainly didn't have the nerve to make such a change myself.

Very shortly after this, Anne asked me to travel with her to her parents' home in another city so that her father could help her purchase a new car. Once at her parents, Anne went with her father to the car dealership to negotiate a purchase. When she returned, she was laughing and told me excitedly that she had bought a sporty little car that was red! Red? Sporty? O my goodness. Red and sporty was definitely not a car that would fit in the church parking lot. Again, I felt a little fearful and was concerned that our talking about legalism was having this effect on her.

When Anne's elder-husband, Guy, saw the car, he was visibly bothered. If I remember correctly, he made her return it.

A Temptation for John

One day while I was at work, John appeared at the garage business office and told me that he had received a call from Steve Smith, asking him to go with him to a conference and "bring back" the messages! John was stunned by this call. (This meant that John would fly with Steve to hear the conference messages and then return to help present them in our meetings.) John had never been asked to do anything like this before. It surprised me also. I had a nagging feeling about the offer. Why after ten years of never acknowledging John in this way, were they calling now? John, like most other brothers, had hoped to advance through the ranks to be a deacon or elder one day, but I think he had pretty much given up on that ever occurring, especially after they ignored his role in the campus work. (It probably didn't help that I had hoped and prayed he would never become a deacon or an elder! I could see the price tag attached to that role.) Anne had a similar reaction to mine and volunteered her thought that this was not a good thing. John decided to refuse the offer and did. We all agreed that the brothers were attempting to pull John into their camp and away from my bad influence.

I felt sad about the way the brothers were treating us and hurt to be losing my good reputation, but I realized that this was not necessarily a bad thing. Hadn't the Lord asked me if what He knew about me was enough for me? Hadn't He asked me how I would respond to being misunderstood? Yes, He had, and I was learning how short I was in that department.

In spite of what was transpiring, Jesus was so real and close that I was doing well. I knew that I loved the Lord and I loved His church. I had a new home, I had a friend, and I had a fun job that was providing us with a little extra money. John and I now lived alone with our children. We even had a dog. Best of all, Jesus was talking to me! God was so good.

Ephraim Is a Deceitful Bow

John and I took a trip to Austin, Texas, because John wanted to talk to a brother named Howard Mays about a personal offense. While John talked with Howard, I visited with three sisters, including Sandra Brown (who had relocated from Houston to Austin) and Diane (Howard's wife). Stephen Thompson, the brother who had been assigned to oversee the Houston campus work, had just been moved to Austin to start a campus work there.

These sisters were concerned that the days of a sweet, enjoyable, family church-life in Austin were going to end because of Stephen's arrival. The campus work was being pushed and promoted in all the meetings. We discussed how the Local Church seemed to be more and more *movement* oriented. It seemed that when brothers and sisters were pressured to participate wholeheartedly in the movements, families and their needs were pushed out of the way.

I told them about my experience with Jesus at the University of Houston, about how the elders had confronted Anne and me, and how they were continuing to talk to me. We were all concerned and realized we needed to pray for the church. We felt like some problems were developing. I told them about a Bible passage I had read recently that said that Ephraim was like "a deceitful bow" (Hos. 7:11–16, KJV).

I told them that to me this Bible passage meant that it was possible for God's people to miss the center of the target for which they were aiming. I thought that "a deceitful bow" meant a bow that was slightly crooked so that an arrow shot from it would appear to go straight, but eventually would veer off course. I told them that we needed to pray that we not become like Ephraim and miss the center of God's target for us. I also told them that I thought that there was a problem with our former elder in Houston, Dan Williams, and that we needed to pray for him.

By this time, John and I were becoming bothered that Dan Williams was trying to correct us when he didn't even live in our city. This practice flew in the face of all we believed about an individual church's ground of locality. He wasn't there actually observing what was happening firsthand, but was getting information secondhand. We didn't understand Dan's behavior. We also were having a problem with his method of dealing with us, with his attitude, and with his willingness to pass judgment on us so easily without ascertaining all the facts by talking to us about specifics. We wondered if maybe he thought he was like an apostle and felt he had a right to exercise authority over churches other than his own.

Witness Lee had taught us that the government or administration of the church was to be local, without any extra-local control. This was the lesson that the brothers in Texas had supposedly learned years before when Leon had tried to take control of the three original churches in Texas. So, according to the Local Church's own teaching, Dan should have had no authority over us because he did not live in our city and wasn't one of our elders.

After our Austin trip, John and I also attended a Local Church conference in Dallas. One day, some sisters had lunch together at a sisters' house; and as we had done in Austin, we talked some about things of concern that were happening in the churches. While we were there, someone suggested that we should get together sometime to pray for the church.

I mention these get-togethers with sisters in Austin and Dallas because these were probably the basis for the elders' later conclusion that we sisters were in some kind of statewide conspiracy.

Questions Turning Into Realizations

All of the things that had been happening were having a profound affect on me. Things had changed: we were a family in suburbia; there was another big *flow* in the church to which I was inwardly resistant; God was showing me truth in His Word that was causing me to ask questions; and I was talking to Anne and John, who had similar concerns about things in the church. My questions were beginning to turn into these realizations:

- Prayer: Sisters, in particular, should be watchful, burdened, and in prayer for the church.
- Individual experience: We should give the Spirit freedom to move in each of our lives and give each other the freedom to have personal experiences with Christ. We had an anointing from the Holy One, who was able to teach each of us (1 John 2:27). We needed to extend to one another the grace to follow the Lord individually.
- Conformity: We needed to feel free to make our own personal decisions about personal matters. For example, I chose my clothing by considering what others would think or by noticing how others dressed. I was afraid to dress differently. Although we said we believed in oneness without conformity, our practices and appearance said otherwise.
- Problems: We needed the freedom to have problems and experience God's help in them without having to keep up an appearance of being always happy and victorious.
- Speaking: We needed the freedom to be able to speak honestly without being afraid of being labeled as negative by the leading brothers.
- Reputation: We should not value pleasing people more than God (1 Thess. 2:4). My sadness about my newly acquired bad reputation showed me that what people thought about me was too important to me. I was not like Christ whose only purpose was to please His Father. He wasn't affected by the praise or rejection of people.

- Loving others: We should be willing to "get our hands dirty," like the good Samaritan (Luke 10:30–37), to care for wounded brothers and sisters who had been labeled as negative.
- Good brothers: Leaders referred to some brothers as "really good" brothers. What were the other brothers? What exactly made a really good brother? Talk like this indicated there were some who were not so good.
- Leaders: We were all accountable to God for how we cared for His flock. God had judged both the shepherds in Ezekiel 34, who cared for themselves and oppressed the flock, and the Pharisees in Matthew 23, who loved themselves rather than God, and oppressed God's people. We could end up under the same kind of judgment if we didn't care for His flock properly.
- Self effort: We should live according to the example of Isaac and not Ishmael (Gal. 4:21–31). Isaac was a result of freely given grace and faith, whereas Ishmael was the result of self-effort and lack of faith in God. It seemed to me that we were busily producing Ishmael rather than letting God produce Isaac.
- Laodicea: We in the Local Church could become, if we weren't careful, like those in the church of the Laodiceans who boasted in their spiritual riches (Rev. 3:14–19). Shouldn't we be on the alert if we saw the symptoms of pride and boasting? Hadn't Brother Lee warned us about this danger?

I was caught in a situation in which my attempt to follow the Lord in the light of the truth that I was seeing in the Bible was bothering some of the leading brothers. There seemed to be no way to handle the situation except just to go on through it.

A Long Night Ahead

One day, when thinking about the dilemma I was in, I remembered an experience I had while driving to attend a training in Anaheim the previous December. In the dark, early morning hours, as I took my turn driving, it occurred to me that I would be able to see a desert sunrise in my rearview mirror, I began to watch, thinking that at any moment the sun would peep up from the long, flat horizon. While waiting, I began to hear this song in my heart:

> There's a light upon the mountains
> And the day is at the spring,
> When our eyes shall see the beauty
> And the glory of the King:
> Weary was our heart with waiting,
> And the night watch seemed so long,
> But His triumph day is breaking
> And we hail it with a song.
>
> — H. Burton

Instead of seeing the sun, I kept seeing distant car headlights appear in the mirror, and these blocked the view of the horizon. Then the terrain changed, and the mountains began to obscure the horizon. After awhile, I became irritated and stopped watching. Later, I once again stole a glimpse in the mirror only to discover that the sun was still not visible. I decided that I did not appreciate the Lord leading me into this frustrating experience. Eventually, I thought, "Just forget about it!" and quit looking altogether. Several hours later, while looking out of my side window, I noticed the sun high in the sky above me. As I looked at the high noon of a brilliant, sun-filled day, I thought, "So, it made it after all!" As I recalled this experience, I thought that maybe it was somewhat prophetic of the "night" I was now experiencing with the brothers. I kept hoping things would change for the better, but it wasn't happening. I was looking for the sunrise, but it just wasn't coming.

God was continuing to give me songs in the night, calling me to take up my cross and follow Him:

Many crowd the Savior's kingdom, few receive His cross;
Many seek His consolation, few will suffer loss,
For the dear sake of the Master, counting all but dross,
For the dear sake of the Master, counting all but dross.

Many sit at Jesus' table, few will fast with Him
When the sorrow-cup of anguish trembles to the brim,
Few watch with Him in the garden who have sung the hymn,
Few watch with Him in the garden who have sung the hymn.

Many will confess His wisdom, few embrace His shame,
Many, should He smile upon them, will His praise proclaim;
Then, if for a while He leave them, they desert His name,
Then, if for a while He leave them, they desert His name.

But the souls that love Him truly, let woe come or bliss,
These will count their dearest hearts' blood not their own, but His,
Savior, Thou who thus hast loved me, give me love like this,
Savior, Thou who thus hast loved me, give me love like this.

— Author unknown

My frustration with the morning sunrise was indeed prophetic. I was on the verge of a very long, lonely, and dark spiritual night. The darkest part would last for more than fourteen years!

Chapter 13
The "Sisters' Rebellion"

My tears have been my food day and night, while they continually say to me, "Where is your God?" (Psa. 42:3)

Something About Oneness

ONE WEEKEND, ANNE ATTENDED AN OUT-OF-TOWN church conference with her husband and some others. After she returned from the trip, she came to my house one night and knocked on the front door. When I opened the door and invited her in, she refused to enter. She stood there on my porch and began to speak very sternly, "Jane, I had a long talk with Dan Williams, flying home on the airplane. I need to tell you something." I responded, "Okay ... what?" She said, "After talking with Dan, I've seen something about oneness. I'm not going to be talking to you anymore." I was stunned and stood there looking at her incredulously for a moment before I said, "What did you see, Anne?" She responded, "I can't tell you. You'll have to see it for yourself." I tried several times to get her to tell me what Dan had said to her and what she had seen about oneness, but she refused to tell me and repeated that I just needed to see it for myself. Then she said on behalf of the leading brothers, "Jane, you are not to talk anymore to anyone—not to Sandra, not to Diane, not to any of the sisters. Sandra and Diane are also clear now about oneness and have repented. You are the root of the problem. You are to stop talking completely! Do you understand?" I just stood there speechless staring at her. She turned and left.

Standing at my door in shock, I watched her as she walked away, down the sidewalk, and ... out of my life. I could hardly breathe. What was that? I moved to a chair in my living room and sat down, reeling from what had just happened. I was very frightened and felt sick at my stomach.

I had seen a glimpse of this side of Anne a few times during our friendship. It usually appeared when we were discussing something related to our church roles or responsibilities that required some kind of a decision. She would get a certain kind of "official" look on her face and tell me in no uncertain terms what needed to happen. She did this in a way to let me know she had made a decision, and I should say no more. Because she was a "deaconess" in the church, I treated her with respect and always deferred to whatever she had decided without further comment. That same look and attitude had been there tonight as she stood on my porch—only it seemed a hundred times stronger. She had given me an ultimatum, a decree from the brothers ... and from her.

I started crying and shaking all over. I knew that this was not good, and that there were some bad times ahead. I dreaded having to face any of the leading brothers. "What had happened to Anne? Why had she done this?" I knew I was going to be disciplined further, and I knew I would have to face it alone. I was scared, upset, and hurt. "How could Anne, my trusted friend and my sister in the Lord, do this to me? How could she treat me like this? Why wouldn't she share with me what she had realized about oneness? I had been sharing with her all the spiritual things I had been seeing for months. Why couldn't she answer my question? What kind of person was she? Was this how Christians were supposed to treat each other?" I had never done anything to her but to love her and be her friend. This hurt was all mixed up with the thought that God had come to punish me for having a friend.

John appeared at the living room doorway and asked me what was wrong. When I told him what had just happened, he couldn't believe it. He also sat down. We both knew this meant we were in a lot of trouble. The leading brothers had officially marked and labeled me as a troublemaker. They had moved to isolate me and prevent me from communicating with anyone else.

Subduing the "Rebellion"

After breaking off her relationship with me, Anne began to help the leading brothers as they took steps to clear up

Chapter 13—The "Sisters' Rebellion"

what they were calling the "sisters' rebellion." It soon became apparent to me that the young sisters with whom I had been closely associated were avoiding me. I understood that most of them now would be afraid of having a relationship with me, once they realized I was in trouble with the leading brothers. I assumed that Anne, where necessary, was doing damage control with these sisters and warning them about talking with me.

After Anne delivered her bombshell message at my front door, John and I still continued to attend the church meetings even though I was emotionally tortured during them. Our attendance was expected. We had been taught that if you were to have a problem in the church where you lived, this never would be grounds for leaving or moving to another Local Church. You stayed put and got through it.

One night in a meeting, not long after Anne's friendship-terminating visit, a special meeting was announced for the coming weekend in which Dan Williams was going to be the speaker. Anne approached me afterwards and asked, "Are you planning to come to that meeting?" I answered, "I don't think so. I think that night will be my turn to babysit." With the official look on her face she said, "You need to get a baby sitter and be in that meeting." With that, she left. I did as she said and went to that meeting.

What happened in that meeting and in the after-the-meeting coffin-closing in the brothers' fellowship room, is indelibly burned into my memory. It is the encounter I described in chapter one of this book. In the blur of all the people in the room that night who had been invited as spectators, the face of my former friend, Anne, and the face of my campus firstfruit, Lana, stand out in my memory. They all sat there with hardened faces and motionless bodies, staring at me as I sobbed my heart out while Dan whipped me with his words. Throughout his reproach and my tears, no one spoke even one word on my behalf. No one even shed one tear with me.

When the meeting was finally over, and I was at home, I wept and wept. How could this have happened? My mind was full of screaming voices, repeating all the things that had been said to me to condemn me. Questions were spinning around in my mind, "What had just happened?

Why? How could Anne just sit there and watch? Why was Lana there? Why wasn't God there with me? Why had He left me alone? Had I really been talking to demons for months? Can demons wake you in the morning and fool you? Can they counterfeit God? Were all of those songs a trick from the devil? Answers were also shouting at me, "Yes. They were from the devil! You were so proud! Who do you think you are that God was telling you things? You are being judged! You are a sister! Sisters are easily deceived. Brother Lee warned you! Remember it was Eve in the garden who caused so much trouble. She was talking to God's enemy! You were so messed up, so deceived, that God had to use the brothers to get your attention!"

Then more questions, "But, maybe those things had been from God? Yes. Maybe it was God. Hadn't He encouraged me to stand one with Him no matter what came? Hadn't he asked me if I was willing to be misunderstood? I definitely felt misunderstood. Yes, He had asked me that ... but ... maybe that was a demon!" The wind of such thoughts had been increasing throughout the events of the evening and now a dark funnel cloud was forming over me. All the thoughts, accusations, fears, questions, and doubts were spiraling around in my mind as I sat there weeping in the pit into which I had been hurled. Then the whirlwind broke out in its full fury as these same thoughts came over and over again, faster and faster. I was being tossed and thrown around in a cyclone of verbiage. I kept reaching out trying to find something to hold on to, something to save me, but I could find nothing.

A Terrible Phone Call

The next day and night were the same. There was no place of escape from the raging maelstrom in my mind. Then unexpectedly, the phone rang with some very distressing news from Dallas. John's mother had been admitted to the hospital. She had developed a serious complication from a recent surgery, and the doctors were giving her just hours to live. We grabbed the children, threw some things in the car, and John sped all the way to Dallas trying to get there to see her while she was still alive.

We arrived in time for him to see her unconscious in intensive care for about a half an hour before she passed away.

We stayed for a week to help wrap up her affairs. I cried throughout the time we were there, mostly because of the verbal beating I had just received in Houston. I was emotionally unavailable for John and was no support for him during the pain of losing his mother. John was in double pain—the church event plus his mother's death. Of all the Christians we knew in the Local Church, not one was there for us. Only David Washington, the older brother in whose home we attended our first Local Church meeting in Denton long ago, acknowledged our loss by sending flowers and a note of sympathy.

After we returned home to Houston, I was devastated. I cried constantly. I wrote letters to all of the leading brothers apologizing for whatever I had done to hurt them and the church. I was extremely confused. I couldn't pray. I couldn't even pick up the Bible, much less read it. All of the thoughts continued. "Who is God? What part, if any, of my morning times over the last few years was from God? What is the church? What is spiritual authority? Have I been praying to and dealing with demons? Have all the songs and verses been sent to me from demons or evil spirits?" I was beginning to fear that I was going to lose my mind if I couldn't stop this vicious circle of questions. Always before when I needed help, I prayed. But I couldn't pray now! I didn't know who I would be praying to!

Gold Tried by Fire

During this time, I don't think I ever made it through an entire day without crying. Gone were my mornings with God. As months passed, nothing changed. The days and nights were filled with bouts of tears. Throughout all of this, we continued to attend church meetings. We were expected to attend the meetings and be supportive of whatever was going on and never again talk as we had done. We did as was expected.

You are probably marveling, as I do now, that we stayed in the Local Church. Why didn't we leave? Isn't this what a normal person would have done? The sad truth is that we never even considered for one moment the possibility of leaving. Our belief system was very strong. We had given our whole lives to the Lord for Him to recover His church, and we were totally convinced that He was going to do this. We were certain that this was His true church. We knew the devil would fight against God's recovery of the true church, and we believed that we had to stand firm no matter what happened. This was our "governing vision," and it was in control of our behavior.

Also, why ever did we comply with the requirement to attend that meeting? For the same reason. There was never any thought that we should not attend when we were summoned. If God's deputy authorities called for a meeting, we went. It was just that simple. We had to submit to the leading brothers in the church.

Attending the meetings, we continued to endure messages that appeared to be delivered with the purpose of correcting anyone who might believe as I had. The leading brothers mocked common Christian terms like "waiting on the Lord." Anyone not actively engaged in the latest flow was a "passive" Christian. There was no need for "spiritual giants" anymore because the age of spiritual giants was over and was too individualistic. We were now in the age of the "corporate Spirit." The battle against what the leading brothers considered to be passivity and individualism was fought in meeting after meeting, both by the leading brothers and the brothers and sisters who gave supporting testimonies.

Suffice it to say that from the night of that meeting, everything changed for John and me. One day, we were appreciated and loved by all our brothers and sisters; the next, we were like outcasts. Everything was different. People were now avoiding us. Before, we had been frequently invited to people's homes for meals and fellowship; but now, no one invited us. No one called. No one spoke to me after meetings. We were shunned as outcasts in the midst of people we loved. We attended the meetings as expected, but we were completely ostracized and might as well have been invisible.

We lost the close daily contact with all those with whom we had served, prayed, eaten, and fellowshipped for the previous ten years. We lost our involvement with the young people, even with those who had lived in our home and with those we had brought into the church. There was nowhere to turn. People I loved were removed from my life, and I was alone in my little, dark pit.

After one meeting, I noticed a sister with whom I had spent a lot of time, standing at a distance looking at me. When our eyes met, she looked teary-eyed. She offered me a partial smile and then looked away. I knew she didn't understand what had happened. I also knew she couldn't ask, and I couldn't tell. I still had John, but we rarely talked about the situation because we were both too wounded and confused to make sense of it. I felt solely responsible for causing our trouble.

As time passed, two clearly opposing trains of thought had formed in my mind out of all the initial chaos. One train insisted that I had been being deceived by the devil for a long period of time. Satan had been appearing to me as "an angel of light" (2 Cor. 11:14). Those thoughts continued to assert that I had reached such a degree of deception that it had become necessary for God to speak to me through His deputy authorities. The other train traveled the tracks in my mind infrequently. It said that all of this somehow was God, in His sovereignty, allowing me to be misunderstood and mistreated.

Once or twice I realized there was one very small, secret thought without much form. This thought seemed to be standing at a great distance away from me. I could never allow myself to actually think it in words, but I was aware it was there. It held this question, "Am I now a bona fide troublemaker? Is God taking me up on my willingness to be identified with those in His body who are like my dear sister Judy?" But, was that little unborn thought conceived by God or the devil?

I think now that this little thought also subconsciously played a part in my belief that we were in the church for the long haul. We had to see this experience through to an end.

I never spoke intimately with Anne again. I only had contact with her when the leading brothers used her as an emissary to communicate something to me, except for one or two other superficial, unavoidable contacts, mainly at church meetings.

As time passed, my tears and confusion remained. One time, I thought about a verse in the Bible that said something about God putting our tears in a bottle (Psa. 56:8); and I risked the request, "Lord, in eternity, may I see my bottle?"

An Angel at My Door

One day, much to my surprise, an angel appeared at my door. It was Sue Wilson. She was a sister who miraculously was oblivious to the leading brothers' actions during the prior months concerning John and me. She had been walking by and decided to stop and say, "Hi." She found me crying. She was very loving and concerned. By the way she talked to me, I realized she didn't know I had been branded as a "leper."

After that day, she would periodically stop by my house and usually find me crying. Although she repeatedly asked me what was wrong, I never told her one word of my trouble, having been forbidden by the leading brothers to talk with anyone about it. She began to worry that I was losing my mind, so day after day, she came, having taken it as her personal mission to encourage me to get a job. She knew I needed to get my mind on something else. Eventually, she helped me make an appointment with a temporary employment agency, and I began working part-time. This was a big step because sisters typically didn't work outside of their homes. I think John only agreed to this because he was also worried about me. This change was indeed a blessing.

Daystar

When I wasn't working, I started to try and find things to do to keep myself busy. My part-time job was providing some extra income, so I could afford to buy a few garage sale furniture pieces and refinish them. John's mother had left us some money in her will, so we had been able to pay off our debt to my father for our house purchase. For the first time in our married life, we actually had a savings account; however, it would have been significantly more if John had not taken an advance on his inheritance in the early 1970s to invest in Witness Lee's business venture named "Daystar."

At that time, the leading brothers had promoted the "Daystar" business for Brother Lee who had told them that the purpose of the business was to raise money for the Lord's Recovery. A number of brothers had worked for his venture. Church members had been told that this was an opportunity that should not be passed by. There was no guarantee of return on any investments made; but because the Lord would surely bless Brother Lee's endeavor for the sake of the Recovery, we were strongly encouraged to do whatever we could to participate. Brothers and sisters from all over the country invested in the venture, which was going to build high-end motor homes. I heard that some church members took out loans and even mortgaged their homes to have funds to invest. Some invested very large amounts of money. In Houston, we were strongly encouraged to participate.

John and I had been living paycheck to paycheck for years and had no money to invest. John, wanting to heed the encouragement to participate, asked his mother if she would give him part of his inheritance in advance. She did so, even though he would not tell her the purpose of the advance. When she died in 1977, we learned that the amount she had given him was one fourth of his inheritance. Daystar was ultimately a miserable failure, and all investments were lost. In Houston and in other churches, those who had invested were asked to release Brother Lee from all obligations, so that he would not feel the need to try to recompense us.

We were being damaged spiritually, psychologically, and materially by our experiences in the Local Church, yet we stayed. This fact shows the magnitude of the deception the devil had achieved in our lives.

Years later, we heard about the Daystar venture's difficulties from a brother who had worked for the business in the overseas factory. He had seen firsthand that reports given to investors misrepresented the real situation.

Chapter 14
Ongoing, Inward Torment

> Now no chastening seems to be joyful for the present, but painful; nevertheless, afterward it yields the peaceable fruit of righteousness to those who have been trained by it. (Heb. 12:11)

Ongoing, Inward Struggle

THE PASSING OF ANOTHER YEAR found me still in emotional turmoil, constantly seeking a way out of my inward struggle. My biggest problem was that I couldn't pray with any confidence. Every time I tried to pray, I always questioned whether I was talking to demons or to the Lord. I was afraid I might get an answer and wouldn't know who it was from. After all, hadn't I been wrong about what I thought the Lord had spoken to me already? Or had I? Maybe it was the Lord who had spoken to me? Then again, maybe it wasn't. If it was, had He possibly led me on this path for a purpose? No, I dared not think like that. If I did, that would be pride, right?

These kinds of crazy thoughts passed through my mind day after day when I wasn't busying myself in some way. I just couldn't seem to find a place of rest from them.

One day, while resting on the couch in my living room, I looked from one corner of the room to the other and said, "Lord, I simply don't know who You are anymore." I looked at one corner and said, "In this corner is a kind and loving God who cares about me infinitely and is full of mercy." I looked at the other corner and said, "In this corner is a righteous, demanding God with a big stick who is ready and willing to smite me mercilessly if I am out of line. Which one are You, Lord? I want You to be the one in the first corner, but I'm afraid You are the second." This was my best attempt at prayer. I thought that if I read the Bible, I would probably get into yet more trouble. The elders and my former friend Anne understood something I didn't. I would just have to hope that someday the turmoil in my mind would end, and I would be able to think straight again.

We were getting ready to attend another semiannual training in Anaheim. I started hoping I could talk to someone there about my dilemma, but I feared that anyone I dared to talk to would report back to the elders in Texas, and my black hole would just get deeper. I couldn't talk to an elder, but I needed to talk to someone who had some maturity in their experience with the Lord.

You may wonder why I didn't go for some kind of professional or psychological counseling. The truth is that I never even thought of going to someone outside the church for help. My strong Local Church belief system told me that the Lord wouldn't be pleased with my seeking help anywhere else. Also, Witness Lee had said that psychology was of the devil.

A Prayer, an Answer, and a Lesson

One day, I thought about Alex Kent, with whom John and I had stayed for three weeks on our first trip to Los Angeles many years before. To my knowledge, he wasn't an elder, so maybe he could just listen to me and try to help me without betraying my confidence. But what if this idea wasn't from the Lord and was just my own desperate attempt to help myself? I decided to pray and ask the Lord to work it out so that our hospitality for the upcoming training would be with Alex and his wife, Sandra. If we were placed with them, then I would know that the Lord was indicating that I could talk to Alex. I asked and waited. We were assigned somewhere else. I wasn't really surprised.

I had a young sister for a roommate at the place where I stayed. By this time, couples frequently were separated so that hosts would have room for more people in each home. They would fill the sleeping quarters with as many brothers or sisters as possible. If couples did stay in the same home, they normally weren't put in the same room, again so that more persons could be accommodated. The young sister was excited about the Lord and the church. I didn't want to put a damper on her experience, so I tried hard to keep my emotions under control. Nevertheless, I had at least one crying spell each day, and she caught me in a couple of those. There just wasn't any private place to go. She talked to me and tried to help me. I told her, "Don't worry about me; I am fine. This crying just kind of comes over me." I am sure she thought I was mentally ill. I was beginning to wonder the same thing.

After we had been in our assigned home for about two days, the wife of the house asked me if I would call Sandra Kent and relay a message to her. "Sandra Kent?" I said, "I know her." She then told me that Alex and Sandra lived right across the street! This was the couple with whom I had asked the Lord to let me stay! I made the call for her. Sandra said to me, "Jane, you and John have to come over for dinner one night while you are here." After the call, I went into the bathroom and wept (again). I couldn't believe it. It looked like the Lord had answered my prayer after all, in His own way. More days passed, and it was nearing time for the training to be over. One day I said, "Lord, if You are going to let me talk to Alex, then let them call and ask us to come for dinner. I don't want to initiate this." The next day, they called and invited us.

Before going to their home that night, I was extremely nervous. I asked the Lord, "Please help me talk to Alex. Please create the opportunity and make it easy for me." When we got there, I was surprised to see a lot of faces from Houston. I was hoping there wouldn't be anyone I knew staying with Alex and Sandra. Instead, many there knew about my "rebellion."

Throughout the meal, I fought to keep my emotional composure. At one point, Alex looked at me and said, "Well, Jane, how is Todd?" In a little voice I said, "He's fine." Alex asked, "Tell me about him. What kind of disposition does he have?" Inside I was screaming, "Please don't do this to me. Don't make me talk in front of all these people." I just sat and looked at him as tears welled up in my eyes. "I don't really know. He's sweet." Alex saw the pain on my face and graciously moved the conversation elsewhere.

Afterwards, as we were leaving, he followed us to the door. I turned and blurted out, "Alex, can I talk to you for a few minutes? Alone?" That was a serious question because brothers were never supposed to talk to sisters alone—in the Texas churches anyway. I wasn't asking for a closed-door hearing but for just a few minutes in a public part of their home. Alex said, "Certainly." John was grateful, hoping Alex would be able to help me.

For ten or fifteen minutes, I poured out my heart to Alex. Without giving any details, I told him that the elders in Houston had disciplined me and that I still was having difficulty getting over it. I explained to Alex that they had said things to me that contradicted my experience with the Lord. When I tried to accept what the elders said with all my heart, I felt paralyzed from talking to the Lord on my own; but when I didn't, I felt guilty and tormented that I wasn't being properly submissive. What could I do? Did he have any help for me? When I finished, Alex began to define church authority, emphasizing the need to submit. I was suspended in another world as I listened, moving farther and farther away, listening to him from a distance, hating him, and hating everything. He basically sounded like the Texas brothers all over again. I wanted to stand up and start screaming at him, but I was in another place. When he finished, I thanked him, excused myself, and went home in tears. He knew he hadn't helped me.

Back at my assigned host's house, I was so upset that I couldn't go into my room and disturb my roommate, so I lay on the bathroom floor. I was cold and numb in my heart. Then suddenly, I got mad. I mean, I got really mad—no, not at Alex—but at God. How could He have done this to me? Then I cut loose and told Him what I thought of Him. "God, I have two children, and I don't claim to be a good mother. I'm just a fallen human being, but never, never would I do to either of them what You just did to me! For the last seven days, You held out hope in front of me like a carrot in front of a starving donkey. You answered my prayer about talking to Alex. You made the way. You dangled the carrot, and I followed, trusting You … and then, again? I was bashed again? What kind of Father are You anyway? Well, as of tonight, I am through. I am sick of all of this. I don't want to follow You. Nothing can be worth this. I quit, and I won't be back!" I meant every word I said. I wasn't playing this game anymore. I felt a great sense of relief, got up, went to bed, and slept like a baby.

About 4:00 the next morning, I opened my eyes. I was wide awake. Something that had happened to me years before began to be replayed in my mind like a video. I watched. The video showed John giving money to his mother instead of to the Lord for our health insurance. When that video finished playing, light had dawned, and I had my answer. My torment was over. In a matter of minutes my heavenly Father had answered my question and ended my mental anguish. He finished the video by asking me, "Now, what kind of Father am I? I answered your prayer to talk to Alex. You were looking for help. You thought it would be from him. Yet, you never asked Me to answer your question. Now, I have answered it." My tears were of a different kind that morning. I felt peaceful.

What had I realized? The Lord had used the mental video to remind me that in the book of Genesis when Sarah had put her hope in God and obeyed the demands of her wrong-hearted husband, Abraham, God had taken excellent care of her. He then showed me that the two things troubling me were reconcilable. Just because the leading brothers had told me something contrary to what I thought God had told me, it didn't mean I hadn't heard God or that God hadn't spoken to me. Years before in Houston, hadn't John told me to give the "heavenly insurance" money to his mother? Hadn't his contrary instruction come *after* the Lord had told me to give that money to Him? I then understood that when I had submitted to John, it hadn't meant that God hadn't spoken to me, nor had it meant I had been deceived. It simply meant that because he was my husband, I could go along with him and hope in God.

Likewise, my going along with the discipline of the elders didn't mean that God hadn't spoken to me or that a demon had deceived me. From that day, I knew that what the elders had done to me was not God's doing, just as Abraham had not been following God when he wronged Sarah. I could still believe what God told me and hope in Him. When Abraham wronged Sarah, she submitted. God had kept Sarah, saved, and delivered her, and eventually, He had corrected Abraham. My hope wasn't in the elders, but in God, who was certainly trustworthy. I had accused the Lord of being a bad Father, but He had shut my mouth.

He was, and always will be, the best Father. I hadn't been talking to demons, but to Him.

The next day, my hosts invited Alex and Sandra to dinner. I was seated next to Alex. My whole countenance must have been noticeably different because he kept watching me. At one point he said, "My, you seem to be a lot better than you were last night." "Yes," I said, "I have been since about four o'clock this morning." He didn't inquire further, and I didn't offer more explanation.

After that experience, I knew that at least one stage of all this ugliness was over. I had just passed through almost two years of mental torture from the things said to me by Anne and Dan, and from the ongoing general rejection of my brothers and sisters. I knew that this had come close to costing me my sanity and had severely impacted John's health. At least now I knew that God was still with me. I also knew He had allowed this trial:

> In this you greatly rejoice, though now for a little while, if need be, you have been grieved by various trials, that the genuineness of your faith, being much more precious than gold that perishes, though it is tested by fire, may be found to praise, honor, and glory at the revelation of Jesus Christ. (1 Pet. 1:6-7)

In spite of realizing these things, I still found it hard to talk to the Lord in the simple, trusting way that I had before. I was like a little wounded animal who didn't want to risk the possibility of being hit again. It was easier to just sit quietly in my cage and not do anything to cause trouble.

The experience with my heavenly Father's video, however, had helped me. After that, whenever I began to feel overwhelmed by our ongoing difficult position among our brothers and sisters, I would remember what God had shown me and be comforted that He loved me and had not left me. We were trying to go on in the church-life as the brothers expected. We continued to go to the meetings. I took cues for my behavior from those around me and carefully filtered everything I said through the elders' prohibitions.

A few times in the months that followed my church discipline, I actually managed to give a few obligatory testimonies when I found something I could say, in good conscience, to support what was being said in a meeting. However, after one of these times, one of the elders stood up immediately after me and said something to correct and adjust what I had said. After that, I didn't venture to speak anymore.

A Passing Ray of Hope

The elders announced one day in a meeting that Brother Lee's right-hand man, Ed Black, had left the church. They said that he had been responsible for a rebellion and had caused division and confusion in the Church in Anaheim and in other Local Churches. We were told that a number of others had followed him in his rebellion. The Lord had come in to judge the situation and save the churches from the things Ed Black had initiated. The once sanctioned Anaheim sisters' flow was stopped. Sheri, Ed's wife, was blamed as the main sister responsible for that flow, which they now said had been exposed as being something that was not from the Lord.

The leading brothers told us that Ed was the one behind brothers and sisters relocating throughout the country and was also responsible for *old* elders being asked to step down to let new *younger* "elders" take their place. Thus, Ed was held responsible for the problems and internal turmoil that the Local Churches had experienced over the previous few years. The elders in Houston stated that they were willing to confer with anyone who had questions or problems as a result of the recent "trying times" and encouraged us to contact them for fellowship.

It was very sad and upsetting to hear these things. John and I decided that maybe we should respond to the brothers' offer as an opportunity to talk with them. Maybe they would be willing to listen to our situation and try to understand it from a new perspective. John contacted Sam Jones to ask if we could come for fellowship. Unbelievably, Sam said to him, "We will meet with you, but not with your wife." John reported this to me and said, "If they will not talk with you, then I will not talk with them," and he didn't.

Many years later, I learned that Ed Black had not simply "left the church" but was publicly humiliated and cut off from church fellowship by Witness Lee. I also learned that one of the precipitating events in Ed Black's expulsion was his discovery that one of Witness Lee's sons, who was then managing the Living Stream Ministry office, was involved in immoral sexual conduct.

Chapter 15
Bruised Reeds and Smoking Flax

A bruised reed He will not break, and smoking flax He will not quench, till He sends forth justice to victory. (Matt. 12:20)

New Elders, Same Trouble

WE WERE BRUISED AND OUR FIRE WAS SMOLDERING, but the Lord wasn't going to discard John and me. He was planning a change for us. In June of 1979, two years after our discipline, my sister Dorothy called from Oklahoma City where she and her family were in the Local Church. In the middle of our conversation, she suddenly said, "Jane, you are not doing well. You have got to get out of Houston." She was aware that I had been in trouble with the elders, but I had never discussed my distressing church situation with her. We were having a mundane conversation when she made this surprising declaration. She said she was worried about my mental health and felt we should leave Houston and move to Oklahoma City. Ultimately, we visited her and her family and decided we wanted to move.

John called Sam Jones again and asked for fellowship with the elders about our prospective move. Sam told John that he would call him back, but he never did. John made the decision that with or without the elders' blessing, we had to get out of Houston. The stress of the prior two years had exacerbated his hypoglycemia to the point that it was almost unmanageable. He was very sick for several years after we moved to Oklahoma City. My mental condition was better after my experience at the training with my Father's heavenly video, but continuing to face the ongoing rejection of the brothers and sisters in the Church in Houston was still very stressful.

Diane Mays, one of the three sisters who had been accused of participating in the "sisters' rebellion" in the

Texas churches, was now living in Oklahoma City. When she heard about our impending move, she called to tell us that there was a suitable house in their neighborhood for sale by owner. We traveled to Oklahoma City to check on the house. Just before we called to make an appointment to see the house, we noticed that the small, homemade for-sale sign which had been in the yard had been removed. We wondered why, so we knocked on their door and asked why the sign was gone. The owners told us that they were Christians who had been praying about selling their house and moving back to Arkansas. They weren't sure what the Lord's will was, so the night before, they had taken the sign down to wait awhile. We laughed and told them we had been praying about moving to Oklahoma City when Christian friends who had seen their sign had called us. We discussed our respective situations. We made them an offer for the house which they accepted the next day. They commented that this event was God's indication to them to move back to Arkansas.

Shortly before our actual move, while we were at my sister's house one weekend, the leading brothers in the Church in Oklahoma City made an appointment to come over and talk to us. It became apparent that the leading brothers in Houston, though unwilling to fellowship with us in person, had been willing to call ahead and warn the leading brothers in the Church in Oklahoma City about our coming. The Oklahoma City leading brothers informed us that we would be allowed to attend the Local Church meetings in Oklahoma City under one condition: I couldn't talk to Diane Mays. The main leading brother, Jerry Hughes, told me that I could not inform her that they were forbidding me to talk to her because she was doing very well and it might upset her. I had remained composed until they gave this requirement; then I began to cry. They weren't moved at all by my tears, but just sat there unsympathetically, waiting on my response. I said in my heart, "Lord, will this never end? I can't do this. Do You want this?" He answered by calming me, and I heard myself saying, "All right." I had already talked to Diane because she had called me about the house, so now I was going to have to stop communication without any explanation.

In August of 1969, we had moved to Houston. Now, ten years later to the month, in August of 1979, we were moving to Oklahoma City. We rented a U-Haul truck and moved ourselves. The church moving service group didn't help us make what was obviously an unapproved move. Imagine our surprise when a number of children on our block appeared to help us empty the house and load the truck! God was taking care of us in His own way.

We moved without John having obtained any employment in Oklahoma, trusting that God would faithfully provide for us. An interview that he had the week before we actually moved ultimately resulted in a job offer. As we drove from Texas into Oklahoma, I felt as if we were driving out of a dark cloud into a place of light. My heart lifted with every mile. I was very thankful to the Lord for rescuing us out of the oppressive atmosphere we were under in the Church in Houston and for working out all the details of our relocation.

Diane, who was excited that her young son and our son Todd would be able to play together again, asked me to be in a babysitting group with her. She was hurt when, in accordance with the elders' requirement, I repeatedly refused. I told her I wanted to hire a baby sitter and attend all the church meetings. I was too afraid of the elders to tell her the truth. Not only did I not want to attend all the church meetings, the money required to hire a baby sitter was needed elsewhere in our budget. Nevertheless, I felt forced to pay for babysitting because it would have hurt Diane deeply if I had joined some other babysitting group. After months of hiring baby sitters, I told Jerry Hughes, the main leading brother in the Church in Oklahoma City, about the economic difficulty this was causing us. He then pronounced, "All right. You can be in babysitting with Diane, but that is all—and no talk!"

Jerry Hughes died several years later. Neither he, nor any of the elders, ever removed the prohibition they had placed on me.

My Job, a Safe Haven

Just prior to our move to Oklahoma City, a single sister named Lanell Allen, who lived and worked in Oklahoma City, had learned that I was looking for a part-time job and called me in Houston. She arranged an interview for me with a company in Oklahoma City that had a word processing position open. I decided to accept the part-time job primarily to avoid daily contact with the sisters. If I spent much time with the church sisters, I was afraid that I would inevitably say something amiss and would find myself in trouble again. By this time, there were some other married sisters who were employed outside their homes, so having a job gave me an acceptable excuse for being unavailable. My job was like a safe haven to me. Outwardly, I was still part of the church and was attending the meetings; but inwardly, I had changed. I did not want to be involved in church service groups, and I was definitely no longer absolutely loyal. I had submitted to the elders' discipline but no longer had any interest in gaining their approval or appreciation. Never again would I carry another report about anyone to them. I had learned this painful lesson and, in the process, had also begun to question the elders' trustworthiness.

It was a huge relief to be away from the people in the Church in Houston who had shunned and pitied us. Most of the people in the Church in Oklahoma City didn't realize who we were or what I had done. However, a few experiences let me know that there had been gossip from some of the brothers to other church members. The result of this seemed insignificant to me when compared to what we had faced in Houston.

Tea with Dan Williams

While living in Oklahoma City, I still had no peace in my heart with regard to Dan Williams, even though I had written a letter to him asking forgiveness, had prayed that the Lord would deliver me and grant me forgiveness, and had done everything I knew to do. I had submitted to him and had forgiven him for what he had done to me, but I still did not trust him or have any respect for him at all. Whenever I heard him speak, a strong wall in me shut him and his words out—a wall I couldn't bring down. I believed such a thing shouldn't be present in the church. This was a serious problem related to oneness, fellowship, and the Lord's blessing. The Word exhorts us to clear up our problems, but this didn't seem easily applicable when the problem was with an elder. I searched the Word and Brother Lee's teachings for help but found nothing that applied. It appeared to boil down to just being my own unsolvable problem.

It seemed that the only solution would be the cross working in my life over time to the point that I no longer had any memory of the situation, but somehow, this just didn't seem possible. On one occasion, I ventured to talk to one of the elders who lived in our neighborhood. I described a hypothetical situation like mine, of someone having a problem with an elder, and asked if this kind of situation could exist in a church without affecting the Lord's blessing on that church. I also asked whether in eternity this person would have no memory of the problem, or would he be left in outer darkness during the millennial kingdom until the problem was cleared up? He didn't have any answers. Ultimately, I decided to avoid all situations in which I might have contact with Dan Williams. Over time, practicing this, I had some success in forgetting what he had done.

After we had been in Oklahoma City for several years, Vera Hughes, the wife of the main leading brother there, told me that a couple of interesting things had occurred related to Dan Williams. Dan, who stayed with them when he was in town, always asked her about John and me. The last time he had inquired, she had asked him why he didn't just contact us himself. Because Vera knew nothing about what had happened to us in Houston, she volunteered this information to me, finding it rather strange. Dan actually called shortly after this and asked to come to see us.

John set up a time with him after I finally agreed, but I determined beforehand that I wouldn't open my heart to him. I wouldn't give him an opportunity to hurt me again. The morning before he was to come, the Lord showed me that I was wrong to predetermine that I wouldn't speak to him. I had to obey if God prompted me to say something to Dan. I finally agreed, "As long as You do the talking."

We sat with Dan at the kitchen table, where I served him hot tea. We small-talked for a few minutes and then we moved to the living room to continue the visit. Dan began to sermonize about how time was the test of everything, saying that whatever was inside a believer as a seed would manifest itself as fruit, given time. As he continued, it became apparent to me that he was referring to what had happened back in Houston. Eventually, I spoke to him from my heart, and in spite of my strong resolution not to cry, I did. I explained that I did not want or need to talk about the particulars of the Houston experience, but I wanted to tell him a story that explained my feelings about it.

I asked him to visualize a war situation in which there were three ships at sea, two friendly, and one an enemy. Both friendly ships, unaware of each other's presence, opened fire on the enemy ship. The enemy ship passed out of the way causing the two friendly ships to strike each other. I suggested that this story might be analogous to what had happened in Houston. We all had been there shooting at our common enemy, Satan; but instead, we had shot each other. Regardless of whether Dan saw it that way or not, I told him that all I had needed then and all I needed now was for someone to say they were sorry if they had hurt me. Dan didn't offer an apology but proceeded by saying: "Brother Lee has said that when you enter into a deception, it takes many years to come out of it—maybe even up to ten years." This was a painful slap to me. It was obvious that Dan still considered me to be in a state of deception. At that moment, however, in my heart, the Lord said to me, "He is speaking about himself." John said to me after Dan had left, "Jane, remember when Dan said that it could take up to ten years to come out of a deception? The Lord told me he was talking about himself."

At another time, Howard Mays, who was an Oklahoma City church elder, expressed his concern to us about what he considered to be our self-inflicted isolation and encouraged us to get fully back into church activities. He also told us about an unusual conversation he had with Dan Williams. Dan now stayed with Howard when he visited Oklahoma City because Jerry Hughes had died. Howard said that every time Dan Williams stayed with him, Dan would eventually inquire about John and me. Howard told us that one time in the middle of a conversation, Dan suddenly changed the subject by interjecting, "You know, Howard, we may have been a little hard on Jane." Howard had suspected Dan's conscience was bothering him and had strongly urged him to call us. Dan never called. Rather, he sent another brother to check on us. We answered the brother's questions honestly, but we could tell by the brother's reaction to our answers that we hadn't passed the test.

My Former Friend at the Door

One day, when I answered a knock on my door, I was stunned to see my former friend, Anne Andrews, and her husband, Guy. They were in town and had just stopped by to say hello. After greeting me, they just stood there smiling. I instantly felt sick at my stomach as the memory of Anne's mistreatment surfaced. I was determined not to cry. We all stood there awkwardly exchanging a few polite comments. I waited to see what the real purpose of their visit was. If Anne had come to say she was sorry for having hurt me, I would invite them in; otherwise, I really didn't want them in my house. My home was a little place of sanctuary into which I didn't want a memory of Anne inserted. They said nothing else but just continued to stand there. I also just stood there with the door held only partially open. After a few minutes, they said goodbye and left.

Tina, a Gift from God

After about two years in Oklahoma City, while we were having dinner in our home with another church couple one day, the wife disclosed how much her three teenage daughters hated the Local Church and would have nothing to do with anyone in it. Few church members had ever laid eyes on these girls because they would hide in their bedroom whenever their parents invited people from the church to their home. Later, as I was doing the dishes, I prayed, "Lord, if You will give me those girls, I will take them." Where had that come from? This was the first time I had felt interested in investing in anyone's spiritual well-being since moving to Oklahoma City. My Houston rejection experience had left me unwilling to have more than a superficial involvement with others in the church.

Chapter 15—Bruised Reeds and Smoking Flax

Not many days later, the wife of the couple asked me if there were any job openings where I worked because she needed a part-time job. There was an opening; but to my surprise, it was Tina, her oldest daughter, who came to the interview when her mother changed her mind at the last minute about wanting to work. Thus began the answer to my kitchen prayer. Naturally, her mother was very surprised when Tina accepted the job with me because I was in the "hated" Local Church. As I trained Tina in her new job, we became friends. God gave me a special love for her. After several months, the leading brothers decided to send Tina's stepfather to be an elder in the Church in Kansas City. Prior to this, the family had already moved from the Church in San Diego to Oklahoma City, a move which had upset Tina tremendously. Now, she was furious that her family would even think of moving at the end of her high school senior year. She refused to go with them and moved in with her aunt instead. But after a week or so with her difficult, demanding, and preaching aunt, who was also in the Local Church, she appeared on my doorstep, angry and crying.

We offered her a place to stay while she decided what to do. This turned into a stay of almost two years. I was happy to have her there and loved her as if she were my own daughter. I was surprised to find that I could feel this way again about anyone other than my own family. People had lived with us before, but this time it was different. Tina wasn't living in our home because of the church; rather, the Lord Himself had entrusted her to us.

As time went on, it became evident that Tina was deeply disturbed. In addition to being upset about her family being in the church, she didn't like or trust men in general and said she would never marry. She didn't ever want to have children because she didn't want to bring them into this "horrible world." One day, to my surprise, she asked me about my being in the Local Church, telling me I was different from other church people she had been around. I told her that I just loved Jesus, that He was first, not the church. We had a nice talk. Shortly after this, the anger she held inside began to brew, and she stopped speaking to me or to anyone. Like a scared animal, she retreated into a dark, little world of silence, not speaking to me for several days.

The office staff noticed her behavior and became very concerned for her. Sadly, this became a pattern with her for as long as she lived with us and we worked together. People in the office would ask, "What have you done to her this time, Jane?" Her silent periods always occurred after we had talked about the Lord—conversations which she usually had initiated. At home, Todd and Matt, who also cared about Tina, began to ask me what I was doing to upset her so. I knew this must be spiritual warfare but didn't know how to fight, so I just kept asking the Lord to make Himself real to her.

After Tina had been with us for awhile, her best friend, Anna, announced she was leaving her husband and invited Tina to go out on the town with her—bar hopping. Tina was a beautiful girl, but she hadn't been dating while she was living with us. Her biological father had physically abused her as a child, generating those ill feelings toward males that she held. I was disheartened that she consented to go with Anna. I think she expected me to disagree with her decision, but I felt I should be quiet and let her go. After she left, I asked the Lord to take care of her and protect her. She returned home several hours later with an amazing story. Apparently, Anna, behaving wildly, had driven them to a bar that was little more than a seedy dive. Tina, not wanting to go into the bar and afraid to tell Anna this, panicked. As she followed Anna towards the bar, she found herself praying, "Lord, please help me. I don't want to do this. Please stop Anna from doing this." Suddenly, Anna turned around, looked at her, and said, "Let's forget this place."

Tina said that the rest of the night, she prayed about everything that was happening, and every prayer was answered. I was thrilled to hear this, noting that Tina was obviously very affected by the experience because she kept restating it. Then she said, "This makes me mad. I don't understand it. This doesn't fit with what I think about God." For several days, she was a different person. Then, slowly, she slipped back into the old Tina. However, a new thought about God had been planted because sometimes, when she found herself in a situation she couldn't handle, she would pray.

Jezebel in the Mirror

While Tina was living with us, God used her to help me in some very practical ways. When I was asked by my employer, a "Big-Eight" accounting firm, to speak at their National Word Processing conference being held in New York City, Tina was adamant that I had to go shopping and buy some *real* clothes. She said, laughing, "You can't stand up in front of people looking like that!" I let her take me shopping. She and the saleswoman had a job on their hands—I looked too "worldly" in everything I put on! Finally, I settled on two very nice suits and a couple of colorful blouses. I thought the colors were too bold, but the church people weren't going to see them anyway. I liked them but was still worried about what I was doing. I was also concerned about the cost. I could have bought ten of my normal Target outfits for what one of these cost!

I was standing in front of the mirror at the store looking at myself in one of the suits when the sales person appeared with some jewelry to wear with the outfits. I said, "No, thank you." Tina said incredulously, "Jane, you have to wear some jewelry. Otherwise, you will look weird! This is the business world!" They put the earrings and necklace on me. I stood looking at the Jezebel in front of me in the mirror and said, "I don't think I can do this." Tina said, "Yes you can!" She turned to the saleswoman and said, "We'll take them!"

I had an amazing experience with the Lord at the New York business conference. I had never spoken in public before and was petrified. On the day I was to speak, I went early to familiarize myself with the conference room for my session. I took one look at it and froze. It was a very formal-looking set-up. I would be standing to speak in an area surrounded on three sides by tables draped in long blue tablecloths. The layout was such that I wouldn't be able to stand or hide behind a podium, but rather would be in full view. I would have to move around and manage a microphone cord and the overhead slide projector! I turned and headed out the door of the conference room. I went to the hotel lobby and looked at the taxi cabs pulling up in front of the hotel. I was moments away from making my escape by running out the door and taking a taxi to the airport to go home! Someone took me by the arm and said, "Jane, it's almost time. Come on." Walking back, I started praying desperately, "Lord, I cannot do this. I am petrified. I don't even remember what I was going to say! Please help me. I need You. I am terrified!"

Moments later, I found myself standing in front of a room full of people. I started talking. It seemed as if only a few minutes passed, and then the two-hour session was over. Afterwards, person after person came up to me and thanked me saying things such as, "I could have listened to you for two more hours! That was great. Thank you so much." In my heart I was saying, "Thank you, Lord. Thank you so much. You were wonderful!" I had been carried through the session effortlessly by Him.

Lest anyone think I am naturally a gifted speaker, the next year I had to do the same thing again. Having been successful once, I waltzed in to do a repeat performance. The only problem was that I forgot to ask the Lord to waltz with me! I managed to make it through the session, but was painfully aware of the time and of my self-effort throughout!

My Isaac on the Altar

Meanwhile, John wasn't well and was having serious spells of exhaustion, tingling, and weakness. Having been diagnosed with hypoglycemia before we left Houston, he was trying to manage his blood sugar problems with a special diet. We went to extremes trying out various health food regimens. Vera Hughes convinced us that John's problems were due to food allergies and showed us how to determine exactly the items to which John was allergic by selectively eliminating foods from his diet. She also introduced John to a juice therapy, which required that we make every day several gallons of "green drink"—a blend of celery, lettuce, carrots, parsley, and so forth. If it was a vegetable and was green or orange, it got juiced! To help John stay on the regimen, I did the same thing. At one point, we even began taking coffee enemas, which were

Chapter 15—Bruised Reeds and Smoking Flax

supposed to cleanse our systems from toxins. I won't go any further into that, but suffice it to say that none of it helped. John was getting worse, and on top of that, his skin was turning yellow from all the carrots in the juice. After Tina had been living with us for almost two years, things reached a climax in our household.

John became so ill that he could hardly get out of bed. Tina also became ill—not surprising, since she routinely ate candy bars and junk food and then skipped meals in order to manage her weight. She was prone to attacks of muscle cramps which were so severe in her legs that she could hardly walk. These would come and go throughout the day at home and work. During this particular week, she decided to do something for her health and started drinking our green drink. She had a terrible reaction to her first drink, and became violently ill with the worst muscle cramps and spasms she had ever had.

I called a brother, who was a doctor, and Vera, the green-drink sister, who had also taken an interest in Tina. The doctor told Tina that she should go to the hospital immediately. Tina dug her heels in, refused to go, and stopped speaking. I sat up with her all night watching her writhe and moan. By morning, she was better, but John was still very sick. In addition to his physical illness, he was feeling the psychological effects of the long-term live-in arrangement with its demands on me and my time. I was so busy trying to help everyone survive that I couldn't see what was happening.

As things went from bad to worse, Vera spent a lot of time at our house helping out. One day she looked at me and said, "Jane, Tina has to go. John is too sick. She is too sick. You have to put John first and take care of him." I said, "Where will she go? We're all she has. I can't do that to her." Tina had told me that in her whole life, whenever she had begun to feel happy or secure in a situation, someone had pulled the rug out from under her. She loved John and me and the kids, and I knew how much she needed us. Again Vera insisted, "Jane, this situation is out of control. Tina has to go. John cannot take this anymore."

Deep inside, I knew she was right. Later, I sat on the bedroom floor crying out, "Lord, what do I do? I can't do this. It will kill Tina. You're asking me to kill her! I can't!" I kept saying over and over to the Lord, "This will kill her. You're asking me to kill her!" Then I remembered the verses in the book of Genesis about Abraham offering up Isaac as a sacrifice to God. As I thought about that passage, I knew it was the Lord confirming that I had to ask Tina to move out. He was asking me to offer her up to Him as my Isaac, and as Abraham had done, I had to obey.

When I talked to John about asking Tina to leave, he started crying and said, "We can't do that to her." I told him I believed it was for the best. Eventually, he agreed. When I told Tina that our situation had to change and that she was going to have to start thinking about another living situation, her reaction was much worse than I had imagined. She began screaming, cursing, and throwing things. She zoomed off in her car.

I was in the kitchen boiling coffee on the stove for its usual ten minutes before using it in our detoxification ritual. Tina returned with boxes and began stuffing her possessions into them. I started crying. Tina was raving. Her grandmother, who was currently in town visiting Tina's aunt, had returned with Tina to help her pack. The whole traumatic situation entered the realm of the surreal when her grandmother, smelling the coffee in the kitchen, asked me if she could have a cup. I said, "I don't think you will want any because it has boiled," allowing her to conclude it was my mistake. I didn't have the courage to tell her the coffee's real purpose. I offered to make a new pot. She insisted on having a cup of the existing brew, indicating that she had never met a cup of coffee she didn't like. I reluctantly poured her a cup, knowing she was about to meet the first one, handed it to her, and watched as she raised it to her lips. She took a big sip, paused, looked up at me, smiled graciously, set it on the counter, turned, and walked rapidly down the hall. I don't know if she swallowed it or not, but I suspect that she made a stop by the bathroom on the way to Tina's room. Tina drove that day to Kansas City, where she moved back in with her family.

I sank into depression after Tina left. Why was the Christian life so hard? Why did things like this have to happen? Then after about three days, the phone rang. It was Tina. She was calm. She said, "Jane, I'm sorry." She then told me something had happened to her she couldn't really explain. She had picked up her guitar two days before, opened a Christian hymnal that was in the house, and started singing. She sang for two days. She could feel the Lord so very real and close. She said, "I understand what you have been saying about Jesus. For the first time in my life, I realize how wonderful He is." God had come to Tina, and she knew it. I started crying. God had given my Isaac back to me in resurrection, just as He had done with Abraham!

Jesus had put us together for our mutual benefit. Tina had gotten her first real view of Him, and I had gotten a renewed one. From that day, I knew I could and would gladly continue to follow and serve Him. I didn't have to understand all that had happened to me in the past in Houston. I had seen Him at work in another person's life, and He was beautiful.

About fifteen years have passed since that time. Tina is now married to a wonderful Christian man and has two children. She is a beautiful person. Her relationship with her parents, who are no longer part of the Local Church, has been fully restored. She has taken steps to clear up the long-term problem with her biological father. I am aware from occasional comments that she still struggles with church issues because of her experience with the Local Church, but the time she spent with us was a major turning point in her life.

Over a period of years, the Lord finished answering my prayer for all three girls in Tina's family. One of her sisters lived with us for a period of time. The other sister became like a member of our family, staying with us on weekends and taking trips with us. I loved all three of these girls like they were my own daughters.

He Needs a Jump Start

John's physical condition continued to deteriorate. One day, he called from work and said, "I cannot go on. I cannot work. I cannot think. I have to do something. I am coming home. I have to see a doctor." Because of the influence of a number of the brothers and sisters who believed the proper approach to health was found in health foods, vitamins, and various dietary supplements, we had come to believe that the standard medical approach should be used only as an absolute last resort.

We decided to see a chiropractor that had been recommended to us, one who apparently had helped a lot of people by using a more nutrition-oriented approach in addition to chiropractic. While waiting to see the chiropractor, John learned about a special diet from the doctor's assistant who also had hypoglycemia. She said the diet had done wonders for her. Both John and I were salivating as we listened to her because she ate good food and didn't drink weird juices or take coffee enemas.

When the doctor took us into his examination room, he put John on a big table and began walking around him and looking him over. He looked into John's eyes with some kind of instrument. He passed his hand around John's head. He told his assistant, who seemed to be in training, to do the same. As she began to do so, he quickly warned her, "Not too close; he will drain you." I thought, "What on earth is he saying?" His comment made me uncomfortable. He moved his hand over John's chest and said, "He needs a jump start. I will need to give him some of my energy." He stood over him, stared into his eyes, then turned to me and said, "He has congestion in his brain." I said, "What do you mean?" He said, "I can't use the words cancer or tumor in a diagnosis, so I am telling you there is a problem in his head. There is serious congestion there. The electrical flow from his head to his body is cut off." I said, "Are you saying he has a brain tumor?" He said, "I cannot use those terms." His comments were extremely upsetting. He began his treatment by thumping John all over his body with what looked like a miniature pogo stick. John was moaning periodically and staring at the ceiling.

Suddenly, the doctor turned and looked at me and said, "He has a physical problem, but his deeper problem is spiritual. I can help him, but only if you are open to me. If you aren't open to me, I cannot help him." At that moment, I knew intuitively that if I opened to this man's help, John would be healed. At the same time, I also knew that this was the devil asking me to open to him. I responded, "I realize that there is a spiritual world in which there are two sides. Which side are you on?" He said to me, "I am from the healing God." I paused, wondering what to say next and then asked, "Are you a Christian?" He said, "Yes." He continued working on John.

I was praying silently, "Lord, help me. What do we do?" The doctor turned and stared at me. He said, "I feel a real resistance from you. If you aren't open to me, I won't be able to help him." I said, "When did you become a Christian?" He said, "As a child, when I was about five." I said, "When you were five, you confessed your sins and asked Jesus to forgive you and cleanse you with His blood?" When I asked this, he became livid. He spoke adamantly, "I have always been a Christian!" I said, "No, no one has always been a Christian. To be a Christian, you must admit you are a sinner, be washed in the blood of the Lamb, and receive Christ as your Savior." He spoke forcefully, "If you think like that—sins, sinner—no one can help you!" He pumped the examination table down and stood John up saying, "You need to leave. I cannot help you. Pay my fee as you go!" We promptly exited that place, leaving a check for his $60 fee and thanking God we had been saved from a big temptation!

As we were leaving, John, who was feeling terrible, groggily said, "What was that?" I said, "It was the devil!" John said, "He said that I have a spiritual problem. I know how to deal with that." Driving home, I made up my mind that I was through with the whole approach to health that included things like weird, meatless diets, nauseating green drinks, and bizarre coffee enemas. When we got home, I opened the freezer and found one lonely package of frozen fish sitting there. I cooked it and some other "forbidden" food and prepared to eat. In the Bible, God told us to eat meat, and I was going to eat meat. John found me in the kitchen and said, "What are you doing?" I said, "I'm eating!" John paused a moment and then said, "Give me some of that!" Our diet trauma was over. John incorporated the food the assistant had told him about, and we were on our way to normal eating again.

Several days later, John came home to tell me he had experienced a spiritual breakthrough. From the time of our visit to the strange chiropractor, he had begun praying intensely. He remembered what the chiropractor had said about him having a spiritual problem, that the flow from his head to his body was blocked. He later told me, "I thought that maybe there was some truth to that, so I started praying loudly that I didn't want the flow from Christ, my Head, to be blocked from me, and I didn't want the flow from my own head to be blocked from the rest of my body. I confessed a lot of things and started feeling much better. I think I have been healed!" John's health improved significantly from that time forward.

God's Economy: The Pinnacle

Brother Lee's main message, the pinnacle of his ministry, was his teaching about God's economy. He continually spoke about the dispensing of the processed Triune God into us to produce the church and the New Jerusalem. He began using the term *divine dispensing* to communicate this concept. Eventually, we had a definition to memorize about God's economy. It went something like this: God's economy is the processed Triune God dispensing Himself into the chosen and redeemed tripartite man for the building of the church and the producing of the New Jerusalem, the mingling of God and man for eternity. To get a taste of his teaching and an explanation of God's economy, here is a quote from Brother Lee:

> God had a desire, a good pleasure, according to which He made a will. Based upon His will, God made a purpose. He then made a plan to administrate His purpose, and this plan is to dispense Himself into all His chosen people. This is the economy of God. It was a mystery because it was hidden. It was never made known to anyone until the time of the apostles. In Ephesians, 1 Corinthians, and 1 Timothy, Paul tells us that God has such an economy which was a mystery but now has been made known to all of us. Now we know this mystery. We know God's economy, and we are now enjoying His dispensing. The Triune God is dispensing Himself into us to be our life and to be our life supply. He is dispensing Himself into us as our food and our drink that we may live by Him. Is this not wonderful? This is much better than religion. We do not come together just to have a kind of religious worship service. But we gather together to enjoy the dispensing of the marvelous Triune God into our being. This is God's divine dispensing. God desires to dispense Himself. In the Lord's ministry

we only care for the divine dispensing of the Triune God Himself into His chosen people. (Lee, *Divine,* 10)

He repeatedly told us that the divine dispensing was the central teaching of the New Testament. This was what Paul received by revelation and taught. It was the apostles' teaching referred to in Acts 2:42. God had now also revealed this truth to Brother Lee, a truth that had been lost for centuries, so that it could be recovered. We came to believe that the Local Church was the only place where the central truth of the Bible was taught and practiced. This teaching became so dominant that we were taught that all we needed to care for was the divine dispensing. This would automatically produce the church and the New Jerusalem. To receive this dispensing, all we had to do was call on the Lord and pray-read the Bible.

Over the years, Witness Lee employed more and more complex terminology to explain God's economy. His terms and phraseology could be seen in large banners that were used in meetings and on wall plaques in members' homes:

The full ministry of Christ is carried out in three stages for the fulfillment of God's eternal economy.

In the first stage of incarnation to bring God into man, to express God in humanity, and to accomplish His judicial redemption.

In the second stage of inclusion to be begotten as God's firstborn Son, to become the life-giving Spirit, and to regenerate the believers for His Body.

In the third stage of intensification to intensify His organic salvation, to produce the overcomers, and to consummate the New Jerusalem.

NEW JERUSALEM, the greatest ultimate sign in the Scriptures, signifying an organic constitution of the processed triune God, mingled with His regenerated, transformed, and glorified tripartite elect.

I heard the phrase God's economy innumerable times while in the Local Church, and I believed the teaching. Yet, no matter how many times I heard it, I still had trouble verbalizing it or understanding how it was the central teaching of the New Testament. Many years later, God would show me what was seriously wrong with this teaching.

The Not-So-Local Local Church

Because the elders in the Local Churches now held Brother Lee's ministry in the place of highest regard, he had a strong influence over them and over the decisions they made. They were always eager to please him. Observing this behavior in the leading brothers, John and I began to consider that the Local Churches had reached the place that they truly were no longer locally governed entities.

The practices of the leading brothers had become very authoritarian. One evidence of this change was in our meetings. Unlike our earliest years in the church, the leading brothers now exercised strong control over the church meetings, to the extent that they corrected and adjusted participants if, in their opinion, they were getting off the track of Brother Lee's ministry. Whatever anyone said in a church meeting was subject to extreme scrutiny and had to pass a litany of tests to be acceptable.

A few years later, in the Church in Oklahoma City, a sheet of paper was distributed which contained a long list of requirements regulating how brothers and sisters could speak in a meeting. Speaking had to be "quick, short, real, and fresh," with no long stories or personal experiences, but only ministry restatements, and so forth. I couldn't believe the contents or the length of the list when I saw it.

The Not-So-Attainable Kingdom

The main elder in Oklahoma City, Jerry Hughes, was a very dominant personality. He fed us a steady diet of teachings about being overcomers. He used Jesus' parables of the five foolish virgins and the unprofitable servant in Matthew 25. Sometimes it seemed to me that he read no other verses in the Bible than these. I became so tired of hearing these teachings that I almost wished that Matthew 25 was not in the Bible. Once the term *overcomer* entered our church vocabulary, the bar was raised. We were constantly reminded of the need to be overcomers.

This was the big carrot held out before us to make sure we kept on track. We believed that overcoming included learning, supporting, and absolutely following Brother Lee's ministry.

One day John said to me, "Jane, I am not going to make it. Since I already know I am going to be in outer darkness for a thousand years, then why should I spend this lifetime struggling to be an overcomer? I might as well enjoy this life as much as I can." I said, "John, if this is the fruit of what we have been taught, then there is something seriously wrong with it!"

I have heard former Local Church members say that they gave up hope because they knew they would never be overcomers. It is interesting that the noun overcomer *does not occur anywhere in the Bible. The Bible only uses the verb* overcome. *Witness Lee introduced the word* overcomer. *To us, it eventually became a term that described a special class of believers.*

As for myself, I found a simple resolution to the problem of being fearful about not being an overcomer and being left behind during the great tribulation, or sentenced to outer darkness. I prayed, "Lord, I don't want to be left here during the great tribulation; but if You want me to be here, for whatever reason, that is all right with me. I am Yours to do with as You please."

I still do not know what I think about all of the kingdom teachings we heard. I don't know who will be where, or when, or why. All I do know is that I want to know Him more and be wherever He is, when He wants me to be there. I want to help others do the same. I also know that for this, I need His grace. The Bible teaches that because God as our Father loves us, He chastens us for our profit (Heb. 12:6-11). I accept this and am secure because of it. I do not fully understand this and many other things, but I am confident that whatever I should understand, He will teach me.

A Child's View

While living in Oklahoma, I continued to want my children to have a walk with the Lord that was their very own, just as I had from childhood. When they became teenagers, we never forced them to attend Local Church young people's conferences. I never made them call on the Lord or pray-read the Bible. I prayed that Jesus, as He had done with me, would visit them personally and make Himself real to them. When they wanted to stop going to meetings, we let them.

This was a blessing to our children, and I believe it spared them from some of the spiritual damage I have seen in other church member's children who were not allowed this freedom.

While we lived in Oklahoma City, I still spent very little, if any, relaxed time with the children. John, who really didn't like me working outside of our home, told me that if my household management started to slip, I would have to quit my job. I couldn't bear the thought of this. My job was my hiding place from the daily demands of the Local Church way of life. So to keep everything running smoothly, I continued in my familiar household captain's role with all my lists and schedules.

One day, Todd found me in one of my rare sitting-down moments in the living room. He came and sat in the chair across from me and said, "Mom, when I grow up, I want to fly airplanes, but that isn't something God will let me do, is it?" I said, "Why do you say that?" He said, "Because everything that is fun, God doesn't want us to do. I don't think God would like that. All He likes is the meetings. I don't really like them that much." I said, "Todd, if you want to fly airplanes, you don't know whether or not God will let you until you ask Him. I think He would let you if you really wanted to." He questioned me further, "Mom, when we are in the New Jerusalem, what will we do? Will we be in meetings all the time?" I felt sad listening to him. I thought about it, and then I said honestly, "I hope not." I paused after thinking about my response and said, "Actually, I don't think we will be in meetings. The Bible says that 'eye has not seen, nor ear heard, nor have entered into the heart of man the things which God has prepared for those who love him' (1 Cor. 2:9). We've already seen meetings!"

Todd graduated from the Air Force Academy about ten years later and became a pilot. God let him fly airplanes for a number of years afterwards. I was right about that, and I hope one day, I will find out I was also right about the rest of what I told him. His question that day gives some insight into a child's perception of the way of life in the Local Church.

Another Texas Casualty

Not long after we moved to Oklahoma, I received a phone call from Sue Wilson. Sue was the angel at my door in Houston who had helped me get a job in order to preserve my sanity. She was very upset and began to tell me about what was happening to her and her husband.

Sue and Bill had moved from Houston to Denver not long after we had moved to Oklahoma City. Their move to Denver had been precipitated by an unusual set of events that had transpired when they were still living in Houston. For most of those years in Houston, Bill was a painter until Guy Andrews hired him to help with his typesetting business (as I had done years before). Bill loved this new job, but when Brother Lee's new ministry center was built in Irving, the elders wanted Bill to move there to be one of the brothers responsible for the Living Stream Ministry's printing work. Bill took a short trip to Irving to see how he felt about moving. After the visit, he told Sam Jones he was going to stay in Houston. However, he soon found out that Guy had given away his job to another church member. Bill couldn't believe this. Guy said that he had understood that Bill was planning to move to Irving. Bill tried to reason with Guy, explaining to him that he had never committed to moving, that he had never given notice, and that he still wanted his job. Guy told him that it was too late.

Bill told me that he found out years later that Sam Jones, the elder who was trying to get Bill to move to Irving, had spoken to Guy and was responsible for having Bill replaced. Sam had done this to pressure Bill into moving to Irving.

Having lost his job, Bill was forced to start painting again. Because painting work was scarce in the depressed economy that existed at that time, it became necessary for Sue to start working for a temporary agency. This went on for months. Then one day, Bill received a call from two brothers in Denver who had moved there from Houston as part of an earlier church migration. They offered him several weeks of painting work. Bill had grown up with these brothers and had introduced them to the Local

Church. They were no longer, however, meeting with the Church in Denver because of a "rebellion" in the church there. They had been labeled as rebellious by the Church in Denver. Bill did not know that brothers and sisters in the Local Church had been forbidden to have contact with these departed "rebellious ones." He needed the income, so he accepted their job offer. After a period of time, Bill decided to move his family to Denver because of the quantity of work available there.

When Bill told Sam Jones he was moving to Denver, Sam displayed his unhappiness with what he was hearing by lowering his head and moving it slowly from side to side while, over and over, he hit one fist into the other palm and intoned, "M-m-m, O Lord, M-m-m, O Lord." This was Sam's signature way of showing his disapproval. Although this bothered Bill, he believed he was to obey God and not man, so he made the move to Denver.

Many years later, Bill told me that when they decided to move to Denver, they became outcasts in Houston. No one called or associated with them any longer except for a couple of brothers that Sam Jones sent to try to talk them out of moving. He said that those brothers could have been nominated for an Academy Award for their efforts.

Shortly after arriving in Denver, Bill was contacted by the elders of the Local Church there who told him that he could not come to church meetings unless he ended his relationship with the two "rebellious" brothers. Bill couldn't believe his ears. When he asked these elders to provide the scriptural basis for their requirement, they were not able to do so. The decision, however, had been made: No one in the church could associate with those who had been in the "rebellion." When Bill called back to Texas to seek Dan Williams' help, Dan told Bill that he had become leprous.

As Sue related this to me over the phone, my stomach knotted. I knew full well what she and her husband were experiencing. Sue said that as Bill had listened to Dan on the phone, tears began running down his face. Afterwards, when he repeated Dan's statements to her, he said, "Sam is behind this." He called Dan back and asked him for the source of his information. Dan refused to tell him. Bill said to Dan, "You don't have to tell me who talked to you, I know. Be warned that you have believed a lie." Bill also told Dan that whoever believes a lie is cursed. For a number of days after this, Bill tried to reach Sam, but Sam never returned his calls.

Bill also told me years later that before all of this transpired, he had such respect for Dan as a leading elder that he had believed Dan would surely listen to his plight and understand, or at least look into the truth of what had happened. "Instead," Bill told me, "Dan blasted me, saying things that I knew were based solely on lies." Not only was he hurt by what Dan said, he also felt disgust for Dan that he had believed a lie without investigating the matter himself to see if the allegations were true. Bill told me that he felt that all of these things revealed what was in the heart of Sam Jones. Also during this process, a brother from the Church in Denver named Greg lied to the elders and told them that he had heard the painters with whom Bill was working say bad things to Bill about the church. The painters, however, were not at all concerned about whether or not Bill went to Local Church meetings. They simply had seen their friend in need of work and had stretched out their hands to help him.

When Bill met for the last time with the Denver elders, he told them they did not have the proper standing as a Local Church because they were not open to receive all believers and were imposing an unscriptural requirement on him. When they would not change their position, Bill decided to stop meeting with the Local Church. As Sue related this to me on the phone, she became hysterical. She cried to me, "Jane, I can't believe this is happening. I never thought we would leave the Local Church. I am afraid. What can we do?" Because I was still under the elders' discipline and required not to talk about what we had been through, I just told her, "Sue, all I can say is just hang on to Jesus."

Years later, after leaving the Local Church, Greg, who was the tale-bearer in Denver, found Bill and confessed that his report to the elders was a lie. Greg asked for Bill's forgiveness. He said that he had invented the story because he wanted to keep Bill from leaving the church by keeping him away from the influence of the so-called rebellious brothers. Years later, the elders who had dealt with Bill in Denver also left the Local Church. They, too, then repented to Bill for what they had done to him and asked for his forgiveness.

Chapter 16
Walking Out the Door

> "I know your works. See, I have set before you an open door, and no one can shut it; for you have a little strength, have kept My word, and have not denied My name." (Rev. 3:8)

Why We Stayed So Long

IN 1987, TEN YEARS AFTER THE DISCIPLINE by the elders in Houston and twenty years after attending our first Local Church meeting, we were about to walk out of the Local Church.

Why did we stay so long? I think there were probably three reasons:

(1) Oneness was paramount. We believed division was an extremely serious sin against God and were very fearful of doing anything that might damage the oneness. The word absolute *was actually a measurement of oneness. We believed that God had placed us in the Local Church, so we needed to remain in oneness with those believers and quietly wait for God to correct anything that was wrong. Life wasn't a fairy tale, nor was the church. Part of the Christian life was the cross, which meant patience, longsuffering, and seeing things through to the end like Job did (Jas. 5:11).*

(2) Leaving was dangerous. We heard this in church meetings: "It would be better for you to have never seen the way of the Local Church than to come this way and leave it. If you leave the church, God is through with you." We were told stories of what had happened to people who left. In our early church years, one couple left the Church in Houston because the wife wanted to move back to her hometown. After about two months there, her husband, who worked on telephone lines, fell from a telephone pole to his death. We heard that this was because the wife had led her husband away from the church. I feared that if we left, we would risk something bad happening to John, the

children, or me.

(3) We had been indoctrinated that the Local Church was God's present move on the earth. It was God's best and was Christ's preparation for His second coming. If we left, there would be nowhere else to go.

It is noteworthy that all three of these reasons were based on fear.

Horrible Events

During our last ten years in the Local Church, some horrible things happened. In one instance, the son of a couple in the Church in Oklahoma City, who was married and was a member of the Church in Dallas, was found dead, hanging from a tree near a lake shore in a large park. The police investigation labeled his death a suicide. In another instance, a sister in the Church in Oklahoma City dropped her children off at another church member's home and then went back home and committed suicide by hanging herself in her kitchen. Her husband found her when he came home from work.

Looking back, it is clear to me now that she needed psychological help. The church, however, didn't believe in this kind of help and, to my knowledge, never offered it to her or encouraged her to seek it elsewhere. We all knew she had psychological problems, but the church's basic answer for every problem was just to call on the Lord. This was one of the striking things about her: she was always continually softly repeating "O Lord Jesus."

The elders quickly hushed these incidents because they reflected poorly on the reputation of the church. I don't know what significance, if any, these events had in the spiritual realm, but it was plain to me that we were not under the Lord's blessing as we had been in our early years.

The New Way

In 1984, we were promised great blessing through the latest and greatest flow—the flow to end all flows—the

Chapter 16—Walking Out the Door

"New Way." This flow began when Brother Lee returned to Taiwan to start a global ministry center and to set up a model for all the Local Churches worldwide. Many individuals and families from the United States moved to Taiwan to help construct the new ministry center. Brother Lee's new vision included a training center where young people could go for two years after graduating from college to be trained in his teachings and become full-time workers. Everyone was encouraged to become either a full-time worker (whom we subsequently called "full-timers") or a full-time money-maker to help support the full-timers. The leading brothers admonished all members to give an extra five percent of their income to the Living Stream Ministry each month, in addition to their regular tithes and offerings, in order to finance this New Way.

In the early years, we never talked about money except to say that we didn't and wouldn't talk about it. There was a slot in the wall of our meeting hall into which we could put our offerings. That was it. By the end of my years in the church, money had become a frequent meeting topic.

As part of the New Way, we started meeting in small groups in our homes during the week. Once a week on Sunday mornings, the whole church came together at the meeting hall. John and I were excited about the home meetings because this was reminiscent of our earliest years in the church. After a number of weeks, reports reached the leading brothers that the small groups were too free and informal; in other words, not focused enough on Brother Lee's ministry. They began reorganizing the various small meetings, trying to place some dependable, absolute members in each home meeting so they could keep the meetings on track with the ministry. When this was unsuccessful, they stopped the small meetings. John and I were really discouraged by this, since the regular church meetings had become dominated by the New Way to the exclusion of everything else. What had happened to Jesus being the Lord of our church meetings? The elders seemed to have usurped that role.

We were pushed to participate in a "door-knocking" campaign, another part of the New Way, to reach our neighbors with the gospel of Christ and bring them into the

Local Church. We were told to go out door-to-door in pairs and to use a pre-defined method, which included how long to stay at each house, exactly what to say, and how to assess the response. If someone accepted the Lord, we were expected to immediately baptize the person in their bathtub. John told me he wasn't going to do any of this. I was glad because I didn't want to do it either. One day after a church meeting, I was accosted by some zealous brothers and sisters and asked with whom I intended to go door-knocking. When I told them I intended to go home with John, they became very judgmental and came close to rebuking me before I escaped.

Also, as part of the new flow, we were encouraged strongly to volunteer for weekend work in the Living Stream Ministry center in Irving. I think John did this once. I never did, being unwilling to have contact with people like Dan Williams and Sam Jones.

Actually, John and I were in serious need of a break from the whole church scene with all the New Way jargon and Living Stream Ministry promotion. We also needed a break from our busy life and work schedules. We needed, dare I say it—a vacation!

Attempted Vacations

During the great majority of our years in the Local Church, we never took a real vacation. We made a few attempts at having a vacation, but always felt guilty about them. At the time we made our final drive moving from Houston to Oklahoma City, we stopped at Turner Falls park with the boys and camped overnight. We took the boys swimming and hiking. Before we left the campsite the next day, I became violently ill with diarrhea. I was so sick that I had to lie in the back of the car for the rest of the trip. John developed the same problem when we got home. We were sick like this for almost seven days before we decided we had to see a doctor. He gave us medicine that immediately solved our problem. I secretly wondered if our sickness was God's judgment on us for our little vacation.

The boys, however, loved camping and wanted to go again, so a few years later, we made another attempt to have a vacation. We decided to take them to Broken Bow State Park in southern Oklahoma for a three-day weekend. They were excited for weeks before we went, making plans and packing their own camping gear. We were planning on just sneaking out of town without telling any of the brothers and sisters where we were going. Then, two days before we were supposed to leave, the leading brothers announced a conference for the coming weekend, which everyone needed to attend. I was sick to my stomach as John told me he was thinking about canceling our trip. Then on the day of vacation departure, John decided we weren't going. He didn't want to have to explain to any brothers why he had missed the conference. The boys cried. I cried and argued with John, telling him it was wrong to do this to the boys. Finally, I prevailed. John angrily piled all of us with our swollen red faces into the car and headed off. He was angry, and I was upset for most of the drive. The boys had a good time in spite of the pre-departure family trauma.

After this, the boys periodically begged us to go camping again. So we planned a real vacation to Colorado! We took them camping and hiking for a week. We told the brothers and sisters that we were visiting the Church in Denver, which we actually did on one of our days. That was our cover story for the vacation.

A Friend on the Outside

During this period of time, as we were becoming more and more concerned about the condition of the church, the Lord gave me a Christian friend who wasn't in the Local Church. I met Emily at jury duty. She had a very joyful heart and a fresh, radiant love for Jesus. She had a beautiful family and was just a very normal person. Whenever I was at her house, I had to struggle to keep from watching the television playing in the background. (It sat in the middle of her den and didn't bother her. Ours was in the closet and was always calling me!) I was so starved for information and entertainment that I was simply fascinated by TV. We weren't supposed to watch it because it was worldly and of the devil. Emily, on the other hand, was oblivious to the television because it held no real attraction for her. She didn't have a rule that she couldn't watch it; she just wasn't interested. How jealous I was of her simplicity! The Christian life to her was not complicated. She wasn't carrying around all the baggage that I was. She was very simple and very happy. I told the Lord how envious I was of her, and wondered if I could ever be like that. Was there any way to unload the heavy cargo of practices and beliefs I had accumulated for so many years? Was it okay for me even to try?

Emily was impressed by my knowledge of the Bible and kept asking me about the Local Church because she wanted to visit it. I avoided her questions because I didn't want her to come. One Sunday morning when I entered the meeting hall, I saw Emily and her family. She had met another Local Church member and had secured an invitation to a meeting. I wanted to run out screaming. Afterwards, she asked me three questions: (1) Why do all the men sit on one side of the room and all the women on the other? (2) Why don't any of the women wear make-up? (3) Who is Brother Lee, and is he the only person your church follows? Good questions. I was glad Emily and her family never came again.

The Final Straw for John

The simple Christian meetings that we had at the beginning of our Local Church experience, in which the Holy Spirit was free to guide our fellowship, were basically a thing of the past. The *ministry* focus had brought things to the point that testimonies of personal experiences with God were openly discouraged in meetings unless those testimonies clearly reinforced points in Brother Lee's messages. There was no need for an individual to receive revelation from the Bible because Brother Lee had all the revelation. In fact, individual light was discouraged and considered as unreliable. In effect, we were no longer allowed to testify freely as we had done in our earlier years in the Local Church.

I was concerned about the situation in the church, but I was more concerned about John's response to it. He was becoming more vocal with me about his unhappiness with the Local Church. I felt the same as he did, but I continued to believe, as I had done for the previous ten years, that we were in God's will for our life. I thought that we just needed to trust the Lord and wait on Him to correct things that were off track. It wasn't long, however, before the final straw came for John. Throughout everything, he had clung to the only remaining church meeting that he still really enjoyed—the Sunday evening Lord's Table. It was the only remaining church meeting that didn't have the focus on the New Way and the Living Stream Ministry.

John really enjoyed this particular church meeting because after we took the bread and wine, time was set aside in which members were allowed to speak freely and give testimonies about their personal spiritual experiences. This gave us a special time of church family interaction, in which our speaking to each other didn't have to be about Brother Lee's ministry.

Then in a church meeting, an elder announced that the time currently being used for such testimonies after the Lord's Table meeting was going to be cut short in all future Lord's Table meetings in order to add an additional Life-Study teaching meeting. He said that this was necessary because there was too much revelation being released by Brother Lee, "God's oracle," to be covered adequately in the other church meetings.

Some had begun by this time to refer to Brother Lee as God's oracle, which meant something like "God's unique spokesman on the earth."

He further emphasized that the time left for testimonies would have to be really short. After the next Lord's Table meeting, as the teaching began, John got up and walked out. I followed him out the door. All eyes followed us. You just didn't get up and walk out of church meetings.

The bottom line was this: John had had it. He said to me, "The Spirit departed a long time ago, and now I am leaving too." I begged him not to talk like that, expecting a bolt of lightning. He told me I was free to continue attending Local Church meetings, but he just couldn't continue. He said, "I just want to have a normal family. After twenty years of church meetings almost every night, I want to come home, sit down, take off my shoes, and rest.

I want to watch some TV. I want to get to know my kids and you. I just want a normal family life."

After our talk about leaving the church, John went to bed. I lay on the couch in the living room, crying. What was our life coming to? We had given twenty years to the Local Church. Now, were we supposed to just walk away? As I lay there, I prayed, "Lord, what is happening? What am I to do? What do You want me to do?" I never wanted to be what I considered a "church widow" (a sister whose husband had stopped going to the meetings). Somehow I knew our marriage would have great difficulty surviving if I remained in the Local Church without him. I would be under the constant indoctrination of the church meetings and would look at him through those eyes. We had enough marital difficulties already without that further complication. As I prayed, I heard the Lord's voice in my heart, "You are to do whatever John does." Once again, the Lord was telling me to go along with John. I was instantly calmed by this thought and slept peacefully that night. John and I never attended another Local Church meeting. Whenever I let myself question my decision, I would lose my inner peace until I retorted, "No, I followed my husband."

Why was it so hard for me to let go? It seems I should have been more than ready to depart. In addition to the reasons given earlier in this chapter, there was another big reason. I never gave up believing it was only a matter of time before God was going to turn the Local Church ship around and correct things. I also believed that the current problems were a result of the leading brothers misapplying Witness Lee's ministry. Because I had learned so much from him about the Bible, I believed there was no wrong on his part—he was just misunderstood and was being misrepresented by the practices that the leading brothers implemented among us.

After missing us at several church meetings, Vera Hughes, the green-drink sister, called me to ask if we were okay. I informed her that we weren't coming to any more church meetings. She was shocked. I explained both John's decision and what the Lord had told me. She asked if I wanted her to keep me abreast of things in the church. I told her no.

The next day, I received a call from one of the elders. Apparently, Vera had told him about our decision. He said, "Jane, just because John wants to leave doesn't mean you need to do the same thing." I told him that the Lord had told me to do whatever John did. He said, "You may be making a big mistake." I answered, "Well, I have made big mistakes before, so it won't be the first time. If it is a mistake, I will just have to find out the hard way."

The comments of this elder reveal the errant belief of the Local Church leaders that loyalty to the church should be given precedence over a marriage relationship! If I had taken his advice, I have no doubt that our marriage would have suffered greatly and might not have survived, especially since this was the case in numerous other marriages in which one spouse remained a member and the other did not.

We Were Out, Now What?

One day, I was in my backyard planting flowers when I prayed, "Lord, what are we going to do now?" The response I heard in my heart was part of 1st Corinthians 13, "If I speak with the tongues of men and of angels and have not love, I am become as sounding brass, or a tinkling cymbal." Then I heard, "Go and learn to love your family. Learn how to love John and Todd and Matt." I started to cry. He convicted me of how miserably I had failed in that area. John and the children had always taken second place to the church. This had remained true, even after I had gotten into trouble in Houston, because we had continued to put the church meetings before everything and everyone else. My family's place of importance had been less than that of the church or of someone like Tina who lived with us, and they knew it. My time hadn't been for them. Nothing in their lives had ever been given priority over my misdirected spiritual endeavors. "Lord, help me learn to love my family."

How dysfunctional our family life was! Neither John nor I had ever seen a Christian family model. We were two love-starved individuals who had been emotionally neglected when we were children. Our resultant weaknesses had made us strong candidates for the kind of warm acceptance initially offered by the Local Church. When it evolved into an extremely aberrational Christian church with unscriptural practices regarding human relationships, we became even more dysfunctional.

John and I had tried to make some improvement in our marriage relationship after moving to Mobud in Houston, but our still too busy church schedules had frustrated us from making much progress. Then for years after I got in trouble, we weren't working on our marriage; instead, we were working on keeping our sanity. After we left the Local Church, our long-term marital difficulties surfaced and our personal conflicts escalated. This difficulty was compounded for me by ever-lurking feelings of guilt and frequent bouts of condemnation over having left "God's best." God had a lot of work to do in us.

We soon discovered that we did not know how to live in the world outside the Local Church. To put it simply: we were misfits. The only people we knew were Local Church people. We never cultivated any relationships outside of the Local Church. We also had neglected our relatives. On top of this, for twenty years, we had developed a lifestyle that existed in an environment of no's. In the Local Churches in which we participated there was:

- No recreation
- No vacations
- No holidays, especially Christmas or Easter
- No birthdays
- No friends
- No close relationships with relatives
- No outside community involvement
- No dating
- No marrying of Local church to non-Local Church people
- No formal weddings
- No pants or shorts for women
- No brightly colored clothing, especially red
- No stylish shoes or clothing
- No sandals or open-toed shoes
- No makeup

- No jewelry, especially earrings
- No nail polish
- No shopping (to shop was to "go into hell")
- No worldly home decorations
- No newspapers or magazines
- No books for light reading
- No ministries other than Brother Lee (or some Watchman Nee)
- No TVs
- No movies
- No swimming
- No expensive cars or homes
- No pets (especially indoors)

There was no written manifesto or credo dictating all these prohibitions. Rather, these behaviors came from illustrations and examples used in teachings and from observing the behavior of those we respected. These were reinforced by the practices of the Local Church deputy authorities in their interactions with members and also misapplied to us by the powers of darkness. The result was that we were practicing asceticism. The book of Colossians makes very clear what we were doing by living in an environment of no's:

> Since you died with Christ to the basic principles of this world, why, as though you still belonged to it, do you submit to its rules: "Do not handle! Do not taste! Do not touch!" These are all destined to perish with use, because they are based on human commands and teachings. Such regulations indeed have an appearance of wisdom, with their self-imposed worship, their false humility and their harsh treatment of the body, but they lack any value in restraining sensual indulgence. (Col. 2:20-23, NIV)

After leaving the Local Church, we made some specific lifestyle changes. For family recreation, we all started playing tennis. I lived in constant fear, however, that someone from the church would see us and report back how far we had fallen—I was actually wearing shorts (long ones) in public. I did have a near miss one day, but I managed to get out of sight before I was spotted. Looking back now, I find my behavior ridiculous. I also went shopping and bought clothes for myself other than the standard blue jean skirt and blouse outfits that were the mainstay of accepted Local Church fashion. I bought some badly needed furniture so that I might be able someday to have guests in my home without embarrassment, that is, if we ever had anyone to invite! We even took a real vacation.

There was also another category of no's:
- *No freedom of expression*
- *No acceptance or appreciation of individuality*
- *No place for questioning or thinking critically*
- *No tolerance for teachings other than those of Witness Lee*
- *No place for Christians who believed differently*
- *No regard for people's feelings, especially those of women*

A number of years after we had left the church, I said to John once, "You know, the Local Church was like a men's club!" He laughed. I responded, "No, I am serious. Think about it. Everything there was for men. Men didn't have to help with household responsibilities. They didn't have to spend time with their children. They had wives who didn't go shopping and didn't spend their money on clothes or make-up or jewelry. They didn't have to celebrate holidays or purchase gifts. They didn't have to put up with home décor issues because only the basics were acceptable. Keeping secrets about church matters from their wives was expected. They met with each other all the time to take care of church business matters. The wives had to prepare good meals every day, work at home to keep a well-run house, and take care of children. This exactly fits most men's natural tendencies and desires. What was there that fit a woman's natural tendencies and desires in the Local Church? Nothing." I don't think John really understood my viewpoint or assessment of the situation, but then, he saw it through male eyes.

To Stone Creek

After we stopped going to the meetings of the Church in Oklahoma City, it became wearisome trying to avoid Local Church members, whether in our neighborhood or in the grocery store, so we decided to move to another part of the city. We wanted to make a break from the past and start anew. For a few months, we looked at houses and tried to figure out how we could afford a move with interest rates that were rising. Finally, we realized we had been getting ahead of the Lord and stopped our house search, deciding to trust the Lord to lead us in His time.

Shortly after this, in answer to John's prayer for a job change, he was offered the possibility of a job transfer to Dallas. I had told him before this that I never wanted to live in Texas again, especially not Dallas, because it was near Irving and the Living Stream Ministry center. But on that day, the prospect of moving to Dallas sounded exciting. He was surprised at my reaction and so was I. Todd was away at college, so a move would not have that much impact on him. We decided to let Matt make the final decision because he was about to be a junior in high school and had just made it onto the tennis team. We weren't going to make him move against his will. After we asked him what he thought, he considered it for several minutes and then said, "I want to go. There are better tennis programs in Texas. Let's do it."

Once again, ten years to the month, we were moving. We left Denton in August of 1969; we left Houston in August of 1979; now in August of 1989, we were leaving Oklahoma City. We bought a home north of Dallas in a suburb named Plano. The Lord took care of every detail of the move. Before this one, our moves (there were thirteen to date) had always been the U-Haul variety. This time, John's company paid for professional packing and moving. God provided immeasurably more for us than we ever could have done by ourselves, considering we had been almost willing to settle for just moving across town in Oklahoma City. John's company even compensated for the interest rate and cost of living differences. Our new street was named Stone Creek.

I still love the name of this street. It has significance to me because our home on Stone Creek turned out to be a place where Jesus, like new, fresh, living water (creek), came to wash and heal and make "living" again two tired, battle-worn Christian stones named John and Jane, as well as many other of the Lord's similarly tired and wounded believers!

The Job from God

Even my job went with me to Stone Creek. In Oklahoma City, I had worked out of my home for the last few years there because most of my work was done via computer modem with the corporate office on the east coast. Because of this, my job easily transferred with me when we moved. As God promised to do when I quit college, He faithfully provided a job for me when I needed to work, and the job God provided wasn't just any job, it was extraordinary.

How did I end up with my extraordinary job? When we were living in Houston, and Sue Wilson sent me to the temporary agency to apply for part-time work, I was very nervous. As she had advised me before my typing test, I glued my eyes on the material to be typed and never looked up at the typewriter. When I reached up to take my test out of the carriage, I saw there was no paper in the typewriter! I wanted to crawl out of a window. Instead, I had to walk across a room full of people to a counter, behind which sat a secretary who was looking down and writing something. I leaned over and said, "Excuse me." She continued to look down and simply reached her hand up and said, "Give me your test." I said, "Well, you see, I have a little problem. My test is on the carriage of the typewriter." I had to explain as everyone in the room listened. I was so embarrassed. She said, "Well, I've heard a lot of things, but this one takes the cake!" She sent me back in the room to retake the test. Incredibly, they still sent me on a job.

When we moved to Oklahoma the following year, the Lord gave me a job with an accounting firm that I would have for the next twenty-five years. After working as a typist, I worked a few years as a word processing supervisor. Then I became bored and started a self-study program to learn computer programming. Later, it occurred to me that I had never prayed about my new course of action. I said to the Lord, "I don't want to talk to You about this because I am afraid You will stop me. I want to do this." But this prayer was contact with Him, and it gave Him the opportunity to speak to my heart: "Didn't I provide the job you now have, as I promised, without your effort? Won't you trust Me to provide any job change you need?" I decided to drop the self-study program. This was hard because I wanted to learn computer programming; but I obeyed as I considered how many times before this I had listened to God regarding practical matters, and things had turned out for the best. I belonged to Him, so I obeyed.

After obeying, I was happy again at work and no longer bored. What a wonder it was when, about two weeks later, the partner-in-charge in the office offered me an opportunity to spend some of my time programming for the company's New York headquarters through my office in Oklahoma City. He also doubled my pay! After a period of time and other opportunities, this pay was tripled. I ended up being trained by my company as a computer programmer and given many opportunities. With each opportunity, my hourly rate also dramatically improved.

One day while still working in Oklahoma City, Andy, one of the firm's partners, who often had befriended me, came by my office to tell me that he had just left a meeting in which the new partner-in-charge, Barry, had announced his intention to find a way to get rid of me. He did not like the amount of money I was being paid. Andy said he shouldn't be telling me this, but he wanted to give me some warning in advance. I surprised both myself and him when I responded, "Andy, as long as God wants me to have this job, I will be here. When He doesn't, I won't." Andy looked surprised and then shook his head and laughed, "Okay, I just wanted to give you a heads-up."

Barry was not able to get rid of me. Rather, a few years later, the company got rid of him. About fifteen years after my statement to Andy, I had occasion to see him again. He had his own accounting firm by then. He was amazed to find out that I was still working for the same company. He shook his head and laughed, as I said something to this effect: "I guess God still wants me there."

Ultimately, I wrote and then updated and supported for twenty years an electronic conference registration system that was used in the firm's headquarters and seventy field offices. Most importantly, I was able to do all of the work on a part-time basis, so I could take care of my children. I worked entirely out of my home for fifteen of those years. By the end of that career, my hourly pay was fifteen times what my initial hourly pay had been.

One day my older son, Todd, said to me, "Mom, do you realize that you have had a job most people would die for?"

What a joy and blessing that job was, and what a testimony to God's faithfulness, not only in keeping His promises to us, but in doing "above all that we ask or think" (Eph. 3:20). He opened all the doors for this job and did so in a way far beyond anything I ever expected. When I surrendered my education to Him, He promised to provide me with a job if I needed one. He more than kept His promise, giving me an occupation that I dearly loved— one that didn't even exist as an option when I was in college. God's postponement of my education was a part of His wonderful plan for my life. When I surrendered my own attempt to learn computer programming, He later fulfilled that desire in an amazing way. How grateful I am for all these experiences of His love and faithfulness!

Part 4

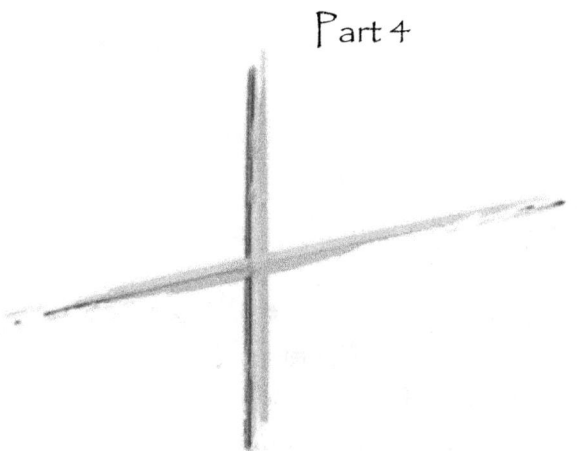

God's Masterpiece

His Purpose, the Cross, and Me

Judge not the Lord by feeble sense,
But trust Him for His grace,
Behind a frowning providence,
He hides a smiling face.

His purposes will ripen fast,
Unfolding every hour,
The bud may have a bitter taste,
But sweet will be the flower.

Blind unbelief is sure to err
And scan his work in vain,
God is his own interpreter
And He will make it plain.

— William Cowper

Chapter 17
The Withdrawn Hand of Fellowship

> Agree with your adversary quickly, while you are on the way with him, lest your adversary deliver you to the judge, the judge hand you over to the officer, and you be thrown into prison. (Matt. 5:25)

A "Rebel" Reunion

During our first year in Plano, I received a call from Lanell Allen. I was surprised by her call because I hadn't talked to her in years and thought that she was still meeting with the Local Church. Her call made me uncomfortable, so I was very non-communicative and quickly got off the phone. I answered a few of her questions and left her with a pretty good indication I wasn't interested in her calling again.

Little did I know that the Lord was preparing Lanell as a wonderful friend for the coming years. I am thankful that she didn't write me off after the way I responded to her call.

Not long after this, Lanell told Sandra Brown (one of the three "rebellious" sisters dealt with in Texas in 1977) that John and I were living in Plano and were no longer in the Local Church. Sandra, the wife of an elder, was still in the Local Church and was very miserable in her marriage. When she confided in Lanell about her marriage difficulties, Lanell encouraged Sandra to call me. Thus it came about that Sandra and I reconnected. She was now living in Fort Worth. We met for dinner at a restaurant and had a very long visit. It turned out to be something like a "rebel" reunion because for the first time in thirteen years, we talked about what had happened to both of us in 1977. We tried to put together the pieces of what we had experienced. I told her what had happened to me in Houston, and she told me what had happened to her in Austin.

First, Stephen Thompson had spoken in a public meeting about the sisters' rebellion, just as Dan Williams had done in Houston. Next, she was further reprimanded in an after-the-meeting meeting with other elders present. Her husband, Bob, who was an elder, had been in that meeting, and he just sat and watched. She was very intimidated by Stephen Thompson, whom she felt could match the best attorney in Texas. She was overwhelmed by all of Stephen Thompson's pronouncements and the judgment that had been made publicly. At the beginning of the after-the-meeting meeting, Stephen asked Sandra if she had anything to say. She told me that she had thought, "What can I say that would make any difference?" So she had answered, "No." Stephen then told her that her talk with others had been extremely divisive and that all such talk should stop. He said that sisters could not be trusted to know their spirit, and that they did not have any discernment. He named several sisters that she was not to have any further contact with, including me. He also forbade her to come to the Lord's Table meeting for a number of weeks.

I was shocked when I heard this. That was a very serious pronouncement and one that I had not experienced in Houston. I could only imagine how terrible that had been for her. She was visibly upset as she repeated this horrible story to me. She continued by telling me that she had left that meeting alone, devastated by the experience. She drove for awhile on a dark country road, confused and weeping. Eventually, she went home and lay down on the floor between the bed and the wall in an upstairs bedroom, where she wept much of the night. After that night, Bob never tried to console her nor did he seek to understand her situation or talk to her at all about it.

I will be eternally grateful to my dear husband, John, and will never forget that in heart and mind he stood with me one hundred percent in my ordeal in Houston. Not only did he not abandon me, he did not allow the leading brothers in the church to come between us as a couple, not even one iota. He did so at a great personal loss to himself.

Sandra later learned that, prior to her disciplinary meeting, the elders had gathered information by privately talking with persons whom they determined had been affected by the "rebellion." However, they never gave Sandra the opportunity in a non-intimidating environment to speak for herself. She was not given any specific information regarding what they considered to be her "rebellious" activities.

Shortly after the disciplinary meeting by the elders, she was sent to Houston to receive further help from Anne Andrews. Anne pointed out to Sandra that her problem was that she was too individualistic. She then instructed Sandra to burn her Darby translation of the Bible. Her use of this Bible, rather than the *King James Version* that others used, was a sign of her individualism. Anne also told her to burn her book about Madame Guyon because this book had fueled Sandra's desire to be a "spiritual giant." Anne also led her to believe that other parties involved in the sisters' rebellion, including me, had already "seen the light." Sandra, in turn, allowed Anne to believe that she was submitting to Anne's correction. From that time forward, Sandra had tried to appear as if she had been reformed; but in reality, she had not changed her thinking at all. As I had done, she had withdrawn from church activities as much as possible. She never did burn her Madame Guyon book or her Darby Bible.

We were surprised at what each of us had been told about the other. We each had been led to believe that the other had repented and was doing well when, instead, we both had been very confused, very hurt, and weren't doing well at all.

After her discipline by the elders, she had escaped some of her daily pain by going back to school to study Spanish thinking she might be able to help in the future with Living Stream Ministry translation. After finishing her studies, she went to the Living Stream Ministry office in Irving and offered to serve. She was sent to the Spanish translation area and began to do some work. Then Sam Jones appeared. When he saw her there, he approached her and asked her what she thought she was doing there. He told her she could not just walk in and serve anywhere she wanted. He sent her out to another area. She told me that she walked from that room straight to her car and never returned. This was not the first time Sam Jones had mistreated her. He knew what she had been through, but instead of welcoming her, he rejected her.

We ended our time together with her telling me about her very unhappy marriage and church experience. It was much worse than I could have imagined. I was very concerned for her as I listened to her, realizing that she was desperately trying to find a way out of both her marriage and the Local Church.

What Did You Do to Steve?

Not long after my talk with Sandra, John and I had occasion to return to Oklahoma City to attend the funeral of a sister who had remained loyal to the Local Church almost up to the time of her death. Her husband had left the church years before. Their marriage had suffered immensely as a result of the church issue. John and I had become good friends with the husband after we left the Local Church. We attended the funeral in spite of the fact that we would see a number of Local Church people there.

One morning during our time there, we went to breakfast with Howard Mays. Howard, an elder, was still hanging on in the Local Church but was struggling with some issues, questioning things, and starting to get into trouble. At breakfast that morning he asked, "Jane, would you mind telling me exactly what it was that you did to Steve Smith in Houston in 1977?" Surprised by his question, I asked him what made him think I had done something to Steve. He told me that in the late 1970's, Dan Williams had told him and a group of other elders that I had ruined Steve's function as an elder. I replied that I did not know for sure what Dan thought I had done to Steve. I told him that when Dan Williams was reprimanding me in 1977, he had said to me, "... and the shameful downfall you caused to one of us." I explained that I had speculated at that time that Dan was referring to Steve breaking down and weeping during a time of fellowship in the Andrews' home. Howard found it hard to believe that this was what Dan could have meant, thinking it must have been something much more serious. I assured him I was aware of nothing else it could have been.

Chapter 17—The Withdrawn Hand of Fellowship

My visit with Sandra and the question by Howard were harbingers of things to come. God was about to bring us into contact with the Local Church elders once again. Before He could do this, though, he had to unshackle me.

My Chains Fall Off

Living in Plano, I was spending my time decorating the house, working in the yard, working on my job from my home office, and trying to forget the painful church past. I was neither praying nor reading the Bible, nor was I interacting with the Lord at all. I still loved Him and knew He loved me, but that was as far as it went. I remember praying twice during that period of time. Each time my prayer was essentially, "Lord, I don't want to pray. I am afraid You might tell me to go back there. I am happy to be away from the Local Church, and I don't ever want to go back. Let's talk later."

One day while cleaning the house, I noticed a small stack of documents and booklets on John's desk. They had been mailed to us several months before by someone who had left the Local Church.

By this time, another "rebellion" was taking place in the Local Church, and some well known leaders had been "quarantined." In other words, they had been labeled and excommunicated. Apparently, Witness Lee felt the word "quarantined" was a more palatable term which accomplished the same objective.

John had read these documents and had tried several times to get me to read them. I had emphatically refused. On this day, when I saw the materials sitting on John's desk, I stood and looked at them for a few moments. Then I picked them up and went outside and sat down in my backyard. I prayed something to this effect: "Lord, I am going to read these now. Please take care of me while I do. I'm afraid of reading negative things."

As I read, the Lord began shining his light and opening my understanding. By the time I finished reading, He had graciously visited me and released me inwardly from the chains that had shackled me since having left the Local

Church three years before. Truth came that day and set me free (John 8:32).

According to one of the articles, it had taken the Lord almost fifteen hundred years to find someone who would stand for the truth of the Bible (Martin Luther) in the face of the error and spiritual darkness in the Catholic church of that day. Why had no one else been willing to do so? The author proposed that it was because of a tremendous fear of dividing the one true church. I knew this same fear was also my problem. I was so deeply convinced that the church and its oneness were of the topmost importance to God, that I had remained paralyzed by the possibility of offending God as a divisive or negative person, even when we were no longer a part of the Local Church! I was also afraid of offending Him by participating in any other church.

That day in my backyard, it became crystal clear to me that any oneness not based on the truth of the Bible wasn't oneness at all. Light began pouring into my thinking. I was free! It seemed like large black clouds had rolled away and light had begun pouring down on me from the clear sky above.

As I sat there in amazement at what had just happened, all of a sudden, Steve Smith's name came to mind, and I began to pray for him. (Steve was the elder in Houston who had been interested in taking care of church marriages and families.) I had not thought of him in years, except for when Howard Mays had asked what I had done to Steve to ruin his eldership. Prior to Howard's question, the last time I had thought of Steve was when we were still in the Church in Oklahoma City, and we heard a rumor that Steve had left the Church in Irving and moved to Tyler, Texas. This event was not discussed openly, so I really didn't know what had happened to him. When I finished praying for him, I considered how unusual it was that God had brought him to mind. I hadn't prayed for anyone that I could remember in almost three years. Maybe this meant Steve was in serious need.

Sitting there looking up at the sky that day, I heard the Lord telling me that I was in His perfect will and plan for my life. All of its steps were part of His plan for me. I knew without a doubt that everything, including leaving the

Local Church and moving to Plano, had been arranged by Him. We were in Plano because He had put us here. We weren't here by accident. I wasn't a spiritual basket case, as it had seemed, just set aside to pass the rest of my days on the earth in a spiritual retirement home!

You can imagine my amazement when the phone rang the very next morning after my backyard deliverance and Steve Smith was on the other end of the line. He confided in me his plan to divorce his wife of almost thirty years as soon as his son graduated from college the next year. It was difficult to believe what I was hearing. His loose, improper, and offensive speaking showed me he was in bad shape spiritually. This didn't sound like the same Steve Smith we had known in Houston. I chose to overlook the offensive details he revealed, focusing instead on his apparent cry for help. The fact that the Lord had surprisingly put it on my heart to pray for him the day before weighed heavily on my mind as he talked. When he asked to meet me for lunch to talk further, I responded that John and I would be glad to get together with him and told him to let us know when.

Back to the Bible

In the days that followed, I started to read the Bible again.

The Living Stream Ministry had published its own translation of the New Testament replete with very long and detailed footnotes that contained Witness Lee's teachings. We used this Bible exclusively in our Local Church meetings. I found it very difficult simply to read this Bible and allow the Lord to speak to me through His own words because the footnotes would always catch my attention. Witness Lee's teachings had become like a veil over my heart. Everything I read in the Bible came through the filter of those teachings. They consistently colored and shadowed the meaning of the Bible's words.

In my backyard that day, God removed the Local Church veil. He wanted me to read the actual words of the Bible and let them speak for themselves without any kind of overlay from another man's teachings and interpretations! With Him, I could discover for myself the truths in it. I put away my *Recovery Version* of the Bible and began reading the *King James Version* again, enjoying every word of it! I was even able to read the book of Ephesians without a Local Church veil over my heart! From that day, by speaking to me directly though His Word, God began helping me clear up many unresolved matters long buried in my heart and mind.

Until the day of my backyard experience, I had avoided being around other people, especially Christians. But that day, my fear of being negative or offending God by fellowshipping with other Christians left. I knew I was free! I knew I could follow the Lord without fear. In one of the first passages I read, I started rejoicing with the father of John the Baptist who said,

> "Blessed is the Lord God of Israel, for He has visited and redeemed His people.... To grant us that we, being delivered from the hand of our enemies, might serve Him without fear, in holiness and righteousness before Him all the days of our life." (Luke 1:68, 74-75)

"Serve Him without fear." How I loved those words!

A Cry for Help

Not long after this, I found out from Sandra Brown, my fellow 1977 so-called rebel, that Steve Smith had also phoned her. What happened over the next year and a half after Steve Smith's phone call to her is a long, complicated, and terrible story. To make a long story short, they ended up having an affair.

When Sandra's husband found out about it, he and another elder confronted Sandra. They told her about previous immoral behavior by Steve of which Sandra was unaware. Steve's sin had been concealed by fellow Local Church elders (in opposition to 1 Timothy 5:20), even from his own wife. When Sandra was able to verify the information, she became extremely upset by all of this. She then called and confessed her sin to me. She broke off her relationship with Steve. She was very confused and was in desperate need of help. She didn't know for sure where she was going, but knew she could not stay with her husband any longer.

Chapter 17—The Withdrawn Hand of Fellowship 257

John and I asked her to come and spend some time with us, hoping we could break the fall she was experiencing and help her regain her spiritual footing. Sandra came and stayed with John and me for a long period of time, agreeing to have no further contact with Steve. We began trying to help her, hoping to rescue her marriage. We were holding on to her to keep her from falling again and trying to help her find a way to reconcile with her husband. She said that the only way reconciliation was a possibility was for her and her husband, Bob, to relocate somewhere far away from the Local Church, so they could try to start over. She was very fragile.

Steve, meanwhile, was repeatedly trying to re-establish a relationship with her. The possible long-term effects of this situation, if it wasn't permanently ended, were so reprehensible to us that John and I felt compelled to do whatever we could to try to rescue her. Sandra agreed to our acting as mediators to talk with Bob, but she believed that their situation was hopeless. She said that Bob would never, ever move away from the Local Church.

John and I ultimately had a very long period of communication with Bob and one of the other elders in his Local Church, Thomas Baker. I had realized from conversations with Sandra that her marriage problem had become much worse after the leading brothers had disciplined her in 1977, especially because her husband, who was an elder and who remained one with the other elders, had stood by silently watching her suffer, never offering her any comfort or help afterwards.

God arranged circumstances that brought about a long period of communication among Thomas Baker, Bob, John, and me in which we all were trying to save Bob and Sandra's marriage. In one of our talks, Thomas learned a little about what both Sandra and I had experienced in 1977. He asked if he could arrange a meeting with all of us and Dan Williams, who was now a sort of regional leader. Thomas insisted that our past experiences were the result of some kind of misunderstanding that could easily be cleared up by talking with Dan. He seemed to believe this would help Sandra, John, and me.

Sandra was completely unwilling to meet with Dan. I was also. After Thomas made the same request several times, I finally told him, very reluctantly, that the only way I thought I might be able to communicate effectively with Dan was to write a letter and read it to him in person with some others present. He encouraged me to do this, saying Dan had agreed to meet with us. So fourteen years after Dan Williams had disciplined me, events had transpired that brought me to the place that I was writing a letter to Dan Williams. I wrote the letter primarily on behalf of Sandra. In part of the letter, I explained the impact that the 1977 event had on her life and marriage, which I understood by my own similar experience.

A Letter to Dan

Sandra participated in the writing of the letter to Dan because she wanted the matter to be addressed. Knowing Dan's mindset, she was positive it would have no effect. She told me that she was certain Bob would never change unless Dan told him the elders had been wrong in 1977. She was certain that would never happen, and if by some miracle it did, it would still be Bob following Local Church leaders, not acting out of love for her. She said, "Jane, I want to do this mainly because it might help others not have to experience what I have been through."

While doing some research related to the letter to Dan, to my surprise, I found that there was a new world-wide "rebellion" that was occurring in the Local Church in reaction to the New Way movement. Some prominent leading brothers, who had been coworkers with Brother Lee from the beginning of his ministry in the United States, were now being labeled as rebellious in a book by Brother Lee entitled, *The Fermentation of the Present Rebellion*.[8] These brothers had stood for the truth of biblical oneness and spoken out against the practice of requiring oneness with Brother Lee's ministry and the Living Stream Ministry business office.

---

[8] *The Fermentation of the Present Rebellion* informed Local Church members that there was a rebellion with a worldwide scope taking place in the Lord's recovery. The first paragraph states, "In this message I will fellowship with you concerning the fermenting events of the present rebellion in the Lord's recovery

and the way to deal with the rebellion. Then we will know what attitude we should take in the present situation. We need to see a chronology of the present trouble, the present rebellion, the present conspiracy, in the Lord's recovery." (Lee, *Fermentation,* 9).

During this time, someone gave me a book entitled, *Speaking the Truth in Love,* by John Ingalls. He was one of the brothers labeled as rebellious in Brother Lee's book. When I first saw John Ingalls' book, I was amazed that he had not been afraid to publish this story. I discovered as I read it that, unlike the things said in Brother Lee's book, it contained verifiable facts, dates, and names. It also provided information about the gross misconduct of Brother Lee's son in the Living Stream Ministry office (Ingalls, 6–7). This book was a tremendous help to me, not only because it was a timely answer to so many questions, but also because someone had dared to speak the truth in love without fear. I was thankful for this and for God having placed a copy in my hands.

I recommend this book to any former Local Church members who might still be seeking help regarding their experience there.

In my research, I also came across a published letter that was written to Brother Lee after an elders' training and signed by 419 elders. It showed me just how far the pre-eminence of Brother Lee and his teachings in the Local Church had progressed. In this letter, the elders agreed that they would be one in every way conceivable. They agreed to support fully Brother Lee's ministry and to be identical with all other Local Churches in "teaching, practice, thinking, speaking, essence, appearance, and expression" (Lee, *Book 7,* 39). The following is an excerpt from that letter:

> We also agree to follow your leading as the one who has brought us God's New Testament economy and has led us into its practice. We agree that this leading is indispensable to our oneness and acknowledge the one trumpet in the Lord's ministry and the one wise master builder among us. (Lee, *Fermentation,* 63)

Brother Lee Warning Himself?

One morning before the letter to Dan was complete, the Lord brought to my mind Matthew 5:22:

> But I say to you that everyone who is angry with His brother shall be liable to the judgment. And whoever says to his brother, Raca, shall be liable to *the judgment of* the Sanhedrin; and whoever says, Moreh, shall be liable to the Gehenna of fire. (RV)

When I read in the *Recovery Version* Brother Lee's footnote to the word, *Moreh,* I was shocked to read that it meant "fool" and was a "Hebrew expression of condemnation indicating a rebel." How could Brother Lee write a footnote like this and then write a book like *Fermentation of the Present Rebellion?* I subsequently wrote about this footnote in my letter to Dan and appealed to him to repent for labeling Sandra, me, and so many other people as rebellious. I begged him to stop doing this.

When the long letter was ready, Dan repeatedly refused to meet with us as had been planned so I could read it to him. Dan continued over a period of months to offer various excuses related to his church and ministry responsibilities. Since the marriage of his fellow elder, Bob Brown, was at stake, Thomas Baker tried several times to facilitate our meeting. At one point, it seemed to us that Thomas was distinctly ashamed to pass along to us another excuse from Dan. Dan never met with us. In the end, my son, Matt, delivered my letter to Dan in person.

Unfortunately, Sandra turned out to be right about Dan. Thomas finally gave up his attempt. He met with John and me for one last time and told us that Dan was just "too busy in the Lord's work" to see us. He also passed on a word from Dan to us. Dan said that we were welcome to come back to the Local Church meetings and be received without any problem as long as we did not bring up our negative past.

When I heard this, I posed a hypothetical situation to Thomas. "Let's say we came back. I could certainly keep from saying anything about what happened to us in the past. I successfully did that for the final ten years that I was in the Local Church. However, if I were to attend a meeting in which I heard anyone say that a brother was rebellious against the ministry of Brother Lee, I would stand up and read both Matthew 5:22 and Brother Lee's footnote. I would say that this practice is wrong." I told Thomas I would never agree with that kind of labeling. Next I asked him this question: "Will I be allowed to stay then?" He didn't answer me.

Tell It to the Church

Unbelievably, Dan Williams had refused to be involved in our attempt to help Sandra and Bob, even though Bob was an elder in his region and the situation involved adultery. By turning his back on the matter, he was also failing to help Steve Smith, a former elder with whom he had been closely associated for many years. This was such a serious matter that we decided to send Brother Lee a copy of the letter to Dan by registered mail under a cover letter signed by John, Sandra, and me. We received a postal notice back with Witness Lee's signature showing that he had received our correspondence, but he never responded to it. Since neither Dan nor Witness Lee would address this matter with us, we decided that we would make an attempt to "tell it to the church," as Jesus commanded:

> "Moreover if your brother sins against you, go and tell him his fault between you and him alone. If he hears you, you have gained your brother. But if he will not hear, take with you one or two more, that 'by the mouth of two or three witnesses every word may be established.' And if he refuses to hear them, tell it to the church. But if he refuses even to hear the church, let him be to you like a heathen and a tax collector." (Matt. 18:15-17)

These verses in Matthew show that it is necessary to further escalate attempts to communicate in order to facilitate understanding and reconciliation. We decided that the way to "tell it to the church" was to communicate with those who had been in the migration to Houston in 1969. These brothers and sisters had known and loved Bob and Sandra for many years. We wrote a shorter letter and included some of the content of my letter to Dan and sent it to them. We had hoped that this further biblical attempt to help Dan hear us would put him in a position that he would feel the need to respond to us.

A few weeks later, Sandra received a letter from a sister in another Local Church asking her about her relationship with Steve! She had heard that Sandra was going to divorce Bob and marry Steve. Sandra was horrified by this letter. She exclaimed to me, "How can she be asking me this, Jane? She's been told something about me that I don't even know! Who told her about Steve and me? How could this happen! Who else knows?" She started to cry, "I know who told her! It's evident! The elders are doing damage control! They've found a way to discredit your letter by telling about my situation!" As the reality of what had happened began to sink in, she became very angry and said to me, "Nothing will ever change there. I don't matter. All they care about is protecting the Local Church. I am through with all of them. I am going to do what I want to do."

The only persons who had known about Sandra and Steve before this were three Local Church elders (Bob Brown, Thomas Baker, and Dan Williams), plus John and me; John and I had told no one else. We had not mentioned Sandra's involvement with Steve in any way in the letter to Dan that we later mailed. The sister's letter to Sandra and the realization it brought was the final nail in Sandra's spiritual coffin. Until the day she received the sister's letter, Sandra had repented and was trying to walk in that repentance. After that day, everything changed.

I heard later that some church members had been told that I wrote my letter to the brothers and sisters in order to justify Sandra leaving Bob and marrying Steve!

Ultimately, Sandra's faith was extremely damaged by her experiences with the Local Church leaders. I will never forget the day she looked at me and said, "I wish the Bible had never been written. What kind of God would allow a book to be written that men could use to lock you into a tormented existence for your whole life?" This came from a sister I loved dearly. She had helped me in my walk with the Lord twenty years before when she had shared numerous personal experiences of how the Lord had made Himself real to her. Shortly after finding out that other brothers and sisters had been told something about her situation, she moved out of our home and began seeing Steve again. She ultimately divorced her husband and married Steve. As far as I know, they both turned away from following the Lord.

A Failed Endeavor?

Overall, our efforts to help Sandra failed. Afterwards, I wondered what, if any, good came out of all our contact with the Local Church about the situation. Maybe God had tried to give the Local Church leaders a look at some of the fruit of their past actions.

One possible outcome was this: In the months after my letter was mailed to "tell it to the church," someone who asked a for a copy of The Fermentation of the Present Rebellion *from the Church in Irving bookroom was told that the book was not available in their inventory. It also was not listed on the Internet as being available from the Living Stream Ministry. This book by Witness Lee did not stand up well in the light of his own* Recovery Version *footnote to Matthew 5:22.*

I had been hopeful that our contact with the Local Church would result in the saving of Sandra's marriage as well as reconciliation with certain people there, but neither occurred. I didn't know for sure if Dan ever read my long letter to him. When all our attempts to communicate with him resulted in complete failure, I wondered why the Lord had led us to confront him in such a serious way.

Prior to Sandra's situation, I had absolutely no desire to have any contact with Dan whatsoever. I was willing to leave all judgment about my situation to the Lord. God used Sandra's situation to motivate me to write as I did. When I saw her beautiful person being damaged to such a terrible extent and her life and family coming apart, I couldn't just look away. Two families were broken apart by this event. Four wonderful children, who had been friends all their lives, saw their families severed through divorce. They watched the mother of two of them marry the father of the other two. Certainly we had to do anything in our power to stop this. We received criticism from a number of people for our role in this. Nevertheless, at least we hadn't watched our neighbor's house burn down without lifting a finger to try to put out the fire.

Dan Williams later said that I was seeking to vindicate myself at that time. It should be noted, however, that my letter to him was written fourteen years after I was accused of being the leader of a sisters' rebellion and that I was encouraged to write this letter by a Local Church elder. God made me willing to write because Sandra's family and future were at stake.

There was another positive outcome of my writing the long letter to Dan: I discovered how much writing helped me. Afterwards, I continued to write. I wrote about things that were happening to us and about the things God was showing me both in the Bible and through my experiences. As I revisited my history with the Lord, I began writing about my past experiences with Jesus, thinking one day it might benefit my children, and maybe even my yet unborn grandchildren! So, although I had no idea at the time, and would not realize it for another fourteen years, that situation actually began the writing of this book.

Lanell's Package

Our period of contact with the Local Church regarding Sandra's marital problem lasted about a year and a half. It was long and complicated and ultimately resulted in a number of letters being written, the first of which was the one to Dan from me in 1991. In 1992, a year after my letter to Dan, we heard that at a regional meeting of Local Church elders, Dan Williams named John and me as persons with whom Local Church members should have no contact because of our "negative" letters.

When former member Lanell Allen heard about this, she became upset because she had witnessed the whole situation with Sandra and had seen how Dan repeatedly refused to be involved with us. In order to clarify the situation for the elders who had attended the regional meeting, she mailed a package of information to each of them, requesting an open meeting with Dan and us. Lanell's package contained further correspondence from both John and me to Dan Williams. Regarding the practice of labeling people as rebellious, I asked him to consider the following quote from a Watchman Nee letter:

> The Holy Spirit alone knows who is not rebellious to His authority, does not grieve Him, and who lives in Christ through Him. And hence, the Holy Spirit alone can decide who may or may not have fellowship. We are not qualified to make such a decision. (Nee, *Back*, 112)

I also had asked him what he thought of what Watchman Nee said in the book, *The Orthodoxy of the Church:*

> The special characteristic of Philadelphia is brotherly love—today this way is the only way for you to walk. But never should you take this kind of attitude: I love the brothers who are clear and the brothers who are lovable, but those who are not lovable I will not love. Whether he is clear or not, that is his business. *We should never say, "You are a rebellious one."* What you have seen this year is what you had not seen last year. Perhaps next year he will also see what you have seen this year. While he reads the Bible, the Lord will also show him the light. God's heart is that great; so ours must be also. We must learn to have a heart large enough to include all God's children. Whenever you say "we" and yet by so saying you do not include all the children of God, you are the biggest sect, for you are not standing in the position of brotherly love but exalting yourself. The way of Philadelphia is the way we must take. (Nee, *Orthodoxy*, 103) [emphasis added]

We were not surprised that Dan did not respond to the above questions or consent to the meeting that Lanell had requested.

The details of Sandra's story, which are not included in this book, give even more insight into the way the Local Church leadership behaves whenever it believes it needs to protect the Local Church's reputation and the ministry of Witness Lee. Their willingness to preserve their cause at the expense of others and even at the expense of truth is more than disturbing. Such behavior, which says that the end justifies the means, brings shame to the name of Christ.

Saddest of all to me is that the leaders appear to truly believe they are serving God when they behave in this way. They indicate that their actions are justified because they believe they are God's deputy authorities who are protecting God's interests on the earth. Because of this belief, they refuse to be accountable for their actions to anyone except God, or someone above them in the leadership hierarchy. If anyone is offended by their actions, then they feel that the offended party has a problem with God. The leaders claim that their actions related to others aren't personal, but simply their obedience to God as they function as His deputy authorities. If they experience any qualms of conscience for such obviously bad and unscriptural behavior, they don't appear to acknowledge them.

Because of our involvement in Sandra Brown's situation and Lanell's package, we were permanently moved from the category of those who had mysteriously left and were to be pitied to the category of those who had attacked the church and were to be considered as opposers.

A Great Calm

I was very saddened by the outcome of the situation with Sandra, but I wasn't discouraged. It wasn't long before God comforted me once again. He assured me that this experience and the one in Houston, with its messed up and undesirable outcome, were in His control. He understood why. He reassured me that the promises He had given me then through the many "songs in the night" would yet come to pass. All in all, I was happy to be walking with Jesus again and hearing His voice in the same simple way I had heard it when I began my journey with Him many years before. I was thankful for the great calm I was experiencing in my heart and mind after so many years of storms while in the Local Church.

I soon began to realize that God was using all that happened with Sandra to help me as well. In writing the letter on her behalf, I had turned and faced the long buried 1977 event. Without Sandra's situation, I would never have taken time to look back there. I had, for all practical purposes, successfully forgotten it. But now God started to show me how all the things that had happened to me then had actually turned out for my salvation. All along, He had been faithfully answering my many cries for help. His answers had been right before me. His work had been strong and thorough. I just hadn't understood it.

Chapter 17—The Withdrawn Hand of Fellowship

Now God began to show me how much He had accomplished by that entire experience. He had used it to begin to answer all my deepest prayers to know Him and to take me up on my consecration to Him. In the blackest night of that time, He had been working mightily in and upon me, saving me from my strong, independent self and from my own zeal to serve Him. I had been a well-meaning servant with a strong desire to know and follow Him, but I hadn't understood His way. All the hymns He had given me before that trial, ones I had loved and treasured, had been to show me the pathway, the way of the cross.

As I looked back, He began to show me that it was my self-centeredness that lay at the root of all the tears that followed that terrible night. Yes, what happened to me was not right, but my response to it showed how very much it mattered to me that I be well-received and appreciated and how very important I was to myself. That experience was actually God's great mercy to me. By it, He began to open my eyes, not only to my sad state of deception, but also to my religious selfishness. In seeking the appreciation and approval of men more than of God, I had sown to my flesh. My tears and sorrow were part of my reaping:

> Do not be deceived, God is not mocked; for whatever a man sows, that he will also reap. (Gal. 6:7)

> "... For whom the Lord loves He chastens, and scourges every son whom He receives."

> If you endure chastening, God deals with you as with sons; for what son is there whom a father does not chasten? But if you are without chastening, of which all have become partakers, then you are illegitimate and not sons. Furthermore, we have had human fathers who corrected us, and we paid them respect. Shall we not much more readily be in subjection to the Father of spirits and live? For they indeed for a few days chastened us as seemed best to them, but He for our profit, that we may be partakers of His holiness. Now no chastening seems to be joyful for the present, but painful; nevertheless, afterward it yields the peaceable fruit of righteousness to those who have been trained by it. (Heb. 12:6-11)

That chastening had not been joyous but grievous, but it had yielded the peaceable fruit of righteousness. Before "that meeting," God had asked me how I would respond if those I loved misunderstood me and rejected me. I now knew the answer. I would respond with self-pity and volumes of tears, as I had done. I thought about Jesus:

> He had no tears for His own griefs,
> But sweat drops of blood for mine.
>
> — Charles H. Gabriel

I began to understand how that black night in Houston had been a turning point for me. Through it, God had set a new path before me. I had prayed to see Jesus as Paul had seen Him. Little by little in that dark time, Jesus had begun to show me Himself in a new way as I found myself alone, without the love of my brothers and sisters. Many times during my long period of rejection, I thought about how Jesus had come to His own, and they hadn't received Him (John 1:11). He came to us and did nothing but love us, but we turned on Him and killed Him. We tortured Him and nailed Him to a shameful cross. While He hung there, we gaped at Him, despised Him, rejected Him, and pitied Him. It appeared to all observers that God had judged Jesus for His claims; then God did not come to his aid. God left Him there all alone, alone with the weight and pain of all our sins upon Him.

Finally, I was able to weep for that, not for myself. My little taste of rejection and despising had opened my eyes to who He was and what He had done for me, and I loved Him more than ever. While chastening me, He also had allowed me by experience to understand a little of the "fellowship of His sufferings" (Phil. 3:10).

For many years after that awful night, I had thought I would never be free from the feelings of shame, humiliation, betrayal, and rejection that had become mine. But God had told me, "earth has no sorrow that heaven cannot heal,"[9] and He had been faithful to keep His promise. Heaven had healed my sorrow. The pain of my dear friend's betrayal had no more sting, and the memory of my brothers' and sisters' rejection and mistreatment could no more disturb my peace.

---

[9] Quotation from the hymn, "Come, ye disconsolate," by Thomas Moore.

Jesus had saved me from the black cloud of guilt and given me peace when I was eleven. Now, He had saved me from the last vestiges of the maelstrom in my mind that began in 1977 and had given me a great inner calm and tranquility. After a long and winding road and a lot of hard lessons, He had brought me back to follow Him in the simple, trusting way in which I had begun. How thankful I was!

Hotel Plano

John and I began to realize our need for Christian fellowship and decided to step out a little. We began meeting weekly with some brothers and sisters we had heard about that were meeting together on Sunday mornings in Garland. Some of them were former Local Church members. We attended these meetings for the next three to four years. God used them to keep us in His Word and in fellowship with others as He continued leading us on our journey to recovery. We didn't have a leader but rather looked to the Lord Himself to direct each meeting. These simple gatherings were blessed by the Lord. We never had a plan for our meetings, but somehow God did. We experienced Him as our Leader and Helper, as He taught us and comforted us through each person's participation in the meeting. Many times by the end of the meeting, we had received a complete and clear message from the Lord—a compilation of the many little parts offered by each person there. It was consistently an amazing experience.

During this time, the Lord reminded me that my material possessions, including my new home, were His. I told him that He could use my home anyway He saw fit. He could bring anyone there He wished; however, I was not going to seek visitors and invite them! He accepted my deal. Suffice it to say that from that time until 1995, we provided a lot of weekend and week-long hospitality to those that the Lord invited to our home.

One night, one of the brothers from Garland called us and asked if we could give hospitality to a former Local Church brother and his wife that were passing through Dallas. We said yes. This brother had been labeled as rebellious in the book, *The Fermentation of the Present Rebellion*. We had never before met him and his wife. When Mark and Linda arrived at our home, we showed them to their room. In the middle of the hall, Mark suddenly stopped and said, "I need to tell you all something before I stay here." He paused and then said, "I have been quarantined. You may not want me here." I quickly responded, "That's not a problem, quarantined people are welcome here!" John was standing there looking a little alarmed. He hesitated and said, "Wait a minute ... well, what is it that you have?" He was dead serious. I said, "John! He means the Local Church has quarantined him!" We all had a good laugh watching John's face as he realized his misunderstanding.

One day I told Mark that God seemed to have a way of bringing people to our house without us taking the initiative to get them there. I told him about my agreement with the Lord—that He could bring His people to our home, but I wouldn't invite them. He said to me, "That's interesting. I have an agreement with the Lord that I will go wherever He wants to send me, but I won't go unless I am invited!" We were both amazed that someone who would go nowhere unless invited was presently staying in the home of someone who would not invite! We revisited how he and his wife had come to be there and had to admit that the Lord was truly amazing.

At times, it seemed we should name our home "Hotel Plano." We had given the Lord permission to use our home, our time, and us, and He was taking us up on our offer.

The Withdrawn Hand of Fellowship

One Saturday morning, several years after the Sandra event, we had an unexpected encounter. John and I were meeting every Saturday morning at a restaurant with some of our Christian friends for breakfast and fellowship. I always looked forward to going, so it was unusual when one particular Saturday morning I couldn't shake the feeling that I should stay home. I got ready anyway but finally decided not to go. John, who went without me, later called me from the restaurant and said, "You will be glad you weren't here when I tell you what happened this morning."

John had arrived at the restaurant that morning and gone to our usual table. One of the brothers there, a former Local Church member, was speaking to another former member, "Did you see who is here?" John looked across the room and saw Dan Williams sitting at a table with three other Local Church elders. The brother continued speaking to the other brother at the table, "Why don't you go say, 'Hi'? He won't bite." When that brother got up to do so, John decided he would go as well. John followed him over to Dan's table. The brother exchanged greetings and shook hands with Dan and those at Dan's table. John also reached out to shake Dan's hand, but Dan drew his hand back and said, "Do you agree with the letters your wife wrote?" John said, "Yes, I do." Dan said, "Then I can't have fellowship with you." John replied, "I didn't come over here for fellowship. I just came to say, 'Hi.'"

When John told me this, I realized that my staying home had been God sparing me from seeing Dan Williams and once again experiencing his judgmental and rejecting attitude. Our friends who were with John had witnessed this event and were shocked at what Dan had done.

We Wrestle Not with Flesh and Blood

While I was writing the letter to Dan, the Lord used the following verse to show me that we weren't dealing just with human beings when we were having contact with the Local Church:

> For we do not wrestle against flesh and blood, but against principalities, against powers, against the rulers of the darkness of this age, against spiritual hosts of wickedness in the heavenly places. (Eph. 6:12)

Then in 1993, I read the book, *War on the Saints,* by Jessie Penn-Lewis. Prior to this, I had been afraid to read this book because Witness Lee, although he had referred to it a few times, had told us we shouldn't read it. After leaving the Local Church and in light of what we had been through there, it had been recommended to me as a must-read. It was very enlightening regarding Satan's methods and strategies against believers. Later the same year, my sister asked me to read two other books about spiritual warfare that had been a help to her when she and her husband had left the Local Church: *Living Free in Christ* and *The Bondage Breaker,* both by Neil T. Anderson. All three of these books were very helpful and gave me a new perspective on spiritual warfare.

While considering what I was reading, God reminded me of an experience I had with Sandra that confirmed what I was reading. Sandra and I were involved in a long and tearful conversation in which I was pleading with her over and over to stop her current path with Steve. I kept saying, "Sandra, this is not the Lord!" She responded, "Jane, I believe that the Lord is in this." I was incredulous and asked her how she could say this. How could the Lord be involved in sin? She then gave me her reason, one that gave me chills. In it I saw a glimpse of how very real the dark spiritual world was and how involved these evil beings could be in the things that happen to us when we are living in the darkness that sin brings.

First she told me something that her husband Bob had said to her when she was still living with him. He had been trying to get through to her, realizing something was seriously wrong with their relationship, but not sure what. (Sandra was secretly involved with Steve at that time.) One day, Bob said uncharacteristically and unexpectedly, "Sandra, you are like a little flower that a man had in his garden, which he forgot to water, and it dried up and wilted." Next she told me her proof that God was involved. She said that a few days after Bob had said this, she received a letter from Steve. In it he wrote, "Sandra, you are like a little flower that a man had in his garden, which he forgot to water, and it dried up and wilted. But then another man came by and watered it, and it responded." From what I had learned in *War on the Saints,* I understood that there was only one way such a communication could have taken place. Evil spiritual beings had transmitted this statement through the spiritual world to Steve. They had succeeded in tricking Sandra into believing that this was a spiritual experience from God.

Bondage Breaking

God began to use what John and I were learning from the three books to practically help us. Mainly we learned that deliverance from Satan's afflictions and attacks came by discovering, with God's help, what sins we had in our lives that were giving the enemy legal ground to afflict us, and then repenting of them. John and I had some major breakthroughs in our marriage relationship as a result. I was inspired to spend more time writing about what we were learning and ended up with what we began referring to as our "Bondage Breaking Notebook."

This notebook contained information that we began to use with other people to help them find freedom from bondage. God arranged that we had a number of what we referred to as "bondage breaking sessions" during these years. Most of these occasions involved former Local Church couples. Some involved adults who had been children of parents who were in the Local Church. We were learning the importance of these words:

> Be sober, be vigilant; because your adversary the devil walks about like a roaring lion, seeking whom he may devour. Resist him, steadfast in the faith, knowing that the same sufferings are experienced by your brotherhood in the world. (1 Pet. 5:8–9)

Chapter 18
The Master Weaver

> Now we are aware that God is working all together for the good of those who are loving God, who are called according to the purpose that, whom He foreknew, He designates beforehand, also, to be conformed to the image of His Son, for Him to be Firstborn among many brethren. (Rom. 8:28-29, CLV)

Our Family Under Attack

IN 1995, OUR LIVES AND OUR COURSE CHANGED as we began to have some very difficult experiences in our family relationships. Hotel Plano was used less and less frequently. Over a short time, the heavenly hospitality arrangements ceased. Hotel Plano was closed.

It soon became apparent that the wonderful calm I had experienced for four years was ending. My long, long night was not over as I had thought. I had only been in the calm eye of the storm. The winds of what lay ahead soon began to blow fiercely. The details of the next part of our journey are another story. To put it simply, our marriage relationship and one of our children came under attack by the devil. The things that began to happen made it apparent that Satan wasn't rolling over and playing dead just because we had made some progress on our path of recovery. He wasn't going to let go of us without a fight to the very last. He was still seeking to destroy us, but God ultimately turned for our good what Satan intended for evil to us.

Two years into this period of trial, we had made some headway in our marriage difficulty, but the situation with our son had not been resolved. It had become worse and continued to surface again and again. One day, the Lord asked me if I was willing to make a change in my life's circumstances that would be very demanding. He assured me that this path was His will and promised to supply me with whatever the change required. I agreed. Three more years passed. The Lord did supply me as He had promised, and I was able to meet the demands placed on me during that time; however, the family problem on which God appeared to be focusing with our son during these three years did not improve but became even worse. Under the continual hammering of it, I eventually became extremely depressed and discouraged. I was in such a low, dark place that I reached the point where, for the first time in my life, I was seriously questioning what I believed about God.

The Master Weaver

When I was a young believer, God had promised to show me the "path of life" that would be "fullness of joy" (Psa. 16:11). He had also encouraged me many times with this verse:

> Trust in the LORD with all thine heart; and lean not unto thine own understanding. In all thy ways acknowledge Him, and He shall direct thy paths. (Prov. 3:5-6, KJV)

Now, however, I was an old and very tired believer. I had reached a point where I didn't want any more direction for my paths. I just wanted a way out. Not only was I tired and extremely discouraged, I was also very hurt and confused. I had a big problem with God. One day, I found myself crying and saying, "Why Lord? Why did You ask me to go through the torture of the last three years? What was the purpose?" I felt that I had been led astray, used, and terribly wronged. I began to question, "Was the course I had taken actually the Lord's leading or just my big mistake?" I even began questioning my ability to follow the Lord at all. "Had I ever really understood His leading? Where was the promised "fullness of joy"?

My discouragement precipitated remembrance of the experience in Houston in 1977. As I pondered the results of that experience and the current one, I decided that if these were representative of following Jesus by faith, I didn't want to follow Him anymore.

What had precipitated all these thoughts? We had just discovered, with help from a Christian counselor, that the serious problem we were having with our son had its roots in what happened to our family during my 1977 church discipline. She had told us that the extreme emotional and psychological distress I experienced as a result of what happened to me had occurred when our son was at a very young and critical developmental age. My constant weeping during the time I was a basket case struggling to remain sane had severely damaged his emotional development. He was too young to understand that his mother was having a serious problem. All he knew was that one day I was no longer emotionally available for him, and subconsciously, he had taken this as my rejection of him. The counselor told us that because he was exceptionally bright, he had made a conscious decision about his relationship with us and had acted on it. He proceeded to actively and aggressively reject both his father and me. From that time until the time of this discovery, he had been at war with us to varying degrees throughout his life. We had all finally become desperate enough to seek professional help. He wanted deliverance from the problem as much as we did. There were other issues involved, but this was the source of the problem!

When I realized after all these years what lay at the root of many years of difficulty with him, I asked myself, "Was it really worth all of this?" I answered my question emphatically, "No!" One night, I blurted out to the Lord, "If I had to live those years in Houston over again, I would no longer be willing to follow You at any cost. It was not worth it!" I regretted everything about that time. Wasn't the present situation just like that one? And nothing good was coming out of it either.

In my discouragement, I started to reconsider all of those promises from the "songs in the night" of years past. Were they really from God? Maybe they had been a result of my own overactive mind. Maybe I had fooled myself into believing they were from Him. What kind of an idiot was I anyway, holding on to some little words from twenty years before! Then two particular lines from one of those songs came into my mind:

> The tangled skein shall shine at last,
> A masterpiece of skill untold.
>
> — E. May Grimes

When setting me free in the early 1990's, God had again brought these two lines to the forefront of my thinking and assured me that He would yet fulfill them. They, above all others, had survived that storm like a well-placed anchor. I had even told Sandra Brown about them, and she had subsequently framed these lines as a gift to me. They had hung on the wall in my home for six years since that time.

But on this night, I found no encouragement in remembering them. Rather, they made me angry. I said, "Lord, it has been twenty years since I believed this promise was from You. Now, I've changed my mind! I don't think it was from You! I think I *was* deceived after all! There is no *masterpiece of skill untold* here! After all these years, what I see is just a tangled mess! I am in terrible shape! And I don't want any more promises from You!"

John and I were now attending meetings at a large Bible church in our area. I fought back tears through much of the church meeting the next morning. Looking at a verse on the wall, "Now unto Him that is able to do exceeding abundantly above all that we ask or think ...," I told myself, "Yes, it says He is *able,* but it doesn't say He *will.*" Not long after this, I awakened one night with this verse in my mind:

> And he said unto me, My grace is sufficient for thee: for my strength is made perfect in weakness. Most gladly therefore will I rather glory in my infirmities, that the power of Christ may rest upon me. (2 Cor. 12:9, KJV)

During the next day, I pondered the phrase "glory in my infirmities." Well, I had the *infirmities* part down, but the *glory* part needed a lot of improvement. How was I to glory in absolute weakness, inability, and unbelief?

Then an amazing thing happened. That night, some of the ladies from church were gathering in one of their homes for food and fellowship. I had declined the invitation but at the last minute decided to go. I was determined not to talk about my situation, but my countenance must have betrayed my condition because I was repeatedly being asked about my well-being. I ended up sharing briefly in tears a little about my family trouble. They all prayed for me and my family.

Then, just as we were about to leave, Joan Craig stopped everyone and told us that the Lord wouldn't let her come that evening without bringing the paper she was now holding in her hand. She had been in her car, ready to leave her house, when God had reminded her that she had forgotten to bring it. She had gone back inside her house and retrieved it. She had expected its content to fit in our fellowship time, but it hadn't. Still believing God had led her to bring it and feeling strongly she wasn't supposed to leave without reading it aloud to us, she asked our permission to do so. We were all standing in a group facing her. I was positioned in front of her and in the center of the rest of the ladies. Joan then read this three-verse poem:

The Plan of the Master Weaver

My life is but a weaving
Between the Lord and me,
I may not choose the colors,
He knows what they should be;
For He can view the pattern
Upon the upper side
While I can see it only
On this, the under side.

Sometimes He weaveth sorrows,
Which seemeth strange to me;
But I will trust his judgment,
And work on faithfully,
'Tis He who fills the shuttle,
And He Who knows what's best,
So I shall weave in earnest,
And leave to Him the rest.

Not till the loom is silent
And shuttles cease to fly
Shall God unroll the canvas,
Explain the reason why

Chapter 18—The Master Weaver

> The dark threads are as needed
> In the skilled Weaver's hand
> As threads of gold and silver—
> The pattern He has planned.
>
> — Author unknown

I stood there dumbfounded. I knew without a doubt why she had been led to read this poem, one I had never before heard. The Lord was responding to my angry, faithless words from a few days before, when I had specifically rejected one of His past promises to me and, in essence, told Him to leave me alone. His response through Joan was an expanded, clarified version of these lines: "the tangled skein shall shine at last, a masterpiece of skill untold." It was as if He had sent the poem through Joan to say, "Jane, I gave you a promise through this one sentence many years ago; but since you have come to doubt that promise and My purpose concerning you, let Me restate it for you in more detail."

I awoke the next morning thinking about the poem again. God had responded to my specifically-voiced doubt with a very specific answer. Once again He had silenced me. The Master Weaver really was in control. In order to make something beautiful and useful to Him of my life, He also needed the dark threads. Their length, color, and texture were under His careful control. What looked like a tangled mess to me did not look that way to Him. He could see the final product. I had surrendered my life to Him many years before, and it was still in the skillful hands of the Master Weaver.

From that day, I knew that the tangled-skein promise had been from Him, and I would see its fulfillment. I remembered these lines:

> "All in his hands"—what confidence it brings
> To tested hearts, to know that all the things
> That make up life and circumstance, He holds
> In His strong hands, and patiently unfolds

> Th' eternal purpose of His sovereign Will—
> That all things shall His grace and glory fill.
>
> — K. O. Macnair

I repented for my upset and my doubt, and thanked Him for the timely presentation to me of "The Plan of the Master Weaver." I was amazed by the way in which this had occurred. God had spoken to me through the simple obedience of another member of His body, very specifically and very clearly. Joan came with no idea why she was supposed to share the poem, and she left the same way. Yet God had communicated to me through her in a way as real as if I had received a written message directly from God Himself.

In my distress, I had been feeling once again as if God had left me alone, without help, but the truth was that He was very present and purposeful. He loved me and was using everything that He had allowed into my life for my highest good. I was at peace again, experiencing His strength in my weakness. The timing of the fulfillment of His promises was entirely up to Him, not me. I understood that my long, long night still wasn't over. Maybe it was going to be a long, long, *long* night. No matter the length, in my heart I knew that the day would dawn in His time and in His way. Whenever that might be, I knew I could now continue in hope:

> So on I go not knowing;
> I would not if I might;
> I'd rather walk in the dark with God
> Than go alone in the light;
>
> I'd rather walk by faith in Him
> Than go alone by sight.
>
> — M. G. Brainerd

A number of years later, God showed me that a part of the Master Weaver poem was to be my title for this book: The Thread of Gold.

The Threads in God's Tapestry

The discovery of the long hidden root of the problem with our son was a turning point for our son and for us. We began to make steady progress in our family relationships as God worked mightily in the years that followed to "restore the years that the locusts had eaten" (Joel 2:25) during our time in the Local Church. Our great Physician applied His skillful surgery and powerful healing. He did a thorough work. Our healing took place in an unpleasant environment of reaping what we had sown, but God worked mightily to "loose the bonds of wickedness, to undo the heavy burdens, to let the oppressed go free, and ... break every yoke" (Isa. 58:6).

He ultimately accomplished a full and complete healing. Our relationship with our son was fully restored. It took ten years from the time that the calm eye of the storm passed by, and I was thrown back into the raging winds of the other side of the hurricane; but God finished His work to heal our family. The storm was over, dissipated, gone forever. The long, long, *long* night passed. We were at rest. The morning broke at last.

> I will extol You, O LORD, for You have lifted me up,
> And have not let my foes rejoice over me.
> O LORD my God, I cried out to You,
> And You healed me.
> O LORD, You brought my soul up from the grave;
> You have kept me alive, that I should not go down to the pit.
>
> Sing praise to the LORD, you saints of His,
> And give thanks at the remembrance of His holy name.
> For His anger is but for a moment,
> His favor is for life;
> Weeping may endure for a night,
> But joy comes in the morning.
>
> Now in my prosperity I said,
> I shall never be moved."
> LORD, by Your favor You have made my mountain stand strong;
> You hid Your face, and I was troubled.
>
> I cried out to You, O LORD;
> And to the LORD I made supplication:
> "What profit is there in my blood,

> When I go down to the pit?
> Will the dust praise You?
> Will it declare Your truth?
> Hear, O LORD, and have mercy on me;
> LORD, be my helper!"
>
> You have turned for me my mourning into dancing;
> You have put off my sackcloth and clothed me with gladness,
> To the end that my glory may sing praise to You and not be silent.
> O LORD my God, I will give thanks to You forever.
>
> (Psa. 30, NKJV)

In my heart, I knew a time of joy lay ahead. By all of the things we had passed through on our journey to freedom and full recovery, He convinced me that, unlike what I had learned in the Local Church, God placed a very high value on me, on my family, and on all the details of our life and relationships. Through all of this, He showed me that I was very important to Him. He loved me and was molding and shaping my experience with Him in a particular way to reach a desired end in my heart and mind according to His purpose for my life.

My Backyard Garden

One day while I was gardening in my backyard, God spoke a clear message to me through His creation about His love for people as individuals. I had just planted some pansies, and I stopped to look closely at a few of them. The differences between them caught my attention. Their sizes, hues, and even the shapes of their petals were not the same. Were there any two pansies exactly alike? No. I looked at the other flower varieties in the garden and thought, "When God created flowers, He made a great many different kinds; and within those kinds, no two are identical. When I looked at all the different flowers in my garden as a group, it was even more beautiful. Not only that, I thought about how He had made so many other kinds and varieties of plants. Then I remembered this verse:

> For the invisible things of Him from the creation of the world are clearly seen, being understood by the things that are made, even His eternal power and Godhead. (Rom. 1:20, KJV)

Seeing this small part of His creation in my backyard, I realized something about the invisible One who created everything. I thought, "God is like this. He appreciates and enjoys tremendous variety. He created millions of unique, beautiful things and then put them together in perfect harmony into this vast and beautiful earth." I said, "Lord, You are so beautiful. Thank You for letting me see that You love beauty and variety. Thank You for loving me and making me one of Your unique little human creatures." That day, I understood something that left an indelible impression on me about what God is like and about His appreciation for every individual person He has created.

God's Purpose for Individual Believers

God later used my backyard gardening experience further to show me why He purposed for every believer to have their own unique story with Him. He did this while I was considering the meaning of Ephesians 3:9–11:

> And to make all men see what is the fellowship of the mystery, which from the beginning of the world hath been hid in God, who created all things by Jesus Christ: to the intent that now unto the principalities and powers in heavenly places might be known by the church the manifold wisdom of God, according to the eternal purpose which He purposed in Christ Jesus our Lord. (Eph. 3:9–11, KJV)

First, God showed me that the "mystery" in these verses is Christ crucified, and that Christ crucified was God's hidden wisdom. Next, He gave me understanding about the meaning of "the manifold wisdom of God" mentioned at the end of this passage. Puzzled by this phrase, I asked, "If God's wisdom is Christ crucified, then what is His *manifold* wisdom? Why does this verse say that God intends to make known His manifold wisdom to the principalities and powers in heavenly places by the church? Hadn't they already seen His wisdom when they saw Christ crucified?" While I was thinking about this question, God turned my attention to the phrase, "God, who created all things." I asked myself, "What does God creating all things have to do with God's hidden mystery and the manifold wisdom of

God mentioned in this verse? Why did Paul mention this?"

I decided to look up the Greek meaning of the word *manifold,* According to the Greek, *manifold* means "much variegated, that is, multifarious" (Strong, G4182). *Multifarious* means "diverse, including parts, things, or people of many different kinds" (*Encarta*). I discovered that the classical Greek word for *manifold* is used to refer to "the beauty of an embroidered pattern or the variety of colors in flowers" (Walvoord, Eph. 3:10).

When I read this, God reminded me about what I had learned in my backyard gardening experience, and I suddenly understood the significance of "the God, who created all things." Through the old creation with its billions of unique and wonderful items, God showed us something about Himself, including His richness and love of diversity. Then, through Christ's death and resurrection, He created something new. When we believe in Jesus, we become a new creation in Christ (2 Cor. 5:17). Through this new creation, with its multitudes of unique and wonderful believers, God will show *the principalities and powers* something about Himself: the depth of His manifold, diverse wisdom. Each believer's story is made up of experiences of Christ and Him crucified. It takes all of these unique individual stories to show God's multifarious wisdom to the principalities and powers.

Each believer's story will be according to the pattern shown in Paul's life:

> However, for this reason I obtained mercy, that in me first Jesus Christ might show all longsuffering, as a pattern to those who are going to believe on Him for everlasting life. (1 Tim. 1:16)

Paul desired to know Christ, "the power of His resurrection, and the fellowship of His sufferings, being conformed to His death" (Phil. 3:10). Each believer's story will be in this pattern. Paul said that it was given to believers to suffer on behalf of Christ:

> For to you it has been granted on behalf of Christ, not only to believe in Him, but also to suffer for His sake. (Phil. 1:29)

He told us to rejoice about this!

> But rejoice to the extent that you partake of Christ's sufferings, that when His glory is revealed, you may also be glad with exceeding joy. (1 Pet. 4:13)

I also noticed something very interesting about the following verse.:

> For we are His workmanship, created in Christ Jesus for good works, which God prepared beforehand that we should walk in them. (Eph. 2:10)

In this verse, the Greek word for *workmanship* is *poiema*, which means "a product ... fabric ... thing that is made" (Strong, G4161). As it dawned on me what this verse was saying, I just sat in my chair for awhile in tears (glad tears!). This verse showed me that the metaphor of a woven fabric, a weaving, to which God had recently likened my own life, was actually in the Bible.

Together, we are His workmanship, a beautiful tapestry. A tapestry is a fabric that is rich, varied, and intricately interwoven. Because it is made by interlacing threads vertically and horizontally, it is filled with crosses. His handiwork will also be composed of many crosses—all the believers' experiences of Christ crucified. I think that God's completed tapestry isn't going to be two-dimensional but multidimensional, having breadth and length and depth and height.

Each of our stories is included in the Master Weaver's universal, multidimensional tapestry created in Christ Jesus. Each of our stories displays the good works He ordained for us to walk in—those that stand the test of fire (1 Cor. 3:13) because they are a result of our experience of Christ and Him crucified. Together, all of our stories with His unique purpose for each of our lives will show to the principalities and powers the manifold wisdom of God, the unsearchable riches of Christ, to the glory of God the Father. The completion of this tapestry will be the fulfillment of His eternal purpose.

What a day of joy that will be when our faith will be "found to praise, honor, and glory" at His appearing! (1 Pet. 1:7). God has been creating His universal tapestry throughout human history, His *masterpiece of skill untold*.

God Approves the Title

As my husband and I were finalizing the title of this book, the Lord gave us a very special experience that confirmed what it was to be entitled and assured us that this book was in His hands. We were about to leave to attend a small gathering of believers in Houston when I told John that I felt the *subtitle* should be changed to *God's Purpose and Me*. John said, "Why not just let that be the main title?" To which I replied, "I think the Lord wants us to leave the main title as it is, *The Thread of Gold,* because of His use of the weaving metaphor in my life." We discussed this a few minutes and then dropped the subject, but not before we had asked the Lord to help us reach agreement on what He wanted the title to be.

Once we arrived in Houston, we had a number of wonderful experiences, but one that stood out occurred in the home where we were staying. Our hosts, Dale and Helen King, made us feel like royalty. Their home and our accommodations, a bedroom and sitting room, were lovely. When I paused to look at what was in a frame on the wall beside our bedroom door, I was taken completely aback by what I saw. I could hardly breathe as I realized what I was viewing. I called John over, pointed to the wall decoration, and said, "Look." John looked and responded, "Jane, how can that be?" I echoed, "Yes. How can that be? What is the possibility that this could happen?"

There on the wall in front of us was a page from a hymnal and some other small items artistically placed inside the frame. We were both staring at the title of the hymn, "Beneath the Cross of Jesus," and at a flowing golden thread on top of the hymn. This perfectly represented my book: a story about the cross that was filled with hymns about the cross, and that showed the thread of gold which God had woven through my life. Was *The Thread of Gold* the main title? We had our answer: a resounding "Yes!" I am still amazed whenever I think of this. By this experience, I also realized that the subtitle should be changed from *God's Purpose and Me* to *God's Purpose, the Cross, and Me*.

The God of All Things

There are no "accidents" in lives given to Him. If we are His, we don't need to blame others for the difficult things in our paths. They are allowed there by Him for our highest good. He is the God who makes "all things work together for good" (Rom. 8:28).

I have heard many of those who were hurt by their Local Church experience blame the Local Church, the church leaders, and Witness Lee for subsequent bad fruit in their lives and in the lives of their children. As far as I can see, blaming others does not help us. What does help us, at any point on our journey, especially if we have not previously done so, is handing over our tangled, messed-up lives to Jesus. He has a wise purpose in view. He can start at any point at which we yield to Him and do His masterful work in our lives.

I have also heard some of the children who spent their formative years in the Local Church voice the same blame. I have particular sympathy for such children because, like my children, they did not experience the Local Church by their own choice. I have seen firsthand the damage caused to some of them.

I recently received a call from Tina, who was a teenager when she lived with us in Oklahoma City. She is now a woman in her forties. We had not talked about the Local Church in a great many years. She called me in distress as I was writing this section about the God of all things. She told me that she had just had an experience that had brought to the surface all of her old pain. She explained how most of the time she successfully kept it shut away. When it had appeared this time, she had decided to call me. Her main question was, "Will I ever be able to get over what happened to me there?"

Tina had come to grips with God being in her life but was still tormented by the church issue whenever it arose. She simply could not connect with any church or other believers who "talked church" in any way. Tina did not choose to be in the Local Church. I still believe, however, that God allowed this for her highest good. I know in my heart that He has a specific purpose for Tina, and that her experience was necessary to produce her life's weaving with her thread of gold. I do believe that God will bring her to a place of full freedom, in His time and in His way, as only He can do.

The truth is that there is no perfect situation or environment available anywhere, for anyone, on this earth. There is no set of circumstances on this planet that is completely secure and that can prevent hurt or suffering. All human beings experience tangled circumstances and situations that cause suffering to one degree or another. Many children are born into terrible situations. The critical question is, "How do we respond to what happens to us?"

In my case, I was responsible for not knowing and not practicing the simple truth in the Bible related to my responsibilities as a human being, wife, parent, and Christian. It was my choice to seek the approval of men more than that of God. These things, of my own making, contributed to the environment in which I was hurt and in which my children were hurt.

My particular life's circumstances include twenty years in the Local Church. I am thankful to Him that I no longer have even one complaint about this. Why? Because I have learned a wonderful secret. Truth has set me free. What have I learned? In the middle of any seemingly hopeless, tangled-up life situation, there is a place of purpose and absolute safety. Where is that place? In the heart and hands of the Master Weaver. With this realization, I wrote this fourth verse to the Master Weaver poem:

> In all things God is off'ring
> His fellowship to me:
> The myst'ry's no more hidden;
> His cross has set me free.
> The purpose for my living,
> Each day unfolds to me.
> His masterpiece eternal:
> My final destiny.
>
> — Jane Carole Anderson

Chapter 19
The Cross

> For the message of the cross is foolishness to those who are perishing, but to us who are being saved it is the power of God. (1 Cor. 1:18)

Christ Crucified: God's Wisdom, Love, and Way

I AM FULLY PERSUADED THAT GOD'S WISDOM is Christ crucified. God's love for us is shown in Christ's death. God's way for us is to know Christ and Him crucified. This is the secret to the meaning of suffering, of death, and of life, and affords us the way into a life of purpose. The Bible says that the "message of the cross" is the "power of God" "to us who are being saved" (1 Cor. 1:18). I find this to be an amazing statement. The power of God in my Christian life comes from the message of the cross. In my experience, it is the message of the cross that has revealed to me the secret of the Christian life and of human life.

God has helped me learn about the secret of the pathway of the cross by observing the lives and testimonies of many people in the Bible, as well as those from many Christian biographies. Their examples didn't give me a method; rather, they gave me a wonderful view of the living and present Jesus Christ and His resurrection power. Their stories made me want to know the One for whom they were willing to give up everything, even their lives. Their love for Christ was like a magnet that drew me to know Him for myself.

He also has taught me by the words of hymns that such Christians have written about their experiences of the cross. I have also come to understand something else very wonderful. Only Jesus Himself can show us the pathway. As one believer wrote:

> Then the Cross! For via Calvary
> Every royal soul must go;
> Here we draw the veil, for Jesus
> Only can the pathway show.
>
> — M. E. Barber

Christ Crucified: The Answer to Human Suffering

I have heard this question asked many times in my life: "If there is a God, why is there so much suffering?" The simple answer is that there is human suffering because there is sin. Sin caused the first human suffering. Since that time, sin has abounded. The Bible says that "the wages of sin is death" (Rom. 6:23). This means that as sinners, every day we are earning death, and one day we will be paid in full for what we have earned. Our suffering in the present reminds us of the ultimate suffering that will come to every man: death. The Bible says that "fear of death" makes us subject to bondage, or slavery, all of our lives (Heb. 2:15). It also says that when we sin, we are slaves of sin (Rom. 6:16). The slave master, Satan, has the power of death. Our sins give him the right to afflict us while we are alive, and then at our end, to take us into the prison of death. We spend a lot of time and energy trying to avoid suffering and trying to drown out our fear of dying.

When God created us, He didn't intend for us to suffer or to die. He created us as dependent beings who would live forever, fully cared for by Him. He warned Adam and Eve not to eat of the "tree of the *knowledge* of good and evil" or they would die (Gen. 2:17). They didn't heed His warning, but were deceived by God's enemy, Satan, and succumbed to the temptation to partake of *knowledge* in hope of becoming like God. As a result, they became separated from God and had to work for their provision. They suffered and died. They sinned when they chose the tree of the knowledge of good and evil, and they and their descendants became slaves of sin.

We may ask why God didn't protect them from Satan and why He allowed them an opportunity to disobey. We may ask why we have to suffer for their sin. We also may ask questions about Satan. I suggest that God does not wish to give us clear answers to these kinds of *why* questions now, or He would have done so in the Bible. He has chosen, for now, only to tell us that which is critical for our salvation and earthly path. As in the Garden of Eden, God is still asking us simply to believe Him and obey, and we are still being tempted by Satan to acquire knowledge and be like God.

Although we don't fully understand why God allowed the deceiver to have access to Adam and Eve after their creation, we do know that God was completely prepared for Adam and Eve's failure. In His omniscience, He already knew what they would do. He had a perfect plan in place—one that would give Him not only a way to rescue mankind, but also a way to fulfill His ultimate purpose.

A first clue to the existence of God's plan came soon after Adam and Eve sinned. God had said that on the day they ate of the tree of the knowledge of good and evil, they would die. They did die spiritually, but they didn't immediately die physically. God's righteousness required their death as payment for their sin. Yet on that day, instead of them, God killed an animal, maybe a lamb, and covered their nakedness with its skin (Gen. 3:21). This was the clue to the existence of His plan. The death of the animal in their place showed that death was necessary to pay for their sin, and that God had a plan to pay the price for what they had done. At an appointed time, because of His great love for mankind, God, in His infinite wisdom, would pay the debt Himself by dying on the cross.

Christ Crucified: God's Lamb

If sin is the root cause of suffering, then the way to end suffering is to remove sin. Whoever can remove sin can remove suffering. We don't have to wait any longer for this to happen because it has already been done. God has taken away sin by Christ's death on the cross.

According to Old Testament law, the Jewish people offered animal sacrifices for their sins. At the first Passover before the exodus from Egypt, each family sacrificed a lamb without spot or blemish and put the blood of the lamb on the doorposts of their homes to save them from the death angel. This foretold of Christ's coming as God's lamb. He became flesh and blood to die in our place and pay the debt for our sins. John the Baptist said,

> "Behold! The Lamb of God who takes away the sin of the world!" (John 1:29)

When Jesus was in the Garden of Gethsemane preparing for His death, He became intensely distressed and sorrowful and went to pray to His Father. He was keenly aware of His coming suffering, to the point of sweating blood, yet His prayer shows that the suffering aspect of His impending death was not His main concern:

> He went a little farther and fell on His face, and prayed, saying, "O My Father, if it is possible, let this cup pass from Me; nevertheless, not as I will, but as You will."... Again, a second time, He went away and prayed, saying, "O My Father, if this cup cannot pass away from Me unless I drink it, Your will be done." (Matt. 26:39, 42)

His request that the cup pass if possible shows that He didn't want to suffer. However, His final prayer was "nevertheless, not as I will, but as You will." In essence, Jesus was saying, "Father, I am willing to suffer and die, if that is what is required to do Your will." Concerning his suffering, the Bible says:

> Who, in the days of His flesh, when He had offered up prayers and supplications, with vehement cries and tears to Him who was able to save Him from death, and was heard because of His godly fear, though He was a Son, yet He learned obedience by the things which He suffered. And having been perfected, He became the author of eternal salvation to all who obey Him. (Heb. 5:7–9)

This was not the first time Jesus had prayed and done His Father's will. This was His way of life. On that day in Gethsemane, God did not force Him to obey. Jesus had the option to avoid the suffering of the cross, but He didn't choose that option. The Bible tells us that when He was being arrested He said, "Or do you think that I cannot now pray to My Father, and He will provide Me with more than twelve legions of angels?" (Matt. 26:53). He could have saved Himself, but He loved His Father and what His Father wanted, so He put His Father's will first. He had become flesh in order to do His Father's will (Heb. 10:9–10).

The terrible situation of darkness, suffering, and death in the whole universe, including humanity's fall, had come from another's selfish will—Satan's will. What did Satan want? He wanted God's place. He wanted to be in the preeminent position.

What did God the Father want? He loved us and wanted the debt for our sins to be paid so that we could be saved and our relationship with Him restored. He wanted Satan to be defeated through His Son, who by becoming flesh was made lower than the angels for "the suffering of death" (Heb. 2:9). The Father did not want His Son to suffer, but this was necessary for our benefit.

As a man in the flesh, Christ learned obedience. Why? So He could be a "merciful and faithful High Priest" who could make "propitiation" for our sins and who could strengthen and help us (Heb. 2:17–18). He faced everything we face in the flesh and remained obedient to His Father. He did not fall to temptation as Adam and Eve did. He never stepped out on His own as they did. He never moved from His place of complete dependence on His Father.

When He was among us, He demonstrated God's love for us by meeting every need of those who came to Him seeking His help. He fed them, healed them, freed them from demonic oppression, and raised them from the dead. He spoke truth to them. Those that heard Him said that no man had ever spoken as He did. Then, He demonstrated His love for us to the uttermost:

> Greater love has no one than this, than to lay down one's life for his friends. (John 15:13)

When He faced a terrible, shameful, painful death, He chose to trust His Father and submit Himself to His Father's will on our behalf. Jesus, the sinless man, God incarnate, chose His Father's will. He loved us and was obedient unto death, even the shameful, excruciatingly painful, and slow death of the cross. He took the place we deserved.

In His death, He was completely alone. He had come to His own, the Jewish people, and they had rejected Him and arranged to have Him killed. He had loved and cherished His disciples for three and a half years, and they forsook Him and fled when He was arrested. "He was oppressed, and He was afflicted, yet He opened not His mouth; He was led as a lamb to the slaughter" (Isa. 53:7). He was mocked as the King of the Jews. His visage was "marred more than any man" (Isa. 52:14). He was "despised and rejected by men, a Man of sorrows and acquainted with grief" (Isa. 53:3). People turned their faces away from Him. "He was wounded for our transgressions; He was bruised for our iniquities" (Isa. 53:5). He was considered to be "stricken, smitten by God, and afflicted" (Isa. 53:4). To all appearances, this was true; in fact, according to His own perception, this also was true because He cried out on the cross asking God why He had forsaken Him. He was "cut off from the land of the living" (Isa. 53:8). "He poured out His soul unto death, and He was numbered with the transgressors, and He bore the sin of many, and made intercession for the transgressors" (Isa. 53:12). He drank the entire bitter cup that we gave to Him.

Hebrews says that Jesus, "for the joy that was set before Him, endured the cross, despising the shame" (Heb. 12:2). Before Him, on the other side of the cross, he saw us. Having done His Father's will, He would have "fullness of joy" in His Father's presence and would present us to Him "with exceeding joy" (Psa. 16:11, Jude 1:24).

Then after three days, God raised Jesus "from the dead and seated Him at His right hand in the heavenly places, far above all" in victory (Eph. 1:20–21). Death could not hold Him because He had no sin. His death resulted in our debt being paid in full. Satan was defeated and lost his right to hold us in death. Death was swallowed up in victory (Isa. 25:8, KJV). He is now on His throne interceding for us (Rom. 8:34) and expectantly "waiting till His enemies are made His footstool" (Heb. 10:13).

Our suffering and our needs bring us to the foot of the cross of the greatest sufferer of all time, where we hear:

> "Come to Me, all you who labor and are heavy laden, and I will give you rest. Take My yoke upon you and learn from Me, for I am gentle and lowly in heart, and you will find rest for your souls. For My yoke is easy and My burden is light." (Matt. 11:28-30)

The "rest" that He gives to us is Himself. When we come to Him, our great High Priest, we come to the throne of grace:

> For we do not have a High Priest who cannot sympathize with our weaknesses, but was in all points tempted as we are, yet without sin. Let us therefore come boldly to the throne of grace, that we may obtain mercy and find grace to help in time of need. (Heb. 4:15-16)

When we come to Him in time of need we receive "the supply of the Spirit of Jesus Christ" (Phil. 1:19). This is grace. His obedience, learned through the things He suffered, becomes ours and saves us through faith:

> For by grace you have been saved through faith, and that not of yourselves; it is the gift of God. (Eph. 2:8)

His wonderful salvation is a gift that is freely ours through faith in all that the Lamb of God has done for us.

Chapter 20
In God's Tapestry

> For we are His workmanship, created in Christ Jesus for good works, which God prepared beforehand that we should walk in them. (Eph. 2:10)

In His Masterpiece: A Multitude of Followers

UNTOLD NUMBERS HAVE FOLLOWED THE LAMB OF GOD and discovered the throne of grace as they lived on the earth. They were supplied by His Spirit and learned to take up their crosses and follow Him. They are in His masterpiece. They have now joined the great cloud of witnesses who are waiting for us. Their lives and testimonies are for our benefit. Over the years, their stories have inspired me and, by example, taught me to follow Him.

In His Masterpiece: Paul, A Pattern for Me

I learned from Paul that he wanted me to know and follow God in the same way that he did. Paul prayed that we would have "the spirit of wisdom and revelation in the knowledge of Him" (Eph. 1:17). As I read all that Paul said to the early believers and saw how he suffered for them, I found myself praying that I could be such a believer. God showed me that he gave Paul to me as a pattern (1 Tim. 1:16) to encourage me. From his example, I learned what a follower of the Lamb should be like. He loved Jesus, and He loved the believers. He gave himself to them and for them so that they could see Christ and their high calling to follow Him. I am called into the same fellowship (1 Cor. 1:9). Like Paul, I also should determine to know nothing except Christ and Him crucified (1 Cor. 2:2). My life should be a living example of the message of the cross. I should share this with others and want them to have the same wonderful experience.

Like Paul, it is my privilege to count everything loss to "gain Christ and be found in Him," and to "know Him and the power of His resurrection, and the fellowship of His sufferings" (Phil. 3:8–10). I saw that Paul wanted me to know I am also called to follow Christ for myself. He told me to make note of those who don't love others and are not willing to suffer for them, who are "enemies of the cross of Christ," and that I should not follow their example. When he talked about such persons, he wept, and I should do the same (Phil. 3:15–18). He encouraged me to have the same mind as Christ, who "humbled himself and became obedient to ... the death of the cross" (Phil. 2:5–8). I saw that my only boast and glory should be in the cross of Christ (Gal. 6:14), and that I should suffer for other believers and for their sake to fill up what is "lacking in the afflictions of Christ" in my own flesh (Col. 1:24–29).

As I saw Paul's love for Jesus and for others, and his single-minded purpose, I found myself praying, "Lord, I want to see You and know You like Paul did." Paul's example attracted me to Christ.

Paul's Love Story

I learned from Paul's biography about his love relationship with Jesus. Paul's love story began with a conversation between Jesus and him. Paul told about a number of such conversations. The conversations took place in real life circumstances, usually difficult ones. I learned from him that as I follow Jesus, I will have my own such conversations with Him. The first conversation Paul had with Jesus occurred on the road to Damascus when he was still called Saul. He was a fully-credentialed person, a highly regarded Jew, a Roman citizen, and a zealous persecutor of the church. While Paul was on his way to persecute more believers, Jesus stopped him in his tracks to have a talk with him:

"Saul, Saul why are you persecuting Me? It is hard for you to kick against the goads."

"Who are You, Lord?"

"I am Jesus of Nazareth, whom you are persecuting."

"What shall I do, Lord?"

"Arise and go into Damascus, and there you will be told all things which are appointed for you to do." (dialogue from Acts 26:14 merged with Acts 22:7-10)

Later, when he was recounting to King Agrippa what had happened on the road to Damascus, he told more about what the Lord had said to him:

"But rise and stand on your feet; for I have appeared to you for this purpose, to make you a minister and a witness both of the things which you have seen and of the things which I will yet reveal to you. I will deliver you from the Jewish people, as well as from the Gentiles, to whom I now send you, to open their eyes, in order to turn them from darkness to light, and from the power of Satan to God, that they may receive forgiveness of sins and an inheritance among those who are sanctified by faith in Me." (Acts 26:16-18)

Jesus talked with Saul, and Saul talked with Jesus. Faith came. Saul believed. He later told us that "faith comes by hearing and hearing by the Word of God" (Rom. 10:17). That first conversation took place in a great light that left Saul physically blinded.

In Damascus, another word from the Lord came through Ananias, who was sent to Saul after Ananias had his own conversation with Jesus. Ananias had told Jesus he was afraid to go to Saul. After Jesus finished talking with Ananias, he was strengthened to obey and went to Saul and told him,

"Brother Saul, receive your sight. The God of our fathers has chosen you that you should know His will, and see the Just One, and hear the voice of His mouth. For you will be His witness to all men of what you have seen and heard. And now why are you waiting? Arise and be baptized, and wash away your sins, calling on the name of the Lord." (dialogue from Acts 22:13-16)

Paul told of another conversation when he was in Jerusalem, praying in the temple. He was in a trance and saw Jesus, who began speaking to him:

"Make haste and get out of Jerusalem quickly, for they will not receive your testimony concerning Me."

"Lord, they know that in every synagogue I imprisoned and beat those who believe on You. And when the blood of Your martyr

Stephen was shed, I also was standing by consenting to his death, and guarding the clothes of those who were killing him."

"Depart, for I will send you far from here to the Gentiles." (dialogue from Acts 22:18-21)

At a later time, after being arrested in Jerusalem, the Lord was with him and said,

"Be of good cheer, Paul; for as you have testified for Me in Jerusalem, so you must also bear witness at Rome." (dialogue from Acts 23:11)

Another word came to him during a terrible, two-week-long storm at sea when all aboard ship had given up hope of living:

"For there stood by me this night an angel of the God to whom I belong and whom I serve, saying, 'Do not be afraid, Paul; you must be brought before Caesar; and indeed God has granted you all those who sail with you.'" (Acts 27:23-24)

Jesus and Paul were in a living, loving, conversational relationship. Jesus was drawing Paul to love Him, and Paul was pursuing Jesus. Circumstance by circumstance, Paul's faith and love increased throughout his life as Jesus revealed Himself to Paul. I learned from his example that my faith and love will increase the same way.

From Paul I learned not to be anxious and to bring everything that makes me fearful to the Lord. Like him, I now know what it is to experience a peace that is hard to explain (Phil. 4:6-7). I also now realize that nothing can separate me from God's love (Rom. 8:35). God had first loved Saul, even when he was killing people in the name of God. Jesus first loved me, even when I was a lying child (Rom. 5:8). Jesus told Paul how much he would suffer for His sake and empowered him to do this. I too have learned that whenever He asks me to suffer something for His sake, He will empower me to do it (Acts 9:15-17). Paul learned that he could "do all things through Christ" who strengthened him. I am learning the same thing day by day (Phil. 4:13). Like Paul, I have come to understand the power in the Lord's words that are spoken to me (2 Cor. 12:9), and I am learning to take those words by "praying always with all prayer and supplication" (Eph. 6:17-18). I realize that the Lord's living words bring me into the experience of His resurrection power and the fellowship of His sufferings.

Paul's Secret

I learned from Paul that there was a wonderful secret of doing all things in Christ. Paul's testimony of how he handled his "thorn in the flesh" has helped me find that same secret when facing my own life's difficulties.

> And lest I should be exalted above measure by the abundance of the revelations, a thorn in the flesh was given to me, a messenger of Satan to buffet me, lest I be exalted above measure. Concerning this thing I pleaded with the Lord three times that it might depart from me. And He said to me, "My grace is sufficient for you, for My strength is made perfect in weakness." Therefore most gladly I will rather boast in my infirmities, that the power of Christ may rest upon me. (2 Cor. 12:7-9)

Paul said he knew that his thorn had been given to him to prevent him from being exalted. He understood this, but he still wanted it removed. He was very troubled by it, so he brought his anxiety and his specific request about this thing to the Lord. He entreated the Lord that it might depart. He waited for an answer. Like Christ in the Garden of Gethsemane, he did this three times.

Then the Lord answered Paul with a few sentences that completely changed him. Some kind of transaction took place between them that I can't rationally explain; but I can see that Paul was changed. There is no trace of fear or anxiety in this statement: "Therefore most gladly will I rather boast in my infirmities, that the power of Christ may rest upon me." He still had his thorn, but He was anxious no more; he was glad! The power of Christ's resurrected life had come to Paul through what the Lord said to him in that situation. I also noticed that the words the Lord spoke to Paul were spoken for his understanding. He explained to Paul that He was going to experience grace instead of thorn removal, God's strength instead of deliverance. (I also couldn't help but notice how different this was from the Local Church teaching that we needed to get out of our mind and get into our spirit.)

I think that because of this experience and probably other similar ones he had, Paul wrote what has helped me in my daily living more than any other statement from him:

> In nothing be anxious; but in everything by prayer and supplication with thanksgiving let your requests be made known unto God. And the peace of God, which passeth all understanding, shall guard your hearts and your thoughts in Christ Jesus. (Phil. 4:6–7, ASV)

Paul's thorn experience showed me that on my journey to know the Lord, every need I face that causes me anxiety, even the smallest thing, is a reminder for me to come boldly to Jesus:

> Let us therefore come boldly to the throne of grace, that we may obtain mercy and find grace to help in time of need. (Heb. 4:16)

When I am in need or when I am weak, I have learned to come boldly—meaning I come in frankness and bluntness with assurance (Strong, G3954)—to His throne. It is a throne of *grace*. There I have found my great High Priest who is touched with the feeling of my weaknesses and who is interceding for me (Heb. 4:15). The Holy Spirit, given as a Helper (John 14:16), is also interceding for me when I pray:

> Likewise the Spirit also helps in our weaknesses. For we do not know what we should pray for as we ought, but the Spirit Himself makes intercession for us with groanings which cannot be uttered. (Rom. 8:26)

My current need brings me to this wonderful throne. Maybe this is why Paul said that "where sin abounded, grace abounded much more" (Rom. 5:20). Neediness, the result of sin and man's separation from God, brings me to Him for help. When I come to Jesus and make my request, something happens that changes me. Grace abounds and fills me with His peace.

I like to ask people what they think my favorite word is in Philippians 4:6–7. To date, no one has been able to guess correctly. My favorite word is *requests*. To make a request is to ask or petition for something to be done or given. I love this word because it reveals something about the heart of God. It shows me how wonderful He is. The God of the universe cares about hearing what I want. All of life's anxieties and needs didn't disappear when I gave myself to Him. Why not? He left these things with me to help me come to the throne of grace every day.

Shortly after I went to work in Oklahoma City, a fellow worker who was a Christian took me under her wing. We ate lunch together and became friends. She wasn't in the Local Church, so I could have her as a friend. She was very curious about me. My appearance was more than a little strange to her. I wore the same pair of shoes every day. I had very few outfits, and they were very, very plain. I wore no makeup or jewelry, and my hair looked similar to a "bowl cut." One day she asked me, "Jane, do you ever go to the store and buy something you want?" I said, "Of course." She asked me to give her an example. I thought and thought and couldn't name one thing. I said, "Well, I buy food I like." She said, "No. I don't mean necessities. I mean something you want. Do you ever go to the store and buy something you like or want?" I danced all around her question, trying to give her the answer she wanted to hear, but I never could. She also asked me what I liked, but I couldn't answer that question either. (I actually think she would have gone and bought it for me if I had been able to tell her something!) I think she asked me these questions because she cared about me.

When in the Local Church, I reached a place where I thought God really didn't care about what I needed or wanted. I didn't think I was supposed to have any requests. I was taught there that God didn't like begging prayers or prayers for help. He didn't want to give us help or things. He only wanted to give us Christ; Christ was all we needed. Did we need patience? Christ was patience. We should not pray for patience but for more Christ, who would spontaneously be our patience. God only wanted Christ! Asking for help or for things was to treat God wrongly, as if He was a personal servant. This was what Christianity did, and it wasn't pleasing to God.

I now know this isn't true. God is always waiting to hear what I want. He already knows my anxieties and my needs. Why doesn't He just wave a wand and meet them? It is because He wants to have a two-way conversation with me. He wants to answer my requests in ways that will teach me about Him and His ways. He wants to have a real, tangible love relationship with me. He wants to teach me that even a "No" from Him is something wonderful because He loves me and is doing what is in my very best interest. When I think that God actually cares about hearing what I want, I feel like crying.

Sometimes, the hardest thing for me to do is to identify what I really want or need. Sometimes it is difficult to determine what is causing my anxiety at a particular time. I think I spent too many years suppressing my anxieties and not allowing myself to admit that I had needs or wants.

A few years ago, I was struggling with a nagging fear about an uncertain future. Finally, I was able to stop and tell Jesus all my fears in detail. I was especially afraid of becoming a burden to my children in my old age. I was eventually able to state what I really wanted: I wanted to be safe and secure and to be cared for by somebody else. I wanted to know my needs would be met. As I told Him all of this, He gave me peace and calmness as He reminded me of His detailed care and tender love for fifty plus years. He asked me, "Do you think that this is the year I stop taking care of you?" When I further confessed my fears about having my needs met at a meager subsistence level, He reminded me that He was the God of the shoes. When I admitted my fear of not having enough to last to the end of my life, He reminded me that He was the God of the washing machine.

The most amazing thing was that, as He comforted me, I found myself loving Him and wanting to follow Him. I wanted others to know His wonderful love—even if that meant giving up what I wanted. How can I explain this? I can't. I think it is His grace that always comes when He shows me how much He loves me.

I appreciate Paul so much for what he shared about anxiety and for his faithful example. Paul counted everything loss for Christ—not because He had to, but because He wanted to. He had been loved, and he loved in return. His heart had been captured by the Lord.

Paul's Suffering for Others

I learned from Paul that I am called to experience the fellowship of His sufferings for the sake of others. When

Paul experienced the fellowship of Christ's sufferings, he suffered for the benefit of others. He said this:

> Always carrying about in the body the dying of the Lord Jesus, that the life of Jesus also may be manifested in our body. For we who live are always delivered to death for Jesus' sake, that the life of Jesus also may be manifested in our mortal flesh. So then death is working in us, but life in you. (2 Cor. 4:10-12)

I saw that like Christ and Paul, I also am called to be a grain of wheat that falls into the ground and dies in order to produce a harvest of many more grains of wheat. I too have been constrained by the love of Christ (2 Cor. 5:14), and His love empowers me to share in the fellowship of His sufferings on behalf of others.

In His Masterpiece: Peter

I learned from Peter that spiritual revelation without the experience of the cross gives opportunity to Satan. Peter told me not to think it strange when I face fiery trials unexpectedly. He knew all about this. From him, I learned that if I run ahead of the Lord, sure that I am in the light, and don't pay attention to what God is saying to me, I will learn the lesson of the cross the hard way. I also learned that I can become a door for Satan to enter.

One such fiery trial that Peter faced and a hard lesson that he learned is recorded in Matthew 16:15–25. First, God told Peter that Jesus was the Christ, the Son of the living God. This was Peter's own personal revelation from the Father. After this, Jesus told Peter that He was going to be killed. Peter didn't like hearing this and began to rebuke the Lord. Then Jesus said to Peter, "Get behind me, Satan!"

Why did Peter argue with the Lord about His statement that He would be killed? Because Peter thought he knew better. Hadn't the Father told him otherwise? He had just received direct revelation from God, not from flesh and blood, that Jesus was the Christ, the promised Messiah. However, there was a problem. Peter jumped to a conclusion. He believed that the Messiah was going to set up a visible, earthly kingdom at that time. Therefore, he was certain that there was no way Jesus would be killed because, according to his revelation, Jesus was the Christ. Peter treasured this revelation—a revelation that Jesus told him was from the Father.

Why did Jesus call Peter "Satan?" Jesus recognized that Satan was behind Peter's contending for his revelation. Satan had taken the opportunity to use Peter's treasured revelation, coupled with Peter's assumption about what it meant, to mislead him. Peter didn't understand that Jesus was working to set up a heavenly kingdom, not an earthly one. This heavenly kingdom could come into being only through the cross. Jesus knew that Peter hadn't fully understood what the Father had revealed to him, so after He heard Satan speaking through Peter, He told the disciples that whoever would follow Him must deny himself and take up his cross. He was telling Peter, at that moment, that he needed to deny himself. Instead of fighting for his God-given revelation, he needed to take up his cross, drop his fight, and let go of what he thought he knew from God.

Peter, however, didn't heed the Lord's word. He heard, but he didn't grasp the meaning of the most crucial point: the cross. When the Lord was arrested, Peter fought with the officials, and then he sought to save himself. He denied the Lord three times, fulfilling the Lord's prophecy concerning him. At the cock's crowing, Peter saw himself a complete failure and wept bitterly. Jesus was crucified.

At the moment of the Lord's death, Peter easily gave up his treasured revelation and his fight for it. Christ was dead. Peter had been wrong after all. Christ was not the Messiah. Peter spent two days in terrible darkness—and then the Lord arose from thc dead.

When Peter saw Jesus resurrected, he understood! Jesus really was the Messiah. In today's language, he would have said, "Now I get it!" He realized that his understanding of the Father's revelation to him had been limited and inaccurate. It had even become a matter of pride and a door for Satan. Peter's understanding of his revelation died on the cross with Jesus; but now his revelation was back, and he understood. It surpassed what he ever could have imagined! Jesus had come out of the grave. The Messiah was the King of a heavenly kingdom! As Jesus had told him, he was no longer Simon, just a natural man of clay; but having been broken through his failure, he was now Peter, a spiritual man of stone (*Peter* means "rock" [Strong, G4074]).

From Peter, I learned that I am prone to treasure what I hear directly from God more than I treasure God's way, the way of the cross. Like Peter, many times I have learned the lesson of the cross the hard way. Too often, I get caught holding on to what I think I know and don't hear His voice. I don't see the need to take up my cross and follow Him until He allows a fiery trial to come and open my eyes. For many years in the Local Church, I was busily pressing ahead, trusting in my own understanding of what it meant to be a consecrated Christian, until God allowed me to have a fiery trial that was specifically designed by Him to burn up my zealous "wood, hay, and straw" (1 Cor. 3:12) and turn me to see Him and His way, the way of the cross.

In His Masterpiece: Abraham

I learned from Abraham that the experience of the cross is about faith and obedience. When God told Abraham to offer up his only son, Isaac, he obeyed by faith. He believed that God was able to raise him up even from the dead. Just before Abraham was about to kill Isaac, God intervened and provided a substitute sacrifice. This was a picture of Christ's death and resurrection that was to come (Heb. 11:17–19). Abraham could offer his son because he believed God's promises to Him. He knew that if he obeyed God, this would not be the end of Isaac because God had promised to bless the whole earth through Isaac. Abraham knew that if Isaac died, in order for God to fulfill His promise, He would have to raise Isaac from the dead.

From Abraham, I learned that I can give up my things, my wants, and even the spiritual things that God has given me by faith (Abraham had received Isaac by faith). I can do this, when He asks me to do so, by faith in who He is and in His promises. Why? Because death is not the end. Whatever I place on the altar at His request, God can give back to me in resurrection in His time. My story shows that this has happened to me a number of times. I gave him John; God gave him back as a believer and as my husband. I gave him my education; God gave me a better one. There are some things I have given Him that have not come back, but He has filled their place with Himself, something much better.

> So Jesus answered and said, "Assuredly, I say to you, there is no one who has left house or brothers or sisters or father or mother or wife or children or lands, for My sake and the gospel's, who shall not receive a hundredfold now in this time—houses and brothers and sisters and mothers and children and lands, with persecutions—and in the age to come, eternal life." (Mark 10:29-30)

In His Masterpiece: John

I learned from the apostle John that the Spirit will guide me into all truth by speaking God's living words to me in the midst of life's situations. Nearing the end of his life, John was exiled on an island and wrote:

> I, John, both your brother and companion in the tribulation and kingdom and patience of Jesus Christ, was on the island that is called Patmos for the word of God and for the testimony of Jesus Christ. (Rev. 1:9)

In this situation, he was our companion in tribulation; he was experiencing the fellowship of Christ's sufferings. During this time, the Spirit spoke the truth to him, and he wrote it down. It is now the final book of the Bible, Revelation. From John's gospel, I learned that the "Spirit of truth" would come to me and speak the Lord's words to me in order to guide me into all truth (John 16:13). John had heard Jesus say before He was crucified that He wouldn't leave them without comfort but would come to them. He would send the Comforter, the Holy Spirit, who would remind them of all the words He had said to them (John 14:26). John's epistles show that the Spirit of truth had been speaking with him. The following quotation shows that he had come to understand the message of the cross and the fruit that would be seen in the life of a true follower of the Lamb:

> We know that we have passed from death to life, because we love the brethren. He who does not love his brother abides in death. Whoever hates his brother is a murderer, and you know that no

murderer has eternal life abiding in him. By this we know love, because He laid down His life for us. And we also ought to lay down our lives for the brethren. (1 John 3:14-16)

In His Masterpiece: Martha, Mary, and Lazarus

I learned from Martha, Mary, and Lazarus that the church which Christ builds is produced by experiencing Him as resurrection life, life out of death. In these three persons in John 11, I saw a picture of believers before and after they experience Jesus as "the resurrection and the life." Martha was a sister who was busy serving others and was "worried and troubled about many things." Mary was a sister who was sitting at Jesus' feet and had "chosen that good part" (Luke 10:30-42). Lazarus was a brother about whom not much was recorded except that he became very ill and died. Martha and Mary had sent for Jesus and, in their opinion, He arrived too late; so, both Martha and Mary let Him know He should have come sooner to prevent their brother's death. They loved Jesus and were following Him, but they really didn't know who He was. Jesus said to Martha:

> "I am the resurrection and the life. He who believes in Me, though he may die, he shall live. And whoever lives and believes in Me shall never die. Do you believe this?" (John 11:25-26)

Then four days after Lazarus' death, Jesus called Lazarus out of his grave. The Bible doesn't record Lazarus saying anything after his resurrection. He really didn't have to. Many saw and believed—he was a living testimony to who Christ was. There is no question that Lazarus was changed by this experience. I think that Martha and Mary were changed as well when they saw Jesus raise their brother from the dead. Martha probably continued to serve busily, and Mary still sat at Jesus' feet; but inwardly, they weren't the same. They had seen who Jesus was—the resurrection and the life.

From them, I learned that by seeing and experiencing Him as the resurrection and the life, I can be busy serving while sitting at His feet. Thus occupied, my life testifies to the principalities and powers that He has raised me from the dead.

In His Masterpiece: The Corinthian Believers

I learned from the Corinthians that the Christian life, without the experience of the cross, produces works of the flesh. This situation makes it possible for the gates of hell to prevail against the church. In Corinth, the church was full of the works of the flesh because the experience of the cross was missing. Paul offered them the solution to their problems: Christ and Him crucified. The Corinthians believed they were following God, but the loveless condition of the church showed that they had not yet learned the way of the cross, the way of God's love (1 Cor. 13). From them, I learned that there is no way for me to be with other believers and glorify Him without the cross working in me personally.

In His Masterpiece: Many Others

I learned from many others that the cross is the power of God unto those who believe. The Bible contains many other examples of faith, and I am thankful for those testimonies. I learned from Moses, who saw the plight of the children of Israel and tried to save them in his own strength. Instead, he found himself exiled and useless to God on the back side of the desert. Many years later, God called him and used him to rescue the children of Israel. From this, I learned that God could use a man for His purpose only after his natural strength had been broken. I learned from Joseph, who was rejected and hurt by his brothers, that God was fully in control of his hurt and had allowed it for his family's highest good. I learned from Esther, who risked her own life to save God's people. I learned from David, who loved God greatly, sinned greatly, and also repented greatly. I learned from Abigail, who risked herself to save others. I learned from Mary, who bore shame by being the willing handmaid of the Lord and becoming pregnant outside of marriage in order for Christ to be born.

In the book of Hebrews, I glimpsed God's big picture of the faithful and also learned what faith is. "Faith is the substance of things hoped for, the evidence of things not seen" (Heb. 11:1). In the list of the faithful in Hebrews,

Sarah stands out to me. From her, I learned that what God remembers is our faith, not our failures. In Genesis, she laughed at God's promise regarding Isaac. When God asked her about this, she lied and said she hadn't laughed. God responded, "No, but you did laugh!" (Gen. 18:15). Hebrews, however, doesn't mention her laughter or her lie—her failure—but only reports that through faith she "received strength to conceive seed, and she bore a child when she was past the age" (Heb. 11:11). (The name Isaac, however, does mean laughter!)

Jesus is the clearest and strongest testimony to God's love and faithfulness. God raised Him from the dead and made him both the King of kings and the Lord of lords. His obedience authored our faith, and His faithful intercession for us as our great High Priest will finish it.

History after biblical times also contains a long list of the faithful. Some of their stories have been recorded. From Hudson Taylor's life, I learned about giving and practically depending on God for financial needs by faith. From Rees Howell's life, I learned about intercessory prayer. From Madame Guyon's life, I learned that in the midst of suffering, it was possible to have a satisfying and joyful relationship with Jesus. From George Mueller's life, I learned about God's practical love for children without families. From Evan Roberts, George Whitefield, and John and Charles Wesley, I learned about the power of the gospel and the power of the Spirit to convict the world of sin, righteousness, and judgment. From Jessie Penn-Lewis, I learned about the cross and spiritual warfare. From Amy Carmichael, I learned about the great love of God, who through her, searched out, rescued, and became a mother to many small children who would otherwise have lived lives of shame in idol temples. Her favorite color throughout her life was blue. From her I also learned that it is okay to have a favorite color! I also learned from many others whose published stories came into my hands. In addition, many believers have conveyed their spiritual experiences to me in the hymns they wrote. My story shows how the Spirit used many of the words in such hymns to help me and teach me.

Chapter 21
You and Me

> I am crucified with Christ: nevertheless I live; yet not I, but Christ liveth in me: and the life which I now live in the flesh I live by the faith of the Son of God, who loved me, and gave Himself for me. (Gal. 2:20, KJV)

In His Masterpiece: Me

MY STORY IS ONE OF LOVE that grew from many conversations between Jesus and me. I love Him because He first loved me and gave Himself for me. He began and is finishing my faith (Heb. 12:2). Until He spoke to me the first time, I had no faith. After He spoke, I had a little faith. Now, many years later, after many more conversations with Him, I have much more faith. Paul told us to continue our walk with Jesus in the same way as we began it (Gal. 3:3). Initially, faith came when I heard Jesus speak to me, and my faith has grown the same way.

From the time I willingly gave myself to Him, He began to make Himself more real to me and to call me to know Him, the power of His resurrection, and the fellowship of His sufferings. Like Paul, I have been through trials and afflictions. Mine have not been in the magnitude of Paul's, but many times they seemed like it to me! Jesus has given me incredible peace in the midst of turmoil. He has carried me through a long, dark valley of suffering to a place of peace and joy. My testimony is that I have been loved with an everlasting love. By His death on the cross, I have been shown the depth of that love. It passes knowledge and my understanding. I can only thank Him and respond in kind.

What a wonder it is that Jesus loved me and died for me—not for who I would be after I became a new creation in Christ, but for who I was when I was separated from Him, when I was at my very worst. He found me to be lovable in that hopeless state.

Did He form me and know me in my mother's womb (Psa. 139:13), love me with an everlasting love, and die on the cross so He could wipe out my person, as I believed in the Local Church? No! He died to set me free, to make me whole. I, Jane, am still here; but I am a new creation in Christ (2 Cor. 5:17), one that depends on Him for everything and loves Him supremely because He first loved me. He loves me intimately. I am His, and He is mine. My story with Him has been, is, and will be for eternity a love story.

In Trouble for Being a Normal Christian

When I got into trouble in the Local Church, I was accused of trying to be a spiritual giant and of seeking my own individual spirituality. I was told that the age of spiritual giants was over and that this was the age of the church, the "corporate Christ." But the truth is that there is no such thing as a spiritual giant. All the believers whose biographies I read only looked like spiritual giants. They weren't. They were normal Christians. It is normal to live by faith. It is normal to know His ways and follow Him. It is normal to love Him above all else, even at the cost of everything. It is normal to have a personal walk with Jesus—my own walk. It is normal to take up my cross and follow Him! It is normal to live according to His purpose for my life. My experience was normal and still is! As a child, I prayed God would just let me be normal. He has answered that prayer! I am a normal Christian, and I am part of His masterpiece, where every Christian is a normal Christian!

Living Testimonies

God has now made sense for me out of my tangled troubles. It was not my brothers in the Local Church, but God's enemy, Satan, who sought to stomp out my normal experience of Jesus. But the strategy of the devil didn't work against me; it worked for me! Satan apparently forgot about the operation of God that raises from the dead.

God's promises were a lifeline to me. When I seemed to be drowning in deep waters, He brought me through to a place of safety. He used the trouble I experienced in the

Local Church to chasten me as a child He loves, to deliver me from deception, and even to introduce me to the fellowship of His sufferings. It was for my benefit in every way.

But it was for more than my benefit. He did more than just save me out of all my trouble. He had a wise purpose in view. One day, while I was writing this chapter, God led me to call Leah, one of the sisters who lived with us in the Harvest and Wheeler houses in Houston, and ask her a question. Leah is no longer a member of the Local Church. He told me to ask her what she remembered about why I had been in trouble in 1977. Her answer surprised me. She said in essence: "What I remember most is that I thought you were in trouble because of all the biographies you were reading and passing to others to read. The brothers thought you were leading people astray from Witness Lee's ministry." After thinking about this, I realized that my trouble in Houston had escalated when I started reading and recommending the life stories and testimonies of other believers. What I read about those believers knowing Christ and Him crucified had fueled my walk with Jesus.

Satan temporarily stopped me from reading such biographies and from recommending them to others. But he didn't stop what God was doing. He couldn't thwart God's purpose. Through it all, God was composing my story, my testimony with Him.

> And they overcame him by the blood of the Lamb and by the word
> of their testimony, and they did not love their lives to the death.
> (Rev. 12:11)

He was adding one more arrow to His quiver. Our life testimonies defeat Satan! They also offer a personal, real, and powerfully attractive look at the Savior as not much else can do.

I once heard Witness Lee say that he didn't think it was a good idea to publish autobiographical material while one was still alive. Because I agreed with this, it wasn't easy for the Lord to persuade me to tell about my experiences with Him. But He finally did persuade me. I am no longer afraid to share my testimony. In fact,

> My heart overfloweth with a goodly matter; I speak the things which I have made touching the king: My tongue is the pen of a ready writer. (Psa. 45:1, ASV)

He has made me glad! I cannot help but tell others about how available and real He is. I cannot help but tell others about the message of the cross and its power. Yes, God had a wise purpose in view.

Although God has caused my experience in the Local Church to work for good, this doesn't mean that God agreed with, approved of, or caused the wrongs that were committed against me by others when I was a member. Whoever commits wrongs is accountable to God for them. One day, we will all be in the light together. There will be no darkness, no misunderstanding, no hurt, no deception, no injustice, and no more tears or suffering. All will be light. My fellowship with all those that I knew and loved while in the Local Church will be restored—yes, even with Anne and Dan—without any bitterness. I look forward to that day.

In His Masterpiece: You

I hope that you are thinking about the wonder of the fact that the God who created the universe loves you and gave Himself for you. It is even more wondrous that He has a specific purpose for your life, one that fits perfectly into His master plan, one that, if He has not already begun to do so, He is waiting to reveal to you.

The New Testament shows that both John the Baptist and Paul finished their courses (Acts 13:25, 2 Tim. 4:7, KJV). According to the Greek, this means they finished their races or, figuratively, their careers (Strong, G1408). All of those in the cloud of witnesses in Hebrews also finished their courses. In her memoirs, Jessie Penn-Lewis wrote:

> There is a "course" prepared for each believer from the moment of his new birth, providing for the fullest maturity of the new life within him, and the highest which God can make of his life in the use of every faculty for His service. To discover that "course" and fulfil it is the one duty of every soul. Others cannot judge what that course is. God alone knows it, and He can make it known, and

guide the believer into it, as certainly to-day as He did Jeremiah and other prophets, Paul and Philip and other apostles. (Garrard, vii)

Yes, you have a career in God, a heavenly career that is uniquely yours to walk in. When you surrender your life to Him, which is the most reasonable thing for you to do with His great love in view, you can be sure that your life will prove "that good, and acceptable, and perfect will of God" (Rom. 12:2).

Chapter 22
The Worthy Lamb

Who is he who condemns? It is Christ who died, and furthermore is also risen, who is even at the right hand of God, who also makes intercession for us. (Rom. 8:34)

... because He poured out His life unto death, and He let Himself be regarded as a criminal and be numbered with the transgressors, yet He bore [and took away] the sin of many and makes intercession for the transgressors—the rebellious. (Isa. 53:12, AV)

The View from the Cross

When You hung there, nailed to that tree,
What did You see? What did You see?
When You hung there, nailed to that tree,
What did You see on Calvary?

Did You see darkness, weakness, pain?
Did You see mankind's cruel disdain?
Did You see those who smiled with pride
Because they had You crucified?

Did You see sin, the filth, the shame:
Your "gift" from those for whom You came?
With all this there, what did You see?
I hear You saying ... You saw me.

— Jane Carole Anderson

The Lamb and His Wife

The Bible contains the wonderful love story of the worthy Lamb of God and His wife. From Genesis to Revelation, the Bible tells this story and reveals God's great love for mankind. His love calls us to love Him in return.

The Bible gives many pictures and stories to help us understand the reality of what Christ accomplished by dying on the cross as God's Lamb. Adam and Eve were saved by the death of an animal. The children of Israel were saved by the blood of the Passover lamb (Exo. 12). We were afforded salvation by the real Passover Lamb, Jesus, who shed His blood on the cross at precisely the same time the Jews were sacrificing a "perfect" lamb to celebrate their Passover. John the Baptist told the Jewish people to behold Christ, the sinless "Lamb of God" (John 1:29).

When the apostle John was on the island of Patmos, the Spirit showed him a vision of the Lamb of God on the throne. Ten thousand times ten thousand, and thousands of thousands, were saying with a loud voice:

> "Worthy is the Lamb who was slain to receive power and riches and wisdom, and strength and honor and glory and blessing!" And every creature which is in heaven and on the earth and under the earth and such as are in the sea, and all that are in them, I heard saying: "Blessing and honor and glory and power be to Him who sits on the throne, and to the Lamb, forever and ever!" (Rev. 5:12-13)

The Spirit also showed John the followers of the Lamb: "a great multitude which no one could number of all nations, tribes, peoples, and tongues." These were those who had been drawn to Jesus by His death on the cross and were standing before the throne and praising the Lamb (Rev. 7:9–12).

The Unveiling

The Spirit then showed John what would happen in the end times to all those on the earth "whose names have not been written in the Book of Life of the Lamb slain from the foundation of the world" (Rev. 13:8). He also showed him those who were before the throne singing the "song of Moses" (sung by the children of Israel after crossing through the Red Sea) and the "song of the Lamb" (Rev. 15:3).

The love story in the Bible culminates in the "marriage of the Lamb" to His bride.

> "Let us be glad and rejoice and give Him glory, for the marriage of the Lamb has come, and His wife has made herself ready." And to her it was granted to be arrayed in fine linen, clean and bright, for the fine linen is the righteous acts of the saints. (Rev. 19:7-8)

She is God's holy city, the New Jerusalem—the bride, the Lamb's wife (Rev. 21:9–10). She will look like Him. All those who love Him will be there. A sister wrote the following hymn, which expresses well the feeling we will have on that day:

> The Bride eyes not her garment,
> But her dear Bridegroom's face;
> I will not gaze at glory,
> But on my King of grace.
> Not at the crown He giveth,
> But on His piercèd hand;
> The Lamb is all the glory,
> And my eternal stand.
>
> — Ann Ross Cousin

Thanks be to God for showing us our Bridegroom, the King of grace, the Holy Lamb of God. May we keep His wonderful death ever in our view and maintain the attitude of love and consecration expressed in the following hymn:

> When I survey the wondrous cross
> On which the Prince of Glory died,
> My highest gain I count but loss,
> And pour contempt on all my pride.

Our God forbid that we should boast,
  Save in the death of Christ our Lord;
All the vain things that charm us most,
  We'd sacrifice them to His blood.

There from His head, His hands, His feet,
  Sorrow and love flowed mingled down;
    Did e'er such love and sorrow meet,
    Or thorns compose so rich a crown?

  His dying crimson, from His head
  Spreads o'er His body on the tree;
    To all the world then am I dead;
    And all the world is dead to me.

Were the whole realm of nature ours,
  That were an offering far too small;
Love that transcends our highest pow'rs,
  Demands our heart, our life, our all.

— Isaac Watts

Part 5

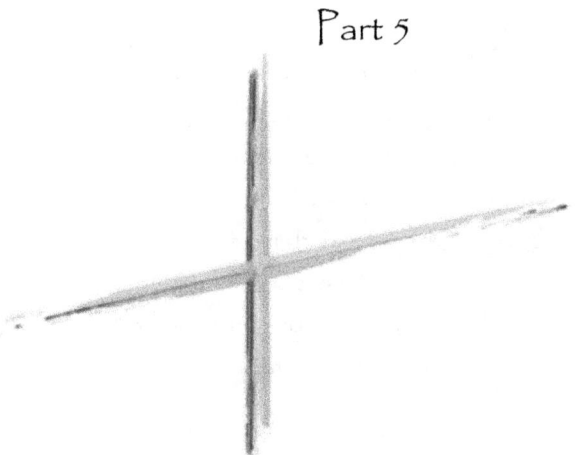

God's Deliverance

Freedom from Deception

His banner over us is love,
　Our sword the Word of God.
We tread the road the saints above
　With shouts of triumph trod.
By faith, they like a whirlwind's breath,
　Swept on o'er every field.
The faith by which they conquered death
　Is still our shining shield.

Faith is the victory! Faith is the victory!
O glorious victory, that overcomes the world.

On every hand the foe we find
　Drawn up in dread array.
Let tents of ease be left behind,
　And onward to the fray.
Salvation's helmet on each head,
　With truth all girt about,
The earth shall tremble 'neath our tread,
　And echo with our shout.

To him that overcomes the foe,
　White raiment shall be giv'n.
Before the angels he shall know
　His name confessed in Heav'n.
Then onward from the hill of light,
　Our hearts with love aflame,
We'll vanquish all the hosts of night,
　In Jesus' conqu'ring Name.

—John H. Yates

Chapter 23
About Deception

> Search me, O God, and know my heart; try me, and know my anxieties; and see if there is any wicked way in me, and lead me in the way everlasting. (Psa. 139:23-24)

Seek and You Shall Find

WE LEFT THE LOCAL CHURCH in 1987. The simple truth was that I had become deceived and needed a full deliverance. It took the Lord a long period of time to set me fully free and bring me back to a simple day-by-day walk with Him. It also took time for Him to heal the damage in my life that was a result of that experience.

I found a measure of freedom as I forgave each person there who had hurt me. However, God was not able to clear up my mental confusion about Him, about His purpose, and about me, until He restored my confidence in being able to hear truth directly and personally from Him. Once this happened, mainly through some writings by other believers who had left the Local Church, I was on the way to full deliverance.

I want to encourage anyone reading this that recovery from deception is possible when you want to know truth and ask Him for His light. He ultimately showed me that the root of all the bad fruit in my life was wrong beliefs I had accepted, which gradually produced wrong thoughts in my mind about God and His purpose, and about myself. Satan used these wrong thoughts to control my behavior and cause me to violate truth and sin against God.

Only as I was able to identify these wrong beliefs and wrong thoughts was I able to find freedom from them. I could never have done this alone. I had a wonderful Helper who answered my prayers from His throne of grace. If you are in need of deliverance (or anything for that matter), I encourage you to go there and tell Him your need.

Susceptible to Deception

I have learned the hard way that even when I am well-intentioned, I am susceptible to deception. I have an individual responsibility to guard against deception. I also have a responsibility to seek deliverance from possible deception in the present (Matt. 24:4).

It is easy to say others are deceived, but it is not always easy to consider my own condition regarding deception. If I am unable or unwilling to humble myself and ask God to shine His light on me, this may indicate that I am in deception. I should always be able to bow to Him and pray for His light to shine on me. I am responsible to God to be right in my relationship with Him, with my family, with other Christians, and with society.

Other Christians that I am associated with may believe the same as I do, but I shouldn't trust in this. I must seek truth for myself. One day, as a believer, I will stand before Christ at His judgment seat to give account for how I lived on this earth. If I have accepted and practiced error because I believed what others taught me without verifying its truth for myself, I will be accountable for this, as well as for the fruit that resulted in my life.

Am I Deceived?

How can I know if I have been deceived or if what I have been taught and believe is in error? The Bible says, "You will know them by their fruits" (Matt. 7:16). This is fundamental. Whenever I note behavior, in myself or others, that is contrary to the plain teaching of the Bible or to the fruit of the Spirit, I must suspect deception. I must pay careful attention to the fruit of my beliefs. If the fruit is not fruit of the Spirit, something is wrong with my belief.

> But the fruit of the Spirit is love, joy, peace, longsuffering, kindness, goodness, faithfulness, gentleness, self-control. (Gal. 5:22-23)

While I was still in the Local Church, God began to open my eyes to the bad fruit in my life and in the lives of others around me. I was in serious violation of God's Word regarding my relationship with Him and with others, but a thick fog was veiling me, preventing me from seeing what I now understand. At the root of this bad fruit was my acceptance of wrong teaching.

The First Deception

The first record of Satan's deception gives insight into how Satan deceives and into what the evidence of deception will be. In essence, by subtly changing God's words, Satan carefully crafted and introduced untrue thoughts into Eve's mind: thoughts about God, about His intention, and about man himself. He then used these wrong thoughts to cause Eve to disobey God. To put it simply, Satan lied to her, she believed him, and she sinned.

His tactic has not changed. Satan deceives us by using God's own words. He slightly alters the truth to solicit our disobedience to God. God's word to Adam and Eve was this:

> "Of every tree of the garden you may freely eat; but of the tree of the knowledge of good and evil you shall not eat, for in the day that you eat of it you shall surely die." (Gen 2:16-17)

Satan drew Eve into a conversation about what God had said: "Has God indeed said, 'You shall not eat of every tree of the garden'?" She answered, "We may eat the fruit of the trees of the garden; but of the fruit of the tree which is in the midst of the garden, God has said, 'You shall not eat it, nor shall you touch it, lest you die.'" Then Satan lied to her, slipping into her mind the first doubt, an untrue thought and slander of God: "You will not surely die." He was hinting to her that God was a liar. He followed this by telling her something further that was true, but which God had not said: "For God knows that in the day you eat of it your eyes will be opened, and you will be like God, knowing good and evil" (Gen. 3:1-5). In this, he was also hinting to her that God's purpose was to keep her from becoming like Him. God did not want her to be wise and therefore was hiding something from her. He also introduced a wrong thought about herself: She could be like God; she could be wise. His carefully planned mixture of truth and deceit worked. She accepted the whole thought he had offered her.

With her new thought, Eve considered the forbidden tree in a new light, noting that "it was pleasant to the eyes, and a tree desirable to make one wise" (Gen. 3:6). She then took a way other than God's way. Instead of continuing to depend on God and talk to Him daily as she had been doing, she made a decision completely on her own. This was a first consequence of her deception. She didn't talk to God (or to Adam) but acted on her own. Satan had told her that she and Adam would be *like God knowing good and evil.* When God appeared, He said, "Behold the man has become like one of Us, to know good and evil" (Gen. 3:22). So, that part of what Satan had told her was true.

Satan repeated his Garden-of-Eden tactic on Christ in the wilderness temptation by using God's words and interpreting them in a way that twisted their meaning. His goal was to cause Christ to disobey the Father. He failed (Matt. 4:1–11).

The New Testament warns us that we are in danger of departing from the faith as a result of listening to doctrines of demons:

> Now the Spirit expressly says that in latter times some will depart from the faith, giving heed to deceiving spirits and doctrines of demons. (1 Tim. 4:1)

The New Testament characterizes deceptive doctrines as follows:

> That we should no longer be children, tossed to and fro and carried about with every wind of doctrine, by the trickery of men, in the cunning craftiness of deceitful plotting. (Eph. 4:14)

Since his conversation with Eve, Satan has continued to use God's words and twist them to produce, manufacture, and originate winds of doctrine with the intention of carrying believers away from God. He uses deceived men to distribute such doctrines in order to cause people to believe lies rather than the truth. Once a lie is accepted, sin will follow, sin that will result in damage to relationships with God and with others.

The Fruit of Deception

Deception results in wrong thoughts about God, about God's purpose and His way, and about ourselves. These wrong thoughts produce wrong behaviors, or sin, that damage our relationships with God and others.

The most easily recognizable fruit or evidence of deception is damaged relationships. Wherever we see damaged relationships, Satan is at work. The first damaged relationship was the one between man and God Himself. This relationship was the real target of Satan in the Garden of Eden. He knew that if he could stop Adam and Eve from spending time with God in the garden, the rest of his plan would fall nicely in place. After he achieved this objective, damaged relationships followed. A rift developed between Adam and Eve when Adam blamed Eve for leading him astray. Eve, no doubt, knew that Adam made his own choice to accept and eat the fruit. Not only that, he had been with her and remained silent when she was being deceived (Gen 3:6).[10] The next damaged relationship was between Cain and Abel. They had the first experience of sibling rivalry. Cain became jealous of his brother, Abel, and killed him (Gen. 4:3–8).

---

[10] Adam was wrong to blame Eve and to indirectly blame God for giving her to him (Gen. 3:12), because he was responsible for his own choice to accept the fruit from her and, thereby, disobey God. Paul wrote that Eve was deceived but that Adam was not deceived (1 Tim 2:14). He also wrote that Adam transgressed and was the one party responsible for the disobedience that made all sinners (Rom. 5:14, 19).

Deception results in obeying Satan instead of God. I will always act according to what I believe. If I have accepted a wrong belief from Satan, he can use that wrong belief to control me. Instead of obeying and serving God, I will obey and serve Satan.

> Know ye not, that to whom ye yield yourselves servants to obey, his servants ye are to whom ye obey; whether of sin unto death, or of obedience unto righteousness? (Rom. 6:16, KJV)

For example, if I believe that a Christian leader is God's authority on the earth, and should not ever be questioned,

Satan can use my belief about that leader to control me. If the leader goes astray, I will follow him and also go astray.

As I embraced, believed, and practiced many of the things I learned in the Local Church, my relationship with God was damaged and my relationship with my family was damaged. My relationships with other Christians were damaged, and my attitude toward society in general was damaged. This was clear evidence of Satan's activity and strong evidence of deception.

> Therefore by their fruits you will know them. (Matt. 7:20)

The Process of Deception

Slowly, Over Time

God has helped me understand that deception in the Local Church occurred slowly, over time, something like the acts in a play. At the opening of the play, the characters were:

- Many young, inexperienced Christians loving Jesus, seeking to know Him more, and ready to learn and follow
- A few older, experienced Christians who were also seeking and were ready to learn and follow
- A much older, experienced, extremely knowledgeable and gifted Bible teacher, ready to pass on his knowledge
- God's enemy, Satan, the great deceiver, watching and plotting to devour these seekers

During Act I, Satan used the gifted teacher to convince the ready learners that they had a unique and special calling to recover the damaged church. He convinced them that they had found God's man on the earth who knew what was wrong with the church and how to recover it. He convinced them the church was to be a round-the-clock experience, more important than anything else in life.

During Act II, God's enemy convinced the seeking Christians that they needed leaders among them to carry out this recovery. He convinced these leaders that they had a responsibility to follow and promote God's man absolutely. He persuaded the rest of the followers that their duty was to follow and to follow well. They must follow the leaders absolutely, even if it hurt their families.

During Act III, the leaders became convinced that the only way to fulfill the vision they had seen from the beginning was to promote to the uttermost the ministry of God's man. When some questioned this, the faithful leaders saw this as an attack by God's enemy, who wanted to frustrate God's move on the earth. They became vigilant to protect the church and the ministry of the man they had been called to follow. To faithfully serve God, they expelled some of their own brethren whom they considered to be deceived. God's enemy also persuaded the gifted teacher to fight for his ministry. During this act, "God's man" and his followers also fought against some of their brethren from Christianity to show them that God would not tolerate anyone questioning them.

By the end of Act III, Satan and his demons had finished their popcorn and were having a good laugh. They sat back and relaxed, knowing that the drama they had successfully produced in the Local Church would be continually repeated there by the faithful. The seekers had been rendered ineffective.

I do not mean by this analogy to make light of what happened in the Local Church. It is not a laughing matter to me. I still love my brothers and sisters there, even though they consider me to be an opposer. Although I am very sad that God's enemy was able to deceive us in this way, I am not discouraged. I know that God is the real director, and He will have the last laugh. The joke will be on the devil and his followers when God reveals Act IV.

Unbalanced Teaching

Another piece of the process of deception was the method by which we were instructed. We heard the same teachings over and over and over again. They were presented in different ways, but there were only a few main themes. It would be untrue to say Witness Lee never taught us other things. He did address a broad spectrum of truth as he gave his Life-Study messages. He did teach, at one time or another, many of the truths that have been gleaned from the Bible throughout Christian history. However, I now believe that his unbalanced repetition of certain teachings gave Satan ground to hurt us.

I believe that his emphasis in teaching should have been governed by the Bible's emphasis. For example, if the Bible uses one hundred verses to tell us something about God's life and one hundred to tell us something about God's love, then Witness Lee's teaching should have been similarly balanced to teach us equally about life and love. Instead, he taught us ninety-nine percent of the time about God's life and one percent, at best, about God's love.

I heard Witness Lee accuse those in Christianity of talking so much about the Trinity, the three Persons of the Godhead, that they came close to sounding like they believed in three gods. Interestingly, he did the same thing when he talked so much about the oneness of the three and their inclusion in the Spirit. He came close to sounding like he believed there was only one God who existed successively in three forms. The Bible mentions the Father and the Son significantly more than it does the Spirit, yet our steady diet was primarily teaching about the Spirit.

We learn mainly by example and repetition, not just by accurate statements occasionally mentioned. Whatever we hear and see most frequently will greatly influence what we believe most deeply. A parent may tell a child that he loves him or her a few times; but if what the child hears most of the time is condemnation and criticism, or if the parent hits the child daily, the condemning and unloving message will be what the child learns.

The Process of Deliverance

Knowing the Truth

How can I find freedom from deception? Freedom comes by knowing the truth.

> And you shall know the truth, and the truth shall make you free.
> (John 8:32)

Deception takes place in my mind, in what I choose to believe, so my deliverance is dependent upon my mind's apprehending and choosing to believe truth.

Chapter 23—About Deception

Recognizing and rejecting false belief systems or wrong thoughts about God, ourselves, and others is integral to finding freedom. Satan hates me, and he hates God. He hates that I would have a relationship with God. He also hates all human relationships: husband and wife, parents and children, Christian brothers and sisters, and neighbors. Satan and his deceiving spirits cultivate wrong thoughts and beliefs in my mind with the intention of damaging me, my relationship with God, and my relationships with others.

I must have direct involvement with the living Word of God if I want to be kept from or delivered from deception.

> For the word of God is living and powerful, and sharper than any two-edged sword, piercing even to the division of soul and spirit, and of joints and marrow, and is a discerner of the thoughts and intents of the heart. (Heb. 4:12)

I must believe that I am individually capable of receiving direct light from God through His Word. If I doubt this, or if I respect the right or ability of others to receive light to the exclusion of my own, then I am in danger. I can be easily deceived and held in a state of deception. It is my responsibility to pray and to use my God-given mind to examine carefully what I believe. Concerning this responsibility, Jessie Penn-Lewis wrote:

> In accordance with these directions of the Word of God, and in view of the critical time through which the Church of Christ is passing, every expression, "view," or theory, which we hold concerning things, should now be examined carefully, and brought to the proof, with open and honest desire to know the pure truth of God, as well as every statement that comes to our knowledge of the experience of others, which may throw light upon our own pathway. Every criticism—just or unjust—should be humbly received, and *examined to discover its ground*, apparent or real; and facts concerning spiritual verities from every section of the church of God, should be analysed, independent of their pleasure, or pain, to us personally, either for our own enlightenment, or for our equipment in the service of God. (Penn-Lewis, 57–58)

Why should we examine and prove all our views, the experiences of others, and every criticism? Why should we analyze the facts concerning spiritual truths from all believers? She continues with the following reason:

> For the knowledge of truth is the first essential for warfare with the lying spirits of Satan, and truth must be eagerly sought for, and faced with earnest and sincere desire to know it, and obey it in the light of God; truth concerning ourselves, discerned by unbiased [sic] discrimination; truth from the Scriptures, uncoloured, unstrained, unmutilated, undiluted; truth in facing facts of experience in all members of the Body of Christ, and not one section alone. (Penn-Lewis, 58)

Whatever is of God can be scrutinized, even as Jesus was. After Jesus was examined, the declaration was this: "I find no fault in this man" (Luke 23:4). Close examination only makes the truth shine brighter.

Renunciation and Repentance

Once truth is apprehended, renunciation and repentance must follow like one footstep follows another. It is not enough just to acknowledge truth; we must reject our wrong belief and repent of the sin that came into our life as a result. I found the book, *The Bondage Breaker,* by Neil T. Anderson, to be extremely helpful on my deliverance journey. I learned from his book that my sin gives Satan and the powers of darkness legal right to afflict me. Only by confessing sin will I be able to find full freedom from the powers of darkness and to continue on my journey with Jesus in the light. I have seen a number of people delivered from spiritual oppression as they applied the truth contained in *The Bondage Breaker,* either alone or with the assistance of others.

Chapter 24
The Ax Laid to the Root

> And even now the ax is laid to the root of the trees. Therefore every tree which does not bear good fruit is cut down and thrown into the fire. (Matt. 3:10)

My Wrong Belief System

THIS LONG CHAPTER WILL PROBABLY BE MOST USEFUL to those who have experienced the Local Church and are seeking both insight into the reasons for their experience and freedom from its distressing aftereffects. However, I believe it may also be useful to others, because those who seek to know God and discover the purpose of life have the potential to become deceived and end up in bondage.

Over time, the Local Church gained a strong and unhealthy holding power over me. Please be clear that I am not saying, nor do I believe, that any of the Christians there planned or intended this. What I am saying is that Satan, the master of deception, managed over a long period of time to deceive and control me. I was attracted initially by good things, but in the long term, I was held in bondage by deception. How was I deceived? Satan used my love for God and my desire to follow Jesus to subtly and gradually veer me and my family (and many others) off course.

My Local Church beliefs had a strong basis in the Word of God, yet many of them contained error. What I believed and practiced in the Local Church grew into a large tree with many branches containing bad fruit. I understand now that Satan was involved in the development of my wrong belief system. Nonetheless, it was my choice to believe what I was taught in the Local Church by Witness Lee and by leaders who followed him, and it was also my choice to follow their example. Thus, I am ultimately responsible for the results in my life. By showing me the bad fruit, God was able to help me realize that I had to lay the ax to the root of the tree of my entire Local Church belief system. As I allowed Him to shine His light on each of the wrong beliefs I held, I was able to humble myself and repent. As I surrendered them, I was set free.

My wrong beliefs resulted in wrong thoughts about God, His purpose, and myself. These beliefs contained truth that was slightly altered by Satan to accomplish his purpose and to bring me into his snare. The part of the belief that was true is what persuaded me and captured my thinking, causing me to overlook the error that was hidden in other parts of the belief. The striking thing about these wrong beliefs is that they all interfered with God's real purpose for me: to know Christ and Him crucified.

In this chapter, I discuss wrong beliefs about the following things and also describe some of the bad fruit that resulted from them:

Wrong Beliefs About:

1. God's Purpose for Me
2. Witness Lee
3. The Local Ground
4. The One Accord
5. Authority and Submission

Resulted in Bad Fruit:

6. Damaged Relationship with God
7. Damaged Relationships with Others

Wrong Beliefs About:

8. God's Way Being Divine Dispensing
9. God's Purpose Being God's Economy
10. Calling on the Lord and Pray-reading

Resulted in Bad Fruit:

11. Wrong Thoughts and Behaviors
12. A "Do-It-All" Method

In the discussion that follows, I frequently refer to what *we* believed because those with whom I was associated in the Local Church held the same basic beliefs as I did. I also offer some examples from the experiences of Local Church members to illustrate the bad fruit I describe. These are not, in fact, isolated examples; they are representative of the experiences of many others.

1. About God's Purpose for Me

In the Local Church, my belief about God's purpose for me governed my whole relationship with God. The basic premise was that God wanted me to give myself to accomplish His purpose and meet His need for the recovery of the true church.

1a. Meeting God's Need: A False Premise

The premise that we need to meet God's need is false. God does not have any need. We are the ones with needs. God, who is love, has poured out His love for us. He has "unsearchable riches in Christ" (Eph. 3:8) to give us for full salvation, every day of our lives and for eternity. C. H. Mackintosh says,

> This is a divine reality, Jesus came into the world to meet our need, to serve us in all that in which we need His precious service, and to give His life a ransom for many; to serve us by bearing our sins in His own body on the tree, and working out a full and an eternal salvation. He did not come to get—He did not come to take—He did not come to be ministered to—He did not come to be gazed at—He came to be used.... (Mackintosh, 95)

He did not come so that we would give Him His church. Actually, Satan tricked us into a very subtle form of "works": We needed to do something for God—to meet His need. No! We are the ones with needs! He is the One with riches! As we ask for His help with our needs, He shows us His love in real, practical ways. As our unsearchably rich Father meets our every need through His Son, we are filled with love for Him. We abide in His love, and we learn to lay down our lives for others that they may know His love (John 15:9–13). This is what He commanded us to do. He did not command us to make the church our purpose:

> This is My commandment, that you love one another as I have loved you. Greater love has no one than this, than to lay down one's life for his friends. (John 15:12-13)

The belief that we embraced about God's need for the church was so strongly implanted in us that some who have left the Local Church are still bound by this thought. Much of their spiritual talk is about the church. They believe God was frustrated in the Local Church from reaching His goal and that He still has this need. This stays in the forefront of their thinking and frustrates their following the Lord and discovering His unique purpose for them. It also hinders their fellowship with other believers, believers who just don't understand the "truth" about the church. They are still focused on the wrong thing.

This situation is like Peter holding his treasured revelation in Matthew 16. In the Local Church, we saw something about the church, but I believe that, like Peter, we misunderstood. Freedom comes when we give up that understanding and give ourselves to know Christ and to follow Him on the pathway of the cross. This is what produces genuine oneness among believers, and this is what makes us fit for the church that Christ said *He* would build.

16. Recovering the True Church

I no longer agree with the premise that the true church has been lost and that our purpose is its recovery. In the Local Church, the recovery and building of the church were our governing vision—one that ultimately diverted our focus from Jesus and our feet from the narrow pathway of following Him. With our eyes set on the wrong goal, Satan succeeded in moving us off course. The focus of the Bible is God and His relationship with us—God with us. This is the gospel. The gospel is *not* that God needs us to recover the true and proper church.

John W. Kennedy wrote in his book, *The Torch of the Testimony,* that the reality of the church for which Christ died has never been lost or broken. It has, therefore, never needed recovery:

> The church of the New Testament is no mere theory. It is a fact of this, the twentieth century, as it was of the first. The principles

of the unchanging Word of God, having been demonstrated and tested for almost two thousand years, have proved themselves applicable to every age and every circumstance. The church authoritative, holy, witnessing, invincible has continued and will continue, not in outward show and ostentation, but wherever the Lord has found a people willing to gather round Him in submission and obedience. It is a church that is indissolubly one, bound by ties of the Spirit. Amid the bitter conflicts and tragedies of so-called Church history, the life of the spiritual movement of the church has flowed on through the ages. The splendid unity of a heavenly race, living a heavenly life passed down from spiritual generation to spiritual generation has never been broken. They are pilgrims and strangers still upon the earth, bearing the reproach of Christ outside the camp, pressing 'on toward the goal unto the prize of the high calling of God in Christ Jesus'. They gather round Christ their Head, owning His Word their guide, bearing the torch of the testimony. (Kennedy, 243-244)

Christ said that He would build His church, and the gates of hell would not prevail against it. In the Local Church, according to our belief about recovery, the gates of hell had prevailed against the church for almost two thousand years. Then, at the very end of time, Christ was finally going to be able to recover the proper practice of the church through us. I believe that this is a deception. Christ has been building His church in love since He rose from the dead, just as He said He would.

1c. My Repentance

I have repented for making the church my purpose and giving it a place of importance in my life that was greater than the place I gave Christ Himself. Repentance for this sin set me free from the power that this errant belief held over me. I am free now to follow Him!

2. About Witness Lee

For many years of my Christian life, I gave myself to follow one man and his ministry. My devotion to him became a vehicle of deception which carried me away from the One I had been called to follow.

2a. Of Witness Lee

The Bible calls us to follow Christ, but history shows repeatedly that God's people are prone to follow men and to become man-centered. Paul said to the early church:

> For when one says, "I am of Paul," and another, "I am of Apollos," are you not carnal? (1 Cor. 3:4)

We in the Local Church repeated this same mistake when we became *of* Witness Lee. Paul was a chosen vessel unto the Lord with a unique purpose in New Testament times that God showed him by revelation. Satan, however, distorted and misused this truth to convince us that God has a unique person like Paul in every time period, and that Witness Lee was that man for our present time. I no longer believe that God has only one man at a time on the earth as His spokesman whom everyone should follow. The Bible does not teach this.

History shows that every period of spiritual awakening on the earth from the time of Christ's resurrection to the present has involved multiple believers. Not one of these was the only man that everyone needed to follow exclusively. I believe, as the Bible says, that Paul was a uniquely chosen vessel whose life was *a pattern of longsuffering for us, a pattern which shows that each of us should follow the Lamb of God* (1 Tim. 1:16, Rev. 14:4). He was not a pattern to show us that God has only one man to follow in each period of time.

Christian history, beginning in Corinth, shows a propensity for believers to conclude that there is only one chosen leader—the one they are following. Our fallen humanity likes to form parties around leaders. When Paul heard about those in Corinth saying they were "of Paul," he did not accept their exaltation of him. Rather, he corrected them for this kind of talk and preached the message of the cross to them. Witness Lee did not do this.

2b. My Offense

I offended the Lord when I believed that being absolute for Witness Lee and his teaching was the same as following God Himself. As a result, I was not open to receive ministry or help from any other teacher, unless that person was a devoted follower of Witness Lee. I did not question Witness Lee's words. I valued what Witness Lee taught me above what I could learn for myself from the Bible and from talking with God.

For almost three years after we left the Local Church, in my heart, I still remained loyal to Witness Lee. As was customary in the Local Church, I continued to refer to him as "Brother Lee." I held to my belief that some of the leaders, not Witness Lee himself, were responsible for the problems in the Local Church. God finally showed me that my total allegiance to Witness Lee was sin, and that what resulted from his teaching and example was at the root of the bad fruit in the Local Church. I don't think Witness Lee intended or purposed to hurt any of those under his ministry; however, the fact is that many were hurt by errant beliefs and practices he introduced and sanctioned in the Local Church.

2c. My Repentance

My declaration of absolute allegiance to Witness Lee and his ministry was a very serious sin. I have repented for this sin and have verbally renounced my previously declared loyalty and allegiance to Witness Lee. By this, God has set me free from the ground that this had given Satan in my life. I have renewed my allegiance to Jesus only, to love Him above all else:

> You shall love the Lord your God with all your heart, with all your soul, and with all your mind. (Matt. 22:37)

I am now able to receive ministry and teaching from other believers. They have helped me find truth and healing from my experiences in the Local Church. However, I will never again treat anyone's writings or teachings as the *only* truth or as infallible. It is idolatry for me to value anyone's interpretation of God's Word, or appreciate anyone's systematized body of knowledge about the Bible, more than the pure Word of God itself. I will not allow anyone or anything to supersede my personal, intimate love relationship with Jesus or my direct involvement with His living Word. My loyalty and obedience are to Jesus.

3. About the Local Ground

In the Local Church, I became completely convinced that God had only one view of the practical church on the earth and that was by city. I believed that when He saw the earth, He saw cities; and in each of those, He saw only one church, not many churches.

I now understand differently. When God sees His children taking up their crosses and following Jesus, He sees the church, wherever that is. The church is not something that can be defined by some kind of man-made border or geographical name. The church is a spiritual reality visible to spiritual beings and also a tangible reality visible to unbelievers by the presence of one thing: the self-sacrificing love of God shown through human beings to other human beings.

As people, we live in space and in time, so it is understandable that Paul addressed physical letters to believers by where they lived and that the Spirit in the book of Revelation told John to do the same. There is no indication in the Bible that these believers had any concept that their oneness was based on the city in which they lived. Paul didn't define their oneness in this way. Rather, he encouraged them to love and follow the Lamb of God. He told them this would result in the love of God among them. The addresses on letters to believers does not dictate the definition of the church.

3a. Local Ground Not Prescribed

The Bible does not prescribe the local ground as Witness Lee taught us. A brother once told me that Bible teachers should not *prescribe* things that the Bible only *describes,* things that can only be observed. Although we can observe that about half of Paul's letters were addressed to a church in a city, it is wrong to teach that the ground of locality is *the* way to practice the church, making it like some kind of a formula. The Bible does not do this. Witness Lee erred when he made the local ground a prescription for oneness.

If God intended to define church form in a prescriptive way, He would have done so plainly in the Bible. The fact that He did not should serve to warn us not to attempt to do so ourselves. The church is something heavenly with a heavenly leader—Christ. He is the Head of the church, and He leads us to gather together with other believers as it pleases Him. The when, where, why, and how of meetings and fellowship with others is up to Him. What matters is not the form of any gathering, but His presence:

> For where two or three are gathered together in My name, I am there in the midst of them. (Matt. 18:20)

36. The Church Built in Love

Christ builds the church in love. He is the Master Builder who knows the details of how each person fits into His masterpiece. He said He would be with us all the days until the "end of the world" (Matt. 28:20). So, I am always with Him, and He is always with me. I am in a continual meeting with Him. As I follow Him, He brings me to know and fellowship with others. The church is His responsibility, and He is supremely capable of orchestrating His work to build up His body in love.

The Bible teaches that all believers are one in Him, spiritually and practically, through love. This is not a man-made, man-enforced oneness. When I meet other Christians, I have an inner witness that we are one.

Paul asked the Corinthians, "Is Christ divided?" The answer is, "No." God does not see us divided because *Christ is not divided* (1 Cor. 1:13). By contrast, in Paul's letter called Ephesians, there is no talk about problems. Rather, he talks about "every spiritual blessing in the heavenly places" (Eph. 1:3) and about down-to-earth, practical relationships: husbands, wives, fathers, children, servants, masters, and fellow Christians. The church is visible in all these relationships with other people as we learn to experience the self-sacrificing love of Christ. It is visible in people who have resurrection relationships and love one another (Eph. 5, 6).

Whatever outward form church gatherings or meetings take is up to Him, not us. We should not claim that we have *it* and that others don't. Instead, we should keep our eyes on Christ and build on the only foundation, Christ Himself. We will love our brothers and sisters in Christ and care for them by experiencing the powerful supply of the Spirit that is ours by Christ's death and resurrection. The love of Christ seen in all our human relationships is the testimony of Jesus on the earth, the church He is building in love.

3c. The Church as Known by Powers of the Air

God has purposed to make known His wisdom "by the church to the principalities and powers" (Eph. 3:10–11). The powers of the air aren't afraid of man-made unity or of believers claiming to be the real church. They know only too well what the church is. The reality of the church exists wherever believers are experiencing Christ's death and resurrection in their lives.

This is the church that principalities and powers seek to prevail against because they fear it. They recognize resurrection life because they saw Christ come out of the grave. He made a "public spectacle of them" (Col. 2:15). This was the first "showing" God gave them of His hidden wisdom, one they will never forget. Christ's death on the cross was a fatal blow to their kingdom of death and darkness. Now, they tremble at the name of the exalted Jesus (Jas. 2:19), the name to which every knee will one day bow (Phil. 2:10).

Satan and his hosts are continually reminded of Christ's victory when they see believers experiencing the power of His resurrection and the fellowship of His sufferings. Every time a follower of the Lamb experiences the power of the cross working in his or her life, the principalities and powers see another display, another one of the many facets of God's manifold wisdom.

This display doesn't fade, but continues to shine like gold. The principalities and powers see Christ in the believer, and they see the believer's unique story with Christ unfolding. No matter what Satan does to those who follow the Lamb, he cannot destroy them or their faith because Christ is in them. When the powers of darkness see such believers gathered in the name of Jesus, they are terrified because they are subject to such believers and their prayers. If God is recovering anything, may He recover this: the pre-eminence of Christ and the message of His cross. If there is a remnant in these times, it is all those who love and follow Jesus, the Lamb of God.

4. About the One Accord

In the latter years of His ministry, Witness Lee began to talk about oneness in a way that stands in opposition to the truth of oneness in the Bible. He said that genuine oneness was based on God's New Testament ministry, which was God's economy. Such ministry was contained in all his publications, so the one accord mainly involved being one with his ministry and his publications.

4a. Unity by Conformity

In our early years, we learned that true unity was "unity without conformity." However, as a result of Witness Lee's extreme teaching and explanation about being in one accord, the Local Church began to practice a kind of unity by conformity. Church oneness was ultimately defined as oneness with Witness Lee and was termed "the one accord." When I read what Witness Lee had said at a training for all the Local Church elders regarding this, God fully opened my eyes to see the source of what I was reading. I knew it wasn't the Lord. Witness Lee said:

> If you believe the Bible, you have to admit that we should be one in teaching, practice, thinking, speaking, essence, appearance, expression. There is not a verse in the Bible that even gives us a small hint that allows the churches to have different appearances. (Lee, *Book 7*, 39)

His definition of oneness allowed for no differences and actually focused people on the evidence of outward, physically visible oneness rather than on Jesus.

Both Witness Lee's attitude and his expectation regarding oneness with his ministry are seen in statements he made regarding publications. He indicated that printed material in the Local Churches needed to be restricted to his publications only. He didn't want others adding their flavor to his teaching. He said he would like for many brothers to publish teachings as he did, but he made it evident that he didn't consider that there were any brothers who had yet received the ability to do this. He also made it clear that he wanted those who were publishing anything on their own to cease, criticizing them for adding their own individual expression to his teachings (Lee, *Book 8*, 161–162):

> I hate to see that some of the brothers would try to publish something by copying my points mixed with their "spices" and their "color." Why do they need to put out some points from my writings in this way? …
>
> … Do not merely speak some points, adding your own "color" and "spices." This changes the taste. It damages my messages. (Lee, *Book 8*, 162)

He continued by telling them, basically, that their publications were worthless and that his were the real item:

> It bothers me that some brothers among us still put out publications. According to my truthful observation there is no new light or life supply there. They may contain some biblical doctrines, but any point of life or light has been adopted from the publications of Living Stream Ministry. There is nearly no item of life or light that has not been covered by our publications. Based upon this fact, what is the need for these brothers to put out their publications? Because all the publications are mine, it is hard for me to speak such a word. But I am forced to tell the truth. By putting out your own publication, you waste your time and money. You waste the money given by the saints, and you waste their time in reading what you publish. Where is the food, the life supply, and the real enlightenment in the other publications among us? Be assured that there is definitely at least one major revelation in every Living Stream Ministry publication. (Lee, *Book 8*, 163)

When I first read these statements, I was struck by how unlike our Lord this attitude is. Jesus was not afraid of what people could do to damage His ministry, because His ministry was the real item, one that could not be damaged or stopped by anything, not even death.

4b. No Tolerance for Differences

Instead of many varied stories woven into one beautiful fabric, the one accord in the Local Church required everyone to be the same. Instead of embracing the beauty and uniqueness in the variety of believers and their experiences, we were all expected to conform to a narrow view of God's purpose, so God could have a corporate expression in which there were no differences.

In the beginning, we were like a beautiful garden, filled with a diversity of flowers; but eventually, some of the flowers exalted one prize rose and led others to do the same. They tried to make every flower in the garden be like the prize rose. They looked at the pansies and said, "You are too individualistic. You need to be on the stems of the rose bush." They looked at the African violets with their need for special lighting and said, "You have to be like the prize rose who basks in the full sun. Stop being unique!" To the century plant that would bloom only once in its life they said, "You are useless, a shame to God for just sitting there passively doing nothing." They pulled the pansies out of the ground and hung them on their rose bush; they forced the African violets into the sun; and they cut the sharp blossomless leaves off of the century plant. They pulled out some of God's plants and discarded them like weeds. The response to the protests of all these plants, who were questioning what was happening in the garden that they loved, was this: "You are negative and rebellious. You must be quarantined or removed so you won't damage the garden! You are not absolute for the garden and the way of the prize rose."

God's garden is not full of identical roses. He loves variety, and He values and gives special care to each plant. In God's creation, nothing is identical. With the billions of human faces, none are exactly alike. Just as a family can have unity without every child being identical, so can the church. Paul was crucified with Christ, nevertheless he, Paul, lived. This is a mystery. I believe that Paul, an individual believer, will be in the New Jerusalem with his own unique "spices" and "color." It will still be him; yet not him, but Christ (Gal. 2:20). Every believer will be there in resurrection with their unique God-given personalities and their unique experience of Christ and Him crucified.

4c. Not Accepting All Believers

We should accept all believers simply because of our common faith in Jesus Christ. We should not define some other standard of oneness to which all believers must conform in order to be accepted. We should not call any believer divisive who doesn't meet the standard that we hold to be true. Our oneness is not in teachings, forms, or practices. Our oneness is in our faith in Jesus.

Oneness is not sameness. How do we have practical unity without conformity? Paul tells us to endeavor to "keep the unity of the Spirit in the bond of peace" (Eph. 4:3). He lists items of oneness that we already have and should keep. After listing the items of oneness, Paul begins his next sentence with the qualifying word *but:*

> But to each one of us grace was given according to the measure of Christ's gift. (Eph. 4:7)

This shows that he understood the fact that, although there is one body, one Spirit, one hope, one Lord, one faith, one baptism, and one God and Father of all (Eph. 4:4–6), we are each unique in God's eyes, each having been given a measure, "a limited portion," (Strong, G3358) of *grace*. In Romans 12:3, Paul also said that we were each given a "measure of *faith*." I think Paul realized that on each of our journeys growing up into Christ in all things (Eph. 4:15), we would be different according to the individual measures of grace and faith we were given. We are to love and receive one another with all of our God-given differences (1 Cor. 12, Rom. 15:7). We can do this because we trust Him, the Author and Finisher of our faith, to grow us up in love into "the unity of the faith and of the knowledge of the Son of God" (Eph. 4:13). He is well able to adjust and correct me when I need it, so He can do the same for others. Mostly, in keeping the unity of the Spirit, I learn the way of the cross, the way of faith in the working of God, and the way of love.

In down-to-earth terms, this means to me that God takes special care of each of us with regard for our differences, differences He gave us for a purpose! His love for each of His children is the same. He asks us to do likewise and to love one another respecting our differences. We have no right to interfere with His care of, or purpose for, another one of His children, one of our brothers or sisters, by stepping in to tell them what *we think* they need to do or be. This doesn't mean we never help one another or that we do not confront a brother or sister when they are living in a sinful way. It does mean, however, that we talk with our heavenly Father and respect Him and His plan for each of His children. Sometimes, He may use us to help another of his children, like He used Ananias to help Paul, or like he used Paul to help the Corinthians when they were receiving a sinful brother. Sometimes, He may tell us to mind our own business, even if we suffer as a result. Sometimes, He may ask us if we would willingly suffer something for the best interests of another. In these ways and so many others in our heavenly interactions with our Father and one another, we are showing that we live by faith, faith in Him, in who He is and what He can do. He is the Lord, and He is *our* Lord. Ultimately, we will all be full of faith in Him and one in that faith. We are our Father's "household of faith" (Gal. 6:10).

5. About Authority and Submission

According to John W. Kennedy in his book, *The Torch of the Testimony,* the kind of belief we held about authority and submission in the Local Church has been one of the things that throughout history has been "a grave danger to the life of the church and a curb on the working of the Spirit":

> The move towards centralization of control and ecclesiastical authoritarianism ... ultimately leads to a dispute with the Lordship of Christ, for He is the Head of the church and is actively present by His Spirit in the midst of His people. Christ alone stands as the Mediator between God and men. The church is vested with the authority to represent God to the world, but no human being or group of persons has the authority to represent God to the church, for Christ dwells there in person. Since ecclesiastical authoritarianism detracts from the incentive from the direct dependence upon God, it is not conducive to the healthy development of spiritual life.... (Kennedy, 46)

To reiterate, "No human being or group of persons has the authority to represent God to the church, for Christ dwells there in person"!

5a. Local Church Leaders and the Lordship of Christ

I wrongly believed, as I was taught, that Witness Lee and the Local Church leaders were God's deputy or representative authorities. When some key leaders among us decided to pledge their absolute allegiance to Witness Lee and to follow him unquestioningly as God's representative or deputy authority and then asked us to do the same, I obeyed them, as did others. We looked to Witness Lee like he was Moses or Paul. The truth is that God does not need to be "represented" to us by other men. He is well able to represent Himself to us in person.

I also wrongly believed that I was not accountable for anything that I did as a direct result of submitting to church leaders or Witness Lee's teaching. I was taught that if I did anything in obedience to them that was ever found to be in error, they, God's deputy authorities, would be accountable for this, not me. I now know differently. I am accountable directly to God for whatever I believe and practice. I will not be able to claim immunity or excuse myself by placing blame on the leaders whom I chose to follow, or by saying, "But Brother Lee said ...."

5b. Misinterpretation and Misapplication of the Cross

As a result of what and how Witness Lee taught about the cross of Christ, I struggled with a wrong view of the cross and its application for many years. He taught us that on the cross, Christ terminated the old creation, Satan, sin, death, the world, the flesh, and the old man, including me, all of which is true. But the problem for me was that I constantly heard Witness Lee teach only about the negative, terminating aspect of the cross. This unbalanced teaching, together with my experience of the Local Church leaders' humiliating application of it, left me with a clear message that the cross was designed primarily to remove everything about me and my person. Witness Lee did tell us that Christ's death on the cross showed us God's love, but this love aspect, the main aspect, he rarely mentioned and, to my recollection, never emphasized.

Many times, I experienced the leading brothers in the Local Church misusing what I now know to be the wonderful truth of the cross and turning it into something else. God's deputy authorities wielded the cross like a disciplinary rod to "cross out" my self, so that only Christ would remain. When all was said and done, the church was supposed to be just Christ, not you or I. I believed that God wanted to nullify me with my "peculiarities" and all my "opinions," and even my natural abilities. He had no use for them. The emphasis on the termination aspect of the cross served to subdue me and bring me into submission.

Even though God was teaching me the real meaning of the cross by my personal experiences with Him, these experiences were continually overshadowed by my experiences in the Local Church that were supposed to be "the cross." The Local Church teachings and practices made it necessary for me to accept every difficulty as God's sovereign arrangement for me without asking any questions or talking to God about them. I was always confused by the contrast between these two kinds of experiences; but I didn't understand until many years later that it was the Local Church experiences, the ones that were to "cross me out," which were the counterfeit ones!

5c. Information Control

I wrongly believed that God's deputy authorities were supposed to protect the church, both from harmful writings and from harmful people. I, therefore, submitted to them when they pronounced certain reading material to be negative. I would not consider reading it or even touching it! I also agreed with them whenever they said that certain people were negative, divisive, spreading poison, or even leprous. It was not my place to understand anything about why. This was not my business. I just trusted them as I was supposed to do. When they stopped or controlled the flow of information, written or verbal, that they considered harmful, especially information that raised questions about Witness Lee's ministry, I understood that they were just doing their job as God's representatives. If they told me not to associate with certain people, I didn't. I had no need to understand why. The fact that the elders said so was enough. I didn't need to know any more. In addition to doing these things, I also reported to them any indications of negativity or divisiveness I observed. I was wrong to follow and submit to them in all these ways. I was wrong to not verify for myself the factual truth of any bad thing I was told about another brother or sister.

One case that illustrates the high level of information control and fear that existed in the Local Church stands out in my memory. Several years after leaving the Local Church, I was in the home of Dot, a sister I had known for many years, when she received a very upsetting phone call. She had made plans for an extended visit with an elder and his wife in another city, but now they were calling to cancel her invitation to their home. Why? They had learned that she had allowed me, the author of a "negative" letter, to enter her home. They were afraid of spiritual leprosy and were protecting themselves. When she asked them if they had read my letter, they answered emphatically that they had not and would not because it was negative. No amount of pleading with them on her part could persuade them to read the letter themselves to see if it was negative.

When Local Church leaders do not allow questions, they are providing fertile soil for deception. When we passively let other human beings tell us what we can read, who we can talk to, or what we can say, we are inviting deception. The Bible charges each individual believer to take heed not to be deceived. In order to avoid deception, it is our responsibility to use our God-given mind to consider what is true, pray about our questions, and, when warranted, ask them.

5d. The Gates of Hell

After Peter had his revelation from the Father in Matthew 16, one of the things Jesus said to him was that the gates of hell would not be able to prevail against the church. Why did He say this? To warn us that there would be a fierce war waged against the church, one in which Satan would seek to overpower God's people. When Peter began to contend for his God-given revelation, Satan immediately appeared at the open gate of Peter's sin. Jesus saw Satan there and rebuked him. Then he immediately turned to the disciples and said:

Chapter 24—The Ax Laid to the Root

> If any man will come after Me, let him deny himself, and take up his cross, and follow Me. (Matt 16:24, KJV)

He was telling them what would shut the gates of hell: each believer taking up his cross and following Jesus. (Maybe this is one of the keys of the kingdom that Jesus had just told Peter that He would give him—a key to shut the gates of hell.)

Witness Lee became like Peter when he fought to defend his treasured revelation. He opened a gate for Satan that resulted in a situation of destruction and darkness in the Local Churches. Many leaders, believing he was infallible, followed him with unquestioning loyalty. They opened many more gates. The flock also followed faithfully. The devil took full advantage of both the sin of the leaders and the followers.

5e. Satan's Most Effective Tool

Satan's most useful tool is deceived men who are functioning as leaders. In 1 Timothy 4:1-3, the Spirit warns us that "in latter times some will depart from the faith, giving heed to deceiving spirits and doctrines of demons." Such men will have consciences that have ceased to function. They will speak lies as if they were truth. It is evident from this verse that such men are recognized as authorities because they give authoritative statements (forbidding and commanding). Such men are weapons in Satan's hands, and he uses them to destroy the flock of God. All he needs in addition to such deceived leaders is a flock that is willing to follow them.

In the Local Church, the devil deceived a number of Local Church leaders to follow Witness Lee without reservation. When Witness Lee and these leaders began to practice things in the name of God that clearly were not, no one could help them. Many of the flock, who loved Jesus, but who also had trusted and had fully submitted to the leaders, were pulled along in the evil tide as its supporters.

Witness Lee and these leaders believed that God had charged them to protect God's interests on the earth and the ministry of His New Testament economy. Satan took the reins of their errant belief and led them into darkness.

In their blindness, they then fought against other Christians outside the Local Church, who were asking valid questions. They even fought with their own brothers and sisters within the Local Church, insisting that everyone stand absolutely for Witness Lee's ministry. Whoever tried to speak truth was labeled as rebellious. When some tried to point out factual errors contained in *The Fermentation of the Present Rebellion,* they would not listen. The errant teaching about authority and submission that had been sown through Witness Lee's teaching bore corrupt fruit. Satan used those he had deceived through it to wreak havoc and destruction among God's people.

In 1988, the Living Stream Ministry published a book entitled *Authority and Submission,* which contained messages given by Watchman Nee. This book contains chapters with such titles as "The Importance of Authority," "Examples of Rebellion in the Old Testament …," "God Intends That Man Submit to Representative Authority," and "The Manifestation of Man's Rebellion…." This book was published after Witness Lee had identified a rebellion that was occurring in the Local Churches. Eventually, to expose and put down the "rebellion," the Living Stream Ministry published Witness Lee's book, *The Fermentation of the Present Rebellion.*

What the Living Stream Ministry did *not* include in *Authority and Submission* is telling. They omitted almost half the messages that Watchman Nee gave in the series. These can be seen in the second half of *Spiritual Authority,* published by Christian Literature Crusade.[11] The omitted messages give another side, a very important one, of Watchman Nee's teachings. The omitted messages have chapter titles like these: "The Character of Delegated Authorities: Graciousness," "The Misuse of Authority and God's Governmental Discipline," "Delegated Authorities Must Be under Authority," "The Daily Life and Inward Motivation of Delegated Authorities," and "The Conditions for Being Delegated Authorities."

---

[11] In 1972, Christian Literature Crusade published *Spiritual Authority,* based on messages given by Watchman Nee. In the front matter is this quote: "The contents of this volume comprise a series of messages which were delivered in

Chinese by the author during a training period for workers held in Kuling, Foochow, China, in 1948, and are now translated from the edited notes taken by some who attended that training." In 1988, Living Stream Ministry published Authority and Submission from the same messages. By the titles of the two books, the difference in emphasis can be seen. Lanell Allen discovered the discrepancy between these two books and pointed it out to me.

5f. Fighting Against Them with the Sword of His Mouth

God does not take lightly people doing unholy things in His name and representing to people that He is doing them. When Moses did this, he paid dearly (Num. 20:7-12). The misuse of authority is a wide gate for Satan. God said that the church in Pergamos was dwelling where "Satan's throne" was, and that Satan was dwelling among them (Rev. 2:13). This word indicates that Satan and his dark kingdom can be present among believers! It also shows that God will suffer this to a point. He is longsuffering and willing to give his people time to shut the gates of hell themselves. He has given them the key to do so. His word to Pergamos shows that He still recognized that there were those in Pergamos who were holding His name and His faith; however, He was also warning them about their sin of allowing men to be among them who were involved with greed and were lording it over the flock, subduing and conquering them. His word also showed that His patience would have an end shortly. He told them all:

> "Repent, or else I will come to you quickly and will fight against them with the sword of My mouth." (Rev. 2:16)

5g. My Repentance

I have thoroughly and completely repented for submitting blindly to the leaders in the Local Church and for believing they were God's representatives on the earth. My acceptance of the lie from Satan that I had to submit unquestioningly to these leaders caused me to be deceived. This gate I had opened for Satan has now been shut. My loyalty, allegiance, and obedience are to Jesus only.

6. Bad Fruit: Damaged Relationship with God

All of the previously discussed beliefs had a very detrimental effect on my relationship with God. In essence, they changed my concept about who He was and how He regarded me. These beliefs gradually changed the way I thought and felt about Him and seriously impacted my ability to properly relate to Him.

6a. No Unique Purpose for Me as an Individual

My thought about God was damaged and the way I related to Him changed when I accepted the belief that God had no purpose for me as an individual. All the teachings about God's need for the church resulted in my holding a wrong thought about God and His purpose for me. I began to believe that God wasn't that interested in my personal spiritual growth or personal victory. All He wanted was His building. From this, a further thought developed in me. My own personal life, with all its small matters, was not important to God. I felt guilty and unspiritual if I asked for something for myself. This kind of thinking became a blockage to my knowing Him as the One who meets every need. When I accepted the belief that the cross was designed to erase me, this strengthened the thought that God had no other purpose for me other than to nullify my individuality and blend me into His corporate expression. I completely stopped feeling the need to follow Him myself and seek His mind about my pathway. I no longer needed to follow Him regarding my "course." I thought I already knew it.

6b. His Word to Me Through an Intermediary

My relationship with God was further damaged when I began to believe that He wanted me to hear His Word from someone who really understood it. That someone was His man on the earth, Witness Lee. He was the only one receiving up-to-date revelation from the Bible. This belief hurt my personal, direct relationship with God and His Word. I began to place my primary confidence in what Witness Lee, God's spokesman, told me, not in what God Himself might try to tell me. As a result, my own interaction with God was hindered. I didn't expect light or revelation or help directly from God through the Bible. All I needed was in what Witness Lee was teaching us.

6c. God's Authority Over Me Usurped

My direct obedience to Jesus as my Lord changed when I began to believe that God wanted me to submit to Him through men whom He had appointed as His representatives. This belief gave ground to God's enemy to usurp Christ's lordship over me. When I accepted the belief that obeying the leaders was the same as obedience to God, Satan had a way to exercise control over me by gaining control over the leaders. I believed that not I, but they, would be accountable to God for things I did as a result of their directives. If the Bible disagreed or my conscience disagreed, that wasn't going to be my problem; it was going to be theirs. This belief made it more difficult for God to convict me if I was sinning in my acts of obedience to the leaders. I could no longer hear the Shepherd's voice and let Him lead me directly. I wasn't really listening anyway. I was too busy following His representatives.

6d. God Misrepresented to Me

The character and person of God were misrepresented to me by men claiming to be His representatives. Their teaching and behavior caused me to believe that God was primarily a stern, demanding, cold, and authoritative disciplinarian. I listened to Witness Lee and those leaders who followed him and observed their behavior thinking that they represented God. I accepted whatever they taught me as one hundred percent from God. Through their example and interpretation of God's word, Satan subtly introduced error into my thinking. Over time, their repetitive teachings, practices, and requirements overshadowed like a dark cloud my initial understanding of God's great heart of love for me. Through them, the devil also shaped a wrong view in my mind of the cross. I lost sight of the cross as the testimony of God's great love for me.

Their teaching and treatment produced in me a fear-based relationship with God, a relationship in which I really was not that important. As I began to question God's heart of love toward me, I held a lurking fear that I would become totally useless to God unless I could measure up to what the leaders expected of me. They told me that God wanted me to be in "one accord." They told me that He had no purpose for my life other than to blend me into a corporate expression of sameness.

In addition to all this, they changed my view of God from One who created the earth for us and gave us all things freely to enjoy, to One who wanted me to spend my life on earth purposely abstaining from whatever I might enjoy. (I already knew God did not want me to enjoy sinful things, but they lumped lawful things with sinful and called them soulish or natural.) Under their instruction, I came to believe that taking time off for a vacation, spending time to enjoy nature, or even laughing too much was sinful. All of these things left me with an overall wrong impression of God—something, no doubt, the enemy of God had intended. I was not drawn to God by these thoughts about Him, but rather was repelled.

6e. In the Name of God

The greatest damage to my relationship with God came from the direct discipline at the hands of God's "deputy authorities," discipline that was done in the name of God. When they finished, I was left completely unable to talk to God for almost two years. I thought it was God who had so cruelly disciplined me and shamed me in the presence of my brothers and sisters. This experience came close to destroying my faith. During the first years that followed that terrible night, the mental and emotional torment I experienced was fiendish. I was under attack in my mind by Satan day and night, left with nowhere to turn. God's deputy authorities had cut off any path of escape by filling my mind with their many years of teachings and directives. I couldn't leave the church. I couldn't move to another church when I had a problem. I couldn't talk to anyone about what the elders and my friend had done to me. I couldn't say I was being tormented by the devil and needed help. I couldn't say I feared I was losing my sanity. I had to act as if all was well and accept the cross. Everyone looked at me with pity and avoided me. But, the absolute worst thing of all was that I couldn't pray. I couldn't pick up my Bible and read it. If I tried, I heard the voice of one of God's deputy authorities saying in my head, "Sisters have no discernment," "Sisters can't get revelation from the

Bible," and "You have become deceived." So, if I prayed, I might be contacting demons or Satan, the angel of light, who might deceive me further with another "revelation" from him. How could I know what was God and what was the devil? God's representatives had told me that I was deceived, and all but a very tiny part of me believed them.

I know now what that little part was. It was my thread of gold, and it ultimately survived that fiery trial. If it had not been for God's great and tender mercy, I might still be there in the Local Church under their "spiritual" control. I might still be there in what had become in many ways like a correctional institution, with guards and an enforcing regional warden. I might still be there supporting absolutely "the only ministry that is producing the church." Instead, I am loving Jesus and following Him each day. I am walking with Him in anticipation of where we are journeying together, as He leads me in the good works He prepared beforehand for me to walk in (Eph. 2:10). How thankful I am to Him for delivering me, even though it was through fire.

6f. Truth About the Cross

My thought about God was wrongly skewed when I accepted the belief that the main purpose of the cross was to remove every problem, including me. God has now completely changed my former belief that the cross is something necessary to terminate me so that only Christ will remain. One day I realized why it was wrong to believe that all God wants is Christ. If all He wanted was Christ, then why did He make you and me? He already had Christ before He made us! He doesn't want only Christ! He also wants you and me, the special and unique individual beings He created!

If I had heard messages about His suffering for me and His great love for me, which He showed on that terrible cross, I would have been drawn to love Him and take up my cross. The main message of the cross is not what was terminated, but what was displayed: the love of God. The message of the cross is powerful and attracts people because it is about the One who died there, the One who loved us to the uttermost.

"And I, if I am lifted up from the earth, will draw all peoples to Myself." (John 12:32)

My testimony today is simply this: When I saw His love on Calvary, I was drawn to love and run after Him:

> "Draw me after you and let us run together! The king has brought me into his chambers. We will rejoice in you and be glad; we will extol your love more than wine. Rightly do they love you." (Song 1:4, NASV)

The truth is that the cross is a not a joy killer; it is a joy producer!

69. H. I. S.

During my recovery process after we left the Local Church, God used a Christian counselor named Elizabeth Baker to finish off one aspect of my old belief about the cross. I had believed that God was sovereign in everything that happened to me, so everything should be accepted without question. This thought from my days in the Local Church still came to haunt me occasionally. One day, Elizabeth told me about something she referred to as H.I.S., which letters stood for "Honesty (or truth)," "Initiative," and "Sovereignty." She said that the Christian life was like a stool with these three legs. My Local Church belief about the cross and about God's sovereignty had resulted in my stool only having one leg!

Regarding the "honesty or truth" leg, she told me to learn to face every difficult situation that comes my way and seek to understand it in the light of the truth of the Bible. I should ask the Lord to help me evaluate my situation according to what the Bible teaches about what is right and what is wrong. For example, it is not right for someone to steal from me or lie to me. Also, it is not right for me to neglect my children (in which case, my own sin is causing my trouble). After I look at the situation honestly, in His light, and understand the right and wrong of it, then I need the initiative leg of the three-legged stool.

Regarding the "initiative leg," if God convicts me that my own sin is the cause, then I should repent. If it is not my sin, but the sin of someone else against me, then I should ask the Lord what He wants me to do. For example, when a crowd was going to throw Jesus off the cliff (Luke 4:29), He didn't say, "God is sovereign, so over I go." Rather, Christ was in communication with His Father and knew His Father's will regarding His death, so he took steps to escape the situation. I should determine the Lord's will in a situation by prayer and His Word. For example, if I have offended someone, Jesus requires me to go to the person and be reconciled (Matt. 5:23-24). If someone has offended me, Jesus commands me to go to the person, several times if necessary, with a view to hearing and reconciliation (Matt. 18:15-17). If I take appropriate action and nothing changes, then I need the last leg of the stool.

The last leg is God's sovereignty. Regarding the "sovereignty leg," if I have done what God has required of me, and He has allowed my difficulty to remain, I then accept it as His sovereignty.

As I considered what she told me, I realized that many times I had actually practiced the honesty leg and the initiative leg, but I always felt wrong or guilty about doing this. In the Local Church, it wasn't acceptable. I wasn't supposed to honestly consider what was right or wrong because that was to partake of the tree of the knowledge of good and evil. I shouldn't take the initiative to address a problem because I was just supposed to submit.

On that wonderful day, my belief stool got two more legs that continue to serve me well as I take up my cross and follow Jesus. The cross is not meant to crush me or eliminate my personality but to bring me to Him, to the throne of grace. This is where I find mercy and grace to help in time of need and where I come to know Him as my *all in all*.

6h. *My Cross*

One day, Jesus finished off another aspect of my old belief about the cross. I had believed that I was supposed to practice the cross by always remembering that everything around me had been terminated and by denying myself everything. He had set me free from this old, wrong thought, but it still occasionally dropped in for coffee. I was reading in the Bible when the word *his* stood out to me in the following verse:

> Then said Jesus unto his disciples, If any man will come after me, let him deny himself, and take up his cross, and follow me. (Matt. 16:24, KJV)

In this verse, *his* referred to *any man*. Jesus was saying that if any man wanted to accompany Him, he must take up *his own* cross. This meant to me that if I wanted to accompany Him, I must take up *my own* cross.

I then remembered that there had been times along the way in my life in which the Lord had given me experiences of death and resurrection in specific things (my job, my washing machine, and so forth). That day, I realized that such experiences had been experiences of *my* cross. In the Local Church, I held the thought that I was basically supposed to deny myself everything. This had been a depressing thought and an impossible task; but taking up my own cross ... this I could understand, and this I could do. Reviewing my history with Jesus, I knew that every experience of *my* cross had been very good and had ended up making me glad!

I also noticed that Luke 9:23 said that a man should take up his cross *daily*. I realized that this meant to follow Him each day in the light of whatever things He had shown me were my cross. On that day, Jesus used the little word *his* to stop once and for all the entrance of my old, lurking, wrong, and depressing thought about the cross! Yes, there has been some sorrow along the pathway with Him, but the main point is that I have been with Him. The joy on my pathway has already far surpassed my tears, and I know my joy will continue for eternity!

7. Bad Fruit: Damaged Relationships with Others

The bad fruit from all these beliefs is also evident in damaged relationships with others. Just as Adam and Eve's relationship was damaged by sin, relationships among us were likewise damaged. As a result of these errant beliefs, we neglected our personal relationship with Jesus and our responsibilities to our families. Leaders violated God-given marriage and parental roles. They rejected other Christian ministries. They eventually even rejected longtime fellow leaders and fellow members. They spiritually killed some of their own brothers, brothers for whom Christ died. Many Local Church members submitted to all of this and, by their silence, supported it. All these relationships were damaged in the name of God.

7a. About Marriage

Regarding marriage, we were told, "If you take care of the Lord and the church, the Lord will take care of your marriage." I now consider this to be a doctrine of demons (1 Tim. 4:1). I cannot find this teaching or anything like it in the Bible. Yet in the Local Church, I heard it, practiced it, and witnessed its bad fruit. We wrongly thought that because Christ loved the church and gave Himself for her that we were supposed to do the same thing. This was Satan's twisting of the meaning of the verses about Christ and the church in Ephesians 5.

While there, I witnessed some cases in the Local Church in which wives listened to church leaders more than to their own husbands. I also saw husbands honor the church leadership more than their wives. Both of these things damaged the marriage relationships God intended. These practices deeply hurt marriages where a spouse's absoluteness was in question or where a spouse was not a member of the Local Church.

The leading brothers also were involved in misusing their position to arrange marriages. A number of the resultant marriages were unsuccessful. Most of them had the same basic characteristic: marriage without love entered into because of pressure from church elders. When these marriages were unsuccessful, not only the spouses but also the children were hurt.

7b. Sandra's Marriage

I won't repeat the story mentioned earlier about Sandra's marriage (see "A Cry for Help" in chapter 17), but I will comment on Bob and Sandra Brown's marriage difficulty with regards to the Local Church. Bob allowed the elders to violate his role and responsibility to his wife. The elders inserted themselves between Bob and Sandra to the extent that Bob was united with them instead of with his wife. The leading brothers' negativity about Sandra became Bob's own. He couldn't trust her. She was God's ordained match for him, yet he couldn't receive any fellowship from her.

Bob came to believe that Sandra was deceived. Sandra was left alone struggling to survive in her miserable existence and recover from the rejection she had experienced from church leaders and her own husband. There was never any follow-up by the elders after her "discipline" to see how she was doing. She was forgotten. Her husband never admitted, or apologized, for failing to love and protect her. After thirty years of marriage, God hadn't been allowed to unite them into the reality of His love. Sandra was devastated by all of this.

7c. Sally's Marriage

After being in the Local Church for awhile, a young brother named Glen became very concerned that he was going to have to marry someone he didn't want to marry. He spent hours talking to John and me about this. We said, "Glen, the Lord will not make you do something against your will." Glen said, "I know, but He might change my will. He might make me want to be married to someone I didn't want to marry before he changed me." From this response, you can get the idea that he was confused and anxious about how people got together and got married in the Local Church.

While living in Oklahoma City, I got to know a young college-aged sister named Sally Martin. I realized that she and Glen had a lot in common and might be interested in each other. Both wanted to be married. He was a warm and kind person, and from comments he had made to John and me about his view of marriage and taking care of a wife, I felt that from a woman's perspective, he would make a good husband.

Glen came for a visit to Oklahoma City, and we introduced them. They spent some time talking to each other and were both very interested in getting to know each other better. However, before this could happen, the main leading brother in Oklahoma City, Jerry Hughes, got wind of what was happening and ran Glen out of town, telling him he was out of bounds. He called Sally's father and told

Chapter 24—The Ax Laid to the Root

her that Glen was not a good brother or a good candidate for marriage. He told him several bad things about Glen that he had heard when he had researched Glen by calling a Houston elder. The things that were said show that Jerry was looking at Glen through a "good brother" filter, and he didn't measure up. After the call from Jerry, Sally's father, who believed all he was told, would not let Sally continue contact with Glen.

Actually, Jerry Hughes wanted Sally to marry a brother named Barry Barnett who was living in Jerry's corporate living home. Barry had been married before and was divorced. He also had a son. Sally had withstood a couple of previous attempts by Jerry to get her to marry Barry, saying that she did not think he was her type or that they had enough in common. Barry had only a tenth grade education. After one of the attempts to put them together, Sally, who was attending college, obtained a college application and gave it to Jerry, saying that after Barry had finished college, she might consider him. She felt that their education level should be comparable.

After Glen's visit, the pressure to marry Barry began again from Jerry and his wife Vera, who talked with Sally on three separate occasions trying to persuade her concerning Barry. Sally said that by the third time, she was beginning to feel very condemned about refusing. She admired Vera and had looked to her as a role model. She considered that both Jerry and Vera, as a leading couple in the church, were very close to God, and that what they were saying must be from God. She finally gave in and agreed to the marriage.

Sally, who knew very little about Barry, was then allowed to have three leadership-approved "dates" with him before they married five weeks later. A short engagement and quick marriage was customary and expected by the elders. Her first date was to a meeting. Her second was to a restaurant. Her third was to look over the house in which they were going to live, in order to see what work it needed. She said that they talked about an hour and a half total during these three times together, and much of the conversation was about the Local Church. Her misgivings never left, and during the week before the marriage, she contemplated backing out. She didn't though, because of the embarrassment that would follow, as well as the fear that she would be going against what the Lord Himself wanted.

About seven or eight years later, they both left the Local Church. Her unhappy marriage became more unhappy when, instead of spending time in numerous church meetings every week, they faced the strain of spending more time with each other in a loveless union. Although she was miserable, Sally determined to stay in the marriage for their children's sakes. Ten years later, they divorced. My husband and I were involved trying to save this marriage. Many years later, after Jerry Hughes died, and after Vera was no longer a part of the Local Church, she apologized to Sally for what she had done to pressure her into marrying against her wishes.

7d. My Marriage

I have done a lot of repenting to my husband and he, likewise, to me. We both have allowed the Bible to change our thought about marriage and reset our focus, not on the difficulties, but on the blessing and the wonder of God's marriage arrangement.

When the Lord told me, after leaving the Local Church, to go and learn to love my family, I obeyed. Now, I can say that over the years since that time, God has worked miracles in my marriage. John and I love each other deeply and are fully committed to each other. We both have learned to experience Christ's self-sacrificing love in our marriage relationship.

While working through the difficulties with our son, we had occasion to have personality tests administered and evaluated by our Christian counselor. After studying both John's and my personality profiles, she pronounced that of all the couples she had ever tested, we were among those that she would have advised never to marry because we were so different. She then said that the fact we were still together after thirty-plus years and loved each other was a testimony to Jesus. We had to agree.

7e. Godly Marriages

In Ephesians 5, immediately after saying that Christ loved the church and gave Himself for her, the Bible tells husbands to love their wives in the same way. This is a picture that shows what a normal, healthy marriage should be like. The husband is not supposed to lay down his life for the church, but for his wife. The wife is supposed to respect and appreciate her husband, not church leaders. A husband who has Christ's death on the cross in his view is enabled to lay down himself for his wife, and a wife whose husband cares for her in this way can't help but submit to him. I believe this kind of marriage relationship is a powerful, visible testimony to the world that shows the reality of Christ's great love for us. We can only have this kind of testimony in our lives as we love Him above all and as He empowers us to do so.

I now believe that, in His sovereignty, God joins two very different people together, a male and a female, so that through the passage of their lifetime together, He can teach them the reality of self-sacrificial love. Marriage, no doubt, exposes our selfishness and our self-centeredness; but primarily, it provides a wonderful environment for us to experience the power of the cross bringing God's love into our marriage relationship. Those whom God has joined together, no church or church leader should separate.

7f. About Parenting

Regarding parenting, there was no help for parents to properly fulfill their roles with their children. One sister, when she asked for help regarding marriage and parenting, was told that all she needed to do was to submit more to her husband. The marriage and children would be blessed; there was nothing else she needed to do.

The elders generally placed demands on members' time without any consideration of the needs of families. If it was perceived to be in the best interest of the church, the elders would take a position on matters regarding children, such as clothing or dating, which the parents were expected to enforce and support. These kinds of things are *bad* fruit. The following stories, of which I have firsthand knowledge, illustrate this bad fruit.

7g. Sally's Discipline as a Teenager

When Sally Martin (the sister whose arranged marriage I described previously) was in high school, she was reported to the elders for being seen kissing a young brother in a car after school. Subsequently, during a conference at the Church in Dallas, she was summoned to a private meeting. When she arrived, she found that her parents had also been summoned. According to her, neither she nor her parents knew what the meeting was about prior to being asked to attend. Sally was seated at the head of a long table. Her parents were included at the table with approximately sixteen Local Church elders from Texas and other states. They proceeded to talk to her about her inappropriate behavior while her parents said nothing.

She told me that the whole time became a big blur to her because she was in so much pain from the embarrassment and humiliation of such a confrontation. She lived with the pain of that memory and suffered under the sanctions they placed on her. She also suffered having to face those elders at other Local Church meetings and conferences.

The appropriateness of Sally's behavior was a matter for her parents to determine, not for the elders in the church. If discipline was needed, it was the parents who should have given it, not the elders. The way that the Local Church elders handled this situation shows a complete lack of respect for her parents' God-given role. I believe that what was done to Sally and her parents was a result of serious deception. It is unbiblical for any church to interfere in any way with the God-given role of parents by circumventing their authority.

7h. Full-timers and Their Children

I believe it is unbiblical for the church to teach that parents should put their involvement with the church or a ministry above their own children. The following statement from a training given by Witness Lee to Local Church elders reveals the kind of thinking that exists in the Local Church:

> Many married sisters pretend and even declare that they love the Lord. Eventually it becomes manifest that what they really love is their children. They do not even love their husbands so much as their children. Such a sister who declares that she loves the Lord yet who really loves her children more is not a full-timer. If a sister is really a full-timer, whether her children live or are taken away by the Lord, it is the same. (Lee, *Book 8,* 112-113)

I believe that a statement like this could produce nothing good in the life of any sister who trusted Witness Lee and was seeking to please the Lord by being a full-timer.

7i. My Children

Both of my children suffered long-term negative effects from their experience growing up with parents who were committed to the Local Church. As a mother, I always met the daily, practical needs of my children. They were bathed, clothed, fed, and educated. However, when I did not spend time with them to love and nurture them as special little human beings, I failed in my most important God-given responsibility to them. Although I had some success in helping them become self-controlled human beings, I failed miserably when they were young in what I now believe is the primary role of a mother, that is, to love and to nurture, and to help them develop into the unique persons God intended them to be.

It was fifteen years after we left the Local Church before I had some assurance that both my children had basically recovered from their upbringing in the Local Church. Each of them did grow up with good character traits, but they both carried the effects of my emotional neglect of them into their adult life. I cannot even think about this now without becoming tearful.

God has been merciful and has been healing them. They were both helped by our leaving the Local Church and confessing to them our sins and failures as parents. They both now love the Lord and have given their lives to follow Him. It took many years, but they are now able to accept, trust, and fellowship with other Christians.

It makes me sad when I consider what I did to my own children in the Local Church environment. It also makes me sad when I look at the fruit in the lives of other Local Church children who have ongoing difficulty following the Lord and trusting other Christians.

7j. Godly Parenting

The Bible teaches fathers to be responsible for the training and discipline of their children and for the children to obey their parents (Eph. 6:1–4). The church should not interfere in these relationships. God places children with parents to care for them, understand and love them. It is the responsibility of the parents, not the church, to find and learn from the Lord the best way to nurture and discipline each unique child. The fact that parents are responsible for these things, and for spending time with their children, is obvious to most people. After spending twenty years in the Local Church, I had to repent for failing in this area of my life. Our exit from the Local Church and my new insights didn't instantly correct everything with our children. We faced many years reaping the undesirable consequences we had sown. God was merciful, however, and worked mightily to heal us and get us back on track.

7k. Other Christians

Our belief that we had a special, unique calling from God damaged our relationship with other Christians. Our special calling was like a mission statement for Christians who came among us to embrace in order to be fully accepted. We didn't have time for anyone who was not interested in "taking this way" along with us. Our belief ultimately isolated and divided us from other Christians. We considered ourselves to be more consecrated and faithful to God than they were. We justified our exclusive behavior by saying we were doing something on their behalf, standing on the ground of oneness.

We are all one in Christ by His death and resurrection, not one in a special calling. The Jews were God's special, chosen people; the Gentiles were not. God removed the differences between them by the cross, creating one body in Christ (Eph. 2:13–16). Any "calling" that causes us to value or appreciate some members of Christ's body more than others is not a calling from God.

Our total loyalty to the Local Church and Witness Lee's ministry gave Satan the way to damage our relationships with Christians who were not in the Local Church. I never heard Witness Lee and the Local Church leaders encourage unity with any other Christian ministries. In fact, I heard them say they could *not* receive other Christian ministries, as in the following quote by Witness Lee:

> Can we in the Lord's recovery, who share in the unique ministry, the continuation of the ministry of the Apostles, accept the ministries of the denominations and divisions? No, we cannot. If we accept them, the recovery will be damaged. The proper ministry, the ministry according to God's New Testament economy, is for the building up of the Body of Christ, but the other ministries are for the building up of the denominations. Because this is the case, we cannot receive the ministries that build up the denominations. (Lee, "Daily")

This stance is evidence of Satan's work to damage relationships with other Christians. I have repented for being party to this kind of thought and practice.

Our belief that we had the one unique ministry combined with the misguided belief that God needed us to contend for it, even to the point of using the legal system, caused the leaders to take action that further damaged relationships in the body of Christ. They brought lawsuits against other believers who, in the late 1970's and early 1980's, published two books that questioned the beliefs and practices of the Local Church: *The Mindbenders* by Jack Sparks and *The God-Men* by Neil T. Duddy. Both of these books contained material that Witness Lee and the church leaders thought was very damaging to the Local Church. We were told by the leading brothers that these books indicated that the Local Church was a cult, and that the church taught heresy. We were told not to read these books because they were "full of poison." The lawsuits were brought against the authors and publishers of these books in order to protect the reputation of the Local Church and Witness Lee's ministry. Ultimately, the books were withdrawn from publication after lengthy legal battles.

In 2001 the Local Church filed a lawsuit against Harvest House Publishers, for publishing a book which included the Local Church: *Encyclopedia of Cults and New Religions* by John Ankerberg and John Weldon. In January 2006, a Texas appellate court ruled in favor of Harvest House. This ruling was appealed, and the appeal eventually went to the U.S. Supreme Court. "On June 18, 2007, the U.S. Supreme Court brought an end to The Local Church's six-year, $136 million legal battle against Harvest House Publishers and authors John Ankerberg and John Weldon" (Apologetics Index website).

By virtue of being a member of the Local Church, I participated in lawsuits against other believers. I have repented for this. The Bible says that the saints in the church are well qualified to judge in a dispute between Christian brothers and that it is a shameful thing to bring suit before the secular courts. If brothers cannot resolve their differences, the solution is simple: It is the pathway of the cross, the one our Lord took for us. We should take up our cross, be willing to be wronged, and follow Him (1 Cor. 6:1–8).

Eventually, and almost unbelievably, the total loyalty to Witness Lee's ministry gave Satan the way to completely sever relationships between Christian brothers within the Local Church. When brothers who had faithfully served with him for over a quarter of a century began to question him, Witness Lee called them rebellious and rejected them. Those who followed him in an absolute way did the same thing.

8. About God's Way Being Divine Dispensing

God has mercifully taken away the God's economy veil from my mind and shown me that His way to accomplish His purpose is not divine dispensing as termed and taught by Witness Lee.

8a. God's Way: Christ

According to Witness Lee, God's way is to dispense Himself into us when we call on the Lord and pray-read the Word (see "'Christ as Life' Versus Religion" in chapter

6). But according to the Bible, God's way is not methods. God's way is Christ, as Jesus taught us:

> "I am the way, the truth, and the life. No one comes to the Father except through Me." (John 14:6)

Christ Himself is the way, not practices or methods or something called divine dispensing. In Greek, the meaning of the word *way* shows us that Christ Himself is our "road" and our "journey" (Strong, G3598). There is no other way. Jesus told us plainly *how* we are to follow Him:

> "Whoever desires to come after Me, let him deny himself, and take up his cross, and follow Me." (Mark 8:34)

Jesus didn't say, "Whoever desires to come after Me, let him receive divine dispensing by calling on My name and pray-reading."

8b. What Paul Meant by Not Teaching Different Things

Witness Lee taught us that in 1 Timothy 1:3–4, Paul said that New Testament ministers and teachers must not teach differently than God's economy (Lee, *Divine*, 13). His *Recovery Version* of the Bible translates these verses as follows:

> Even as I exhorted you, when I was going into Macedonia, to remain in Ephesus in order that you might charge certain ones not to teach different things nor to give heed to myths and unending genealogies, which produce questionings rather than God's economy [Gk: *oikonomia*], which is in faith. (1 Tim. 1:3-4)

Regarding what "not to teach different things" means, Witness Lee stated:

> As we have seen, Paul tells Timothy in 1 Timothy 1:3 that he left him there in Ephesus to charge certain ones not to teach differently. What then, we may ask, is the unique thing which all the Christian teachers should teach? ... There is only one ministry which always builds up, edifies, and perfects with no destruction at all. There is only one unique ministry that is justified, promoted, uplifted, and even glorified in the New Testament. In 1 Timothy 1:4 Paul went on to tell Timothy what those ones who were teaching differently should be occupied with—God's economy. (Lee, *Book 3*, 43)

Is this explanation by Witness Lee what Paul really meant when he wrote to Timothy in Ephesus?

God showed me another verse which made it clear that Paul's letter to Timothy was not about God's economy as defined by Witness Lee. In the following verse, Paul explains why he sent Timothy to the believers in Corinth:

> For this reason I have sent Timothy to you, who is my beloved and faithful son in the Lord, who will remind you of my ways in Christ, as I teach everywhere in every church. (1 Cor. 4:17)

It makes sense that whatever Paul taught "everywhere in every church" would be the same thing he was referring to in 1 Timothy 1:3–4 when he said to "charge certain ones not to teach different things." So, to identify a *different teaching,* you would need to compare it to what Paul taught everywhere about his ways in Christ.

As I looked at the teachings of Paul and the other apostles throughout the New Testament, it was obvious to me that the main message they taught was *not* divine dispensing. Paul did not teach everywhere about the meaning of *economy* (*oikonomia*) and try to define God's purpose in terms of methods such as calling on the Lord and pray-reading the Word. Instead, Paul consistently taught about and experienced Christ and Him crucified (see "In His Masterpiece: Paul" in chapter 20). Also, he demonstrated for us that the result of his walk was love, and he plainly stated that love is the goal of his commandment not to teach differently (1 Tim. 1:5). Paul stated very clearly what the apostles taught when he said, "we preach Christ crucified" (1 Cor. 1:23). He emphasized that he did not speak or preach using persuasive words of "man's wisdom" but words the Holy Spirit taught (1 Cor. 2:13). He further said:

> For Christ did not send me to baptize, but to preach the gospel, not with wisdom of words, lest the cross of Christ should be made of no effect. For the message of the cross is foolishness to those who are perishing, but to us who are being saved it is the power of God. (1 Cor. 1:17–18)

Paul's message was clear. It was the message of the cross, which was the power of God. This message empowered people to perform all the instructions he gave in his letters regarding their relationships with God and with one another.

The New Testament contains many, many verses that reveal what the apostles taught about Christ and the cross, and that show how they lived this message.[12] The main teaching of the apostles was not mingling or the divine dispensing of the processed Triune God. They preached the message of the cross, a message that was considered to be foolish. They testified about their own experience with Christ and encouraged others to experience Him as well. They did not systematize an explanation of God's purpose with wise words and offer guaranteed methods to accomplish it.

---

[12] Verses that show the apostles taught and lived the message of the cross: Acts 1:22; 2:14–27, 31–32, 36, 42; 3:15, 18, 26; 4:2, 10, 33; 5:30, 41; 9:16; 10:39–41; 13:30–38; 17:3, 18, 31–32; 26:23; Rom. 1:4; 4:24–25; 5:6, 8; 6:4–6, 9–10; 7:4; 8:11, 17–18, 34; 10:9; 14:9, 15; 1 Cor. 1:17, 23–24; 2:2–5, 8; 4:8–16; 5:7; 6:7, 14; 8:11, 13; 9:12; 10:16, 33; 11:23–26; 12:26; 13:4; 15:1–58; 2 Cor. 1:4–10; 2:14–16; 4:7–17; 5:14–15; 6:4–10; 8:2; 10:1; 11:23–30; 12:8–10, 15; 13:3–4, 9; Gal. 1:1; 2:20; 3:1; 5:11, 24; 6:12, 14–17; Eph. 1:7, 19–20; 2:6, 13–20; 3:3–6; 4:2; 5:2, 25; 6:20; Phil. 1:13–21, 29; 2:5–8; 3:7–11, 17–18; 4:9; Col. 1:14, 20–22, 24–29; 2:12, 14–23; 3:1–3, 5; 1 Thess. 1:10; 4:14; 5:10; 2 Thess. 1:5; 1 Tim. 1:16; 2 Tim. 2:8, 12; 3:12; Heb. 2:9–10, 14, 18; 5:8; 9:12–28; 10:19; 11:1–39; 12:2, 24; 13:12, 20; Jas. 5:10; 1 Pet. 1:2–3, 11, 19, 21; 2:19–23; 3:14–18; 4:1, 13–19; 5:1, 10; 1 John 3:14; Rev. 1:5, 2:10; 5:9; 7:14; 12:11; 19:13.

8c. Witness Lee Taught Different Things

> Even as I exhorted you, when I was going into Macedonia, to remain in Ephesus in order that you might charge certain ones not to teach different things nor to give heed to myths and unending genealogies, *which produce questionings rather than God's economy* [Gk: *oikonomia*], *which is in faith*. (1 Tim. 1:3-4, RV) [emphasis added]

This verse was one of Lee's foundational verses for his contention that only the apostles' teaching, which he said was "God's economy," should be taught. It is noteworthy that, in this verse, Paul does not actually say to teach something called "God's economy." Paul charges Timothy to tell some (1) not to teach different things and (2) not to give heed to myths and unending genealogies. He then clarifies what he means by pointing to what will be produced by wrong teaching. "Different teachings" can be identified by looking at what is produced.

According to Paul, a "different teaching" will produce questions (disputes). It won't produce God's economy which is in faith. So Paul was not exhorting Timothy to charge others to teach God's economy; rather, he was exhorting Timothy to charge certain people not to teach things that didn't *produce* God's economy. Or, to make it more clear (by removing the double negative from this sentence), Paul was indicating that things should be taught that *produce* God's economy.

Paul proceeds in the next verse to tell us what the desired product looks like:

> But the end of the charge is love out of a pure heart and *out of* a good conscience and *out of* unfeigned faith... (1 Tim. 1:5)

This verse clearly shows that the teaching Paul is talking about will produce *love* (and this love will come out of people with pure hearts, good consciences, and unfeigned faith). God's economy is simply God's love seen or demonstrated through His holy, faithful people.

> Love worketh no ill to his neighbour: therefore love is the fulfilling of the law (Rom. 13:10)

What does God's love look like? Look at Calvary. There you see God's love for man.

If you want to know if someone is teaching "differently" you should check what is produced. If the end product is not the love of God, as demonstrated on Calvary, the teaching is a "different teaching."

What has been produced in a whole movement under Witness Lee's teaching is strong evidence that Witness Lee was teaching differently than what Paul and the other apostles taught. Witness Lee taught different things. His teachings are not like those of the apostles who taught about Christ and Him crucified. Instead, Witness Lee taught about his version of God's economy—what he called the divine dispensing—and used many terms to explain it, words that needed explanation and clarification. For example:

- eternal economy
- organic salvation
- blending
- mingling
- processed Triune God
- Triune God's organism
- tripartite man
- God-men
- consummate divine multiplication
- organic constitution of the processed Triune God
- three stages of incarnation, inclusion, and intensification

Paul, Peter, and John did not teach with these kinds of terms or concepts. Paul spoke of the Spirit and the riches of Christ in numerous places, but he didn't build a "processed Triune God" theology with complicated terms and explanations about Christ and the Spirit.

Several times in his epistles, Paul did use the Greek word *oikonomia* (which can be translated as "administration," "dispensation," "stewardship," or "economy"), but he did not major on its meaning or importance. I think Paul's point in using this word was to show that all of God's actions are part of God's overall plan for His household. In its most straightforward definition, *oikonomia* (economy) means "house law" [*oikos* (house), *nomos* (law)]. So, God's *oikonomia* is His house law. The law of God's house is love. God is love, and the most excellent way is love, love which never fails. His love is displayed in Christ crucified, which is what the apostles all taught.

Witness Lee erred when he formulated his teaching about God's economy and divine dispensing. He constructed this teaching primarily by taking a number of verses from Paul's writings, putting them together, and trying to explain his concept about them with his own unique terms. Paul was certainly qualified and capable of formulating a systematic *oikonomia* theology if he had wanted to do so, but he didn't. Instead, he preached Christ and Him crucified.

9. About God's Purpose Being God's Economy

Witness Lee used Ephesians 3:9 to support his claim that God's economy, the divine dispensing of the processed Triune God to produce His building, was the central teaching of the New Testament. He also used it in conjunction with Ephesians 3:11 to say that God's economy was the eternal purpose of God.

Because I had never done this before, I decided to thoroughly investigate his economy of God teaching. As I did, God showed me two problems with his interpretation of Ephesians 3:9. The first problem was about Witness Lee's definition of the word *mystery*. The second problem concerned which Greek word belongs in this verse, *oikonomia* or *koinonia*.

9a. First Problem in Ephesians 3:9: The Meaning of Mystery

In chapter one of Witness Lee's book, *The Divine Economy,* I found his explanation about the first part of Ephesians 3:9 which says:

> And to enlighten all *that they may see* what the economy of the mystery is ... (Eph. 3:9, RV)

In his discussion about the meanings of the words *economy* and *mystery,* he ascribes to them both the meaning of "divine dispensing" (Lee, *Divine,* 9–10). If this is true, then this verse is saying:

> And to enlighten all *that they may see* what the divine dispensing of the divine dispensing is ...

Obviously, this is not right. After further looking into the meaning of the word *mystery* in Ephesians 3:9, I became convinced that he had misinterpreted this word. The mystery was referring to something else. What did I discover about the word *mystery?*

In Ephesians 3:9, Paul says the mystery had been hidden from the beginning of the world in God. In Corinthians, he says:

> But we speak the wisdom of God in a mystery, even the hidden wisdom, which God ordained before the world unto our glory. (1 Cor. 2:7, KJV)

Revelation 13:8 tells us that the Lamb was "slain from the foundation of the world." This indicates that God's plan from the beginning of the world was for His Lamb, Christ, to be slain at a certain point in time. His wisdom was hidden until Christ came and was crucified. Paul continued to say that if the fallen spiritual rulers of the world had known God's hidden wisdom, they would not have crucified Christ:

> Which none of the rulers of this age knew; for had they known, they would not have crucified the Lord of glory. (1 Cor. 2:8)

Why not? Because His crucifixion would mean their end. Through death, Christ destroyed the devil (Heb. 2:14). If they had understood the mystery that Christ crucified was God's wisdom, they would not have crucified Him. The cross was God's wisdom to destroy Satan (Heb. 2:14). What was the hidden wisdom that was ordained before the world? Christ crucified. Paul tells us plainly that Christ crucified is the wisdom of God:

> But we preach Christ crucified ... the power of God and the wisdom of God. (1 Cor. 1:23-24)

These verses, together with the fact that Paul consistently preached about Christ and the cross throughout the New Testament, convinced me that *the mystery* is Christ crucified; and the "fellowship of the mystery" (Eph. 3:9, KJV) to which Paul referred is the fellowship of Christ's death and resurrection.[13] Christ crucified is God's wisdom that was hidden from the beginning of the world. Hiding it made it a mystery. God revealed the mystery to Paul and told him to preach it. What did Paul preach? Christ and Him crucified. Once I understood this, the meaning of the whole passage of Ephesians 3:8-11 became clear to me (see "The Threads in God's Tapestry" in chapter 18).

---

[13] The *King James Version* of the Bible recognizes a Greek word in Ephesians 3:9 that is different from the one the *Recovery Version* of the Bible recognizes. The *King James Version* uses *koinonia* and translates it "fellowship," whereas the *Recovery Version* uses *oikonomia* and translates it "economy."

Many Bible scholars agree that the mystery Paul was talking about in Ephesians 3:9 was the Gentiles being "fellow heirs, of the same body, and partakers of His promise in Christ by the gospel" (Eph. 3:3–6). I also agree with this. Paul had just explained this in chapter two of Ephesians, where he had written about his understanding of all that Christ accomplished on the cross. He had explained the mystery that, by the cross, God had abolished "the enmity" between the Jews and the Gentiles and reconciled "both to God in one body" (Eph. 2:15–16). This is the *objective* truth of the mystery that God had shown Paul. But there is also a *subjective* side to this truth. The subjective side is what Paul was talking about in Ephesians 3:9 when he referred to the *fellowship of the mystery*. Doctrinal understanding of the truth about God's mystery is not sufficient. Each believer should have subjective experiences of Christ's death and resurrection in order to participate experientially in the reality of the one body. Paul's teaching and his life show he was subjectively experiencing Christ's death and resurrection.

Witness Lee said, "Although the divine economy is the central topic in the New Testament, it has not been touched that much among the Christians in past centuries" (Lee, *Divine*, 7). Does this mean that Paul failed? Could it be that only Witness Lee could explain what Paul was saying? Did only Witness Lee apprehend God's eternal purpose? If what Witness Lee said is true, then Paul mostly failed in his God-given commission to enlighten all concerning this mystery. History, however, shows that Paul did not fail! He was given grace, and grace succeeded. Paul said he finished his course successfully. History makes it plain that for centuries believers have experienced Christ and the way of the cross through Paul's teaching and example, and also through the teaching and fellowship of the other apostles.

Who can believe that God's purpose remained concealed, waiting for Witness Lee, with all his terminology about "God's economy," to explain it at the end of the twentieth century? This would mean that nearly twenty centuries of believers had almost no possibility of participating in God's eternal purpose!

In his ministry, Paul called others by example to imitate him as he imitated Christ. He did not say to the Philippians that his goal was to "know Him and God's economy, the divine dispensing." He did not tell the Corinthians that he determined to "know nothing among them but Christ and God's economy, the divine dispensing," nor did he tell the churches that all they had to do was to "take care of the divine dispensing." Rather, by his teaching and his example, Paul called them to subjectively experience the mystery of Christ and Him crucified.

In Colossians 1, Paul preached at length about the cross of Christ and about his participation in the afflictions of Christ for His body's sake. He then said that he became a minister according to the *oikonomia* of God. His ministry, however, as he had just demonstrated, was not to preach about *oikonomia;* it was to preach about Christ and Him crucified.

9b. Second Problem in Ephesians 3:9: Oikonomia or Koinonia?

I was surprised to discover that there is a question as to which Greek word belongs in Ephesians 3:9. Some Greek manuscripts have the word *oikonomia;* others have *koinonia*. Witness Lee and the *Recovery Version* translators render the verse as follows:

> And to enlighten all that they may see what the economy [*oikonomia*] of the mystery is ...

The *King James Version* translates it this way:

> And to make all men see what is the fellowship [*koinonia*] of the mystery ...

Witness Lee didn't tell us that scholars disagreed as to which Greek word should be in this verse even though he used it and God's economy (*oikonomia*) as a cornerstone of his ministry about God's eternal purpose.

Once I understood that the mystery in Ephesians 3:9 is Christ crucified, I better understood what Paul meant by making all men see the fellowship of the mystery. He was referring to the believers needing to be established according to the revelation of the mystery:

> Now to Him who is able to establish you according to my gospel and the preaching of Jesus Christ, according to the revelation of

the mystery kept secret since the world began. (Rom 16:25)

The Greek word for mystery, *musterion* (Strong, G3466), implies individual initiation into a secret.[14] Paul had received such an initiation into the mystery. He had prayed that God would also grant the Ephesians "the spirit of wisdom and revelation" (Eph. 1:17). He asked that God would reveal to them His hidden mystery, that they would receive their own initiation into His secret. Paul wanted everyone to see something particular about this mystery. Depending on which Greek word belongs in Ephesians 3:9, Paul either wanted people to see the "fellowship" (KJV) or the "economy" (RV) of the mystery.

---

[14] In Greek, *musterion* is "primarily that which is known to the mustes, the initiated.... In the N.T. it denotes ... that which, being outside the range of unassisted natural apprehension, can be made known only by Divine revelation, and is made known in a manner and at a time appointed by God, and to those only who are illumined by His Spirit" (Vine, 769).

Although the meaning of *oikonomia* can make sense in this verse, the use of the word *koinonia* now makes the most sense to me in light of my understanding that the mystery in Ephesians 3:9 is Christ crucified. What did Paul want us to see? He wanted us to see the *koinonia* of the mystery—the fellowship, participation, or sharing in the mystery which is Christ crucified. This is the same fellowship Paul wanted to know when he spoke about knowing the *koinonia* of Christ's sufferings in Philippians 3:10. [Footnote 16: The use of *koinonia* in Philippians 3:10 means "that Paul's 'own actual sufferings are a real participation in Christ's sufferings, suffered by virtue of his communion with Christ.'" (*New Bible Dictionary,* from George, 184).] Paul wanted us to see that we were also called to know the same thing.

The use of *koinonia* in Ephesians 3:9 also seems to fit better with Paul's composition of his letter to the Ephesians. First, he talked about the objective truth of the cross in the beginning of Ephesians (Eph. 2:13–16). Then, he talked about the subjective experience, the *koinonia* of the cross in Ephesians 3:9.

Paul wanted each individual believer to be initiated into the secret of experiencing Christ crucified. In this context, Witness Lee seems to have missed the importance to God of individual believers having their own personal experiences of Christ crucified and thus fulfilling their own unique role in God's eternal purpose. He neglected the importance of the individual and stressed the church to such an extent that the role of the individual was lost. Paul, however, knew that each believer's own subjective experience of the cross was necessary to produce the real experience of the one body that was created by Christ's death and resurrection. He knew that this was how God would show the principalities and powers His manifold wisdom by the church.

10. About Calling on the Lord and Pray-reading

Witness Lee taught us that there were two ways to participate in God's economy: calling on the Lord and pray-reading the Word. He told us that this was how we would receive the processed Triune God and how God would complete His purpose.

10a. Calling on the Lord

One of the ways to be mingled with God, or receive divine dispensing, was to call on the Lord (Lee, *Christ*, 118-119). He also taught us that to call on the Lord was to repeat out loud, "O Lord Jesus," usually numerous times in a row. I no longer believe these things, and I have come to realize the diversity of meaning involved in truly calling on the name of the Lord.

There is much more meaning to the phrases, "calling on the Lord," and "calling on the name of the Lord," than the simple definition that Witness Lee gave us. The most important words in these phrases in the New Testament are "the Lord" and "the name of the Lord." Witness Lee, however, majored on the "calling" part of the phrases. He explained that the root word of the Greek word for *calling* is *kaleo* (Strong, G2564), which means "to call out loud." So, according to him, to call on the Lord was to call out, "O Lord Jesus."

I discovered that the meaning of *epikaleomai* involves much more than just to call out. According to Strong's concordance, *epikaleomai* also means "to entitle," "invoke," and "appeal" (Strong, G1941). After looking at the definitions of these words, I felt that a more accurate explanation of the phrase, "call on the Lord," would be this: to honor Jesus with the title, "Lord" (to entitle); to use His name, Jesus, the name above every name in power and authority, when asking for help (to invoke); or to make an earnest or urgent request for something in the name of the Lord Jesus (to appeal). In addition, according to W.E. Vine, *epikaleo* can mean to make use of the Lord's name to express adoration (Vine, 156).

As I revisited each verse in the New Testament in which I could find the word *epikaleomai*, I realized that each one was easily and sometimes better understood with the meanings of the words *entitle, invoke,* or *appeal,* instead of the meaning "to call out loud." I also noted that none of these verses indicate that calling on the Lord causes divine dispensing to occur, or that the motivation for calling on the Lord should be to receive divine dispensing. For example:

> And they stoned Stephen as he was calling on God and saying, "Lord Jesus, receive my spirit." (Acts 7:59)

In this passage, Stephen is clearly calling the Lord's name to appeal to Him to receive his spirit. There is no indication that he was calling to receive more of the processed Triune God or divine dispensing, as if he needed to get as much dispensing as He could at the last minute before dying. Another example is in Acts 22:16: "Arise and be baptized, and wash away your sins, calling on the name of the Lord." Here the phrase "calling on the name of the Lord" can be better understood with the meaning of honoring or confessing Jesus as the Lord rather than with the meaning of crying out to receive more of the Lord or of divine dispensing.

Nowhere in the Bible do I see the concept of saying, "O Lord Jesus," repetitively and continuously, something we were constantly admonished to do. Witness Lee equated our calling to breathing, something we do constantly, because God is Spirit and is like the air. This *may* be a valid analogy, but it does not prove his claim that calling the Lord's name dispenses more of the processed Triune God into us, nor does it support his claim that this is the purpose of calling on the Lord.

Witness Lee focused us on the calling part of the phrase. The focus should be on the One being called. The logical implication of calling on or upon someone is to make contact with that person, with a specific matter in mind. It means that we are contacting that person for a reason, with something that we want to communicate. When the widow in the Bible repeatedly bothered the unjust judge with a request, he eventually responded to her by granting her request (Luke 18:2-5). What would he have done if the widow had just repeatedly said, "O Judge, O Judge, O Judge," without telling him what she wanted? Maybe he would have committed her to an institution. Instead, she asked him for something specific, and he granted her request.

In the Local Church, I heard people calling incessantly, sometimes fretfully, saying, "O Lord Jesus," over and over again. It was apparent that they were in real need and were having a very hard time. They believed, as I did then, that help from God would come in the form of divine dispensing that would eventually "do it all" and supply whatever the need was. I now think that, instead of divinely dispensing Himself, Jesus was there listening to the incessant repetition of His name and was responding, "Yes? What do you want? What is your request? You have my attention. What is your need?" He was ready for personal interaction and conversation in which He could make Himself known in a real and specific way.

Witness Lee told us that the prayer for "help" was a pitiful, low kind of begging prayer. We were not supposed to ask or beg for help but to ask for more of Christ. I still remember when, after leaving the Local Church, I prayed a simple prayer, "Help me, Father." I had the thought, "You have really fallen to a low place, Jane. You are now asking for *help.*" You can imagine my surprise when God answered my "pitiful" prayer and helped me. I was overcome by this. And what was the result? It was simply this: love for Him. My faith increased, and I worshipped Him. I never had this kind of experience as a result of seeking divine dispensing by calling, "O Lord Jesus."

10b. The Mighty Name of Jesus

My explanation of an expanded definition of calling on the Lord shows clearly that the focus of this phrase is the Lord and His name. He is the Lord! He is the One who can answer our earnest requests and help us. He is the One on the throne of grace. The One we call out to is the One whom God raised from the dead and made both Lord and Christ, the One to whom God gave a name that is above every name! He has been given the highest authority and has all power.

In our practice in the Local Church, we placed so much importance on the supposed result of our calling (receiving divine dispensing) that we ended up focused on ourselves—our breathing, our eating, our drinking, our receiving. When we entitle Him as Jesus the Lord, we give Him first place, and He gets the glory. When we cry for help in His name and He answers us tangibly in our time of need, we spontaneously give Him praise and honor and glory.

The truth has set me free to invoke, appeal to, and call upon Him for whatever I need and to entitle Him as my Lord. I have purposed never again to use the Lord's name in a vague, empty, meaningless, and repetitive way (Matt. 6:7). Like Paul, I will make known my requests and appeal to Him to answer me in His mighty name. I will also freely use His name to acknowledge His lordship, to praise Him, and to adore Him. I will not be deluded to think that calling on the Lord brings divine dispensing that will do it all!

10c. Pray-reading the Word

Pray-reading the Bible was the other way Witness Lee taught us to be mingled with God or receive divine dispensing. I no longer believe this. He taught us to take any verse or verses from the Bible and speak them aloud, interspersing the words with "O Lord," "Amen," and "Hallelujah." He mainly used John 6:63 and Ephesians 6:17-18 to support the practice of pray-reading:

> It is the Spirit who gives life; the flesh profits nothing; the words which I have spoken to you are spirit and are life. (John 6:63, RV)

Chapter 24—The Ax Laid to the Root

> And receive ... the sword of the Spirit, which *Spirit* is the word [*rhema*] of God, by means of all prayer and petition, praying at every time in spirit ... (Eph 6:17-18, RV)

Witness Lee said that in these verses Jesus was revealing to us that "the Word is the Spirit, and the Spirit is the Word" (Lee, *Christ*, 103). He said that because of this we needed to contact it with our spirit, not our mind (Lee, *Christ*, 104). We were often told to "get out of our mind" and "into our spirit."

I do not believe that we should forget about our mind when we contact the Bible. Why? In the New Testament, there are two Greek words that are translated into English as *word*. These are *logos* and *rhema*. *Logos* means "the expression of thought" (Vine, 1241). It is "something said (including the thought)" and indicates "reasoning (the mental faculty)" (Strong, G3056). *Logos* is "living and powerful, and sharper than any two-edged sword, piercing even to the division of soul and spirit ... and is a *discerner of the thoughts* and intents of the heart" (Heb. 4:12) [emphasis added]. *Logos* operates specifically on our thinking and understanding. The whole Bible contains the expression of God's thought in words.

W. E. Vine states that *rhema* is distinct from *logos* in that *rhema* does not refer "to the whole Bible as such, but to the individual Scripture which the Spirit brings to our remembrance for use in time of need...." (Vine, 1242). So, what exactly is *rhema*? *Rhema* is a specific instance of God's speaking to us in a time of need. Because *rhema* also expresses a thought of God, it is spoken for our understanding. According to these verses, the words that we should take by means of all prayer and petition are *rhema*, those that God speaks when we are in need, not *logos*. Why is this difference important? Because it is the *rhema* of God, His living, instant speaking to us, that gives us faith. "Faith comes by hearing, and hearing by the *rhema* of God" (Rom. 10:17). Ephesians 6:17-18 shows how much we should value God's personal speaking to us.

By telling us to pray-read anything in the whole Bible, Witness Lee was teaching us to pray-read as if Ephesians 6:17 contained the word, *logos;* when, in fact, it contains the word, *rhema*. His *Recovery Version* footnote to

Ephesians 6:17 acknowledges that the word here is *rhema*, but he did not teach us accordingly, that is to say, to pray and petition with the *rhema* we hear from God. Not only that, his other main support for pray-reading, John 6:63, also contains the word *rhema* instead of *logos*.

When Paul was in a time of need with a "thorn" in his flesh, God spoke *rhema* to him. This word was spoken for Paul's understanding. He never forgot those words and even recorded them for us. God didn't tell Paul to go pray-read and get more divine dispensing. He didn't tell him to get out of his mind or to turn to his spirit!

I no longer believe that John 6:63 and Ephesians 6:17-18 support the practice of praying the words of the Bible in the way Witness Lee taught us. Neither do I believe that these verses prescribe a method by which the Triune God will dispense Himself into man. This does not mean, of course, that it is wrong to pray as we read *logos*. Jesus told those who love Him to keep His word (*logos*) (John 14:23). We do need to treasure the *logos* of God and pay careful attention to it. How we do this is not prescribed as a methodology in the Bible, however. We just need to keep His words and hide them in our heart by reading, memorizing, meditating, praying, or whatever way we can. This is especially important because, much of the time, it is the *logos* of God that is the basis for His *rhema* to us.

10d. The Bread and the Wine

So, what does happen when the Lord speaks His *rhema* to us? He not only teaches us something that we can understand in our walk with Him, He also supplies us with the strength to obey His speaking. This is what the Lord did in answer to Paul's prayer about the thorn in his flesh. He spoke to Paul, "My grace is sufficient for you." This statement was not just a nice teaching for Paul. It was *rhema*; it was *spirit* and *life*. These words actually gave him an experience of the power that raised Christ from the dead, an experience of the saving life he wrote about in Romans 5:10, which resulted in his glorying in his weaknesses.

This is what Jesus talked about with His disciples before He was crucified when He said, "The words [*rhema*] that I speak to you are spirit, and they are life" (John 6:63). He made this profound statement to them after they had become upset. What were they upset about? They were upset because He had just said to them,

> "Most assuredly, I say to you, unless you eat the flesh of the Son of Man and drink His blood, you have no life in you. Whoever eats My flesh and drinks My blood has eternal life, and I will raise him up at the last day. For My flesh is food indeed, and My blood is drink indeed. He who eats My flesh and drinks My blood abides in Me, and I in him." (John 6:53-57)

He then explained these words saying, in essence, "I do not want you to eat my physical flesh and drink my physical blood. I want you to eat the words that I speak to you." When He told them they needed to eat His flesh and drink His blood, He was actually telling them that He was God's lamb. The Passover Lamb was sacrificed by the children of Israel and then eaten. Jesus was indicating to them, "I am the Lamb of God. After I am sacrificed, you will be able to *eat* Me."

He was telling them ahead of time that they were going to benefit from His death and resurrection in a great way. They were going to experience the spiritual reality of what the children of Israel had experienced. They weren't going to be saved from Pharaoh and Egypt; they were going to be saved from Satan with his world system and kingdom of darkness. He was telling them how they were going to partake of this great salvation. They would experience His great salvation as they ate His *rhema*.

How would they remember His words? He promised them that the Comforter, the Holy Spirit, would bring His words to them, His words that were spirit and life. This is how they would live their new life. They would live by *rhema*.

> "Man shall not live by bread alone, but by every word [*rhema*] that proceeds from the mouth of God." (Matt. 4:4)

The effectiveness of His death and resurrection would be available to them when they ate the Lamb by eating the *rhema* He spoke to them.

Today, whenever I eat the bread (symbolic of His flesh) and drink the wine (symbolic of His blood) in remembrance of the Lord (1 Cor. 11:26), I understand that I am symbolically showing that this is how I live and walk with God, that is, by the death and resurrection of Jesus. Whenever I receive the *rhema* of God, I experience in my own life, as Paul did, the result of what Christ accomplished by His death and resurrection. His *rhema* helps me in the same way it empowered Paul regarding his thorn. It supplies me with grace and strength.

God usually speaks *rhema* to us that is based on words of the Bible. Sometimes He speaks *rhema* to us with words that are not a direct quote from Scripture. For example, when God said to Paul, "My grace is sufficient for thee ...," this was not a quote from Scripture. I also remember reading about another such example when God spoke to Hudson Taylor, "Then go for me to China." This was also not a quote from Scripture, but God's work in China through Hudson Taylor was testimony to its truth. Any such speaking must be discerned to be from God and not His enemy. If it is from God, it will not contradict the Bible or God's character; it should be confirmable in fellowship with others; and if it is directive, it should be confirmed by our environmental circumstances. It will result in gladness, not frustration or oppression.

I have learned to treasure the words (*rhema*) that God has spoken to me during my lifetime. Remembering them has carried me through long and difficult periods of time when God seemed to be absent. I have also learned to treasure the written Word of God, the Bible, with all its wonderful promises.

His Word has been a light to my path (Psa.119:105), even in the darkest times. He promised He would be with me all the days of my life, and I have learned to believe Him, even when my circumstances are screaming otherwise. In dark times, I have learned to ask Him to shine on any sin that may be separating me from Him. I have learned that when He enlightens me, I simply need to repent. If He doesn't make me aware of any sin, I walk on by faith in His Word (*logos*), which is full of rock-solid promises. I store His Word in my mind by reading and meditating on it. His Word is a wonderful treasure, a truly living book, like no other book ever written! (Heb. 4:12).

I no longer believe that all I need to do is pray-read the Bible, as defined by Witness Lee, or that pray-reading automatically causes some kind of divine dispensing to occur. Instead, I believe that God's Word is the means by which He communicates the thought of His heart to me and the way in which He interacts with me in real situations. When He communicates with me, He always respects my understanding. Through His words, He reveals truth and supplies me both the *grace* and *strength* needed to walk in His truth and experience His great salvation. I am transformed by the renovation of my understanding and my ways of thinking (the renewing of my mind) (Rom. 12:2).

11. Bad Fruit: Wrong Thoughts and Behaviors

The fruit of a teaching reveals whether or not it is of God. In my life and the lives of others, the divine dispensing teaching resulted in wrong thoughts about God, about man, about love, about the cross, about leadership, about the worth of the individual to God, and about individual responsibility. It also resulted in wrong attitudes and ungodly behaviors.

The intended result or fruit of Paul's teaching was love: love for God and love for all people (1 Tim. 1:5). In the Local Church, the fruit of the divine dispensing teaching was not self-sacrificial love for all. Instead, the fruit was a zealous love for the ministry of one man and mutual "love" among his absolute followers. The devotion to this man's ministry superseded loving *all* those for whom Christ died. This is clearly evidenced by the Local Church's history of hurting and rejecting real believers in order to protect the ministry of Witness Lee.

11a. Wrong Thought About God

My belief about divine dispensing resulted in my holding wrong thoughts about God. By the end of my time in the Local Church, whenever I heard Witness Lee say God's economy was the processed Triune God dispensed into the tripartite man, I had a picture in my mind of a processed multi-ingredient liquid in a bottle ready to be dispensed. The processed Triune God was like a special elixir that would automatically cure any and all of my maladies just by drinking it. Rather than God being shown to me as Someone who wanted to relate to me on a person-to-person basis, who loved me and died on the cross for me, God was shown to me as a processed product ready for easy consumption.

Additionally, because the Father was included as an ingredient in the processed Triune God, there was no need for me to pray to Him as Jesus taught (Matt. 6:9–13). I didn't even need to think about God as the Father, except when we sang a hymn to Him or prayed a few prayers to Him at the end of the Lord's Table meeting.

These kinds of wrong thoughts about God ultimately shut Him out of our lives. They hindered Him from developing a personal, intimate, and uniquely purposeful relationship with each one of us.

11b. Wrong Thought About Man's Being

Where did I receive divine dispensing? As a "tripartite man," I believed I was made up of three parts, shown in a diagram as concentric circles. The little circle in the middle of me was my human spirit. It received the divine dispensing and was like a beachhead from which the processed Triune God could spread into the second circle. This circle, which surrounded my spirit, was my soul and was made up of my mind, will, and emotions. The last and outer circle was my body.

I still believe that man has all these "parts," but I no longer think about myself that way. I no longer wonder which part is currently functioning, like I did while in the Local Church. I have a physical heart, a stomach, and a liver; but if I constantly think about each of these parts, questioning which part is functioning, it indicates that there is something wrong with me. After my experience in the Local Church, God had to put my parts back together again. In other words, He had to change the way I had come to think about myself. He didn't view me in parts. He saw me as a person, as Jane. One day, I noticed something in the verse which Witness Lee used when teaching us about the three parts of man. I saw that the phrase, "spirit, soul, and body," had a modifier, the word *whole:*

> Now may the God of peace Himself sanctify you completely; and may your whole spirit, soul, and body be preserved blameless at the coming of our Lord Jesus Christ. (1 Thess. 5:23)

While this verse does refer to the three parts of man, it also indicates that these parts make up one *whole,* an entire being. God showed me it was not healthy to think of myself in *parts* and wonder which part I am "in," as I learned to do in the Local Church. Since this realization, I have not spent even one second wondering if I am *in my spirit* or *in my soul.* I have completely stopped trying to determine which part might currently be in operation. I am sure this talk sounds strange to anyone who has not experienced the Local Church, but I'm just as sure it doesn't sound strange to those who have. The truth is that the Bible tells me to look away to Jesus, not to look at my parts and figure out where I am.

11c. Wrong Thought About the Cross

Witness Lee taught us that Christ's death was included as an ingredient in the "life-giving Spirit." He taught that we would automatically experience the cross by continuing to receive the divine dispensing of the processed Triune God. I now see that this is a very serious error because it causes people to think wrongly about how to walk with Christ and experience the cross in daily living. Such a walk does not happen automatically without our awareness. It happens by conscious specific interactions between us and the Lord as He speaks His *rhema* to us in specific situations. We should relate to the Lord as a person in real life situations, not just drink some kind of an elixir. In our walk with Him, He wants to teach us something about the cross that we can understand. He also wants us to know the power of His resurrection, which supplies us with the strength to obey His speaking in real situations.

The belief that divine dispensing is the only way to really subjectively experience the death of Christ is prevalent in the Local Church. Some members published on a website the following statement in which they refer to Christians throughout the centuries:

> Many have had the realization that they were crucified on the cross with Christ, according to Galatians 2:20 and Romans 6:6, but have never been able to enter into the experience of this precious fact. (Christian Websites)

This website proceeds to explain the way to enter into this precious fact, indicating that "many" believers couldn't enter because they didn't have the key.

For centuries, however, believers who didn't understand the "key" have entered into the experience of being crucified with Christ. They have learned to follow the Lamb of God through the lives and teachings of Paul and the other apostles. They have had personal, specific interactions with Jesus by which they experienced the reality of the cross. Untold numbers of believers have walked with Jesus and been empowered to live a crucified life. A clear example of this is found in the book, *Mimosa: Who was Charmed,* by Amy Carmichael. Mimosa was a Hindu in India who, after a fleeting introduction to the gospel as a child, somehow accepted Christ and walked with Him for twenty years afterwards without having any further Christian instruction, except that which came directly from her heavenly Father. Her life showed the fruits of the Spirit and evidence of the crucified life.

11d. Wrong Thought About Love

Witness Lee taught us not to express our natural love. He taught that a Christian who received the divine dispensing would spontaneously express God's love. He said that we should not talk about *love* or encourage one another to *love*. Instead, we should talk about *life* and encourage one another to eat and drink the Spirit.

The bad fruit of this teaching can be seen in a story that Sandra Brown told me. She stayed home one night from a church meeting because she was very sick. She bathed her children and put them to bed. As she tried to finish the dishes so she could go to bed, her husband, who knew how sick she was, returned from the meeting. He paused to see her slaving away at the kitchen sink doing dishes, and then he turned and went on to bed. Years later, when she was leaving him, she asked if he remembered that night. He did. She asked, "Why didn't you offer to help me? You knew how sick I was." He answered, "I wanted to help you, but I wasn't sure whether it was something of life or of my natural love, so I just didn't do anything." She said, "Please! I would much rather have received your natural love than none at all!" Her husband truly believed he was following God when he ignored her need! He was apparently still waiting on the dispensing of the Triune God to produce real love in him. He wasn't sure whether that had happened yet, so he just left her to suffer and went to bed.

In this situation, Satan used the divine dispensing teaching to produce a situation where the opposite of love was shown. What might Jesus have wanted to speak to her husband? "Bob, love your wife as I loved the church and gave Myself for her." Bob might have helped his wife instead of trying to care for his own "spirituality." The divine dispensing teaching affords the way for a person to excuse obviously bad behavior; and in essence, put the responsibility for it on God, because He had not yet produced love by the dispensing of divine life. Life was constantly trumpeted as the focus, to the exclusion of love. The strength of the thought that we held regarding this can be seen in some of the classic hymns we sang. For example, one of the hymns in our hymnal was changed from "O Christ, He is the fountain, the deep sweet well of love" to "O Christ, He is the fountain, the deep sweet well of life."

Jesus, Paul, and the other apostles, however, *did* talk about love. They exhorted us to love our neighbors and even to love our enemies. The Bible exhorts us to love, lest we forget. We should be reminded of the commandment to love one another. If we had heard this as frequently as we heard we must spiritually eat and drink, we might have noticed when this fruit of the Spirit—love—began to be missing among us. We might have repented.

11e. Mistreatment of Fellow Believers

Bad fruit from the divine dispensing teaching can be seen in an encounter I had with a sister after we had left the Local Church. This sister had lived with us in the Wheeler House by the University of Houston, and she was still a member of the Local Church. The following experience with her occurred about thirteen years after my 1977 discipline. It was the first time I had talked with her since that time.

When our brief conversation began, she was very cool and guarded. At one point, she said she had not really understood what had happened to us. When I tried to offer a few sentences of explanation, she became very tense and immediately cut me off in a very unkind manner, telling me she didn't really want to know. She stood up and began to say over and over, "I only know one thing—calling on the Lord and the divine dispensing." This was interspersed with her repeatedly saying, "O Lord Jesus." She said that this was all she knew, this was what God wanted her to do, and she didn't allow herself to think about other things.

In this encounter, she exhibited a complete absence of love. I had given her a great amount of my time, love, and care while she lived with us, yet all she could give me was rudeness and coldness. She was much more interested in protecting her "spirituality" than in considering me. I responded, "Please don't say there is only one thing. If you say 'divine dispensing' to me, then I say to you there should be another thing: love. God is love. Where is God's love?" She didn't answer me but proceeded to depart quickly.

11f. Authoritarian Leadership Practices

Another result of the divine dispensing teaching is that some Local Church leaders exhibit undesirable fruit in their leadership practices. The ones with whom we've had contact are very matter-of-fact and cold in their dealings with others whom they consider to be in error. They also have an unusual mindset regarding their responsibility to respond to the teachings of the Bible.

Because of the teaching about divine dispensing, they have a way to avoid facing any issues raised about matters that are obviously wrong according to the plain words of the Bible, or even according to common sense. They are able to reject the logical understanding of a situation by saying, "This is something from the mind, not the spirit. There is nothing of life in such speaking." For them, since the source is the *mind,* this means that the content has no validity whatsoever. As a result of this mindset, they can remain in a state of disobedience to the Word without a qualm of conscience.

119. A Boasting Leader

In the early 1990's, when the Lord opened my eyes to see that not only Witness Lee's teachings, but also his attitude and example were different from those of the apostles, I was fully set free from my feeling of loyalty to him and his teachings. In messages he delivered at an elders' training to over four hundred attendees, he did not display an attitude befitting a servant of the Lord or a Christian leader. If this attitude was the fruit in his life after years of practicing his own teachings about God's economy and divine dispensing, then it was plain to me that these teachings were not of God.

In these messages, when he was strongly contending for his teaching about God's economy being *the one* teaching, he stated:

> If anyone of you could rise up to render the Lord's recovery the proper leadership, I would be the first to follow you, to take your leadership. But what kind of direction can you give us? How much truth do you know? Could you open up the entire New Testament from Matthew to Revelation in a detailed way to bring the churches into the depths of God's New Testament economy? If I am boasting, I am forced to be a fool like the Apostle Paul (2 Cor. 12:11).
>
> There is no hint in the New Testament telling us that in the Lord's move there could or should be more than one leadership. No one can deny this truth. Even the Devil, Satan, has to admit that two plus two is four. If you are going to express your opinion, you must annul the truth I put out. Do not express your opinion; express your knowledge of the truth.... My point is this—since the revelation is here, the teaching is here, the leadership must be here. (Lee, Book 7, 127-128)

In these statements and a number of others in this elders' training, I saw clearly, in contrast to Paul's example, an example I did not want to follow.

11h. Witness Lee's Experience

In *Living Christ*, Witness Lee says that "man has only two sins before God": not being a believer and, as a believer, "the sin of not living Christ" (Lee, *Living*, 11–12). In this book, he gives his own testimony about not living Christ. His testimony, which follows, was given after he had been a believer for more than fifty years. After saying that the Lord had asked him whether he had confessed the sin of not living Christ, Witness Lee said this:

> From that day on, I would confess this sin thoroughly before the Lord. Then I found out that there is no end to the daily confession of this sin. It is extremely difficult for us to live Christ every moment of the day. I did a little calculating for myself and for others as well. There are twenty-four hours in a day. After deducting eight hours for sleeping, there are still sixteen hours. How much of the remaining sixteen hours do I spend living Christ? I found out that I may not even have two hours of living Christ. In the other fourteen hours although I did not commit any sin, neither did I live Christ. Do you see this? Within the sixteen waking hours, I had only two hours at most in which I was living Christ.
>
> These two hours of living Christ started with my prayer time. In fact, at the beginning of my prayer time, I was not in my spirit but still in my mind. Then gradually I prayed myself into my spirit. When I prayed myself into my spirit, I lived Christ in my spirit. When I prayed, I lived Christ. After praying, I was living in my spirit, but this did not last long. After five minutes Sister Lee asked me, "Yesterday you gave some money to So-and-so. Why did you not discuss this with me first?" Her questioning halted my living of Christ. Immediately I turned to my mind, asking, "What is this?" This was not to live Christ. I spent the next fifteen minutes telling her all the reasons, and in those fifteen minutes I did not live Christ. What did I live? Even I myself do not know. I did not sin or lose my temper, but neither was I in my spirit living Christ. This would go on until two or three o'clock in the afternoon; then I sensed something was wrong. I turned to the Lord to confess, "Lord, I did not live Christ throughout the day. Although I did not do anything wrong, I have been living in myself. Lord, I am not trustworthy. Lord, forgive my sin! Lord, remind me that I am one spirit with You, and You are one spirit with me. I do not want to live

outside of this spirit. I want to live only in this spirit." After my confession I felt much better within and sensed the Lord's sweetness, and I was again in my spirit living Christ. However, at this moment the phone rang, and I picked up the receiver. That one phone call got me out of my spirit again. Also there were times when the telephone did not ring, and I was just working and not committing any wrong, yet I still was not living Christ. (Lee, *Living*, 12-13)

He proceeded to state his fear that even the best brothers and sisters in the church only "live Christ" five percent of the time (Lee, *Living*, 13).

In this testimony, I saw a man who was not at all like Paul. He wasn't glorying in his weaknesses, nor was he experiencing God's grace and the power of Christ resting upon him. Rather, he was struggling under the need of constant confession, trying to do something he called *living Christ*, failing in his attempt, repetitively analyzing the matter, and then telling others they were failing in a worse way. He was certainly not preaching Christ or words of faith. His testimony was one of hopelessness and futility. This testimony was actually his own admission that what he had been teaching for many years was not working well at all.

12. Bad Fruit: A "Do-It-All" Method

Witness Lee told us that divine dispensing would do it all. This simply is not true. There is no practice or method given in the New Testament that will *do it all*. There is, however, "the supply of the Spirit of Jesus Christ" (Phil. 1:19) which is available to me to meet every need. Paul was definitely in a time of need in prison when he told the Philippians that his need would be met through their prayer and the supply of the Spirit of Jesus Christ. God also meets my needs through this supply when I ask.

If what Witness Lee prescribed is *the only way*, then when the Spirit spoke to the seven churches in Revelation 3, He should have told each church the same thing: "Just call on the Lord and pray-read the Word. The divine dispensing will do it all." But instead, the Spirit spoke specific, meaningful, and different words to correct each particular problem in each church, and He promised to reward the individuals who heard and responded to His words regarding their problem.

If Witness Lee was right, when Paul prayed three times to be delivered from the thorn in his flesh, the Lord should have said to him, "Just call on My name and pray-read My Word." Instead, the Lord conversed with him and gave a specific answer to his prayer, saying that His grace was sufficient. He didn't bypass Paul's thought process but gave him an explanation of why He wasn't removing the thorn—because His strength was made perfect in Paul's weakness. If Paul believed that divine dispensing would do it all, he shouldn't have prayed about his personal problem, nor should he have told us about this *old* way of praying. Neither did God need to explain anything to Paul about what He was doing.

12a. Mind Renewing Not Divine Dispensing

According to the teaching of divine dispensing, the Spirit of God comes into my spirit first, and from there, spreads into my mind, will, and emotions by His divine dispensing. I am thus automatically changed as He spreads into me and replaces me.

I no longer accept this explanation. Instead, I simply believe that Christ is in me (Col. 1:27) because the Bible tells me so. I believe that the Lord Jesus Christ is with my spirit (2 Tim. 4:22). As for what He is doing in the rest of me, I believe what Paul said in Romans 12:1–2:

> I beseech you therefore, brethren, by the mercies of God, that you present your bodies a living sacrifice, holy, acceptable to God, which is your reasonable service. And do not be conformed to this world, but be transformed by the renewing of your mind, that you may prove what is that good and acceptable and perfect will of God.

I have presented my body a living sacrifice, and I am allowing Him to transform me by renewing my mind. Paul was concerned that we would be deceived, and that our minds would be corrupted from the simplicity that is in Christ.

> For I am jealous for you with godly jealousy. For I have betrothed you to one husband, that I may present you as a chaste virgin to Christ. But I fear, lest somehow, as the serpent deceived Eve by his craftiness, so your minds may be corrupted from the simplicity that is in Christ. (2 Cor. 11:2-3)

Paul said that we have the "mind of Christ" (1 Cor.2:16), and he prayed that Christ would dwell (take up permanent residence) in our hearts by faith (Eph. 3:17). So, I believe that Christ is making His residence in my heart by renewing my mind as I, by faith, choose to believe His Word, both *logos* and *rhema*. His Word contains His thought, and through it, He speaks to me and my understanding. Christ's redeeming, sin-cleansing death has made this wonderful communication between God and me possible.

12b. Blocking Interaction with Jesus

As His believers, we are called to have living, meaningful interactions with Christ Himself, not to receive a processed product by certain prescribed methods. Christ is our way to the Father, our way to know the love of God. The errant belief that divine dispensing will automatically do everything actually gives Satan the way to block us from having real, practical experiences that come from communicating with Jesus.

This belief can easily result in avoiding the personal responsibility to face actual problems and difficulties. It can hinder us from bringing our problems to the Lord by prayer and supplication with thanksgiving. It can hinder us from making our needs known directly to God. It can hinder us from hearing the Spirit speak to us directly about personal matters and cooperating with Him to put to death specific fleshly deeds (Rom. 8:13). It can hinder us from taking up our cross and following Him. In essence, it can become a way to avoid facing the very things that God wants us to talk to Him about in our time of need. This is why we have times of need! He wants to know us and be known by us in everything. He wants to make Himself real to us in our ordinary, daily lives.

12c. Christ, the Way

Jesus has shown Himself and His love to me most plainly in the little things that He has done for me in life's practical situations. I call them little only because they probably don't matter to anyone but me and those who care about me. He has walked with me closely through my childhood, my marriage, giving birth, speaking in public, learning to be a parent, learning computer programming, and writing. He has been and still is my very best friend, my best counselor, my provider, the giver of songs in the night, the keeper of every promise, and the greatest lover of my soul. He has personally taught me, in so many things and ways, what it means to take up my cross and follow Him. I have not known Him as a processed product but as my way to the Father, who is love.

Paul's walk by conversing with Jesus demonstrates the truth that Christ is the way. Paul didn't preach other ways. He preached Christ. Paul didn't practice *methods;* he took up his cross and followed Christ. He was following His course by following *Someone*.

12d. Touching Him

Many were thronging Jesus, maybe even calling His name, but only she touched Him:

> So Jesus went with him, and a great multitude followed Him and thronged Him.
>
> Now a certain woman had a flow of blood for twelve years, and had suffered many things from many physicians. She had spent all that she had and was no better, but rather grew worse. When she heard about Jesus, she came behind Him in the crowd and touched His garment. For she said, "If only I may touch His clothes, I shall be made well."
>
> Immediately the fountain of her blood was dried up, and she felt in her body that she was healed of the affliction. And Jesus, immediately knowing in Himself that power had gone out of Him, turned around in the crowd and said, "Who touched My clothes?" (Mark 5:24-30)

When she touched His clothes, Jesus perceived that power (Gk: *dunamis*) went out of Him. She had connected with

Jesus in a way that caused a transfer of something from Him to her that healed her. The Greek word indicates that a miraculous strength or power passed to her. From what she did, can we prescribe a method to receive power?

Paul also experienced a similar transfer from Jesus. After he prayed about the thorn in his flesh, Jesus told him, "My grace is sufficient for you, for My strength [*dunamis*] is made perfect in weakness" (2 Cor. 12:9). Jesus told Paul that this transfer of strength was His grace. It made Paul glad in spite of his infirmity. Paul wanted us to know this same strength when he prayed that we would know the "exceeding greatness of His power [*dunamis*] toward us" (Eph. 1:19).

Christ lived, died, and rose again that we might have a rich, abundant supply of grace. That supply is now available at the throne of grace for our times of need.

12e. The Most Excellent Way

The most excellent way is the way of love—the way that never fails. Love is simply God Himself. God demonstrated His love by becoming flesh and dying on the cross for us. Regardless of what we do or what we have—even if we "understand all mysteries and all knowledge"—if we don't have love, we are nothing (1 Cor. 13:2). I may think I know all about the processed Triune God and how to receive Him and to be built up into His church, but if I cannot love every believer in deed and truth, I am in error. If we love God, we will also love *all* of our brothers and sisters in Christ (1 John 4:21, 5:1). We can evaluate our walk with Christ by looking at our love for God and others.

Christ is a living person who knows the heart of every person. He loves us, but we cannot use Him for our own ends or manipulate Him. He relates to us in honesty. Because He is the truth (John 14:6), His relationship with us will be a true one. He loves us far too much for our relationship with Him to be otherwise. He longs for us to know Him intimately and genuinely, not methodologically. If we have a relationship with Him in this earthly life, it will be a true and honest one, one in the light, one filled with real mutual communication and love.

How can we find Him as our way? By telling him we want to know Him above all else and seeking Him with all our heart.

Dear Jesus,

Open my eyes that I may see You as You are. Grant me a heart that loves You and wants only to follow You at any cost. Make me a person who presses through the crowd of all that blocks You from my view and who reaches out in faith to touch You.

Chapter 25
Faith Is the Victory

> Then I heard a loud voice saying in heaven, "Now salvation, and strength, and the kingdom of our God, and the power of His Christ have come, for the accuser of our brethren, who accused them before our God day and night, has been cast down. And they overcame him by the blood of the Lamb and by the word of their testimony, and they did not love their lives to the death. Therefore rejoice, O heavens, and you who dwell in them!" (Rev. 12:10-12)

Faith—The Victory

THE SPIRIT PRAISED THE CHURCH IN PHILADELPHIA because they had a little strength and kept His word and did not deny His name (Rev. 3:7–8). That little strength is our faith, the faith that comes when God speaks to us. Faith is a small but powerful thing. Faith the size of a mustard seed can move a mountain (Matt. 17:20).

> For whatever is born of God overcomes the world. And this is the victory that has overcome the world—our faith. (1 John 5:4)

The powers of darkness fear our little strength, the thread of gold, our living faith. They know only too well that faith enables people to obey God at any cost, even at the cost of their lives. They have seen what it can do. The dark powers in the air didn't just read about faith in the book of Hebrews, they were firsthand witnesses to all of the events recorded there. What did they see? They saw people who

> through faith subdued kingdoms, worked righteousness, obtained promises, stopped the mouths of lions, quenched the violence of fire, escaped the edge of the sword, out of weakness were made strong, became valiant in battle, turned to flight the armies of the aliens. Women received their dead raised to life again. Others were tortured, not accepting deliverance.... Still others had trial of mockings and scourgings ... and of chains and imprisonment. They were stoned, they were sawn in two, were tempted, were slain with the sword. They wandered about in sheepskins and goatskins,

> being destitute, afflicted, tormented.... They wandered in deserts and mountains, in dens and caves of the earth. (Heb. 11:33-38)

How did these people do these things?—by *faith!*

We overcome by the blood of the Lamb and the word of our testimony, and we will not love our lives unto death. The author of Hebrews continues:

> And all these, having obtained a good testimony through faith, did not receive the promise, God having provided something better for us, that they should not be made perfect apart from us. Therefore we also, since we are surrounded by so great a cloud of witnesses, let us lay aside every weight, and the sin which so easily ensnares us, and let us run with endurance the race that is set before us, looking unto Jesus, the author and finisher of our faith, who for the joy that was set before Him endured the cross, despising the shame, and has sat down at the right hand of the throne of God. For consider Him who endured such hostility from sinners against Himself, lest you become weary and discouraged in your souls. (Heb. 11:39-12:3)

His Coming

The Bible asks a very compelling question, one we should stop and consider:

> ... when the Son of Man comes, will He find faith on the earth? (Luke 18:8, NASV)

When Christ comes, will He find us weary and discouraged? Will He find us faithless? Or, instead, will He find us full of faith?

He will find us full of faith if, during our days, we "consider Him" and the hostility that He endured from "sinners against Himself" (Heb. 12:3). Just one look at His love for us, which He displayed in His death upon the cross, is enough to begin our thread of gold and our walk of faith. Our thread of gold grows as we continue to walk in the same way: looking away from all that is around us, away to Him, and coming forward boldly to His throne of grace.

The love of God shown in Christ's death on the cross has been speaking for centuries and has caused multitudes of people to believe in Him:

> When I call to remembrance the genuine faith that is in you, which dwelt first in your grandmother Lois and your mother Eunice, and I am persuaded is in you also. (2 Tim. 1:5)

Like a thread of gold connecting them, the faith that lived in Timothy, also lived in his mother and in his grandmother. Such faith has continued unbroken for centuries. This faith is not something we work up, muster up, or manufacture by our own efforts. It is a living and increasing faith, one that comes as a gift when we hear God speak to us. We are progressing from faith to faith.

> For in it the righteousness of God is revealed from faith to faith: as it is written, "The just shall live by faith." (Rom. 1:17)

As I look back at my life, I see my wonderful thread of gold. How did it come to be? It came into being, as Jesus spoke His words to me through the course of my life, in both good times and bad. The first thread began when I was a child, filled with guilt from lying. Then I heard His words to me for the first time, "God forgives." I repented and was saved. Then He told me, "Have no fear. I am with you." These were specific, meaningful, and powerful words that He spoke to me, a little eleven-year-old with a big problem. He used these words to take away my fear and tell me that He was with me. I knew what had happened and who had done it. I understood it, and I never forgot it. From my childhood until now, I have continued to learn to receive prayerfully the words He speaks to me, and He has continued to weave His thread of gold into my life. My love for Him and my faith in Him have continued to increase.

The pain of that dark time in my young adult life, when I was wounded by my own brothers and sisters and left in a pit, is not what is prominent in my remembrance anymore. What stands out in my memory about that time is one brief promise that came from Jesus to me: "The tangled skein will shine at last, a masterpiece of skill untold."

I now understand that there have been no accidents in this little life of mine. He had His own purpose in view.

Through all of the roughness of the journey, He has shown me His "good and acceptable and perfect will" (Rom. 12:2). The greatest privilege in the universe has been mine—to know Him.

> Yes, Lord, it's now as I was told.
> Your purpose did to me unfold.
> When I saw You upon that Tree,
> My heart was won, You conquered me.
> The long, long night? It now has passed.
> The tangled skein? It shines, at last.
> A masterpiece of skill untold!
> My faith, Your gift: the Thread of Gold.
>
> — Jane Carole Anderson

Gal. 2:20
I have been crucified with Christ; it is no longer I who live, but Christ lives in me; and the life which I now live in the flesh I live by faith in the Son of God, who loved me and gave Himself for me.

Heb. 12:2
Looking unto Jesus, the author and finisher of our faith, who for the joy that was set before Him endured the cross, despising the shame, and has sat down at the right hand of the throne of God.

Rom. 1:16–17
For I am not ashamed of the gospel of Christ, for it is the power of God to salvation for everyone who believes, for the Jew first and also for the Greek. For in it the righteousness of God is revealed from faith to faith; as it is written "The just shall live by faith."

I Cor. 13:13
And now abide faith, hope, love, these three; but the greatest of these is love.

Index to Hymns, Psalms, and Poems

First line:

"All in his hands"—what confidence it brings	279
A little bird I am	139
He giveth more grace when the burdens grow greater	179
His banner over us is love	322
How firm a foundation, ye saints of the Lord	168
How sweet, how heavenly is the sight	159
In all things God is off'ring	288
I will extol You, O Lord for You have lifted me up	281
Judge not the Lord by feeble sense	248
Loved with everlasting love, led by grace that love to know	2
Many crowd the Savior's kingdom, few receive His cross	188
My life is but a weaving	278
Near after distant	180
She kissed His feet, with tears she washed them	175
So on I go not knowing	280
The Bride eyes not her garment	318
The Lord will silently plan for thee	179
Then the Cross! For via Calvary	290
There's a light upon the mountains	187
When I survey the wondrous cross	318
When You hung there, nailed to that tree	316
Yes, Lord, it's now as I was told	406

BIBLIOGRAPHY

Bibles and Hymnals

American Standard Version. In e-Sword, ver. 7.1.0. Franklin, Tennessee: Rick Meyers, 2004. (See <http://www.e-sword.net> for this free Bible software.)

The Amplified Bible. Grand Rapids, Michigan: Zondervan Bible Publishers, 1965.

Concordant Literal New Testament. Saugus, California: Concordant Publishing, 1966.

The Holy Bible, The New International Version Study Bible. Grand Rapids, Michigan: Zondervan Bible, 1985.

Holy Bible: Recovery Version. Anaheim, California: Living Stream Ministry, 2003.

Hymns. Los Angeles: The Stream Publishers, 1966.

King James Version. In e-Sword, ver. 7.1.0. Franklin, Tennessee: Rick Meyers, 2004 (See <http://www.e-sword.net> for this free Bible software.)

New American Standard New Testament. Grand Rapids, Michigan: World Publishing, 1995.

The New Testament: Recovery Version. Anaheim, California: Living Stream Ministry, 1985.

Other Materials

Anderson, Neil T. *The Bondage Breaker*. Eugene, Oregon: Harvest House Publishers, 2000.

Ankerberg, John and John Weldon. *Encyclopedia of Cults and New Religions*. Eugene, Oregon: Harvest House Publishers, 1999.

Bright, Bill. "Have You Heard of the Four Spiritual Laws?" Orlando: New Life, 1994.

Brown M. D., Rebecca. *He Came to Set the Captives Free*. Chino, California: Chick Publications, 1986.

Carmichael, Amy. *Mimosa: Who Was Charmed*. Fort Washington, Pennsylvania: Christian Literature Crusade, 1976.

Christian Websites. "Experiencing Christ's Death." 1999. Available on the following website on July 16, 2005: <http://www.christsdeath.org/experiencing/index.html>.

Encarta Dictionary. In Microsoft Office Word 2003 SP1. Microsoft Corporation, 2003. (software program)

Garrard, Mary N. *Jessie Penn-Lewis, a Memoir*. Ontario, Canada: Ontario Christian Books, 1930.

Grubb, Norman. *Rees Howells Intercessor*. Fort Washington, Pennsylvania: Christian Literature Crusade, 1973.

Guyon, Jeanne Marie. *Autobiography of Madame Guyon*. Chicago: Moody Press, n.d.

Hsu, Lily. *My Unforgettable Memories: Watchman Nee and Shanghai Local Church*. Xulon Press, 2013.

Apologetics Index. "U.S. Supreme Court Rejects Local Church Lawsuit against Harvest House." 2013. Available on the following website on May 29, 2015: <http://www.apologeticsindex.org/545-local-church-loses>.

Ingalls, John. *Speaking the Truth in Love: A True Account of Events and Concerns Related to the Local Churches: 1987–1989*. Anaheim, California: The Word & the Testimony, 1990.

Kennedy, John W. *The Torch of the Testimony*. Auburn, Maine: Christian Books, 1965.

Lee, Witness. *Christ Versus Religion*. Taipei, Taiwan: Gospel Bookroom, 1971.

Lee, Witness. "Daily Reading Portion in the Ministry for 07/13/2005": Available on the following website on July 16, 2005: <http://steward.emanna.com/7ministry-readings.cfm>. From *Truth Messages*. Anaheim, California: Living Stream Ministry, 1992, 40–44.

Lee, Witness. *The Divine Economy*. Anaheim, California: Living Stream Ministry: 1986.

Lee, Witness. *Elders' Training: The Way To Carry Out the Vision—Book 3*. Anaheim, California: Living Stream Ministry, 1985.

Lee, Witness. *Elders' Training: One Accord For the Lord's Move—Book 7*. Anaheim, California: Living Stream Ministry, 1986.

Lee, Witness. *Elders' Training: The Life Pulse of the Lord's Present Move—Book 8*. Anaheim, California: Living Stream Ministry, 1986.

Lee, Witness. *The Fermentation of the Present Rebellion*. Anaheim, California: Living Stream Ministry, 1990.

Lee, Witness. *Living Christ*. Anaheim, California: Living Stream Ministry, 2000.

Lee, Witness. *The Vision of God's Building*. Taipei: Gospel Book Room, 1972.

Mackintosh, C. H. "The Ministry of Christ: Past, Present, and Future (Exodus 21:1–6; John 13:1–10; Luke 12:37)." *The Mackintosh Treasury: Miscellaneous Writings of C. H. Mackintosh*. Neptune, N.J.: Loizeaux Brothers, 1978.

Miller, Andrew. *Miller's Church History*. Addison, Illinois: Bible Truth Publishers, 1977.

Nee, Watchman. *Authority and Submission*. Anaheim, California: Living Stream Ministry, 1988.

Nee, Watchman. *Back to the Cross*. New York: Christian Fellowship Publishers, 1988.

Nee, Watchman. *The Orthodoxy of the Church*. Anaheim, California: The Stream Publishers, 1970.

Nee, Watchman. *Practical Issues of This Life*. New York: Christian Fellowship Publishers, 1975.

Nee, Watchman. *Spiritual Authority*. New York: Christian Fellowship Publishers, 1972.

The New Bible Dictionary. Wheaton, Illinois: Tyndale House Publishers, 1962. From A. R. George. *Communion with God in the New Testament*. In Logos Research Systems. Logos Library System 2.1b. 1997. (software program)

Penn-Lewis, Jessie. *War on the Saints*. With Evan Roberts. 9th ed. New York: Thomas E. Lowe, 1991 (or Christian Literature Crusade abridged edition).

Strong, James. *The New Strong's Exhaustive Concordance of the Bible*. Nashville: Thomas Nelson Publishers, 1990.

Taylor, Howard. *J. Hudson Taylor: God's Man in China*. Chicago: Moody Press, 1965.

Vine, W.E. *An Expository Dictionary of New Testament Words*. Nashville: Royal Publishers, 1952.

Walvoord, John F. and Roy B. Zuck. *The Bible Knowledge Commentary*. Wheaton, Illinois: Victor Books, c1983–c1985. From Scripture Press Publications, 1983. In Logos Research Systems. Logos Library System 2.1b. 1997. (software program)

Webster's New World Dictionary of the American Language. 2nd ed. Cleveland: William Collins + World Publishing, 1974.

Glossary

The following list contains some of the Local Church terms that are used in this book with definitions according to the author's memory of what she learned about them. Most of these terms are explained in the book the first time they occur.

Absolute. A description of a member's loyalty to the Local Church. A member was either absolute or not absolute, meaning either completely loyal or not. The status of a member's loyalty was monitored by the leaders and by fellow members. Members desired to be considered absolute for God and "one" with His church. Outsiders considered Local Church members' absoluteness to be blind following.

Body-life. Our church experience was "the body-life" because we were living members of the Lord's living body on this earth. We were not an organization, but an organism. See also Church-life.

Brothers. Men in the Local Church, meaning brothers in God's family. See also, Elders.

Burning. See "Our First Burning" in chapter 6.

Buried. Baptized.

Built together. Local Church members were being built together to produce God's building, just as God built the tabernacle in the Old Testament. The tabernacle was built with boards paired and standing together in silver sockets. A single board was not complete unless it was paired with another board. We were not complete as an individual but needed to be paired with at least one other to make a useful unit.

Calling on the Lord. The practice of calling "O Lord" or "O Lord Jesus" out loud, usually repetitively. This was the way to be born again, as well as the way to be saved daily from one's self. See "About Calling on the Lord and Pray-reading" in chapter 25, item 10.

Capture. To catch people for the church by helping them "see the church" and give themselves fully to it.

Church-life. The way of life in the church, which meant a life involved with the church every day of the week. The church was more than just going to a meeting as a duty once a week. The church was Jesus living His life in us together with other Christians. Christ was our life, and we were His way to express Himself on the earth today.

Christianity. Organized groups of Christians outside of the Local Church. Christianity was considered to be blind, fallen, poor, and degraded. It was also considered to be spiritual Babylon, a place where Christians were held in captivity.

Claim the ground. To declare, mainly to the principalities and powers, that we were meeting as the Local Church in a new city to which we were moving with the purpose of establishing a new Local Church. We usually claimed or took the ground in a meeting by praying and praising.

Come into the church. To see the vision of the Local Church and to become a committed member.

Corporate expression. God being expressed in the Local Church in all the members as a whole. Members were blended into one and did not stand out as individuals. The corporate expression was to be a testimony that the world could see, mainly visible in the meetings.

Corporate living. Arrangements where a married couple had single brothers or single sisters living with them in their home. Sometimes these living situations included only one unmarried person; oftentimes, three or four; and sometimes, as many as nine or ten or more, but always of the same sex.

Delegated authority. See Deputy authority.

Deputy authority. The role that Local Church leaders have as God's representatives on the earth in their respective churches. It also referred to Witness Lee's authority as the apostle of the age and as the oracle of God. See "About Authority and Submission" in chapter 24, item 5.

Divine dispensing. The ongoing dispensing of the Triune God into us in order to produce the church and ultimately the New Jerusalem. See "God's Economy" in chapter 9.

Door-knocking. A part of the New Way which Witness Lee initiated in the Local Churches in the 1980's. This was a way to reach new people by going door to door in neighborhoods and preaching the gospel by a predefined method which included baptizing any converts in their bathtubs. See "The New Way" in chapter 16.

Economy of God. See God's economy.

Elders. Leaders in the Local Church. In line with the belief about one church in one city, there was one eldership per city made up of several elders. We referred to these leaders as "the elders," "the leading brothers," or "the leading ones." However, most often, we just referred to them as "the brothers." These brothers were the main decision-makers among us and were responsible for the administration of the church. In addition to this, among the leading brothers in each Local Church, there was normally one brother who was recognized as the main leading brother. This brother was looked to by all as the leader with the final say in a Local Church.

Eating Jesus. To partake of Jesus as the "living bread" (John 6:51). Witness Lee taught that those in Christianity were busy studying and learning about Jesus, but they weren't eating or enjoying Him. In the Local Church, members ate Jesus by calling on the Lord and pray-reading the Bible.

Enjoy the Lord. To feel happy by eating and drinking spiritually. This usually involved calling on the Lord or pray-reading. Witness Lee taught that those in Christianity were busy studying and learning about Jesus, but weren't enjoying Him. The way to enjoy Jesus was to eat Him.

Exercise the spirit. To use the human spirit to contact Christ as the life-giving Spirit. This was mainly done by calling on the name of the Lord and pray-reading.

Flow. Move of the Holy Spirit. In a meeting context, the moving of the Spirit toward the purpose the Lord had for each church meeting. Members were to support the flow with appropriate songs, prayers, and testimonies. In a larger church context, this term indicated the direction that the leading brothers believed the church as a whole should be going. The flow was whatever they believed was the "current move of the Spirit." A flow was typically the result of a teaching from, or fellowship with, Witness Lee. The flow changed directions when some new major practice or movement was introduced. It was often called a "turn" or a "new move."

Full-timers. Local Church members who forsook regular employment to devote all their time to learning and spreading Witness Lee's ministry. They were typically supported by gifts or offerings.

God-men. Witness Lee's description of believers as beings who were both divine and human by virtue of being mingled with God through eating and drinking Him.

God's economy. Describes God's ultimate purpose: The processed Triune God dispensing Himself into the chosen and redeemed tripartite man for the building of the church and the producing of the New Jerusalem, the mingling of God and man for eternity. See "God's Economy" in chapter 9.

Gospel march. See "A Gospel March" in chapter 7.

Ground of the church. The belief that the church can only be built on the ground of a locality or city (sometimes called the ground of locality). See also Local Church.

Hospitality. The practice of Local Church members opening up their homes, usually to other Local Church members who needed food and lodging. Hospitality was most frequently given during church conferences or trainings. Hospitality was sometimes offered to new prospects to help capture them.

Human spirit. The innermost part of man. God had made man with three parts: a spirit, a soul, and a body (1 Thess. 5:23). The human spirit was the key to eating Jesus and experiencing Christ as life. We "exercised our spirit" in order to contact Christ by calling on the Lord or pray-reading.

Leading brothers. See Elders.

Leprosy. See Quarantining.

Living Stream Ministry. Publishing organization established by Witness Lee to produce and distribute written materials and audio and video media containing his ministry. It is headquartered in Anaheim, California.

Life-giving Spirit. The Spirit that Christ became after his death and resurrection, according to Witness Lee's interpretation of 1 Cor. 15:45.

Local Church. The name given to the movement by those outside of it. We did not claim any official name. We referred to an individual church by the name of its city, for example, "The Church in Dallas." The name, Local Church, was derived from our belief that there could be only one church in each city that is the true expression of the body of Christ in that city. We also believed there could be only one eldership per city. Although we recognized that there were real Christians who were not part of the Local Church, we considered all other organized churches to be fallen, divisive, and sectarian. We would associate with individuals who attended such organizations in hopes of helping them see the vision of the Local Church, but we did not recognize other Christian organizations as being authorized by God.

Local ground. See Local Church.

Lord's Recovery. See Local Church. See "Our Vision: The Lord's Recovery" in chapter 7.

Lord's Table. Biblical term used to refer to breaking bread and drinking wine to remember the Lord's death until He comes, as He commanded the disciples to do.

Love feast. A meeting held for the purpose of bringing non-Christians to eat dinner and then hear a gospel message in the hopes of capturing them for the Local Church.

Meetings. Meetings of the Local Church. Many Christians say that they go to church. Local Church members do not "go to church" but "go to the meetings."

Meeting hall. Building used for the purpose of holding Local Church meetings.

Message. Long teaching or inspirational word spoken in a church meeting, conference, or training. Used in place of the word sermon.

Mingling. The ongoing sanctification or filling by which members receive more of the Lord and become one with Him. This term is based on Leviticus 2:4, where fine flour was mingled with oil, typifying Jesus' fine humanity being mingled with the Holy Spirit. See "'Christ as Life' Versus Religion" in chapter 7.

Ministry, The. The teachings and ministry of Witness Lee as published by the Living Stream Ministry.

Morning watch. Prayer and pray-reading in the morning before beginning the day's activities. This was, if at all possible, to be done with others and was, as such, sometimes referred to as "corporate morning watch."

Natural. Relating to our physical birth. Christ's life was the life we had by our new spiritual birth. Whatever we could do for God without experiencing Christ as our life was natural and, therefore, unacceptable.

Negative. Label for anyone or anything that the leaders perceived as being against the Local Church or the ministry of Witness Lee, usually involving speaking out or asking critical questions. See also Quarantining.

New Way. See "The New Way" in chapter 16.

Oneness. See "Oneness" in chapter 7.

Opposers. People who have openly spoken or written anything that questions the Local Church and its practices. An opposer can be a former member, a concerned family member, another Christian ministry, or a researcher—anyone who takes a critical look at the Local Church and the Living Stream Ministry.

Pray-reading. See "We Find the Best Way to Eat" in chapter 6, and "Pray-reading the Word" in chapter 24, item 10.

Processed Triune God. God after having gone through the process of incarnation, human living, crucifixion, death, resurrection, ascension, enthronement, and outpouring as the life-giving Spirit in order to make Himself available to be dispensed into believers as their life when they called on His name or pray-read His Word.

Quarantining. Officially labeling persons as negative, divisive, leprous, rebellious, or poisonous, and warning "healthy" Local Church members to keep away from them so that they will not be infected or damaged.

Recovery. See "Our Vision: The "Lord's Recovery" in chapter 7.

Religion. See "'Christ as Life' Versus Religion" in chapter 7.

Representative authority. See Deputy authority.

Saints. All believers as sanctified ones in Jesus Christ, but used mainly to refer to Local Church members.

Self-life. See Soul-life.

Service groups. See "Service Groups" in chapter 7.

Sisters. Women in the Local Church, meaning sisters in God's family.

Soul-life. The psychological life of a person, consisting of the mind, will, and emotions.

Spirit, human. See Human spirit.

Spiritual authority. See Deputy authority.

Take the ground. See Claim the ground.

Tree of life. A tree that God named in the Garden of Eden that Adam and Eve were allowed to eat of but did not. After they disobeyed God, they were barred from access to it.

Tree of the knowledge of good and evil. A tree that God named in the Garden of Eden that Adam and Eve were forbidden to eat of. They disobeyed and ate; the result of this sin passed to all their descendants.

Training. See "More Ministry" in chapter 9.

Worldly. Usually activities or material things that were a part of Satan's world system, sometimes referred to as just "the world." Any activity that was not related to the church and that provided a form of enjoyment was considered to be worldly. Material possessions were considered "worldly" unless they were absolute necessities. For example, decorations, jewelry, and pictures were worldly; they were vanities, not necessities. Local Church members were expected to abstain from worldliness.

Young people. Junior high, high school, and college-aged persons in the Local Church.

www.ingramcontent.com/pod-product-compliance
Lightning Source LLC
LaVergne TN
LVHW051540070426
835507LV00021B/2341